REBELS AGAINST
THE RAJ

REBELS AGAINST THE RAJ

WESTERN FIGHTERS FOR INDIA'S FREEDOM

Ramachandra Guha

ALFRED A. KNOPF   NEW YORK   2022

Library of Congress Cataloging-in-Publication Data
Names: Guha, Ramachandra, author.
Title: Rebels against the Raj : Western fighters for India's freedom /
Ramachandra Guha.
Description: First edition. | New York : Alfred A. Knopf, 2022. | Includes
bibliographical references and index.
Identifiers: LCCN 2021047324 (print) | LCCN 2021047325 (ebook) |
ISBN 9781101874837 (hardcover) | ISBN 9781101873526 (trade paperback) |
ISBN 9781101874844 (ebook)
Subjects: LCSH: Dissenters—India—Biography. | Europeans—India—
Biography. | Americans—India—Biography. | Europeans—Political activity—
India. | Americans—Political activity—India. | India—History—
British occupation, 1765–1947—Biography.
Classification: LCC DS479.1.A2 G83 2022 (print) | LCC DS479.1.A2 (ebook) |
DDC 954.03—dc23/eng/20211027
LC record available at https://lccn.loc.gov/2021047324
LC ebook record available at https://lccn.loc.gov/2021047325

Original jacket art by Tarini Sharma, based on an image
from The Stapleton Collection/Bridgeman.
Jacket design by Janet Hansen

Manufactured in the United States of America
First Edition

For Jean Drèze

A foreigner deserves to be welcomed only when he mixes with the indigenous people as sugar does with milk.

Mohandas K. Gandhi, speaking to a friend in January 1946

If India had been deprived of touch with the West, she would have lacked an element essential for her attainment of perfection. Europe now has her lamp ablaze. We must light our torches at its wick and make a fresh start on the highway of time. That our forefathers, three thousand years ago, had finished extracting all that was of value from the universe, is not a worthy thought. We are not so unfortunate, nor the universe, so poor.

Rabindranath Tagore, writing in 1908

Contents

List of Illustrations

Anne Besant sitting in the gardens of the Theosophical Society (courtesy of the Theosophical Society)

Annie Besant lecturing to a crowd after her release from internment (courtesy of the Theosophical Society)

Studio portrait of Annie Besant (courtesy of Theosophical Society)

Studio portrait of B. G. Horniman (author's collection)

Madeleine Slade as a young woman in London (courtesy of the Sabarmati Ashram Archives)

Samuel Stokes in his Gandhian phase (courtesy of Professor Vijay Stokes)

Satyanand Stokes with wife Agnes and daughter Satya (courtesy of Professor Vijay Stokes)

Mira Behn helping Gandhi repair his spinning wheel (courtesy of the Sabarmati Ashram Archives)

Mira Behn feeding a calf in her Pashulok Ashram (author's collection)

Mira Behn being visited at her Himalayan ashram by the President of India, Rajendra Prasad (author's collection)

Philip Spratt and his wife Seetha (courtesy of Bob Spratt)

Philip Spratt at work (courtesy of Bob Spratt)

R. R. Keithahn and his wife Mildred (author's collection)

Citation of award presented to Dick Keithahn (author's collection)

Sarala Behn (courtesy of Lakshmi Ashram, Kausani)

Sarala Behn with her students and disciples (courtesy of Lakshmi Ashram, Kausani)

Prologue

Loyalty is a virtue much cherished by humans, and those who are disloyal often face criticism. In the modern world, the gold standard of loyalty is loyalty to one's nation. Men are chastised for leaving their wives, politicians attacked for changing their parties. But the scoldings they face are nothing compared to those aimed at individuals who betray their countries. From Benedict Arnold to Lord Haw-Haw, there is a veritable rogues' gallery of men (and they are virtually all men) who threw in their lot with a country at war with their own.

Very occasionally, however, history and morality permit, and even encourage, individuals to identify with, and devote their energies to fulfilling, the aspirations of a country that is not their homeland. Among these exceptions is the International Brigade which fought on the Republican side in the Spanish Civil War. Here were Frenchmen, Britons, Irishmen and Americans who took up arms to defend the democratic traditions of Spain and the individual liberties of Spaniards. Their heroism and sacrifice were much celebrated at the time, and have since been commemorated in a steady stream of novels, memoirs, biographies, historical studies, and films.

The International Brigade was formed in September 1936. It was disbanded two years later, by the Spanish Government, as a tactical move, in the hope that this would shame Hitler and Mussolini into stopping the sending of troops and money to the other side in the Civil War. Before the foreigners left for their own countries, they were given a stirring farewell in Barcelona. At a massive public gathering, Prime Minister Juan Negrín promised Spanish citizenship to those who chose to return. Then the celebrated orator Dolores

Ibárruri, 'La Pasionara', spoke in praise of these foreign fighters. In years to come, she said, Spaniards would tell their children of

> how, coming over seas and mountains, crossing frontiers bristling with bayonets . . . these men reached our country as crusaders for freedom. They gave up everything, their loves, their country, home and fortune . . . they came and told us, 'We are here, your cause, Spain's cause is ours.' It is the cause of all advanced and progressive mankind.[1]

Rebels Against the Raj tells the story of another group of people who chose to struggle for the freedom of a country other than their own. This story remains much less known, although it is in some ways more remarkable. Those who joined the International Brigade came to Spain as temporary travellers. They would, sooner or later, go back to the nations from which they had come. The men and women profiled in this book came to India for the duration. They exchanged their old homeland for their new one unreservedly, and unequivocally – once in India, they knew they would almost certainly die in India too. The foreigners who fought in Spain stayed for the most part within their racial and religious boundaries, whereas the freedom fighters of my narrative turned their back on their compatriots to identify with people who were neither Christian nor white. They did so for what should certainly have been 'the cause of all advanced and progressive mankind'; namely, the ending of European imperialism and the liberation of colonized people.

One of the battalions in the International Brigade was named for Abraham Lincoln. Its members were all Americans. Yet, as the very name of the *Lincoln* Battalion suggests, for these fighters identification with the Republican cause in Spain did not mean a disavowal of their own country, but, rather, an affirmation of its noblest values. Abraham Lincoln was an American president who stood forthrightly for democracy and justice, at home; these compatriots who invoked his name would struggle for democracy and justice, abroad. To keep at bay the Fascists, to save Spain from the awful fate that had befallen both Italy and Germany, was therefore an act of transnational solidarity through which universal values could be pursued regardless of an individual's background or theatre of enactment.

In the same manner, by coming out to India the renegades of this book were not necessarily rejecting their land of origin. British fighters for India's freedom were upholding the dissident culture within Britain itself, which urged them to be identified with the underdog.[2] By doing what they did in India, for India, they were calling their British compatriots to their better selves. And the Americans in my story saw themselves as acting in the anti-imperialist tradition of their homeland. Like the foreign radicals in 1930s Spain, these foreign radicals in colonial India were not being 'disloyal' to the nation of their birth; rather, they saw in another nation the possibility of pursuing social and political ideals that make human life more appealing everywhere. If imperialism was immoral and unjust, then ending it was in the interest of the colonizer as well as the colonized. If women sought equal rights in Britain or America, then surely they should get equal rights in India too.

The thirty thousand-odd foreigners who came to Spain in the 1930s left behind memories, warm and affectionate memories no doubt. However, they did not have any tangible influence on the history of the country whose cause they briefly made their own. The Civil War was lost by the Republican side they fought for. On the other hand, the seven individuals featured in this book did much more than bravely take a stand for Indian freedom. Through their work, and through their writings, they contributed enormously to public debate within India. They challenged Indians to pay closer attention to the fault lines of class and gender that preceded the coming of the British and which would – if left unattended – persist after the British left. They offered fresh, arresting, insights into how a free India could best promote economic development, equal access to education, and (most farsightedly) environmental sustainability.

The lives of these white-skinned heroes and heroines of India's past may yet be relevant for India's future. And – since the ideals they strove for were universal rather than parochial – for the future of the world too.

In December 1945, Mahatma Gandhi met with a group of British Quakers in Calcutta. Animated by ideals of peace and brotherhood, these social workers had come to aid the victims of the Bengal famine. The Second World War had just ended; there was a rising tide of nationalist aspirations awaiting fulfilment. One Quaker asked whether it was better if non-official Englishmen stayed away from India for the time being. Gandhi answered: 'Any friend, who is a real friend, and who comes in a spirit of service, not as a superior, is bound to be welcome.' He gave the example of the Anglican priest Charles Freer Andrews (1871–1940), who had worked as a bridge between the Raj and Indian nationalists. A close friend of Gandhi as well as of the great poet Rabindranath Tagore, Andrews worked tirelessly to end indentured labour in the colonies. His Indian admirers lovingly named him 'Deenbandhu': friend of the poor.

Gandhi told the Quakers that anyone of any nationality was welcome, so long as they came, like Andrews, in the spirit of disinterested service. He added: 'India, when she comes into her own, will need all such assistance.' Aside from C. F. Andrews, Gandhi also mentioned a man named Samuel Stokes, a lapsed missionary, originally from Pennsylvania, who lived for many years in the mountains around the imperial summer capital, Simla. Stokes concluded that if he wished to serve India he had to become Indian in character and orientation. So he married a local Rajput woman, for which, said Gandhi, 'he was boycotted by the Rajputs. The Government distrusted him too in the beginning. But he has lived down the distrust of both the Government and the Indians.'

Gandhi told the British Quakers who had come to see him in Calcutta that

> if then, even a C. F. Andrews and a Stokes and others had to labour under distrust, for you to be distrusted may not be wondered at. So far Indians have known Englishmen only as members of the ruling race – supercilious when they were not patronizing. The man in the street makes no distinction between such an Englishman and a good, humble European, between the Empire-builder Englishmen of the old type that he has known and the new type that is now coming into being, burning to make reparation for what his forefathers did. Therefore if one has not got the fire of sacrifice in him I would say to him: 'Do not come to India just now.' But if you are cast in a heroic mould there will be no difficulty. You will in the end be taken at your worth if you persevere.[3]

Of the duo mentioned by Gandhi, Samuel Stokes is a central character in this book, whereas C. F. Andrews is not. For all his love for India and Indians, Andrews remained within the Church, and maintained close relations with viceroys and archbishops. It was Stokes who more radically transgressed the boundaries of race and religion. He married an Indian named Agnes, and raised a large family with her, of children who grew up as Indians. He left the Church, and grew ever closer to Hinduism in his spiritual outlook, even changing his first name from Samuel to Satyanand (meaning 'the joy of truth'). And, perhaps most significantly, he took part in Gandhi's anti-colonial struggle, and spent a spell in prison as a result.

Charlie Andrews was a bridge-builder. There is a wonderful book waiting to be written about him and his ilk. It might include Sister Nivedita (Margaret Noble), the Irishwoman who attached herself to the great Hindu monk Swami Vivekananda, moving to Bengal to work for and with him; Marjorie Sykes, the Quaker teacher who translated Tagore and ran schools in the Nilgiris before joining a movement to save the Narmada valley from being destroyed by large dams; Laurie Baker, the Quaker architect who ran a clinic with his doctor wife in the Himalaya before returning with her to her native Kerala to become a pioneer of low-cost housing; or Verrier Elwin, the Gandhian theologian from Oxford who was thrown out of his Church and cast out by the Mahatma en route to becoming the foremost authority on the tribes of India.[4]

The focus of this book, however, is on individuals who decisively changed sides, identifying completely with India, meeting Indians on absolutely equal terms as friends and lovers, and as comrades on the street and in prison too. Detention in British India (or externment from British India) is a sine qua non for inclusion here. Imprisonment or banishment signified the depth of their commitment to the cause.

The rebels of this book are to be distinguished from bridge-builders on the one side; and, on the other, from those whom the writer William Dalrymple has called 'White Mughals', who 'responded to their travels in India by slowly shedding their Britishness like an unwanted skin, and adopting Indian dress, studying Indian philosophy, taking harems and adopting the ways of the Mughal governing class they slowly came to replace'.[5]

If 'White' represents the skin colour of these adventurers, then 'Mughals' accurately captures their luxurious lifestyle. On the other hand, the rebels I write about endured poverty and hardship, disease and incarceration. (Even the men among them could not have remotely contemplated 'taking harems'.) To live like the Indians whose struggle they made their own was at once a manifestation of their courage and the source of their credibility.

The 'White Mughals' of Dalrymple's construction came to India in the late eighteenth and early nineteenth century, when racial boundaries were more fluid. At the time, much of the subcontinent was still under the rule of native princes; even the parts controlled by foreign mercenaries were governed loosely rather than rigidly. However, in 1858 all of India came under the direct rule of the British Government; now, racial boundaries became ever more fixed and exclusive. To live like a White Mughal in the early days of colonial expansion was one thing; to become a renegade when the clash between imperialism and nationalism was at its most intense, quite another. The first path was associated with romance and a certain kind of hedonistic voyeurism; the second path with idealism and a certain kind of reckless bravery.

Of the seven rebels featured in this book, four were men and three were women. Five came from Great Britain, while two were Americans by birth. Some came from elite families – one was the daughter of an admiral – while others came from more plebeian homes. In terms of religious affiliation, two arrived in India as Christian missionaries, one as a militant atheist, a fourth as a Theosophist.

These renegades came to the subcontinent from diverse social and intellectual backgrounds. In India, they all combined writing with activism; otherwise, what they did in their new homeland varied greatly too. Two worked up north, in the high and cold Himalaya; two in deepest South India, close to the hot and humid coast. Of the women, one based herself in the great cities of Madras and Banaras; the other two were inspired to settle in villages instead. Two men married Indians and raised children with them; another brought his white-skinned wife and sought to make her an Indian too. One woman fell passionately in love with an Indian man but could not marry him; one man stayed unmarried and was almost certainly gay, taking Indian lovers.

The first of these rebels arrived in India in 1893, the last died in India in 1984. Their lives thus span a century of tumultuous history for India and Indians, incorporating the two World Wars, the rise and maturation of the freedom struggle, Independence and Partition, and the emergence of a state and society.

In this shaping and re-shaping of modern India these individuals were active participants. Their work spoke directly to what was happening on the ground. For these men and women were anti-colonial crusaders as well as nation-builders. The education of the girl child was an abiding passion for at least three of them; building the country's intellectual and scientific capacity an abiding passion for two others. For them all, freedom from British rule was only the first step for India; they wished also for their adopted country to be free of injustice, inequality, poverty, ignorance, and disease. Notably, in their conscious endeavour to change India they unconsciously changed themselves too. Two Christians became former Christians as a result of their experiences; a fanatical Communist became a vigorous anti-Communist.

The lives and doings of these individuals constitute a morality tale for the world we currently live in. This is a world governed by paranoia and nationalist xenophobia, with the rise of jingoism in country after country, and a corresponding contempt for ideas and individuals that emanate from outside the borders of one's nation. Narendra Modi and the Rashtriya Swayamsevak Sangh in India, Donald Trump and the white supremacists in America, Boris Johnson and the Brexiteers in England, Xi Jinping and his Confucian Communist Party in China – all see themselves as uniquely blessed by history and by God. No foreigner, they believe, can teach them anything.

This book tells us that they can.

PART I
CROSSING OVER, CHANGING SIDES

CHAPTER I

Mothering India

I

In the year 1893, three Indians destined for greatness made their mark in countries outside India. In April of that year, Mohandas K. Gandhi enrolled as a lawyer at the Natal Bar, en route to becoming the leader of the Indian community in South Africa and in time the leader of the freedom movement in his homeland. In July 1893, his fellow Kathiawari, Kumar Shri Ranjitsinhji (always known as 'Ranji'), played for Cambridge versus Oxford in the annual University Match at Lord's, en route to becoming the first great cricketer of Indian origin. In September of that year, Swami Vivekananda made a stirring speech in the World Parliament of Religions at Chicago, en route to becoming the authoritative voice of a Hindu Renaissance.

These overseas debuts, all in the same year, were intimations of much more than personal fame. They presaged three different ways in which Indian culture was to profoundly impact the world. Gandhi's leadership of the freedom movement inspired anti-colonial struggles across Asia and Africa, as well as movements for racial justice in North America. Ranji's success on the playing fields of England was the forerunner of the emergence of cricket as India's national sport, and of India as the epicentre of world cricket. Swami Vivekananda blazed the trail for other Indian seers and prophets to travel overseas, taking their ideas with them. The subsequent spread of Hindu spirituality and of the practice of yoga across the world, owe their distant origins to that famous speech made by the Swami in Chicago.

In a striking juxtaposition, even as Gandhi, Ranji and Vivekananda were seeking to take their ideas and expertise outside India, a Western woman was making the reverse journey, bringing her ideas and (as it were) expertise to India. For it was also in 1893 that the first of our renegades, Annie Besant, arrived on these shores.

Mrs Besant (as she was usually known)[1] was born Annie Wood in London on 1 October 1847. She was three-quarters Irish. Her father, a doctor who went into the City, died when she was five. Annie was brought up by her mother and a wealthy aunt. As a teenager, she travelled with her aunt in Germany and France, while reading widely and learning the piano.

The young (and talented) Annie was courted by a Cambridge-educated priest named Frank Besant. They married in December 1867, and moved to Cheltenham, where Frank had a job as a teacher. The bored housewife wrote short stories while having two children – a boy and a girl – in quick succession.

By 1871 – merely four years into the marriage – Annie and Frank had begun to quarrel. The next year she became interested in Nonconformism, before moving on further afield, to atheism. In September 1873 the couple separated, each keeping one child. Annie was now living in London, spending long hours in the British Museum, reading Darwin, Spinoza, John Stuart Mill and the like. In August 1874 she heard the legendary atheist Charles Bradlaugh speak for the first time. He was forty; she, just twenty-six. Soon Annie became an active member of Bradlaugh's National Secular Society. Before the year was out, she was speaking from its platforms, and making a name as an orator. With Bradlaugh she travelled up and down the country, speaking on secularism, science, and the rights of women. Her mentor was a famous public speaker, but his young protégée was not far behind, being described in the provincial press as 'a lady of refinement [and] genius' with a 'matchless power of reasoning and eloquence'.[2] Audiences were not always so generous; at several places the duo were heckled by devout churchmen and even had stones thrown at them.

Under Bradlaugh's influence, Annie became a fervent republican, opposed to imperialism and all its works. In 1876 she organized a petition to oppose the Prince of Wales's forthcoming trip to the subcontinent. She got more than 100,000 people to sign the petition, which, almost a mile in length, was presented to the House of Commons. (The Prince's trip went ahead regardless.)

In 1877 Mrs Besant's first book appeared, a collection of her essays called *My Path to Atheism*. She was now seriously studying religious texts, all the better to refute them. Her critical gaze began turning Eastwards, as she read books on Buddhism and Hinduism and the religions of ancient Egypt. A newer faith that came to her notice was Theosophy, a mystical movement begun by a Russian émigrée called Madame Blavatsky and her American associate Colonel H. S. Olcott. Apart from the United States, Blavatsky also found disciples in Ceylon and in India, where her Theosophical Society had purchased a large and beautiful tract of land on the banks of the Adyar river in Madras.

Culturally as well as geographically, India was vital to the development of Theosophy. Mrs Blavatsky spoke of being in communion with spiritual masters in the Himalaya. She was inspired by the Bhagavad Gita and by the works of the great Oxford Sanskritist F. Max Mueller, and herself visited India in 1879–80. Among the early converts to Theosophy was Allan Octavian Hume, the ornithologist and reformist civil servant who helped found the Indian National Congress. As one historian of Theosophy has written: 'India, Blavatsky maintained, was the source of all human knowledge. Everything the Egyptians, Phoenicians, Jews, Greeks and Romans knew, they had learned from the Indians.'[3]

Annie Besant's own first impressions of Theosophy were underwhelming. In an article of 1882 she dismissed it as 'a dreamy, emotional, scholarly, interest in the religio-philosophic fancies of the past'.[4] She was herself now moving rapidly to the Left, befriending Karl Marx's disciple (and future son-in-law) Edward Aveling and the socialist playwright George Bernard Shaw. The playwright had great affection and admiration for Mrs Besant, for her intelligence and force of character, and especially her oratorical skills. Of one public debate where he had to take the podium after her, Shaw wrote that when a speaker on the other side had finished, 'Mrs Besant got up and utterly demolished him. There was nothing left to do but gasp and triumph under her shield.'[5]

In 1885 Mrs Besant joined the Fabian Society, and threw herself into socialist causes, leading marches of underpaid workers and craftsmen. In 1888, Theosophy entered her life once more. Sent a book by Madame Blavatsky to review, she was drawn to, indeed enchanted by, its contents, writing in her autobiography of how

> as I turned over page after page the interest became absorbing; but how familiar it seemed; how my mind leapt forward to presage the conclusions, how natural it was, how coherent, how subtle, and yet how intelligible. I was dazzled, blinded by the light in which disjointed facts were seen as part of a mighty whole, and all my puzzles, riddles, problems, seemed to disappear.

Mrs Besant asked to meet the author of the book. The meeting took place in a house in London, where Mrs Blavatsky – a large, corpulent figure dressed in black, with her head covered and her piercing eyes looking out – 'talked of travels, of various countries, easy brilliant talk, her eyes veiled, her exquisitely moulded fingers rolling cigarettes incessantly'. One meeting was enough to convert the once sceptical Irishwoman, and two months later Mrs Besant was formally inducted as a member of the Theosophical Society, kneeling before Madame Blavatsky and receiving, through her, the blessings of the Himalayan Masters she claimed to communicate with.[6]

When Mrs Besant joined the Theosophical Society, its three aims were: 'To found a Universal Brotherhood without distinction of race or creed; to forward the study of Aryan literature and philosophy; to investigate unexplained laws of nature and the psychical powers latent in man.' (The second aim, with its unfortunate racial tinge, was later modified to mean the study of comparative religion.) By June 1889, the middle-aged convert was writing essays for *Lucifer*, the magazine of the Theosophical Society. In the same year, Mohandas Gandhi, then a law student in London, was writing a series of essays for the journal of the Vegetarian Society of London. The young Gandhi was becoming increasingly interested in Theosophy, and almost certainly attended a series of lectures that Annie Besant delivered in August 1889, of which *Lucifer* remarked that 'the Hindu gentlemen who were present, conspicuous by their quiet mien, nodded their frequent approval in silent but significant manner'.[7]

In her early years as a Theosophist Mrs Besant retained her interest in socialist causes. However, after Madame Blavatsky's death in May 1891, she 'perceived she had a higher mission'. She undertook three lecture tours in the United States in quick succession, her words and her energy leading to her being hailed by the *Chicago Tribune* as 'the most prominent theosophist of the day . . . on whom the mantle of Madame Blavatsky has fallen'.[8]

The moving spirits of the Theosophical Society, Colonel Olcott and C. W. Leadbeater, wanted Mrs Besant – at this time regarded 'as the greatest speaker of her sex in either Europe or America'[9] – to tour India, where, they thought, the growing English-speaking middle class could provide ready converts to this hybrid faith, which (unlike Christianity) treated Hinduism with respect. Mrs Besant herself was extremely keen to visit the land where her teacher's own teachers were believed to reside. On 20 September 1892 she sailed from New York to London, and, after a brief halt there, carried on to Marseilles, where she took the steamer *Kaiser-i-Hind*, bound for Colombo. The plan was for a brief, six-week tour of Ceylon and India in the cold weather, following which she would return to England.

She stayed forty years.

II

Annie Besant first saw the country she made her own on the morning of 16 November 1893. On this day she landed at the southern port town of Tuticorin, before making her way up the coast to Madras, where the Theosophical Society had its headquarters, in a plot of land along the Adyar – now a stinking sewer suffused with the city's wastes, but then a briskly flowing stretch of mostly clean water.

Madras (still many decades away from being renamed Chennai) was the third largest city in the subcontinent. It was from here that the British administered the southern parts of their Raj. In 1893 Madras had a population of about half a million; employed in the colonial government and in the colonial army, but also in trades and services. The city was a centre of textile and leather production, and had a whole array of English-language educational institutions, the products of which were potential recruits to the Theosophical cause.

In her first winter in India, Mrs Besant toured South India by train and occasionally by bullock-cart. She spoke in (among other places) the cities of Madurai, Tirunelveli, Bangalore, and Hyderabad. Early in the new year she headed north, making her first acquaintance with Banaras. She also made a detour to see the Taj Mahal in Agra.

In her first years in India, Mrs Besant spent much time attending to, and seeking to resolve, the factional conflicts within the Theosophical Society, these partly based on personal rivalries, and partly on whether to adopt the Buddhist or the Brahminical approach to reincarnation. She also made long tours overseas – to New Zealand and Australia, to the United States, and of course to England and Europe, seeking to build the network of the society and enlarge its membership base.

In the wider international fraternity of the Theosophists, Mrs Besant came to be known as 'Mother'. In Madras, which was in effect her main base, she was known as 'Periamma', the Great Mother; in North India, as Bari Memsahib, the Big (or Biggest) Lady Sahib. She toured the country 'lecturing on Hinduism, Mesmerism, Temperance, Vegetarianism, etc.'. One early report on her activities says she 'consistently covered Hindus and their religion with almost sickening flattery'. The flattery was returned, with interest, an Indian newspaper calling her 'the veritable goddess of Ind coming from the far off West for the spiritual regeneration of the land'.[10]

In England, Mrs Besant had been prevented from obtaining a degree from the University of London. This prompted an intense ambition to start a university of her own in India. When wealthy Hindus evinced an interest in funding such an enterprise, she took it up more seriously. In July 1898 – less than five years after landing in India – she announced the establishment of a 'Central Hindu College' in the ancient temple city of Banaras. The Maharaja of Banaras chose to gift her land and buildings – although he later had misgivings. The Maharaja of Kashmir chipped in with funds. Hostels and classrooms were built, to which students came from across India. The University of Allahabad – seventy miles upstream on the River Ganga – gave the new college accreditation. The institution had boys alone; so, in 1904, Mrs Besant started a residential Hindu Girls School, a revolutionary idea at the time.

In 1895, barely a couple of years after she moved to India, Annie Besant gave a lecture in several cities bearing the title 'The Means of India's Regeneration', a talk radiating prescriptive energy about what her adopted land could do to recover her place as one of the great nations of the world. Mrs Besant wanted a strong classical core to Indian education, hoping that 'a public opinion could be formed, sufficiently strong, which made a knowledge of Sanskrit a real necessity, so that no man would be regarded as an educated man unless a knowledge of Sanskrit formed part of his education'. Turning to secular learning, she deplored the fact that the history and geography textbooks in use were so utterly alien to Indian realities. These books acquainted the schoolboy with English kings and queens, English towns, and English industries, 'leaving him without any knowledge of the detailed history and geography and products and industries of his own country, where the whole of his life is to be spent, and to which his thoughts should be ever turned'.[11]

In another lecture, Mrs Besant explained how the Central Hindu College would blend the modern with the traditional, with the curriculum being equally strong in classical Sanskrit texts as well as in modern works in English. 'Do you not see', she remarked:

> that there are two Hindu nations in this land – one of Pandits, profound in their learning, scholarship, thought and knowledge, but knowing nothing outside Samskrit literature. They know nothing of modern thought, modern life, the modern spirit. On the other side there is a Hindu nation growing up, knowing nothing of Samskrit literature and of the sacred Books, growing up utterly westernized. There is a great gulf between them and the nation of Pandits. The Pandit cannot influence the English-educated boy, because he does not sympathise with him in his hopes and aspirations. You cannot influence the young unless you sympathise and feel with them. We want to bridge the gap between these Hindu nations, and we build this double bridge of Samskrit and English. We lead both classes, so that both shall know English and both shall know Samskrit; we thus hope to join the two Hindu nations and make them one in the service of their Motherland.[12]

These words were spoken in 1903, by which time Mrs Besant had been a decade in India. She had started a college for boys as well as several schools for girls. Her views on gender relations had markedly changed from her days in the West. As a socialist and suffragette, she had demanded full equality between the sexes. Now she was more inclined to the Hindu view that women's roles and responsibilities were different from (and somewhat subordinate to) men's. So, as she wrote in 1904, 'the national movement for girls' education must be on national lines: 'it must accept the general Hindu conception of woman's place in the national life'. That is to say:

> It must see in the woman the mother and the wife, or, as in some cases, the learned and pious ascetic, the Brahmavadini of older days. It cannot see in her the rival and competitor of man in all forms of outside and public employment, as woman, under different economic conditions, is coming to be, more and more, in the West. . . . [T]he national movement for the education of girls must be one which meets the national needs, and India needs nobly trained wives and mothers, wise and tender rulers of the household, educated teachers of the young, helpful counsellors of their husbands, skilled nurses of the sick, rather than girl graduates, educated for the learned professions.

While most girls had to be prepared through education for a life of motherhood and household management, there would, admitted Mrs Besant,

> always be some exceptional girls who need for the due evolution of their faculties a more profound and wider education, and these must be helped to what they need as individuals, each to her own line. Such girls may be born into India in order to restore to her the learned women of the past, and to place again in her diadem the long lost part of lofty female intelligence.[13]

Mrs Besant's emphasis on the spiritualization of education was at odds with the colonial curriculum, and – as notably – with the views of Indian liberals who believed in shunning the religious dogmas of the past while embracing the rational, sceptical, scientific approach of the modern world. Writing to the great Poona liberal Gopal Krishna Gokhale, Mrs Besant proclaimed: 'I believe that India has been materialised, vulgarised and denationalised by leaving religion out of education; and all my efforts are turned to restoring religion to its proper place.'[14]

III

In her lecture of 1895 on the 'means of India's regeneration', Mrs Besant had asked her audience to affirm the national spirit by 'maintaining the traditional dress, ways of living and so on, by promoting Indian arts and manufactures, by giving preference to Indian products over foreign . . .' Here, the Irishwoman turned Indian was anticipating the Swadeshi movement of 1905–7, when nationalists organized flamboyant bonfires of foreign cloth in protest against the political and economic exploitation of India by colonial rule.

The Swadeshi movement was at its most intense in the Bengal Presidency, where the anger against foreign goods, foreign ways of life, was compounded by the partition of the province in 1905, which had been bitterly opposed by the intelligentsia.[15] Although sympathetic to nationalist sentiment, Mrs Besant did not want to put her institutions at risk by associating publicly with it. She still wished to stay on the right side of the British Raj. The Hindu College in Banaras now had more than a hundred boys, and Mrs Besant sternly warned her Bengali students not to take part in popular protests against the Government. At this stage she was a Hinduphile (rather than Indophile), as well as an Empire Loyalist, careful not to explicitly foster sentiments of secession and independence among her wards.

While opening these schools and colleges Mrs Besant continued to be very active in the Theosophical Society. When the President of the Society, Madame Blavatsky's long-time collaborator Colonel Olcott, died in February 1907, Mrs Besant's supporters claimed that the Mahatmas in the Himalaya wanted her to be his successor. An election was held nonetheless, about which an industrious biographer provides some telling details. We thus learn that the Dutch section of the society chose Mrs Besant over her opponent by a margin of 781 votes to 1; the Germans by 583 to 20; the Cubans by 188 to 14. The Indians were thunderingly behind their *Periamma*, 3,571 to 47, and the British supported her solidly too, 1,189 to 261. The only substantial opposition to Mrs Besant came from the United States, but even here she won quite comfortably, 1,319 to 679.[16]

By now, the society's headquarters at Adyar had expanded and consolidated itself quite considerably. It stretched for a full mile along the river; its eastern side abutted the ocean, with a private beach for the society's members. The fields and gardens provided vegetables and fruits aplenty. Electric lights had replaced kerosene. There was even a dairy on the premises. When in town, Mrs Besant held court on the second floor of the handsome main building, sitting cross-legged on a cushion, speaking to visitors and admirers, or writing letters.

In 1909, Mrs Besant's colleague in the Theosophical Society, C. W. Leadbeater, bumped into two beautiful young boys on the beach in Adyar. They were sons of a Telugu-speaking member of the society. Leadbeater thought the younger of the brothers had a wonderful aura about him; when Mrs Besant met him, she agreed. The boy, Jiddu Krishnamurti, had a lovely face and a serene countenance. Mrs Besant had always thought that the new World Teacher, the twentieth-century reincarnation of a Buddha, a Jesus, a Zoroaster, would come from India. She was easily convinced that the boy Jiddu would, under her tutelage, become the One.

Over the next two decades, Mrs Besant's life was deeply intertwined with Krishnamurti's. She founded an Order of the Rising Sun and anointed him its President (she herself was the Order's Protector). Krishnamurti's father took her to court, alleging that she had adopted his sons through fraudulent purposes; she fought him all the way to the Privy Council, retaining custody. She tried to get the boy admission into Oxford; according to one story, when she told the President of Magdalen College that her ward was the Son of God, the grandee replied: 'Madam, we have the sons of many important people in our College.'[17] Eventually, the son himself walked out on the Mother, with Krishnamurti telling a massed audience of Theosophists that he was not anybody's teacher, and they'd better find their own individual routes to enlightenment, without his assistance.[18]

Krishnamurti and his brother were found for Mrs Besant. Other young Indians joined her on their own, and with great enthusiasm. Their recollections speak of the enormous appeal that this renegade Irishwoman had for a certain kind of educated Hindu. The Bombay writer Kanji Dwarkadas joined the Theosophical Society in 1912, aged twenty, being admitted by Mrs Besant herself. Half a century later he recalled

> the inner experience that came to me on account of her wonderful personal magnetism. The mighty figure with deep penetrating eyes, silvery hair shining on her head, clean unruffled face, looked as if a great messenger, who had her head with the high and mighty to the clouds, spoke to me once more after ages, with a view to showing me and leading me on to the path that one must tread if one has to reach the goal of the union with the One Life of which no creature is bereft.[19]

Among Mrs Besant's closest companions in Banaras was the philosopher Bhagwan Das. His son Sri Prakasa joined the Theosophical Society as a boy, and came to regard Mrs Besant as a Mother. He admired many things about her, not least her oratory. As he wrote in an adoring biography, Mrs Besant

> never carried any papers as she spoke. Her memory must have been remarkable, and I believe she just rehearsed her lectures to herself once, before going into the lecture hall; and that was enough for her. She never faltered for a word and her voice never broke. She told us in one of her talks how she was fond of beautiful perorations; how she liked to end her speeches by working up her audience to a certain pitch, leaving their minds in possession of some peculiarly tragic or pathetic scene created by the magic of her words.

Sri Prakasa added: 'Mrs. Besant did not like any one to speak after her; and quite rightly too, for who could heighten the impression and the effect, of her speech? They could only mar them.'[20]

IV

Her former friend and erstwhile comrade George Bernard Shaw once described Annie Besant as 'a woman of swift decisions', who 'always came into a movement with a bound, and was preaching the new faith before the astonished spectators had the least suspicion that the old one was shaken'.[21]

Mrs Besant's abandonment of Socialism for Theosophy was at once a move from West to East, and from politics to spirituality. Indeed, it was because she had been so intensely engaged in public affairs before she came to India that she sought so resolutely to stay away from controversy once she was here. However, the subcontinent was no peaceable haven of freedom, where she could endlessly and unproblematically experiment with moral or religious ideas. It was a colonial regime, run on racist lines. So long as she focused on expanding the membership of the Theosophical Society or on getting more boys and girls into school, the facts of Indian subjecthood could be temporarily brushed aside. In the end, though, she could not escape them altogether.

In October 1902, Mrs Besant gave a talk in London on what she had learned from a decade in India on 'the relations which exist between one of the greatest of conquering nations and the greatest of subject peoples'. The venue was the South Place Chapel in Finsbury, a district that had famously elected an Indian, Dadabhai Naoroji, to the House of Commons in 1892.

In her lecture, Mrs Besant analysed the relations between England and India under three heads: that of religion, that of education, and that of political relations. On the first count, she remarked that 'India has more to teach than she has to learn'. She thought there was nothing in Christianity that did not already exist in Indian spiritual traditions. With regard to education, she said that modern Western learning had to be adapted to Indian conditions. With regard to political relations, she observed that the destruction of Indian industries and high taxation had been among the unhappy consequences of British rule.

At this stage, Mrs Besant's criticisms of colonial rule were gentle and understated. She urged, on the ruling race, greater respect for a people with an old and sophisticated culture of their own. While she accepted that many British officials in India were hard-working and motivated by a sense of justice, nonetheless 'they have a tendency to think they are so immensely superior to others that whatever is good for them is good for everybody else; they fail to understand the traditions and the customs which must exist in an ancient people, a people of high and complicated civilisation . . .'[22]

These well-meaning, politely worded, feelings were soon put to the test. For the first decade of the twentieth century witnessed an intensifying opposition to British rule; as in the aforementioned Swadeshi movement, which was both preceded and followed by bomb attacks in the three great Presidencies of Bengal, Madras and Bombay. Tempers ran high, nerves were fraught; and the colonial state sometimes reacted with excessive force. In 1910, there were a series of incidents wherein British officials harshly abused and even physically attacked Indians. Mrs Besant drafted an appeal urging the rulers to show respect and restraint. This angered the Governor of Madras, who wrote to her that 'your words may be used to stir the impressionable youth of India to revolt. Some of your sentences shorn of their context may be seized upon and turned to undesirable purposes by those who are engaged in the task of stirring up strife.' The Viceroy, weighing in, told this Irish defender of Indian freedoms that since the cases of official abuse 'are comparatively rare', giving them publicity was likely to vitiate relations between Europeans and Indians.[23]

Some students of Central Hindu College were itching to join the growing movement against colonial rule. When, also in 1910, Mrs Besant asked the Viceroy, Lord Minto, to become a patron of the college, he wrote back (via his Private Secretary) saying that since the students' magazine had praised the militant nationalist Lala Lajpat Rai, he was therefore 'doubtful whether he should support the institution, until the management has been brought more into line with the views of the Commissioner of Benares, who is evidently anxious to help the College in every way'.[24]

In 1907, the country's main political organization, the Indian National Congress, had split into two wings. While Lajpat Rai was an Extremist, wanting to sever all connections with British rule, Mrs Besant was now engaging actively with the Moderates, liberal incrementalists who wished for greater self-government while retaining their ties with the Empire. Prominent Moderates like Tej Bahadur Sapru and Motilal Nehru had made donations to Central Hindu College.

Several Indian Theosophists were active in Congress affairs, which encouraged Mrs Besant to involve herself in the party too. Having dipped her toenails in these waters gingerly already, she now prepared for a more active engagement. Theosophy and education would no longer suffice to sustain her energies and her interests.

In January 1914, Mrs Besant announced that a new weekly would be published from the headquarters of the Theosophical Society in Adyar. It was to be called *Commonweal*, and its aims as enunciated in Mrs Besant's first editorials were: 'To hold a free platform for the expression of varied opinions on religious, educational, social and political problems, so that burning questions in all parts of the world may be threshed out, and truth elicited by a thoughtful discussion.'[25]

The pre-eminent Extremist leader of the Congress was the Poona firebrand Bal Gangadhar Tilak. In 1908 Tilak had been shut away in a prison in Mandalay on charges of sedition. He was released in June 1914, whereupon the waters of Indian politics began to be stirred more actively than ever before.

When Tilak came out of prison, Mrs Besant was in London. So was Tilak's great rival, the Moderate leader Gopal Krishna Gokhale. Gokhale was sensible of the enormous prestige this Irishwoman had acquired among the Hindu middle classes. Were young patriots to be weaned away from extremism towards moderation, Annie Besant could be of enormous help. The two met several times in London in the summer of 1914. When Mrs Besant prepared to depart for India, Gokhale wrote saying that he planned to visit Madras for the annual meeting of the Congress in December, when, he hoped, 'we may succeed in devising some new scheme which will bring together the more earnest spirits in the country in active cooperation in the service of the Motherland – yours now no less than mine and of other Indians'.[26]

Mrs Besant was now in her late sixties, yet entirely prepared to throw herself into the Congress movement. She bought the title of a defunct newspaper, the *Madras Standard*, and proclaimed her desire 'to make it a power in the land'.[27] The paper was renamed *New India*, signalling that its editor's ambitions were not provincial but properly pan-Indian. 'Please do not have a fit', she wrote to a Theosophist friend in England, 'but I have bought a daily paper in Madras. It is needed for the work. It was a rag, but it will be a power. . . . It is quite exciting to edit a daily paper! I expect to make it good. I have cleared off all the coarse advertisements . . .'[28]

Writing to the Bengali Moderate Bhupendranath Basu in September 1914, Mrs Besant worried that 'the Congress is losing touch with the younger men of India, and no longer raises the enthusiasm which was caused by it in its earlier days'. Two months later, she told Basu of her desire to bring 'the Left Wing people' back into the Congress. 'The thing is to persuade our Left friends to come inside', she said, 'so that they may be represented in the discussion . . . Mr. Tilak is quite ready to talk things over, and with good will on all sides, a way should certainly be found.' She concluded the letter with these emphatic words: 'It will be a great thing for India if the whole Nationalist party is united.'[29]

V

In the late summer of 1914, as war broke out in Europe, in India Annie Besant had begun to see herself as more – much more – than just a member of the Congress. She was – or had decided – to be its glue, the healer of its divisions, the torch-bearer of its desire and ambition to represent all of India and all Indians.

In November 1914, Mrs Besant wrote to Gokhale that it was time to 'close the breach between the Extreme Wing and the Moderates', and 'in view of the political changes which will follow the War to have a United India and to formulate its wishes'. The previously recalcitrant Bal Gangadhar Tilak, she said, was now prepared to ask for self-government within the Empire, and not separation or full independence for India. In early December she wrote again, saying she was coming to Poona to meet Tilak, since she would not think she had done her best 'unless I try to persuade

Mr. Tilak to behave reasonably, and fail'. If 'the attempts to make peace fail', she wrote, 'it is necessary that India should know that Mr. Tilak is irreconcilable and that the fault lies with him'.

Sensing that Gokhale would be nervous about an out-reach to his bitter rival, Mrs Besant added this significant postscript: 'Don't forget <u>re</u> Tilak, that I have been in politics all my life, and worked closely with Charles Bradlaugh. You need not fear his making any capital out of my visit that I am not prepared for, and have discounted.'[30]

Gokhale remained deeply sceptical of Tilak's intentions. As he wrote to Mrs Besant, 'if the door was opened to him [Tilak], he would renew his attempts of 1906 and 1907 to capture the Congress for his views'. These views did not preclude opposing colonial rule by violence, if necessary. 'Well, having experienced the full bitterness of that struggle', continued Gokhale, 'we should, I felt, be traitors to the cause we then saved from destruction after great exertions, if we offered, in the name of unity and reconciliation, another opportunity to men who will learn nothing and unlearn nothing to renew once again the old struggle.'[31]

Mrs Besant came to Poona and met Tilak. The talks failed, as Gokhale had warned that they would. Tilak saw her coming all the way from Madras as a sign of weakness, and made it clear that he would rejoin the Congress only if he and his group were in control of the party. After their meeting, Tilak wrote defiantly to Besant saying:

> We do not wish to join the Congress as dummies who will admiringly look at the grave faces of the Moderate leaders and enthusiastically applaud their elegant speeches. . . . If we join the Congress, we shall do so for working out our programme by persuading the majority – if it be possible to do so – to our side.[32]

Mrs Besant had entered the Congress as a Mother, seeking to reconcile its squabbling children. Always secure in her self-belief, she thought that she would succeed where others had failed. Gokhale repeatedly warned her that the road would be far rockier than she presumed or hoped. A letter of January 1915 has him saying to her:

I fear I have been writing to you about Tilak much more than I should
care to do to any one and I need not assure you that it is all done
with extreme reluctance. But now that you have come into this
Congress movement, it is necessary that you should know these things.
As I said to you personally here the other day, I have no wish to treat
Tilak ungenerously. In fact, it goes against my grain to take the line
I am often forced to take. But by bitter experience ranging over nearly
30 years now, I have learnt that not generosity but caution has to be
the key-note of our dealings with him.[33]

Although he was a decade younger than Mrs Besant, Gokhale
was in much poorer health. The factional quarrels within the
Congress had worn him down enormously. His new friend, the
Irishwoman settled in Madras, worried for him, writing: 'You must
guard your body for future work, and your life is a thousand times
more important than Tilak's presence in, or absence from, the
Congress.'[34] The affection was manifest, but the warning came too
late. In the second week of February 1915 Gokhale died, ostensibly
of a heart attack, but in truth from exhaustion. He had given his
life in the cause of his country-in-the-making.

VI

Gokhale's death served to strengthen Mrs Besant's commitment to
the nationalist movement. In the first week of April 1915, while
inaugurating a conference in the United Provinces, she spoke of
India as 'our Motherland', and of her hope that a free India would
be on a 'footing of equality with the other Self-Governing
Dominions' such as Canada and Australia; indeed, because of her
size and the antiquity of her civilization, 'the centre of a federated
Empire'. She then turned to the subject of Hindu–Muslim relations,
which were particularly contentious in the United Provinces.
Warning that 'a continuance of strife' would 'bar all Self-
Government', she called for 'a generous forgiveness of past injuries
on both sides, and a resolute determination to cease from the
mutual infliction of injuries in the future'.

Mrs Besant ended her address by affirming her own patriotism, her *Indian* patriotism. She said:

> To be a Servant of India is the deep wish of my heart, and the oppor-
> tunity to serve India is the greatest guerdon [reward] you can give
> me. . . . The love of India, born in early womanhood, embodied itself
> in eager defence of her in my English political life, flowered when
> Theosophy made Hinduism for me a living philosophy and religion,
> and for the last two-and-twenty years has made me consecrate to her,
> seeing in India's greatness and in India's Liberty the surest pledge for
> the progress of the world. When Mr. Gokhale lately, in an affectionate
> letter, spoke of India as 'your Motherland as much as mine, or any
> Indian's', I felt as though he had given me a patent of nobility.[35]

Mrs Besant saw her own political service to her adopted motherland as two-fold: uniting the Congress within, and presenting its case to the world without. Because of her experience of British politics, she thought herself uniquely qualified to persuade the 'Home' public of the justice of the Indian demand for freedom. In the summer of 1915 she began tapping wealthy Indians for support in presenting the Congress case to the British people. After the war was over, she told these donors, 'every Colony will claim its right in an Imperial Parliament. India should do the same. But unless in England there is now an active educational agitating body, to convince the democracy of India's right and her resolution to have them, the opportunity will be lost, and India will remain "our great Dependency".'[36]

In September 1915, Mrs Besant proposed that a Home Rule League be set up in India. Her inspiration was her native Ireland, where the cry of 'Home Rule' was then being heard more energet-ically than ever before. India, she urged, should be 'mistress of her own household'; it should become a free nation, while remaining within the framework of the British Empire. She asked:

> Will Indian leaders in every town and village take up the cry of 'Home
> Rule for India', hold meetings and explain to the masses and make
> them demand from the liberty-loving British race self-government for
> our country? Will Indian newspapers, zealously and perseveringly,

keep on writing, writing, writing till the idea permeates Indian society as a whole and the demand is clearly echoed 'Home Rule for India'![37]

Mrs Besant took the idea of Indian Home Rule on the road, speaking about it in Bombay, Allahabad, and Calcutta, among other places. A report of her speech in the last-named city began:

At a crowded meeting held at the Star Theatre on Wednesday last [6 October], Mrs. Besant explained her ideas about the proposed Home Rule League. For an hour and a quarter she held spellbound the vast audience which had come to listen to her, with an eloquence all her own. India is fortunate in having so powerful an advocate of the cause of self-government.

This report appeared in *The Bengalee*, a newspaper which (as the name shows) was run by and for Indians. The rulers, on the other hand, were rather less enthusiastic about Mrs Besant's campaign. Particularly agitated was the Madras Government, since it was in this Presidency that Mrs Besant resided, and where she had the most influence. On 8 October 1915, the Chief Secretary of Madras sent a long letter to the Government of India urging that this troublemaker be deported to Britain. 'Mrs. Besant is not without opponents', the letter noted, 'but a number of prominent men follow her leadership in the political or religious field or both, and their association with her cannot fail to increase her influence, especially the young men to whose immature and impressionable intellects her crude views and passionate denunciations are likely to be peculiarly acceptable.'

So long as Mrs Besant was starting new branches of the Theosophical Society, running schools, and opening a Central Hindu College, there was, from the perspective of the colonial state, no particular cause for worry. But this movement for Home Rule was, the Madras Government insisted, 'fraught with danger to the public peace and the public safety. . . . Mrs. Besant is now committed to this agitation and is evidently reckless as to the consequences which may result from the means which she employs to attain her ends.' The Governor of Madras therefore thought that 'the most satisfactory way of checking her activities both in the Press and on the platform would be to forbid her under the Defence of India rules to remain in British India'.

The Madras Government's proposal was actively debated in the Viceroy's Executive Council. One British member concurred, saying: 'If Mrs. Besant were forced to leave India, she will no doubt continue her campaign in the English or American Press, but we shall be spared her ravings on the Indian platform and her writings will lose a great deal of their danger on account of the distance between herself and her audience.' A second British member disagreed, saying that if the Government 'send her Home with a little halo of martyrdom', then the 'next thing we shall have is reports of speeches at Home, probably more violent that those delivered here'. A third wrote on file that 'Mrs. Besant's Home Rule League is foolish and wild, and I doubt whether even the National Congress will adopt it. I do not fancy that the Indian politicians will much relish being tied to the apron strings of an elderly European lady who in her time has had many evanescent enthusiasms.' While this official was 'not in favour of packing off the lady to Europe', he thought that 'she might now be warned in much more formal fashion, that she must restrain both her oratory and her articles, failing which section 108 of the Criminal Procedure Code and the Press Act will have to be resorted to in her case'.

A long and most interesting comment on the case came from the sole Indian member of the Executive Council, C. Sankaran Nair. He suggested that the authorities were to blame, by having unnecessarily boosted up Mrs Besant's image in the first place. Thus he wrote:

> The Government of India placed her on a high pedestal when she was ensuring her position as a great spiritual teacher. The King-Emperor and Empress honoured her college with a visit . . . This has produced a great impression. . . . I think in the present condition of the country it is unwise to provoke the volume of feeling that would be roused now by any action against her.

Nair sardonically added that 'I am the more inclined to suggest this course as I am unable to choose any definite statement made by her and say it is malicious or absolutely false.'

The file containing all these varied opinions ends with a definitive one-line verdict by the Viceroy, Lord Hardinge: 'Order: That no action [against Annie Besant] be taken at present.'[38]

VII

The debate within the Government of India about whether or not to extern Annie Besant took place behind her back. She had no clue about it; indeed, while the debate was being carried out, she was preparing for publication a 700-page book called *How India Wrought for Freedom*. Ostensibly a narrative history of the Indian National Congress, based largely on the proceedings of its annual meetings, it also sought to legitimize her own growing involvement in the movement for self-rule in India. The book was

DEDICATED
With Profound Devotion to the
MOTHERLAND
And with Respectful Admiration to her Noble Son
DADABHAI NAOROJI
By her Servant
ANNIE BESANT

The singling out of Dadabhai Naoroji was sincere as well as strategic. Now in his ninetieth year, Naoroji had a record of public service longer than anyone else in India. He had been active in politics in his homeland – serving three terms as Congress President – and in England, as the first Indian Member of the British Parliament. He had written major works of scholarship, and had an enduring interest in social reform. He was above scandal and intrigue; his character was absolutely beyond reproach.[39] Although a self-professed Moderate, even the most extreme of Extremists would not dare criticize him. By compiling a history of the Congress and then dedicating it to Naoroji, Besant was, among other things, telling her Extremist rivals that she was here for the duration.

How India Wrought for Freedom had twenty-seven substantive chapters, one for each session of the Congress held thus far. They were preceded by a fifty-page 'historical introduction', where Mrs Besant set out the case for India to be a self-governing nation. She began by tracing the antiquity of Indian civilization. India's claims to nationhood, she argued, were far older than any country in the West. Epics such as the Mahabharata and Ramayana continued to live 'vitally in Indian hearts and prayers and ceremonies of to-day', a historical continuity signalling 'only this one fact writ large: *It is on this literature and the past embodied in it that the foundation of Indian Nationality is indestructibly laid.*'

Mrs Besant insisted that 'India is a continuum, and her Aryan civilisation an unbroken whole'. She wrote of how this unity and continuity persisted through the rise and fall of empires; even Muslim invasions could not disturb or destroy it. While the coming of a foreign religion, Islam, 'caused inevitably disturbance and much evil feeling on both sides', at the same time the new rulers 'brought to the building of the Indian Nation most precious materials, enriching the Nationality and adding new aspects to its many-faced splendour'. Only the British were different; since they did not assimilate into the Indian soil, and since they went back to where they had come from.

There was, noted Mrs Besant, another difference that came with British rule; for the first time, the *whole of India* was under foreign domination. Under Mughal rule, many of the most important posts in the administration were reserved for Hindus. No longer. 'It has seemed', wrote Mrs Besant sarcastically, 'as though it were the British aim to turn the Indian Nation into a race of clerks.' The usurpation of all power, all decision-making, by the European colonists had created a pathetic feeling of dependence among the subject population. Thus 'Indians hesitate, where they should act; they ask, where they should take, they submit, where they should resist; they lack self-confidence and the audacity that commands success'. Quoting Gokhale's remark that 'a kind of dwarfing or stunting of the Indian race is going on under the present system', Mrs Besant insisted: 'This is the deepest, gravest, wrong that Great Britain has inflicted on a once mighty and imperial race. Unless Indians can again develop the old vigour, courage and initiative, India can have no future. But the old spirit is awaking on every side, and therein lies our hope.'

Annie Besant ended her 'historical introduction' with a balance sheet of colonial rule, which was decidedly biased towards the negative side of the ledger. The British conquest of India, she argued, had deliberately destroyed indigenous arts and industries, to 'favour the importation of cheap foreign goods'. The rulers had neglected irrigation, thus undermining food security, and neglected education · too; only 3 per cent of the population were literate in India, whereas 'Japan, under eastern rule, has educated her whole population in 40 years'. British rule was extremely costly; the high salaries and pension benefits of colonial officials constituting a massive drain of money and capital away from India.

India, concluded Mrs Besant, was 'getting very tired of English domination'; she was 'determined to get rid of coercive legislation, and to enjoy Self-Government'.[40]

After the book was published, Mrs Besant set·about organizing a 'Conference for the formation of a League for Self-Government'. She approached Dadabhai Naoroji to be its first patron, and he, after some hesitation, agreed. The conference was planned for the last week of December, in Bombay. Mrs Besant sent letters of invitation to many middle-class, English-speaking men from different parts of India. (Among the few Indian women active in public affairs at this time was the poet Sarojini Naidu, who did not figure in Mrs Besant's list of invitees.)

Most who had been asked to come for the meeting readily agreed. There were, however, a few dissenting voices, such as Cassamally Jairazbhoy from Bombay, who wrote to Mrs Besant saying her initiative was 'premature and ill-timed': premature because the Congress and the Muslim League already existed as representative organizations, and British statesmen had promised these bodies that they would give Indians greater representation at all levels of Government after the current war in Europe had ended; ill-timed because the British people were presently absorbed in winning the war. Mr Jairazbhoy told Mrs Besant that her campaign 'will be misunderstood in England, and it would weaken the momentum of future constitutional movements and would be fraught with real danger to the cause of ultimate progress. As an English woman, I think you should be the last person to embarrass British statesmen while their minds are pre-occupied with the war and the Empire is in danger.'[41]

Mrs Besant's conference 'for the formation of a League for Self-Government' took place in the Bombay locality of China Baug on Christmas Day 1915. The meeting discussed what form the organization would take, what the criteria for membership should be, and who its officials might be. To assuage British concerns, it was stated that the proposed 'League for Self-Government' was being established for 'the good of both Nations [India and England] and for the Safety of the Empire'. Among those in attendance were the prominent lawyers M. A. Jinnah, M. R. Jayakar, Chunilal Mehta, and Sachidanand Sinha, and the Parsi millionaire J. B. Petit.[42]

A hundred miles away in Poona, a rival conference was held the same week in December, convened by Bal Gangadhar Tilak. Its aim was to set up a Home Rule League. How this differed, in spirit and method, from the 'League for Self-Government' was not specified. But clearly Tilak wanted to have his own organization, distinct from and independent of the show orchestrated and directed by Mrs Besant.

VIII

Annie Besant published her autobiography in the year she first came to India, 1893. A third impression came out in 1908, by which time she had been in the subcontinent for a decade and a half. In the preface to this reissue, she described her work in India as being of two kinds: 'first of all, the revival, strengthening and uplifting of the ancient religions – Hinduism, Zoroastrianism, and in Ceylon and Burma, Buddhism'; and 'in the second place, educational, and the note of this has been the wedding of Western education with Eastern religion and Eastern ethics, and the carrying on of colleges and schools under the control of Indians, instead of under the control of Government or of [Christian] missionaries . . .' It is significant that, in 1908, her ambitions excluded the political. She had stayed away from questioning the legitimacy of British rule in India and from asking for self-government for Indians.[43]

Mrs Besant never wrote a sequel to her autobiography. She never explained, in her own words, why after twenty years in India she suddenly turned, or rather re-turned, to politics. It seems however that there was no one cause, no particular epiphanic movement, but rather a series of events and influences that prompted this move back from spiritualism to activism. We know that she was outraged at the casual racism of British officials in India; that she admired Gokhale and other Moderates; that her native Ireland was itself experiencing a movement for Home Rule. And let us not exclude the possibility of her being bored. Educational curriculum, Theosophical Society elections and conclaves, et al., while important in themselves, could not provide her with the excitement that public meetings and political campaigns so manifestly did.

By 1915, Annie Besant was at the very centre of political debate in British India. Towards the end of the year she composed an Indian National Song, 'God Save Our Ind', set to the tune of 'God Save the King'. Its words went:

> God save our Motherland,
> God bless our much-loved Land,
> *God save our Ind!*
>
> Sing of her story old,
> Sing of her heroes bold,
> Sing of her hearts of gold,
> *God save our Ind!*
>
> Sing Ramachandra's praise
> Sing of the Rajput days
> *God save our Ind!*
>
> Sing of great Akbar's sway,
> Sing of Shivaji's day,
> Sing boldly Freedom's lay,
> *God save our Ind!*

Lord of the Burning-ground,
Send forth Thy damru-sound,
God save our Ind!

Grant us the hero-heart,
Careless of loss or smart,
As men to play our part,
God save our Ind![44]

This 'national song' died a quick and unmourned death. Perhaps it deserved to die, for the words were hackneyed and the tune derivative. But that it was composed at all must compel some admiration. There were no half-measures with Mrs Besant; once she had chosen to become an Indian, she would be an Indian all the way through.

CHAPTER 2

Home Ruler, Congress President

I

In the year 1915, while Annie Besant was establishing her mark on Indian politics, Mohandas K. Gandhi was travelling through the subcontinent, getting to know a country he had been away from for more than two decades. The two were aware of one another; indeed, the younger man had a certain veneration for the older woman. As a young law student in London, Gandhi had heard Mrs Besant speak at Theosophy meetings. Later, as a lawyer in South Africa, Gandhi had a photograph of Mrs Besant up in his chambers, as a mark of respect for what she was doing to promote spirituality and social renewal in India.[1]

In 1905, Mrs Besant's book on the Bhagavad Gita was reprinted by a press in Durban with which Gandhi was associated. She wrote complaining that her permission had not been asked for, and that they should not have used her portrait in the book. The letter was sent to the manager of the press, who forwarded it to Gandhi, who wrote to Mrs Besant taking full responsibility. An Indian merchant had offered to fund the printing of the book 'for distribution among Hindu boys'. As Gandhi now told Mrs Besant, 'I felt that the motive of the management was pure, and that when the circumstances, under which the edition was published, were brought to your notice, you would overlook any apparent impropriety.' As regards the inclusion of the portrait, Gandhi said 'that, if a mistake has been committed, it has arisen from excessive reverence for yourself'. He added: 'Rightly or wrongly, as you are aware, publication or printing of such portraits in sacred works is not uncommon in India.'[2]

The name and work of Mrs Besant often featured in *Indian Opinion*, the journal that Gandhi had founded in South Africa. In February 1907, the lawyer translated an article by her on nation-building. In introducing the article to his Gujarati readers, Gandhi said Mrs Besant 'enjoys the reputation of being one of the world's great orators and most of her writings, too, are very instructive'.[3]

In April 1915, now back in India, Gandhi spoke at a meeting in the town of Nellore, up the coast from Madras. He was introduced by Mrs Besant, who called the speaker's work in South Africa 'an inspiration to self-sacrifice, an inspiration to the following of a great ideal', which would 'strengthen the Indian nation in future'.[4] I suppose the praise was sincere; although there were those in Mrs Besant's circle who had a less flattering view of Gandhi. When Gokhale died the previous February, V. S. Srinivasa Sastri was chosen to succeed him as President of the Servants of India Society. Mrs Besant's paper *New India* hailed the election of Sastri, adding that the suggestion, made by some, that Gandhi should have been chosen instead was 'sentimental and impractical', since that would have been akin to making the Archbishop of Canterbury the head of the Bank of England.[5]

In Nellore in 1915, it fell to Mrs Besant to introduce Gandhi at a public event. Nine months later, it fell to Mrs Besant to stop Gandhi in mid-stream while he was speaking at a public event. This was at Banaras, where a new Hindu university was being established. The university was co-founded by Mrs Besant and a nationalist named Madan Mohan Malaviya, who was a scholar of Sanskrit, a trained lawyer, and a past President of the Indian National Congress. Back in 1905, the two had independently proposed the creation of a properly *Indian* university; they amalgamated their schemes, with Malaviya taking the lead in raising funds from Hindu princes, land-lords, and merchants. By 1916 the money was in place; the land had been acquired; the buildings had been designed; and it was time to inaugurate the Banaras Hindu University.[6]

The university was formally inaugurated by the Viceroy, Lord Hardinge, amid much pomp and splendour. After the Viceroy, his duties done, had departed for New Delhi, a series of smaller cere-monies were held, at one of which Gandhi was the featured speaker.

He was expected to talk about his work with the diasporic community in South Africa, but he chose to focus on issues closer at hand instead. Indeed, Gandhi made this the occasion to announce himself as the coming man in Indian politics. He did so by attacking the patrons of the university, who had come suitably overdressed for the occasion. Was it necessary, asked Gandhi of the assembled Maharajas, 'that in order to show the truest loyalty to our King-Emperor, it is necessary for us to ransack our jewellery-boxes and to appear bedecked from head to toe'? 'There can be no spirit of self-government about us,' he carried on, 'if we take away or allow others to take away from the peasants almost the whole of the results of their labour.'

After targeting the Princes Gandhi targeted colonial officials, of whom a fair sprinkling were also present. As he chastised them for being so indifferent to the plight of ordinary Indians, Mrs Besant, who was also sitting on the stage, said 'Stop! Stop! Stop!' The students, on the other hand, asked Gandhi to continue. So he did. But when he characterized British officials as 'tyrannical and overbearing', Mrs Besant intervened once more. The chairman, the Maharaja of Darbhanga, now asked Gandhi to stop, once and for all.[7]

After the event, Mrs Besant told a friend that Gandhi was a mere 'child in politics, a dreamer wandering in a world he did not know or understand'.[8] In public she defended her intervention as being in the interests of decorum. Since the university's patrons were in attendance, as a member of the Reception Committee she had to make sure things did not get out of hand.[9]

II

In the last week of December 1915 Annie Besant had organized a conference seeking a 'League for Self-Government' for India. By the time the new year had dawned this had been renamed the Home Rule League, an apparent nod to the movement for Home Rule in Ireland. Under that scheme the Irish would have their own parliament, while their Government would be run by Irish, rather than

English, civil servants. However, Ireland would still be part of the Empire, with the British monarch as Head of State.

Annie Besant had first announced a Home Rule League in an article in *New India* published on 25 September 1915. The League was formally inaugurated a year later, on 3 September 1916. By this time Bal Gangadhar Tilak had started an organization of his own, with a similar aim and name. On 28 April 1916, Tilak established the Indian Home Rule League; when Mrs Besant inaugurated her own show five months later, she called it the All India Home Rule League.

The two organizations were competitive, but in a friendly rather than rivalrous manner. Tilak knew that he commanded greatest influence in western India; Mrs Besant knew that her domain was Madras and the United Provinces. The British Raj was hostile to both Home Rule Leagues. In July 1916, bonds of Rs 40,000 (a considerable sum) were placed on Tilak's newspapers on the grounds that they were seditious. He was externed from Punjab, the province from which Indian soldiers for the First World War were principally recruited. Fines were also imposed on Mrs Besant's paper *New India* (for writing sympathetically of the Home Rule movement in Ireland), and she was barred from entering the Central Provinces and the Bombay Presidency.[10] She remained defiant, writing to a Tamil friend: 'I am still alive, and so is *New India*. "Threatened men live long," they say. But for all they can do, India will win Home Rule.'[11]

The All India Home Rule League hoped to achieve self-government within the Empire through constitutional means. Mrs Besant had maintained her connections with her old Socialist friends in England, now part of the rising Labour Party. The Labour leaders Philip Snowden and George Lansbury agreed to be vice presidents of the London branch of her All India Home Rule League. Scotland Yard prepared a report on this branch, terming it 'potentially very dangerous', as well as 'irresponsible and ignorant'. This outfit, claimed the Yard, 'will be exploited by cranks of all kinds, pacifist, socialist, labour, feminist . . .'[12]

Through the first half of 1916, *New India* regularly carried sympathetic articles on the Irish rebellion.[13] Because it now vigorously advocated Home Rule for India, Mrs Besant's journal was subjected to regular harassment under the Press Act. Several articles were deemed to be seditious or charged with 'stirring up racial animosity'.[14] The paper was asked to pay substantial sums as a security deposit, and Mrs Besant made to appear in court. Her appearances further impressed her Indian admirers, with her oratory apparently displaying 'the tongue of Demosthenes and the brain of Plato and Socrates combined'.[15] She continued to write against press censorship. After one case brought against *New India*, Mrs Besant wrote: 'Queen Mary thought she was blowing out candles when she burned her heretics. She blundered; she was lighting them. Government thinks it will destroy *New India* by forfeiture; it blunders; *New India*, its body struck away, will assume a myriad subtle forms, and will breathe life and inspiration into myriads of Indian hearts.'[16]

Mrs Besant saw the struggle in intensely personal terms. In June 1916, she wrote an essay on what she called 'the great struggle for liberty, for Home Rule, that has begun in India'. The 'people have chosen already', she said, 'and their cry is ringing through the land. What will the leaders do? Will all step forward and lead, or will some hesitate and fall back?' These questions she answered on her own behalf as follows:

> To be chosen to bear the standard [for Indian Home Rule] is the good karma which grows out of a life that has never shrunk from sacrifice for Freedom's sake. Turned out of my home because I would not pretend to believe in a Christianity which I had rejected; winning my war on press and platform as a soldier of political liberty; fighting beside Charles Bradlaugh for the right to Free Speech and Free Thought, and then for the right to Free Discussion on social matters; fighting beside him for the right to the seat he had won; fighting for [a] decent life for match-girls, for dockers, for the unskilled and the helpless, for Free Speech again in the last great London struggle; fighting against the treatment of India, the invasion of Afghanistan, the theft of Egypt, for Ireland in the early dangerous days when Home Rule was 'the march to the dismemberment of the Empire through rapine', for Internationalism and Socialism in France, in Holland, in Britain – I have won the right again in the [battle] for Free Speech in India.

Mrs Besant continued:

> I am not wont to boast of my past, nor to claim to lead when the
> way is easy; but in the day of peril, when Liberty, my life's mistress,
> calls, I claim my place in the front of the struggle. . . . 'Materialised
> Mystic' as I am, I believe that God has given me this glorious struggle
> for India for the last of this life's efforts, and that none can prevent
> this beloved Motherland from winning the Home Rule that He has
> awarded to her as her Right.[17]

As autobiographical narratives shall, this retrospectively imposed
order and coherence on what had in fact been a very meandering
life's journey. In Mrs Besant's rendition, an absolutely straight line
led from the first rejection of her familial faith via her struggles with
socialists and atheists on to the crowning achievement of her being
in the vanguard of the fight for India's freedom.

Mrs Besant was now increasingly losing patience with the slowness
of constitutional reform. The suppression of the Easter Rising in
Ireland affected her greatly; as did the punitive actions on her newspaper, the fines and closures levied on it by the Government of
Madras. In October 1916, when an Indian friend asked whether she
would attend a reception in the Viceroy's honour, she angrily
answered:

> How could you suppose that I could accept an invitation to do honour
> to a man who had tried to intern me, and is trying to ruin me? I am
> free-born, and bow to no coercionist. So long as Indians do not resent
> coercive legislation, but flatter those who resort to it and do them
> honour, there is little hope of India's freedom. . . . I think you hardly
> understand how we, who are Irish, feel about oppression, and I resent
> it for Indians far more than I do for myself.[18]

III

As Mrs Besant became ever more prominent in public affairs, she was the subject of acclaim as well as criticism in the press. Some loyalist papers in India thought this Home Ruler to be a dangerous radical. Writing in March 1916, the *Cochin Argus* claimed 'Mrs. Besant has been doing her best to bring British rule in India into contempt and disrepute'. Referring to a speech she had made attacking Government education policy, the paper said that 'presumably, she thinks that Home Rule will come sooner the more the Government is attacked and vilified, the more its motives are attacked, and the more people of this country are rendered discontented and restless . . .'

In its issue of 29 May 1916, *New India* charged a rival Madras paper, the *Indian Patriot*, of being excessively obsequious towards the Government of India and especially its powerful Home Secretary, Sir Harold Stuart. The next day, the *Indian Patriot* responded with a splendidly splenetic attack on Mrs Besant, where it said, among other things:

> May we suggest to Mrs. Besant that she must have as much tolerance for difference of opinion as she expects Government to show towards her. . . . She has absolutely no claim on us: she has no right to expect us to follow her. She came into our politics only yesterday. The editor of the *Indian Patriot* has been in public life for nearly thirty years . . . There is not a prominent journal or a prominent public man whom she has not attacked when they ventured to differ from her. She is after all an Irish woman whom nobody beyond her Theosophical Society is bound to revere; and her claim to lead the whole of India setting aside all old leaders and public workers is most preposterous.

Other Indian periodicals were more appreciative of Mrs Besant. In May 1916, the respected Tamil paper *Swadeshamitran* said that *New India* 'has been doing immense good to the people after it was purchased by Mrs. Besant. It is through this paper and her lectures from time to time that Mrs. Besant has created a national consciousness among the people of this country.' In the same month, a Kannada paper published in the princely state of Mysore remarked of Mrs Besant that 'in the British Empire there is no one of either sex who can equal her in capacity or scholarship'.[19]

Another Kannada paper, published from Bellary, offered this encomium for the Irish proponent of India's freedom:

> Mrs. Besant is sowing the seeds of self-government in the heart of every Indian. She is going from house to house, from village to village, and from bazaar to bazaar, and like electricity she is drawing the student population towards the current of liberty. Her strength does not lie in mere eloquence. She fully practises what she preaches.[20]

IV

In November 1916, Mrs Besant was prevented from entering the Central Provinces. In protest, a public meeting was held in Allahabad, presided over by the Congress leader, Motilal Nehru, at which 'all the leading Hindu politicians of Allahabad and the members of the Lucknow Home Rule deputation were present'. Mrs Besant's work for the country was praised and the demand put forward for her being elected the next Congress President.

A report on this meeting promoted the Home Member of the Viceroy's Executive Government to write:

> I regret very much that we did not take the advice of the Madras Government a year ago and send Mrs. Besant home. The general view then was that she would fall foul of the Congress and lose her influence. What has really happened is that although she may have, owing to jealousy, lost some of her personal ascendancy, yet her Home Rule programme is practically being adopted by the Congress and the Muslim League. . . . The demand for Home Rule as an ultimate ideal cannot be called unreasonable; but the demand for immediate Home Rule which is now coming to the front is assuming a revolutionary aspect.

The Home Member could not 'help feeling that Mrs. Besant would be better out of the country, or failing that, that the Madras Government should intern her'. As things stood, she could not be kept out of the annual meeting of the Congress, to be held in Lucknow in December 1916. As the Home Member said in exasperation, it would be

> inconsistent to keep Mrs. Besant out, and to allow Tilak and other extremist leaders to speak to their heart's content at Lucknow. If Mrs. Besant is allowed to come, Tilak can hardly be excluded. But I feel that we are rather drifting into the position in which political leaders will soon work up the feeling that anything short of Home Rule at the end of the war will be a justification for violent agitation, and violent agitation is sooner or later accompanied by actual violence. The cause of the anarchists in Bengal will be greatly strengthened and the secret applause which they receive will be much increased. I cannot help feeling that this rising Home Rule ardour requires to be damped.[21]

At the Lucknow Congress, the Extremists and Moderates were under one roof for the first time in a decade. Tilak and Mrs Besant, in that order, were the stars of the Congress. The annual meeting of the Theosophical Society was held in the same week in Lucknow, with the matriarch hopping from one venue to the other, and back again.

Through the winter of 1916–17 the Home Rule movement grew rapidly. Every district town in the Madras Presidency opened a branch of the League. The participation of young men in the movement particularly unnerved the authorities. 'There is no question', wrote an intelligence report in alarm, 'as to the hold which Mrs. Besant and her followers are acquiring on the rising generation.'[22]

Mrs Besant's ability to impress the young was regarded with particular dread in the princely state of Mysore, which bordered the Madras Presidency. The students of Bangalore town wanted her to come and speak to them; the British Resident to the Maharaja had the invitation scrapped. 'Personally I regard Mrs. Besant as a very real political danger', wrote the Resident to the Government of India:

Her speciality seems to be to get hold of young and impressionable students and to inflame their minds against our rule. It is dangerous to predict; but, unless I am mistaken, the culte of Annie Besant is a stepping-stone to political assassination. It is high time her mischievous propensities were stopped finally. A policy of 'wait and see' is bad in England. In India, it is a positive danger.[23]

In the spring of 1917, the Madras Government banned colleges from inviting Indian politicians to give lectures to students. Annie Besant now worried that there was a danger of 'the youth of the country [being] divided into two groups: one servile and cringing, useless to the country and fit only to be the servants of the bureaucracy; the other high-spirited and patriotic but desperate, clinging to anarchical violence'. To 'save these unfortunate youths from becoming either slaves or rebels', she thought of promoting a scheme of National Education, 'entirely apart from, but not in hostility to, the official system', and which would offer as 'an alternative to the government and missionary schools, an education which will train Indian students as students in other countries are trained, to look forward to a life honourable to themselves and useful to their country, nourishing in their boyhood and youth a noble ambition to be worthy citizens of a great and powerful Nation'.

Writing in *New India* on 1 March, Mrs Besant offered 'three outstanding reasons why we should demand Home Rule after the War'. The first reason was that Indians were less free than when the British Crown took over from the East India Company in 1858; the right to bear arms had been taken away, and there now were increasing curbs on the freedom of the press. The second reason was that demands for greater access to education, for protection of Indian industries, for more army commissions, for enhancing local self-government, etc., had been ignored, with the Raj showing 'stolid indifference' to 'Indian aspirations'. The third, and most important, reason for Indians to demand Home Rule was 'because Liberty is man's birthright, and because the rule of another Nation is inconsistent with National self-respect, National dignity, and unfettered National development'.[24]

In May 1917, Mrs Besant drafted a scheme for National Education, whose curriculum would 'place Indian interests in the forefront', and 'make India the centre of study, and study of other countries adjuncts instead of primaries'. A 'special stress' would be laid 'on the commercial, trade and agricultural side of education . . . but the Arts will not be forgotten, and a broad foundation will be laid on which culture may be built'. All subjects would be taught in the vernacular of the province, with English as a compulsory second language.[25]

The Government was planning its own scheme, in order to silence this troublemaker. With a war on in Europe, the British did not want to be embarrassed with a rising tide of nationalist sentiment in their largest and most lucrative colony. They blamed Mrs Besant for stirring up passions, and thought that if they shut her up, and shut her away, the movement for Home Rule might die down.

On 16 June 1917, the Governor of Madras called Mrs Besant for an interview; and told her that out of his 'great consideration' for her, he would give her a chance to reconsider the statements she had recently made, failing which she would be served with an order of internment. Mrs Besant answered that she had nothing to regret in anything she had said or written. The Governor offered her safe passage to England for the duration of the war. She said she did not want to go to England.

After the meeting, Mrs Besant returned to her home in Adyar, where the internment order was served on her an hour later. She was offered a choice of six places to be confined in. She chose the hill town of Ootacamund, proceeding there by train with her two associates George Arundale and B. P. Wadia. Here, she would stay in a cottage originally owned by the Theosophist Colonel Olcott. She was allowed to meet visitors, but her letters were censored and no trips to other towns permitted.[26]

The Madras Government sent the Government of India a dossier hundreds of pages long, outlining the reasons why they had taken action against Mrs Besant. They charged her with 'employing every means to inflame racial animosities', with offering 'a series of disgraceful comments on the Irish rebellion', and with conducting a 'persistent campaign' to 'foment discontent and indiscipline among students'.

The dossier drew attention to Mrs Besant's influence on Government servants, many of whom were Theosophists. 'No less deplorable is

Mrs. Besant's influence on teachers', it added. The Government worried that Mrs Besant's style was being imitated by vernacular writers 'to infect the masses of the Presidency' with subversive ideas. And so the Governor had acted to restrain her, since 'strong measures against the misguided people who were only imitating Mrs. Besant, would be neither fair nor likely to be effective, unless the principal offender, Mrs. Besant herself, was first dealt with. So long as she remained unpunished, Indians who merely copied her example would believe themselves safe and see no reason for discontinuing their activities.' This was a remarkable, albeit unwitting, acknowledgement of Mrs Besant's standing among middle-class, politically conscious, English-speaking Indians.[27]

As the news of Mrs Besant's internment spread, it led to a series of protest meetings across southern and western India. Large cities like Bombay and Madras, small towns like Calicut, Gooty, and Salem, all witnessed demonstrations demanding her immediate release. Several provincial Congress committees resolved to have her elected President of the next annual session of the party, due in December. The Government had hoped to quell Mrs Besant's influence; instead, they greatly enhanced her standing and reputation. That the State would seek to silence her was seen as decisive proof of her deep love for, and her total identification with, the Indian people.[28] As the prominent Moderate Surendranath Banerjee observed:

> The internment of a gifted lady who was serving the motherland with unexampled devotion set the whole country ablaze with excitement. The general feeling was that by her internment the Government sought to aim a deadly blow at the agitation for self-government, which she had so vigorously championed; and the utterances of provincial rulers, which had a wonderful family likeness in their tone of disparagement, if not of ridicule, deepened the public impression and intensified the public agitation. . . . Could the bureaucracy have anticipated the agitation that Mrs. Besant's internment gave rise to, it would probably have left her alone.[29]

One would have thought that, confined to her cottage in Ooty, Mrs Besant could give the authorities no trouble at all. But there was a cordite factory on the outskirts of the town, and the Madras Government worried that the presence nearby of this old, but undeniably combative, lady would stir the workers to industrial action. 'Under existing conditions', wrote the Chief Secretary, 'it seems highly probable that Ootacamund will develop into a place of pilgrimage.'

The Madras Government had Mrs Besant shifted to the town of Coimbatore, at the foot of the hills. But this didn't quieten their fears; since, even when confined to her cottage, she apparently continued 'to be a dangerous source of inspiration'. The Government now thought that the only solution was to extern Mrs Besant from the province, and preferably from India itself. The Governor of Madras wrote to the Viceroy advising such a move. Since Mrs Besant's 'opportunities for mischief at home would be infinitely less than they are here', he remarked, it would be 'highly politic, were the Government of India to send Mrs. Besant home with as little delay as possible'.

The Viceroy shot down the proposal. 'There are obvious objections to deportation to England', he told the Governor:

> Mrs. Besant is an old lady and we must have regard to her health. The monsoon season is now on and we could scarcely force her to take a voyage at a time when we would not send our own womenfolk. Moreover, the submarine peril is a very real one, and we should incur grave criticism if we were to submit her to chances which we forbid women generally to take at this time.[30]

Mrs Besant's internment dismayed sections of the British Establishment. She had many influential friends; among them Emily Lutyens, wife of the architect who was then designing the imperial city of New Delhi, and a considerable figure in her own right. A month after Mrs Besant's internment, the Liberal statesman Edwin Montagu was appointed Secretary of State for India. Emily Lutyens immediately wrote him a letter of congratulation, praising him as a true 'friend of India'. The formalities out of the way, Mrs Lutyens came to the main point of her letter. 'Indeed, it is time that sympathy with Indian National aspirations should be shown from high quarters', she wrote,

and some encouragement given to constitutional agitation for reform
or I fear a very dangerous situation will arise. . . . I wish you could
do something to procure Mrs. Besant's unconditional release. Her
power in India is immense both as a religious teacher and a political
leader. She is loved and reverenced as 'Mother' from one end of India
to another, and do you think those who regard themselves as her
children are going to stand quietly by and see her persecuted by the
Government?

Appealing shrewdly to imperial interest, Emily Lutyens claimed
that 'the first result of her removal has been a tremendous wave of
enthusiasm for the Swadeshi movement', adversely affecting the sale
in India of British goods, and a second result that recruiting for the
war, 'of which Mrs. Besant was an enthusiastic advocate, is being
stopped'. More broadly, 'the question arises now that Mrs. Besant's
restraining hand has been removed will it be possible to keep that
movement within constitutional limits? The advocates of violence
are many, but of such methods Mrs. Besant has always been a
determined opponent.'

Emily Lutyens then alerted the Secretary of State to the international aspects of the case. For Mrs Besant had

thousands of devoted followers all over the world who are burning
with indignation at the treatment meted out to one whose life and
teachings are an inspiration to thousands. What can they think of
England who proclaims that she is fighting in this War for the freedom
of Nations and for democracy and yet allows actions to be taken in
her name worthy of pre-revolution Russia and Prussia rolled into
one.

Mrs Besant's seventieth birthday was due to fall on 1 October.
Her followers all over the world were going to organize special
celebrations to mark the occasion. These, warned Mrs Lutyens, might
now turn out to be protest meetings against the harsh treatment of
her by the British Government. 'Is this going to help England?' she
asked.

Emily Lutyens ended her artfully worded letter to Edwin Montagu with this clever plea: 'If you could inaugurate your reign at the India Office by procuring Mrs. Besant's release I believe it would do more than anything else to win you the sympathy and confidence of the Indian people – and you would start your reign of Office with blessings instead of curses.'[31]

V

Emily Lutyens sent her letter to Edwin Montagu in the last week of July 1917. His reply is unavailable, but in September he gave instructions that Mrs Besant should be released as a gesture of goodwill. She was freed from internment on 17 September, where-upon meetings to celebrate her release were held in many towns of the Madras Presidency. The president of the meeting in Guntur said: 'Christ was subjected to many troubles and was crucified and killed. . . . When a great deed has to be done, some sacrifice has necessarily to be made. In *yagnams* our countrymen make sacrifices. In the present great *yagnam* of political agitation, Mrs. Besant was the offering and she sacrificed her body.'[32]

In November, the Secretary of State, Edwin Montagu, came out to India for a close look at the massive and diverse territory under his command. He stayed several months, travelling across the subcontinent, combining shikar with work, meeting all the important public figures in India.

Annie Besant had a long conversation with Montagu on 26 November 1917, in New Delhi. She met him at his hotel, and then drove with him to the temporary home of the Viceroy, in the north of the city, across a forested ridge. In the car Mrs Besant urged the Secretary of State to attend the Calcutta Congress, due the next month, and of which she had been elected President. He replied: 'Mrs. Besant, my work is already very difficult. I do not want to make it impossible.' He had, he said, to bring the bureaucracy around, which meant avoiding large public meetings such as the Congress.

After the new Viceroy, Lord Chelmsford, had joined them, the three sitting on large sofas, Montagu immediately asked: 'When I was here last, Mrs. Besant, you were engaged in educational work.

Why did you go into politics?' Mrs Besant replied that when she came to India, she had political ideas, but wished to know the country first, and hence focused on educational matters. She however insisted that even in their educational work 'all the time we were troubled by the suspicions, doubts and questionings on the part of Government'. Then she met Gopal Krishna Gokhale and other Congressmen, and became more involved in political questions. Both Gokhale and she wished to draw patriotic young Indians away from 'the more violent and showy methods'. Gokhale was keen to bring the Extremists back into the Congress, and asked Mrs Besant to speak to Tilak and his friends, which she did. Then Gokhale died, and 'I was left to carry out our plans alone.'

Chelmsford and Montagu listened patiently to this extensive recapitulation of Mrs Besant's life in India. She moved on next to the formation of the Home Rule League, which she said was partly inspired by a visit to Bengal, where she sensed a growing anger among the youth. She claimed that 'the Home Rule League had drawn many young men away from the desire to join the revolutionary party, and therefore that it had been of immense service both to this country and to the Empire'.

At this point Montagu asked Mrs Besant her opinion of local government. Mrs Besant underlined its importance; noting that 'villagers were not so densely ignorant as was made out; they had their own culture; they were shrewd and knew their business'. She urged the handing over of more power to District Boards and village councils.

The Viceroy now asked: 'Suppose we gave you the whole of that scheme, why do you want Provincial autonomy as well?' Mrs Besant answered that this too was necessary, since programmes of education, health, etc. needed supervision, direction, and the ability to raise funds within the province. The Viceroy then asked: 'If you are given provincial autonomy, why do you want also to change the Imperial Council?' Mrs Besant said it was for the same reason. 'Your Government have the largest sources of supply. Unless we have a large majority and can control the purse, how are we able to get the money?'

The meeting had gone on for several hours already. Chelmsford and Montagu indicated they had other engagements. 'There is one thing I want to say before I go', said Mrs Besant, 'India is determined to be free, and if you do not meet her, you will be up against a <u>Nation</u>.' 'Well, Mrs. Besant', answered the Viceroy, 'it is we who have made that unity.' To which she responded: 'It is not a question of who made the unity, the point is that it is here. Granted that you made it, how are you going to face it now?'

On her way out, Mrs Besant said she was soon to leave for England, and wanted an assurance that she would be allowed back to India on her return. Her notes of the meeting conclude with this exchange:

> The Viceroy laughed: 'Mrs. Besant, if you only knew how often we have wanted to deport you. We should have been so glad to get you out of the country so often!'
>
> 'Yes,' I said. 'But I won't leave here, until I am quite sure that I shall be able to come back.'
>
> 'Well, you know,' he said, 'it is a very difficult matter for any woman to travel to England just now.'
>
> 'Oh, it is not the danger that I mind,' I said. 'I don't care about that at all.'[33]

VI

Of Annie Besant's standing in India in 1917, one historian has written: 'At the time of her release it seemed she had the national movement at her feet. The internment had united Moderates and Extremists as never before, and her popularity swept her into the Presidential chair of the Congress session in Calcutta at the end of 1917.'[34]

Mrs Besant was the first woman to be elected President of the Indian National Congress. She began her presidential address in Calcutta by focusing on something else that was singular; that, 'for the first time in Congress history', the members had chosen one, who when the choice was made, 'was under the heavy ban of Government displeasure, and who lay interned as a person dangerous to public safety'. With a (not unmerited) sense of self-satisfaction, Mrs Besant proclaimed: 'While I was humiliated, you crowned me with honour; while I was slandered, you believed in my integrity and good faith; while I was crushed under the heel of bureaucratic power, you acclaimed me as your leader; while I was silenced and unable to defend myself, you defended me, and won for me release.'

Mrs Besant represented her election as Congress President as a harbinger of happier relations between Great Britain and India. Most Indians knew Englishmen only as rulers and conquerors, who sought to chain and control them. Drawing the audience's attention to another England, 'the England that is the enemy of tyranny, the foe of autocracy, the lover of freedom', Mrs Besant said 'that is the England I would fain here represent to you to-day'.

After this emotional beginning, Mrs Besant turned to a more dispassionate analysis of the cost of British rule. For the past century, Indians had paid, in money and blood, for a series of wars that were not of their creation and not in their own interest; fought by the British against the Afghans and the Nagas, in Africa and in the Middle East. At the same time, India had seen its handicrafts destroyed under British rule; and got little by way of education or health care in return. They were not prepared to accept all this any more. There was, remarked Mrs Besant, now a 'New Spirit in India', represented in the awakening of the merchants, of the women, and of the masses, all representing in different ways 'the cry of a Nation for Freedom, for Self-Rule'.

In her presidential address, Mrs Besant argued that 'India demands Home Rule for two reasons, one, essential, and vital, the other less important but weighty: First, because Freedom is the birthright of every Nation: secondly, because her most important interests are now made subservient to the interests of the British Empire without her consent, and her resources are not utilised for her greatest needs.' What the Home Rulers were now telling the British was this: 'You have not succeeded in bringing education, health, prosperity, to the masses of the people. Is it not time to give Indians a chance of doing, for their own country, work similar to that which Japan and other Nations have done for theirs?'

Mrs Besant ended her two-hour-long address with a stirring

anticipation of the redemption of a land great in the past and destined to be even greater in the future: 'India, which has been verily the Crucified among Nations, now stands on this her Resurrection morning, the Immortal, the Glorious, the Ever-Young; and India shall soon be seen, proud and self-reliant, strong and free, the radiant Splendour of Asia, as the Light and the Blessing of the World.'[35]

VII

The anointment of Annie Besant as Congress President showed the profound respect and admiration she commanded among educated Indians across the country. However, there was one element of the politically alert middle class which did not warm to her, who were in fact strongly opposed to her. This was the non-Brahmin intelligentsia of the Madras Presidency. They had recently formed an organization, known as the Justice Party, which pointed out that the Brahmins of Madras, though a mere 3 per cent of the population, commanded a disproportionate share of Government jobs. The Brahmins dominated the professions too. Senior lawyers, college and school principals, editors of newspapers, successful doctors, all tended to be Brahmin.

In her writings and speeches, Annie Besant interpreted the history of India in Hindu, even Brahmanical, terms. She went so far as to claim that it was Brahmins who had 'given to India all that was greatest in her literature and arts'; that Brahmins were the 'natural leaders of the people' owing to their 'high education', their 'brilliant intelligence', their 'powers of speech'.[36] These sentiments justly provoked the ire of the emerging non-Brahmin movement in the Madras Presidency, especially since Mrs Besant seemed to think that only Brahmins could lead India in the present as well.[37]

The Justice Party's house organ regularly attacked Mrs Besant. When *New India* ran an article claiming that 'the anti-Brahmana movement preaching the Crusade of Hate . . . is essentially foreign in spirit, not Indian', *Justice* rebutted this vigorously, saying: 'We know more about what is Indian than Mrs. Besant. We have not renounced our country, and we never will, and we have no respect for those who renounced their own, their native land.' *Justice* insisted that, far from promoting hatred, the non-Brahmin communities were 'trying to improve their own position in their own way without . . . provoking any feeling of hostility towards any other community, Indian or non-Indian'. *Justice* dismissed Mrs Besant's influence on the grounds that 'the people of India are very amenable to flattery especially by a European. It is by flattery that Mrs. Besant has secured so many Indians to follow her lead.'

Also very critical of Mrs Besant was a Madras weekly named *Non-Brahman*, edited by a young man named C. Sarangapani Mudaliyar. This argued that *New India* was controlled and directed by 'a stinking combination of Brahman vakils [lawyers] and vakilets'. Mudaliyar urged 'Non-Brahmans to show that they deserve self-government by refusing to be sung into sleep by Besantine lullabies'. While Madras politicians were 'immersed in Annie Besantism', remarked the *Non-Brahman*,

> our sturdy thinkers from the *mufassal* [small towns] still continue to think for themselves, and do not let Mrs. Besant or her emissary Mr. Wadia think for them. . . . The time is not far off when she will be thrown off like a sucked orange by those who now call her mother and make her pierce the bureaucratic lines, so that they may take possession of the breach.[38]

The Justice Party's charge that Anne Besant was particularly well disposed to Brahmins and Brahminism was not without foundation. Yet it was expressed in perhaps excessively polemical language. Writing to her friend P. Kesava Pillai, Mrs Besant said: 'Don't trouble about the attacks on me in *Justice*; I do not mind them in the least, and they injure *Justice*, not me. I am entirely indifferent to what [the Justice Party leader] Dr Nair and his young men say or write.' In another letter, she hoped that the non-Brahmin movement would become 'a movement for the improvement of the status of the non-Brahmanas, and not one of attack on Brahmanas'. In a third letter she claimed that the denunciations of her as pro-Brahmin had done 'great harm' to 'the National cause'. In a fourth letter she said of the Justice Party leader Dr Nair, that 'he strikes at everyone who stands out a little above the crowd – a policy of mere jealousy'.[39]

These attacks had evidently hurt Mrs Besant, despite her protestations to the contrary.

VIII

In the past, the person chosen as Congress President had 'regarded it as essentially a one-day or at the most a one-week job'; performed only when the Congress was actually in session, as a reward for past services. Mrs Besant, however, argued that the President should be continuously active for a whole year, from one session to the next, deepening the Congress's roots and organization across India, and working full-time for Home Rule.[40] In keeping with this aim, she wrote several letters to the Viceroy in January 1918, complaining of ill-treatment of political prisoners. She provided details of several such cases, which had caused 'bitter resentment' among those Indians who heard these stories. She combatively asked: 'If Germans ruled in England, and such stories leaked out as to the treatment of untried Englishmen, would you not all be furious?'[41]

In March 1918, Mrs Besant visited Ahmedabad, where Mohandas Gandhi was in the midst of organizing a strike of disaffected textile workers. The two met in the home of the textile magnate Ambalal Sarabhai. Gesturing towards their host, Gandhi told Mrs Besant: 'They were prepared to crush the millhands out of existence.' Ambalal responded: 'And they were prepared to crush the millowners out of existence.' Mrs Besant asked Gandhi whether she should ask the Government to intervene between the striking workers and the millowners. Gandhi answered there was no need, since 'there has been perfect good humour between us'.[42]

Later, Annie Besant wired the Ahmedabad mill-owners: 'Do not sacrifice a great man to a small cause.'[43] That the cause was 'small' the capitalists (or the workers) may not have agreed; but of Gandhi's growing stature there was no longer any dispute. He had already successfully organized peasants in Bihar and Gujarat; this struggle in Ahmedabad was further proof that he was the rising man in Indian politics.

In 1918, a Franchise Committee appointed by the Imperial Government toured India. They concluded that the vote should not be given to Indian women. Native-born feminists were furious, and so was the Indian by domicile, Annie Besant. The following spring she travelled to England to testify before a Parliamentary Committee that the omission of women's suffrage was a grievous blow to Indian hopes and aspirations. In a public speech in London entitled 'Indian Women as Citizens', Mrs Besant argued that Indian women who met the education and property criteria that allowed Indian men to vote should be enfranchised immediately. She told her audiences that Indian women needed the vote 'even more than English women'.[44]

As Congress President, Mrs Besant had established fraternal relations between her party and the Labour Party in Great Britain. The hope was that Labour would send delegates each year to the annual meeting of the Indian National Congress, as they already did to meetings of fraternal parties in Canada, the United States, and France.[45]

In further pursuit of this internationalist agenda, the wealthy American branch of the Theosophical Society had written to the US President, Woodrow Wilson, about the justice of the Indian demand for self-rule. President Wilson was asked to support this cause, out of his own 'love for freedom and fair play', and because the movement was being led by 'that illustrious protagonist of the rights of men, Annie Besant'. Wilson was told that 'the hopes of India's teeming millions now lie in the hands of the greatest living advocate of Democracy and Living Responsibility – yourself, Mr. President'.[46]

Ironically, even as the Indian cause was being taken overseas, fissures had emerged – or re-emerged – at home. The uneasy compact between Moderates and Extremists had broken down. In a public statement, Mrs Besant said:

> I regret extremely that his followers have broken off my co-operation with Lok[manya] Tilak. I respect him for his flawless courage, his intense patriotism, and his utter self-abnegation in the cause of the Motherland, and I believe that he and I formed a strong combination, over the disruption of which the enemies of India, though also some of her friends, will rejoice.[47]

Mrs Besant thought Bal Gangadhar Tilak was her main rival. So he had been – in the past. But now both Maharashtrian man and Irishwoman were being rapidly put in the shade by the Gujarati out of South Africa via London, Mohandas Gandhi. As the new year dawned, Gandhi began making preparations for his first all-India campaign, the Rowlatt Satyagraha of 1919. A planning meeting, held at his ashram at Ahmedabad in the last week of February, was attended by, among others, Jamnadas Dwarkadas, a Theosophist and Home Ruler and a devoted disciple of Annie Besant. Dwarkadas was deeply impressed by Gandhi's ideas and example, and signed the 'Satyagraha Pledge'. This called for civil disobedience against the harsh new sedition law the Government proposed to enact, known as the 'Rowlatt Act' after the British judge who had helped draft it.

Jamnadas Dwarkadas knew that Mrs Besant (whom he called 'Mother') would be lukewarm about signing such a Satyagraha Pledge herself. So he now wrote to her: 'Your attitude is quite correct so far as you are concerned. You cannot take part in a movement like this, because you do not know the language of the people you are speaking to.'[48]

Dwarkadas knew that Mrs Besant, now in her seventies, was not comfortable with street protest any more. But surely he was also implying that she was now out of touch with the popular mood, which included, of course, the language in which the popular mood was expressed. Gandhi had signalled that political discourse between Indians would henceforth be conducted principally in the vernacular, in Gujarati or Tamil or Hindi as the case might be. The language of the people was necessary to take the Congress out of its middle-class, English-speaking cocoon and embrace peasants and artisans and workers as well. In this endeavour an Irishwoman who spoke no Indian language would no longer have a place.

Dwarkadas was not the only follower of Mrs Besant to embrace Gandhi's Satyagraha Pledge. So did many other young men, among them quite a few from her own bastion of Madras. Mrs Besant felt injured and ignored, communicating her feelings to the veteran Madras Congressman S. Subramania Iyer, who in turn passed them on to Gandhi. Gandhi replied to Iyer:

Will you please tell Mrs. Besant this movement is not a party movement, and those who belong to particular parties after joining the
movement cease to be party men? She will find, as the movement
progresses, that satyagrahis will endeavour to purge themselves of
acrimony and other such delinquencies. I entirely agree with you that
however much we may differ from her, no Indian can help feeling
grateful to her for her wonderful services to India.[49]

The month of April saw well-attended protests against the Rowlatt
Act conducted in towns and cities across India. The cry on the lips
of those participating in public meetings was 'Mahatma Gandhi ki
jai', 'Glory to Mahatma Gandhi'. This seems to have angered Mrs
Besant even more. She now wrote to Gandhi accusing him of irre-
sponsibility and polluting young minds through his satyagraha
campaign. 'You little realise', she said, 'how you have led young men
of good impulses but thoughtless, to break their most solemn pledges
by inducing them to take your vow.'[50] Gandhi, in reply, said:

> It saddens me to see in your writings a new Mrs. Besant who in utter
> disregard of man-made laws, whether social or political, stood for
> Truth against the whole world. It is tragic to think that you should
> now turn back upon your own teachings and accuse me of 'leading
> young men of good impulses to break their most solemn pledges'. I
> cannot accept the charge, but I would certainly advise everyone to
> break all the pledges he might have taken if they are contrary to
> Truth. . . . Surely your past life is a striking demonstration of the
> truth of my remark. Is not every reformer an avowed law-breaker?

'But I do not want to strive with you', added Gandhi: 'I shall continue
to think of the Mrs. Besant whom from my youth I had come to
regard as a great and living illustration of fearlessness, courage and
truth.'

At this time, both Gandhi and Mrs Besant were in Bombay. Gandhi
concluded his letter thus: 'Should you want to see me, I am at your
service. I have not a free hour today. I am free only after 10 p.m. I
am free tomorrow morning.'[51]

Mrs Besant's reply to this letter must be quoted in full:

Dear Mr. Gandhi,

I am perfectly willing to see you, if you wish to come.

I am sorry you think I have changed. I have always been ready to break a bad law & suffer the penalty; I have never been ready to break all laws (without moral sanction), leaving my conscience to be ruled by a committee. The first is the action of a reformer; the second of an anarchist.

As to courage, it needs far more courage to face a misled crowd & stand alone, than to win always plaudits by fine phrases misapplied. You do not do this, I know, but some of your followers do. Such phrases stir the crowd to passion, & it strikes blindly at authority, while the phrasemongers salve their consciences by selling tracts, where the only penalty is confiscation.

It is a pity that both you & I have lost our ideal of the other. Time will tell which of us has been the more faithful to India & to Freedom.

Yours sincerely

Annie Besant.[52]

Gandhi may have been a Mahatma to others, but to Mrs Besant he was merely 'Mr. Gandhi'. In suggesting a meeting, the younger man had left open the question as to where it would take place, while the older lady was insisting that he must come to her. In the event, the meeting did not take place. The exchange as a whole revealed a striking reversal of roles; in a matter of weeks, Gandhi had supplanted Annie Besant (as well as Bal Gangadhar Tilak) as the pre-eminent leader of the Indian freedom struggle.

CHAPTER 3

Freedom-Loving Englishman

I

In 1918, a book was published in Bombay bearing the title 'A Friend of India': Selections from the Speeches and Writings of B. G. Horniman. The book had a preface by Annie Besant, where she called Horniman 'one of those all too few Englishmen who carry their British principles with them when they come to India and keep them in the open air during the years of their stay in this land'. Liberty of speech, of person, and of the press, which in England are 'taken for granted', wrote Besant, were in India 'matters of grace', held 'at the mercy of autocrats, little and big, white and brown, from the "Lat Saheb" [Viceroy] enthroned in Simla . . . down to the constable who takes toll of the coolie's basket and cuffs him if he complains'. But 'to Mr. Horniman', added Besant, 'these Rights are still Rights, and their effacement is a matter of constant pain. He feels, as though inflicted on his own person, the wrongs suffered by the Indian, and with passionate insistence seeks to arouse in the injured the courage to assert their God-given manhood.'[1]

Benjamin Guy Horniman was to journalism what Annie Besant was to public affairs: a free-born, white person who had made it his mission to see that Indians were given the same rights of liberty and freedom that Englishmen took for granted. Horniman was born in the town of Dovercourt, in Essex, on 17 July 1873. His father worked as a senior paymaster in the British Navy; his mother was the daughter of a British engineer seconded to the Greek Navy. He was particularly attached to his mother, who taught him Latin and French at home. He attended Portsmouth Grammar School and passed the examination for the Royal Military Academy in Woolwich, but then chose to become a journalist instead, beginning his career as a reporter on the *Southern Daily Mail* in Portsmouth. He later worked in several London papers, including the *Morning Leader* and the *Daily Express*, before going to India in 1904 to join *The Statesman*, then the leading English newspaper in the subcontinent.

The Statesman was published in Calcutta, the capital of British India and the second city of the Empire. Its senior management enjoyed a comfortable, not to say luxurious, lifestyle, writing sonorous editorials in the mornings before going to the races in the afternoon and to the Bengal Club for drinks and dinner after that. Horniman, however, liked to get out into the field. He travelled widely through the Presidency, making his name writing about rural distress and Hindu–Muslim conflict in the districts of Comilla and Mymensingh.[2] When a popular movement was launched to undo the partition of Bengal, 'Horniman identified himself with the agitation. In sympathy with the mourning Bengalis, he too walked on the streets of Calcutta barefoot, dressed in a white *dhoti* and *kurta* and *chadder* like an Indian patriot.'[3]

Calcutta was the political epicentre of the Raj; Bombay its commercial hub. Here, the leading English-language paper was the *Times of India*, a solidly Establishment outfit and a thoroughgoing apologist for British colonial rule. In 1913, a group of liberals in Bombay, headed by the Parsi lawyer Pherozeshah Mehta, decided to start a paper offering the Indian point of view. Characteristically, they wanted an Englishman to edit it. The person they first approached was S. K. Radcliffe, the incumbent editor of *The Statesman*. Radcliffe was loath to leave the comforts of Calcutta, so he recommended his deputy instead. Horniman accepted, and in 1913 moved across the subcontinent to become the first editor of the *Bombay Chronicle*.

In Bombay, Horniman settled down in a bungalow in Worli – then a charming seaside suburb – with his dogs and his servants. He was unmarried, in fact gay, though in the homophobic world of colonial India he kept his sexual life and preferences private and discreet. In any case he was consumed by his work. Since the new paper was projected as a rival to the *Times of India*, and the latter was priced at four annas an issue, Horniman decided to price the *Bombay*

Chronicle at a mere one anna. The *Times* promptly reduced its price to one anna too.

Apart from sending reporters out into the field and soliciting articles from across India, Horniman also wrote often for his paper, in unsigned editorials as well as opinion pieces under his own name. His writings attracted admiration from Indian readers as well as anger and hostility from officials of the British Raj. The progressive Bombay industrialist L. R. Tairsee said the *Chronicle* was at once 'an appetiser to a hearty meal for the public and a paper which destroyed the appetite of the Government and its sycophants'.[4] Tairsee described Horniman as a 'sincere champion' of Indian aspirations, who, when he got up to make a speech, usually had a roll of paper in his hands, these akin to 'the title-deeds of India's right to equal treatment as any other nation on the face of the earth'.[5]

After the First World War broke out in July 1914, the autocratic Governor of Bombay, Lord Willingdon, imposed a regime of press censorship. Horniman protested vigorously against the new restrictions. In 1915 he founded the Press Association of India, a union of working journalists that aimed at 'protecting the press of the country by all lawful means from arbitrary laws and their administration, as well as from all attempts of the legislature to encroach on its liberty or of the executive authorities to interfere with the free exercise of their calling as journalists'. When the *Chronicle* published reports of brutalities by British soldiers, the Bombay Government threatened action under the Defence of India Act, but Horniman refused to be intimidated.[6]

As President of the first trade union of working journalists in India, Horniman fought fiercely for the freedom of the press, sending petitions to the Viceroy and the Governor 'protesting against the misuse of the Press Act by Government and against the constant abuse to which the Defence of India Act was put'.[7] He brought this fight to his own paper, where he battled continually with the board of directors of the *Chronicle*, who wanted to curb his editorial independence. So long as he was alive, Pherozeshah Mehta backed Horniman; but after Mehta died in 1915, the board grew more restive. Alarmed at Horniman's combative support to the Home Rule movement, they asked him to tone down his editorials in support of Besant and Tilak. He threatened to resign, announcing his decision in a public meeting in a workers' colony known as Shantaram's Chawl. The board backed down, and asked Horniman to resume his duties. The directors hostile to the editor resigned, being replaced by men closer to him in their political sympathies.[8]

Under B. G. Horniman's editorship the *Bombay Chronicle* covered politics avidly, while also giving ample space to the two great, emerging, popular passions of Bombay (and India): films and cricket. The prose was racier than in the *Times of India* and the editorials more pungent and the cartoons much funnier. In a matter of months, the new paper had become the preferred reading material of the modernizing middle class. Many Englishmen in the city read it too.

While published in English, the *Chronicle* sided with the subaltern classes of the city who did not read or speak that language. As one historian of Bombay writes, Horniman's paper 'amended the official sociology of the city to include workers and the urban poor. It repeatedly emphasized the plight of various groups of workers – millhands, labourers, railway workers, as also the vast numbers of low-paid clerks employed in government, municipal and private offices – reeling from price rises and commodity shortages during the war.' The editor himself often addressed workers' meetings, where he spoke of how unions and organized action had helped European labour materially improve their working and living conditions.[9]

Like Annie Besant, Horniman nurtured the hope that the British would redeem themselves by granting Indians the rights they themselves enjoyed at home. Thus, when the First World War broke out, he warned those who were fighting for India's freedom not to have delusions about the Germans. If the Germans won the war, he said, it would be far worse for Indians than if the British were the victors. He pointedly asked:

> Have you more to hope from a Prussia weltering in the blood of her victims, triumphant over fallen democracy, casting her greedy eyes on the wealth of India; or, worse still, from a Prussia which has already over-run your borders and found you unprepared? Will Prussia wish to see you free? What of Roumania; what of the poor, deluded, tricked Bolsheviks; what of the Ukraine; what of Finland, what of the peasants

of the Baltic Provinces and Livonia, handed back to the tender mercies of their old despotic bestial masters, the German landed proprietors? That is what Prussianism means.[10]

On 16 June 1917, Annie Besant was interned under the Defence of India Act. B. G. Horniman proceeded the same night to Madras. Travelling with him was the prominent liberal P. K. Telang. Telang assumed the editorship of Mrs Besant's journal *New India*, where he printed a stirring article by Horniman entitled 'Resurgam' (I shall rise again). Horniman said the Madras Governor, Lord Pentland, and his advisers had not apparently learned the lesson that history should have taught them: 'that you may strike down, imprison or place in fetters the leaders of great causes a hundred times, but the cause itself will live; and that the banner of freedom, once unfurled, though it may fall in the dust again and again, will always be uplifted afresh, to be borne and carried forward by brave and willing hands'.

Pentland thought that, by arresting Mrs Besant, he would drive a wedge between the Moderates and the Extremists; in fact, as Horniman noted, the two sections had closed ranks and together condemned her detention. For, as Horniman now reminded the Government of India,

> it is not merely a troublesome old lady with a bee in her bonnet. It is the champion of a great movement . . . We do not disguise the loss to the cause of Home Rule which the removal of Mrs. Besant involves; we do not ignore the immensity of the gap which is left by the deprivation of her organising genius, her guiding hand, her never-failing energy and indomitable courage, her inspiring leadership; but we cannot ignore the immense strength and impetus, which has been given to the cause she led by the blow sought to be aimed at it through her.

The larger lesson that Horniman drew from Mrs Besant's detention was that

> a system of Government which has reached a stage, where it must rely for its safety on internments without trial and the suppression of speech and writing, is bankrupt, and stands in need of radical

reform. The only remedy is to confer on the people of this country that liberty and control over their own affairs, which British statesmen have declared to be the right of every people; for which right they are waging the most stupendous War known to history. It rests with the men and women of India whether that issue is brought home to the people of England. We have no misgivings, despite temporary checks, of the ultimate outcome.[11]

II

In December 1916, B. G. Horniman had attended the Lucknow session of the Congress. Here, he met Motilal Nehru, a star at the Allahabad Bar and an active Congressman and Home Ruler. Horniman got to know (and like) Motilal's son Jawaharlal as well. The younger Nehru had come back from England after studying at Cambridge and qualifying as a barrister; however, unlike his father, he was not a particularly effective lawyer. He was looking for a more creative outlet for his energies, which he found in nationalist politics.

In July 1917, Horniman wrote to Jawaharlal Nehru about a scheme to launch a 'Passive Resistance movement' to get Mrs Besant freed from house arrest. He had difficulties persuading the veteran Congressmen Madan Mohan Malaviya and Mohammed Ali Jinnah to join. Writing to the younger Nehru, he said the movement would be 'a good idea if we can only inject some virility into these old stagers'. He wanted help in giving these 'elder Congressmen . . . a good shaking up'.[12]

The movement was not needed, since the pressure from nationalist newspapers and town hall meetings, and the intervention of Edwin Montagu, persuaded the Government to release Mrs Besant anyway. Now, in emulation of what Horniman was doing with the *Bombay Chronicle*, the elder Nehru, Motilal, decided to start a nationalist newspaper of his own in Allahabad. This would be to the United Provinces what the *Chronicle* was to the Bombay Presidency: a vocal, articulate, professionally run Indian alternative to pro-Raj papers such as *The Pioneer* of Lucknow (where Rudyard Kipling had once worked).

In setting up this paper – to be called *The Independent* – Motilal sought the help and advice of B. G. Horniman. Horniman sent his talented young protégé, Syed Hossain, to help launch the new paper. He also made several trips himself to Allahabad, advising the Nehrus on the purchase of paper and printing machinery, and on circulation and distribution as well.[13]

Horniman had also befriended Mohandas Gandhi. When Gandhi returned from South Africa in January 1915, the receptions held in his honour in Bombay were extensively covered by the *Chronicle*. Horniman himself attended at least one of these receptions; although we do not know whether the newspaper's editor and the returning hero actually met or spoke.[14] Shortly thereafter they came into close and regular contact. In June 1916, when Gandhi spoke at a public meeting in Bombay urging the loosening of the state's curbs on a free press, Horniman was in the chair.[15]

As the war was winding towards an end, Horniman was hopeful that it would lead to meaningful political reform in India. In a speech of 15 December 1917 he said that

> it would be a sad day, if it ever dawned, that found the British Empire, which has made such colossal and noble sacrifices in this great battle for freedom, remaining at the end of it the champion of freedom for the weaker peoples of Europe, but condoning racial privilege and dominion within its own borders. But that such a day can ever dawn I do not believe.[16]

Horniman's paper was now paying increasing attention to the doings and sayings of the rising man of Indian politics. For his part, Gandhi was aware of the importance of the *Chronicle* as a vehicle for his various causes.[17] In 1918, when Gandhi organized a peasant protest in Kheda district against the land tax, Horniman's newspaper gave it wide and sympathetic coverage. After printing a series of detailed reports on agrarian distress in Kheda, the *Chronicle*'s editor added a commentary of his own, where he urged officials to put their pride aside and recognize the suffering of the peasants due to crop failure. Some officials had cast aspersions on the leaders of the peasants, but Horniman said this 'is no time for acrimony', for 'thousands of people are in very dire distress', and 'there is something at stake far graver than official prestige'.

In April 1918, Horniman and Gandhi spoke together at a public meeting held in Shantaram's Chawl in support of Kheda's peasants. The Indian focused on the anguish of the peasantry, whereas the Englishman focused his ire on the officials who had caused it. Horniman was particularly harsh on the Commissioner, a man named Pratt, whom the editor referred to 'as the auto-Pratt'. This man, said Horniman, was assigning to himself powers of infallibility which even the Pope did not claim; the peasants 'should remind him that tomorrow another Commissioner, a Mr Flatt or a Mr Matt, may change his decision, while in any case he was answerable to the British Parliament'. Horniman asked the audience 'not to be unduly alarmed by the appearance of this new disease of auto-prattism', for bureaucracy was dying in India, 'it was heaving its last moments and Mr. Pratt's ecstatic claim to divine powers was evidently the swan song of bureaucratic tyranny'.[18]

The struggle in Kheda in 1918 was a localized affair. The following spring, Gandhi organized a more ambitious, all-India movement; against the draconian new legislation known as the Rowlatt Act. This legislation prescribed harsh measures to deal with dissent; including trial without juries and *in camera*, with the public and the press excluded. In his campaign against the Act Gandhi drew into his fold some supporters of Mrs Besant; and the editor of the *Bombay Chronicle* too. B. G. Horniman attended the preparatory meetings in Gandhi's ashram in Ahmedabad, and threw his newspaper into the campaign. His participation was consistent with his love of liberty, and with his horror at the harsh laws prevailing in British India. He had written several searing pieces on the detention without trial of political workers. 'By what right', asked Horniman of the Government, 'do you lock men up indefinitely without the semblance of a trial or judicial enquiry?' He warned: 'For every *detenu* you seize and lock up you create a hundred revolutionaries in mind and spirit . . .'[19]

In March 1919 Gandhi wrote to the Viceroy, Lord Chelmsford, urging him to withdraw the offensive new Acts. When the Viceroy refused, Gandhi chose to mark Sunday, 6 April, as a day of protest. In towns and cities across India, nationalists held public meetings where they resolved to court arrest in protest against the Rowlatt Act.[20]

Gandhi himself chose to lead the protests in Bombay. The next day's *Chronicle* began with this report:

> Bombay presented the sight of a city in mourning on the occasion of the day of national humiliation, prayers and sorrow at the passing of the Rowlatt Bills . . .

> Long before the sun had risen, the Back Bay foreshore was humming and throbbing with life, for it was full of people. From an early hour in the morning, people had come to Chowpatty to bathe in the sea . . . It was a Black Sunday, and the day's programme had to begin with a sea bath . . .

> Mr. M. K. Gandhi was one of the first arrivals at Chowpatty with several volunteers, and by 6.30 a.m. or earlier he had taken his seat on one of the stone benches with about a hundred satyagrahis around him . . . As the day advanced people kept pouring in on to the seashore. Every new arrival took his bath in the sea first and then came and sat around Mr. Gandhi. In this manner the crowd swelled and swelled until it became one huge mass of people. Mr. Gandhi, as the time for the meeting on Chowpatty sands neared, moved in that direction . . . It was a splendid sight at this time, for the whole Sandhurst Bridge swarmed with people and there must have been approximately one-and-a-half lakhs of people . . . All communities were represented there – Mahomedans, Hindus, Parsis, etc., and one Englishman . . . At exactly eight o'clock, Mr. Gandhi made his speech.[21]

The 'one Englishman' participating in this very Indian protest was the newspaper's editor Benjamin Guy Horniman.

III

Gandhi had canvassed support for this movement in Bengal, Madras, Bombay and the United Provinces. The one province of British India he had not yet visited was the Punjab. After the great meeting in Bombay on 6 April, he took a train to Delhi, hoping to proceed from there to Lahore and Amritsar. The authorities, fearing trouble, stopped him at a station short of Delhi, served an order externing him from the Punjab, and sent him back to Ahmedabad. This act provoked an angry article in the *Bombay Chronicle*, unsigned, but almost certainly written by B. G. Horniman. This declaimed:

> Mr. Gandhi, with his body in police custody and his self free, at this moment symbolises India, where the forces of right – of Government based on moral laws – and of wrong – Government depending entirely and ultimately on the sanction of brute force – are locked in a struggle which stands on a higher plane than even the great war of arms that has just ended.[22]

On 13 April, a peaceful crowd of nationalist protesters was fired upon in the city of Amritsar in Punjab, an event that came to embody the infamy and illegitimacy of British rule in India. News of this 'Jallianwala Bagh massacre' was slow to come out of Punjab. Among the first Indian journals to print details of the killings was the *Bombay Chronicle*. By now, Horniman was openly, explicitly, identifying with the nationalists against the Raj, and with India against England. This angered the authorities, who sought to get him out of their skin and out of their way. In the third week of April, the Governor of Bombay wrote to the Viceroy, suggesting that Horniman be sent away to Burma, at this time also a province of British India. The Viceroy, after consulting with his advisers, wrote back that 'the general impression is that to deport Horniman to England straightaway would be more advisable than to take two bites at the cherry. It might provoke renewal of excitement if you were to deport him to Burma and then have second deportation.'

The Governor of Bombay concurred, urging only that action be taken immediately. 'The early arrest and deportation of Horniman', he told the Viceroy, 'is now doubly urgent inasmuch as he is now publishing very inflammatory articles in the "Chronicle" and causing serious reaction in public feeling in favour of lawlessness.' He added: 'We have to face very anxious months ahead not only in regard to Moslem question but also famine disturbance, and if Horniman is not got rid of before these mature things may become more serious.'[23]

On the afternoon of 26 April 1919, F. C. Griffiths, the Commissioner of Police, came to Horniman's house accompanied by several other officers as well as two doctors, both Englishmen. The editor was served an order of deportation, charging him with bringing 'into hatred and contempt the Government established by law in India'. The order adduced as evidence editorials in the *Chronicle* calling the Rowlatt Act a 'Black Bill', supporting the satyagraha against it as an expression of the 'national conscience', and praising the circulation of prohibited pamphlets, since 'those who know the works will have no doubt as to their moral value and their title to free dissemination'.[24]

Horniman was examined by Government doctors, who declared him fit to travel by the SS *Takada* the next day. The Police Commissioner then formally placed the editor under arrest; he gave the prisoner half an hour to pack his belongings, whereupon he would be taken to the ship, and spend the night on board before sailing for England on the morrow.

Horniman now asked his servants, 'who were in a very confused state', to 'put together as quickly as possible as much as they could'. He was then conveyed to a waiting ambulance, which took him to the docks from where he boarded the ship that was to take him away from India. Before leaving home he had emptied his purse, giving all he had, some one hundred and fifty rupees in all, to his servants.[25]

Shortly before he was taken aboard ship, Horniman hurriedly wrote a note to Gandhi, which read:

My dear Mahatmaji,

They are taking me away at last. I have been rushed off without notice. This is only to say 'Au Revoir' and to ask your blessing. God speed you in your work for the Indian people.

I shall do what I can wherever I am.

Ever Yours affectionately

B. G. Horniman.[26]

On hearing that Horniman had been deported, Gandhi issued a public statement, which began:

With great sorrow and equal pleasure I have to inform you that the Government have today removed Mr. Horniman from Bombay and he has been placed on a steamer bound for England. Mr. Horniman is a very brave and generous Englishman. He has given us the mantra of liberty, he has fearlessly exposed wrong wherever he has seen it and has thus been an ornament to the race to which he belongs, and rendered it a great service. Every Indian knows his services to India. I am sorry for the event because a brave satyagrahi has been deported while I retain my physical liberty. I am glad because Mr. Horniman has been given the occasion of fulfilling his [Satyagraha] Pledge.[27]

How Horniman occupied himself on the SS *Takada* has not been recorded. We do know, however, that he arrived at Gravesend on 26 May 1919, exactly a month after he left Bombay.

IV

The arrest and deportation of B. G. Horniman provoked a veritable storm of commentary in the Indian press. *The Hindu* of Madras called it a 'rank injustice', adding that 'we cannot find an atom of justification for the drastic manner in which the rights of the Press and the liberties of the people are being dealt with in this country'. The Telugu paper *Desabhimani* (published from Guntur) said that 'there is no doubt that all Indians are immersed in an ocean of sorrow on account of this [deportation of Horniman]. His unsurpassed love for the people of India seems to be the only reason why the authorities are indignant towards him.'[28]

The most intense coverage took place, naturally, in the Bombay Presidency, where the editor had lived and worked. One Gujarati paper, *Sanj Vartaman*, called the deportation a 'grave blunder' that had 'deeply wounded' many Indians. Another, *Hindustan*, said 'every Indian will be grieved' at the Government's action, which was apparently motivated by 'panic and wrath'.

While deporting Horniman the Government had also suspended the publication of the *Bombay Chronicle*. The *Praja Mitra*, deeply regretting the order, observed that under Horniman's editorship, the *Chronicle* 'had played a great part in the public life of India in general, and this presidency in particular'. The paper thought that 'much of the liberalism and progress observable in the administration' of the Bombay Presidency in recent times could be attributed to the *Chronicle*'s 'fearless and vigorous advocacy of the people's rights', adding that 'the whole political consciousness, during recent years, of our presidency, is due largely to its spirited and stimulating columns'.

On Sunday 11 May, the city of Bombay observed a total strike in protest against the deportation of B. G. Horniman. Both Hindu and Muslim establishments shut down for the day. The call for the strike had come from Gandhi himself. With a group of volunteers, Gandhi went around the city to make sure the protests were peaceful.[29]

In the third week of June, the order of suspension on the *Bombay Chronicle* was lifted. On 19 June it made its reappearance, the first issue of the paper for thirty-four days. The paper noted, with slight but pardonable exaggeration, that its editor's deportation had 'been universally condemned by Indian public opinion as a most arbitrary exercise of executive authority'. It committed itself afresh to the ongoing struggle to substitute 'popular will for executive fiat', urging constitutional reforms whereby 'the rights and liberties of the Indian people as British citizens must be secured to them'. *Kesari*, the newspaper founded by the great nationalist Bal Gangadhar Tilak, urged the Government to cancel the order of deportation on Horniman and allow him to return to India and resume the editorship of the *Bombay Chronicle*.[30]

V

When he was deported, Horniman had been out of England for fifteen years. His heart was in India; politically and spiritually, and perhaps also emotionally and romantically. He desperately wanted to return. In October, he filed a petition to the Privy Council challenging his deportation. The petition had been drafted by his solicitor, David Graham Pole, a close associate of Annie Besant.

The appeal was rejected. Horniman now asked Liberal and Labour MPs to pose questions in Parliament. When the Secretary of State for India said Horniman's paper had caused riots and sought to excite 'disaffection and insubordination' among British troops, Colonel Wedgwood asked: 'Why not prosecute him?' (instead of summarily deporting him, that is). Other MPs pointed out that with the war now two years in the past and with the Defence of India Act having lapsed, surely it was possible for Horniman to be granted a passport and return to Bombay? The Secretary of State answered that the Government of India 'do not consider that Mr. Horniman's return to India is compatible with the public safety'.[31]

The Secretary of State for India, Edwin Montagu, a Liberal himself, might have allowed Horniman to return. But the high officials of the Raj were in no mood to relent. When Montagu asked the Governor of Bombay whether the editor should be granted a passport valid for India, he wired back saying that 'it would be highly dangerous for Horniman to return and shall therefore be glad if you will refuse passport'.[32]

Gandhi, characteristically, did not forget his English friend, now exiled from his adopted homeland by the authorities. The people of India, he proclaimed, 'will never forget what Mr. Horniman has done for them'. Gandhi urged his supporters in India to demonstrate for the editor's return to India, but to do so peacefully and without violence.[33]

On 30 May 1919, Gandhi wrote to his other (and older) English friend, Henry Polak, his comrade from South Africa who was now based in London, saying: 'I hope, you have sought out Mr. Horniman if he has not sought you out. Please keep him informed of all the doings here.' A week later he wrote to Polak deploring 'the horrible misrepresentations about Mr. Horniman. The real reasons for his deportation will probably be never given.'[34] A week later still, he sent a message to a public meeting in Bombay in support of the deported editor, which read:

> Of Mr. Horniman, I can say that the more I knew him, the more I loved him. Few Englishmen have served journalism, and through that gift India, with such fearlessness and strength of conviction as Mr. Horniman, and this I am able to say, although I often disapproved of his strong language and invective of which he was a master.[35]

In London, Horniman's correspondence was being tracked, with some letters withheld and others going through. A letter to Gandhi written on 30 July 1919 says he was 'anxiously waiting to hear what developments there may have been of the Satyagraha movement'. Horniman passed on a report of a meeting between the Moderate politician Vithalbhai Patel and Edwin Montagu, where the Secretary of State had promised to consider an amnesty of political prisoners and ensure the Rowlatt Act became a 'dead letter', but refused to cancel the order of deportation against Horniman himself. He was now thinking of approaching the Privy Council to seek redress.

Also in London at this time was Horniman's fellow renegade Annie Besant. Despite her reservations about the Rowlatt Satyagraha, Mrs Besant was working in her own fashion for Home Rule for India, speaking about it to audiences in England. 'Mrs Besant and her friends are holding some good meetings', wrote Horniman to Gandhi, 'and she has been taking on the whole a satisfactory attitude on most questions and, I think, is doing useful work.'[36]

Gandhi himself had gone on from opposing a single (albeit awful) Act to organizing a movement for Non-Cooperation with British rule. He asked Indians to stop paying taxes, boycott colonial courts, and burn foreign cloth while spinning and weaving their own. While engaged in planning and mobilizing for this countrywide campaign, he had not forgotten Horniman. On 26 April 1920, exactly one year since the editor had been deported, Gandhi wrote a signed piece in his magazine *Young India*, asking that meetings be held in towns and villages across the Bombay Presidency, demanding 'that Mr. Horniman's deportation should be cancelled without delay'. He followed this up with another piece, this time in Gujarati, where he observed:

> A great principle is at stake in Mr. Horniman's return, namely, the freedom of the citizen. . . . If Mr. Horniman wrote anything unlawful, he may be tried and sentenced, but the people ought not to tolerate punishment without a trial. In defending Mr. Horniman's freedom, therefore, the people will be defending their own freedom, and so we hope they will not forget his case, but strive hard and take effective steps to secure the withdrawal of the prohibitory order against him.[37]

In England, biding his time, Horniman kept engaged with Indian affairs by writing a book on the causes and consequence of the Jallianwala Bagh massacre. The man who had ordered the shooting, Brigadier General Dyer, had become a hero among conservative circles in England, who were raising a public subscription for a man they believed had helped to save the Empire. Horniman was appalled by the lionizing of Dyer, and determined to tell the truth to the British public about what had really happened in Amritsar.

Horniman's book – published in London in 1920 under the title *Amritsar and Our Duty to India* – began with the contributions made by the Indian people to the winning of the war. A million soldiers from the subcontinent had fought for the British on the battlefields of Europe, and India had contributed mightily in material terms too. For this act of loyalty and sacrifice, the Indians were rewarded with the Rowlatt Act, whose harshness and discriminatory nature Horniman excoriated. The movements led by Gandhi against the Act, insisted his English admirer, were of an 'absolutely peaceful character'. Gandhi's philosophy of satyagraha he described as 'a sublimation of the Christian doctrine. By suffering and soul-force and conversion, through these and love, one must conquer; not by destroying one's enemies or oppressors.'

The book gave an account of the events in the Punjab, focusing on the unprovoked shooting in which more than four hundred innocent Indians died. Dyer, said Horniman, 'had no evidence at all to justify his assumption that it was a seditious assembly'. A reign of terror was imposed by the military authorities, under martial law, on a province that had so recently provided so many recruits to help the British win the war. As ordered by the autocratic Lieutenant Governor, Michael O'Dwyer, British officials in the Punjab outdid one another in repression, and 'each distinguished himself for individual originality in devising special atrocities and methods of frightfulness . . .'

Horniman urged the British people to 'vindicate their humanity in the eyes of the world by the trial and punishment of the guilty'. While the officials of the Punjab, both civilian and military, were of course the principal culprits, Horniman argued that both the Viceroy and the Secretary of State for India also bore some responsibility. Beyond punishing the guilty, the authorities must, he insisted, protect the people of India from 'liberty-destroying laws and the recurrence of such oppression as that inflicted on the people of the Punjab last year'.

Horniman ended his book by saying that if the British wished to retain their connection with India, 'the only assurance of that connection lies in the full recognition of India's right to responsible government now, and without equivocation'. As he put it:

> Let those who can be moved by the knowledge of what India has been made to suffer, at the hands of people wielding power in their name, ponder whether, in the light of that knowledge, they can still acquiesce in the denial to her people of that full freedom for which they have fought, not only to win for the oppressed peoples of Europe, but to preserve for England herself.[38]

Reviewing Horniman's book, the *Manchester Guardian* observed that it was written 'with notable clearness and economy of words; and, although his own convictions and his personal career are both alike deeply engaged, his tone is free from violence and bitterness'.[39]

VI

In the autumn of 1920, Horniman told friends that he was disappointed that the Congress and Gandhi had not done more to secure his return to India. These comments, made in private, were reproduced in the *Bombay Chronicle*, and when the newspaper reached him he wrote a long letter to Gandhi by way of apology and explanation. 'I assure you that I have no complaint to make at all', he said, adding:

> I have wondered sometimes why you call me 'reckless', but I have never thought seriously about it. The last thing in the world that I would wish anyone to think is that I am not fully appreciative of all the love and kindness that the people of Bombay in particular have always shown me, and as long as that lasts I am content.

Embarrassed by his private thoughts being made public, and worried that the great Gandhi would think ill of him, Horniman now hastened to assure the leader of Indian nationalism of his own undying support of him and his cause. 'I have just been reading your articles in "Young India" of September 1st', he wrote, 'and feel greatly refreshed by such a clear exposition of the situation we have to face.' He agreed with Gandhi about the 'wrongness and futility of all violence', and was certain 'that, if India remains true to the ideals of Satyagraha and Ahimsa, she will win the greatest victory for humanity that the world has seen in our time'.[40]

In December 1920 Horniman attended a public meeting in Manchester held in support of India's freedom. He was one of the speakers; the radical Labour politician Fenner Brockway another. The meeting passed a resolution sending 'greetings to the people of India and wishes them well in their struggle for political and economic freedom'. It further denounced 'the tyranny of British rule', protested 'against the scandalous condition of poverty under which millions of Indians are forced to live as the result of exploitation by Capitalist Imperialism', and underlined 'that it is the glory of the Labour movement that it is the champion not merely of freedom at home but of freedom elsewhere'.[41]

Gandhi and his Congress party were now preoccupied with the ongoing Non-Cooperation movement. Horniman's return was not a priority for them. But it was for some other Indians, among them, quite remarkably, the textile workers of Bombay. In April 1921, a meeting was held in a labourers' colony in Parel, chaired by the mill-owner L. R. Tairsee, an old friend of Horniman's. The speakers included the women's rights activist Avantikabai Gokhale. The meeting passed a series of resolutions. The first expressed a 'deep sense of gratitude to Mr B. G. Horniman' from 'all classes of workers in Bombay . . . for his valued services for the cause of working men'. The second resolution condemned the 'unjust and arbitrary attitude of the Governor of Bombay in refusing to allow Mr. Horniman to return to Bombay'; the third urged that this 'wrong' be undone; the fourth authorized Tairsee to communicate the workers' sentiments to the Viceroy and the Secretary of State; the fifth and last asked him to forward the resolutions 'to Mr. B. G. Horniman with a special expression of Indian labour's affectionate regard and loving remembrances of his many-sided labours for their uplift'.[42]

Horniman was cheered by these resolutions, which made him even keener to return to Bombay. Rebuffed by the India Office, Horniman now tried the Foreign Office, who replied, in a letter of 13 October 1921, that the Bombay Government and India Office had to agree to issuing a passport, which they would not do. Horniman angrily wrote back that there was 'no authority under the Statute Law of the United Kingdom for the refusal of a passport to a British subject', and therefore 'the refusal to issue a passport to me constitutes a direct interference with the exercise of my legal right to leave England and proceed to India or elsewhere'.[43]

Horniman had begun writing on Indian affairs for the *Daily Herald*, the London newspaper, close to the Labour Party, which was then at the height of its influence. An article describing the horrific conditions of work in the tea gardens of Assam ended with this pointed question: 'What has British Labour to say of the maintenance of this abominable system, for which every British man and woman bears an individual responsibility?'[44] In the *Labour Monthly*, he wrote a long, critical, assessment of a book on Indian affairs by the Establishment journalist Valentine Chirol. Here Horniman argued that the British must recognize that 'Indians are, after all, ordinary human beings like ourselves, with minor psychological differences, who want to manage their own affairs; and want it all the more because others have made such a shocking mess of the business.'[45]

This article was published early in March 1922. Later the same month, Gandhi was arrested in his ashram in Ahmedabad, and sent off to prison in Poona. In May of that year, the Afghan Foreign Minister, Sirdar Abdul-Hadi Khan, visited the United Kingdom. It appeared that (at least according to Scotland Yard) B. G. Horniman met him, and through some high-placed British friends (a 'Lord Clifford' was mentioned) asked him to grant him a diplomatic passport to enter Afghanistan, from where he planned to cross over into India.

Through 1922, Horniman applied repeatedly to the Foreign Office for a passport. As before, the request was passed on by London to Bombay. In June, the Governor of Bombay wrote saying: 'The political situation has greatly improved, but is by no means firmly established yet. Such bitter and unscrupulous propaganda as Horniman would certainly embark upon on his return would do more than anything else to rally the Extremists, and to encourage a fresh recrudescence of lawlessness and disorder.' A passport for the renegade would still not be forthcoming.[46]

The year 1923 came and went with B. G. Horniman still in England, chewing his nails. In January 1924, Horniman applied again for a passport to allow him to return to India. The request was refused, based on the Viceroy's saying of Horniman that 'he was throughout his career in India an evil influence, and his return will definitely set back the general settling in which has been [a] marked feature of politics since Gandhi's arrest. The man is an adventurer unworthy of any sympathy . . .'[47]

On 4 February 1924, Gandhi was released from prison in Poona. This excited Horniman's hopes; now he might be allowed to return to India. On 6 February, he wrote to S. A. Brelvi of the *Bombay Chronicle*. 'Mahatmaji's release is, of course, a great thing', said Horniman. He thought that 'there ought to be no doubt about my getting my passport now but they are delaying the matter for some reason or other. If I don't get it in the next few days I shall stir things up in Whitehall and in the House.' He added: 'I need hardly tell you how much I am looking forward to my return and longing to be back again. Every day's delay is most galling.'

Horniman's letter ended with these telling lines:

> There is one thing in which you might be of great help to me. When I do get my passport I shall be in great need of money – as, of course, I have nothing. I hope you will do your best to impress on our friends who <u>can</u> provide the sinews of war to see that I get without publicity what ever it may be necessary for me to ask for. I shall have a good deal to clear up here.[48]

Horniman also wrote to the London *Times*, disputing a recent report that he had been 'deported [from India] during the war' for ostensibly opposing it. He noted that the paper he had edited, the *Bombay Chronicle*, had 'consistently supported the cause of the Allies throughout the war'. He had in fact been deported several months after hostilities ended, under the Defence of India Rules, 'a grave abuse of a war-time measure'. Now that those Rules had lapsed, surely he should be allowed to return to India? As a British subject, he had the right of free movement throughout the King's dominions. Yet he had been repeatedly denied a passport. By keeping him out of India, said Horniman, the authorities in London seemed only to want to oblige the Bombay Government 'which is anxious to get rid of an inconvenient critic of its policy and acts of administration'.[49]

VII

In the third week of February 1924, the Moderate leader Vithalbhai Patel introduced a resolution in the Imperial Legislative Assembly, asking the Viceroy to take steps to 'remove all restrictions in the way of Mr. B. G. Horniman [to allow him] to return to India'. Now that Gandhi himself was no longer in jail, the Bombay Government should allow Horniman to return. Patel said in the Assembly that Horniman 'was deported because he was a lover of liberty. He loved the liberty of person, he loved the liberty of the press and he loved the liberty of speech, the three inalienable rights of every person on the earth.'

After several other speakers had spoken in support of Horniman, the Home Member, Sir Malcolm Hailey, spoke on behalf of the Government. He admitted that the legislation under which Horniman had been deported, the Defence of India Act, had lapsed. However, he reminded the Assembly that the grounds for deporting him was that 'the course of conduct for many months was such that it was dangerous to the public peace and leading to serious disaffection against Government'. In any case, now that he was in England, said Hailey, the matter was out of the hands of the Government of India – 'the decision lies really with the passport authorities [in London] acting on the advice of the Secretary of State'.

Hailey was being evasive, if not downright dishonest. His remarks provoked a spirited rebuttal by M. A. Jinnah, who pointed out that 'no Secretary of State for India will go against the Government of India in this matter'; if Delhi was happy to allow Horniman back, London could not and would not stand in the way. Jinnah then continued, addressing Hailey and his Government:

> You refused to give him a trial and you made allegations against that man. You deport that man, a most horrible procedure to adopt, and I say no civilised government in any country should resort to that. You have deprived that man of his livelihood. You have prevented that man from going out of England. How do you justify that? And you have done it for four years. That is what I want to know from the Government. How do you justify that? I am really shocked at the manner in which the Honourable Member has pleaded his case. It is not worthy of a responsible government to put forward.

Pitching in on Hailey's side was a nominated European Member, W. S. J. Wilson, who was from the Associated Chambers of Commerce. Wilson told the Assembly that Horniman was 'not admitted to any of our clubs and was not a man that we have any pride in having in this country, and we prefer to be without him'. This was too provocative to go unanswered, and it wasn't, C. S. Ranga Iyer acidly remarking that 'when Mr. B. G. Horniman identified himself with the national movement which every English gentleman thinks jeopardises his existence, naturally he would not have been admitted to any of the English clubs'.[50]

A month later, the same matter was discussed in the Bombay Legislative Council, where the brilliant lawyer-patriot K. F. Nariman introduced a resolution in the provincial council recommending that the Government remove the ban on B. G. Horniman's entry into India. Nariman pointed out that

> the case of Mr. Horniman is really a strange anomaly in this country. The strangeness of the anomaly lies in the fact that the whole Indian inhabitants of this country of whatever caste or creed, of whatever political opinions they may have, are to-day standing up to fight for the rights and privileges of an Englishman . . . But the anomaly goes further than when Indians of all castes and creeds are fighting for the rights and privileges of an Englishman, strange enough we find the opponents to those rights are some of his own countrymen.

Once Horniman's supporters had spoken, the Government's representatives rose to reply. The Home Member of the Bombay Government, Sir Maurice Hayward, launched a savage personal attack on Horniman, claiming that the editor's 'indebtedness, general incapacity to live out here on the salary he was given and other misfortunes embittered him', and then, 'after the death of [the Liberal] Sir Pherozeshah Mehta, after the removal of his restraining influence, Mr. Horniman took to violent politics and his writings became a source of serious danger'.

Hayward started his speech on the 19 March. Continuing the next day, he reiterated his 'particular points in regard to this particular man – his perpetual financial troubles, shunning his own society, seizing on false rumours to rouse the fears and passions of the illiterate masses, quarrelling with his own employers . . .' The resolution was put to a vote, losing by 38 to 43, with all 18 nominated European Members of the House voting against, supported by a bunch of Indian loyalists. The consolidated Indian vote in the House was 38 to 25 (so Nariman had somewhat exaggerated when he said *all* Indians were for Horniman's return).[51]

In exile in England, Horniman kept himself going by reading the *Bombay Chronicle*, which reached him by sea mail, each issue getting to him a month after it had been printed. When he read in the paper of the debate in the Bombay Legislative Assembly, he was moved to reply to the charges made against him by Sir Maurice Hayward. He wired his old paper a short rebuttal, which they naturally printed. He said here that Hayward, realizing that the stated reasons for excluding him from India did not hold water (since the Defence of India Act no longer existed), 'deliberately and wickedly decided to throw aside all pretence of justice and decency and to resort to vulgar abuse, insinuation and mud-throwing – the invariable resource of unscrupulous and unprincipled people who have a bad case to defend'. Horniman, in injured tones, said: 'I make him [Hayward] and the Government a present of my financial difficulties. They can make as much capital, in their sordid way, out of them as they can. The fact remains that they are nothing whatever to do with the Government, and it is laughable to suppose that they provide a reason to exclude me from India.'[52]

Englishmen in India, whether official or non-official, wanted to keep this renegade out of the subcontinent. On the other hand, there were some liberty-loving Englishmen in England who fought for Horniman's right to return. The colonial archive has representations on his behalf sent in March 1924 by, among other such bodies, the National Co-operative Men's Guild of Birmingham and the Duddleston Labour Assembly.

The (ostensibly freedom-loving) Labour Party was now in power, heading a coalition government with Ramsay MacDonald as Prime Minister. Writing to a journalist friend, Horniman suggested a petition to the Prime Minister signed by 'as many Labour men as possible in and out of Parliament. I can also get some good signatures of Liberal M. P.'s. It would also be useful to get the signatures of as many prominent journalists as possible . . .' If, even after that, the passport was refused, the matter could be taken up afresh in the House, and by the National Union of Journalists. 'I have a right to a passport', wrote Horniman plaintively, 'and I do not see why I should have to tout for it at the India Office.'[53]

In the third week of July 1924, a memorial regarding Horniman was sent to the Prime Minister, Ramsay MacDonald. The celebrated writer

H. G. Wells was the first signatory. The others included as many as nineteen Members of Parliament, as well as prominent journalists. The petitioners said they would not debate here the merits of Horniman's writings in and on India. Rather, they questioned his punishment by executive fiat without trial or legal process, this 'a grave infringement of the liberty of the subject and, in this case, of the liberty of the press, and contrary to the principles and traditions of the Constitution'. If the Government had a case against Horniman, then they should prosecute him in the courts in the UK or in India. 'In any event', they argued, Horniman was, 'entitled to a full public statement in England of the reasons for which he was removed and is still excluded from India, with the material on which they are based, as well as an opportunity of refuting them before an impartial public enquiry.'

The file which contains this memorial does not have a record of any reply. It must have been in the negative, since 1924 came and went with no sign of a passport for Horniman.

VIII

It was now more than five years since B. G. Horniman had been forcibly externed from India. Countless petitions and representations asking for his return had been ignored or rejected. Fed up with waiting, bored, lonely and without work in England, desperate to resume his interesting and active life in Bombay, he now decided to use less than straightforward means to go back to where he belonged.

In September 1925, Horniman applied for a passport to enable him to travel to France and Italy 'for reasons of health'. A passport was granted to him on 13 October, endorsed for France and Italy, but not for India. After some weeks on the Continent, on 18 December Horniman sailed eastwards from Paris on a French boat, and without a passport valid for India. However, he did have a passport valid for France, and when the news of his adventure reached the India Office, they worried that he might land at a French settlement in India (such as Pondicherry), and from there cross over by land into British India.

His Majesty's Government were worried that Horniman was seeking to exploit a loophole in the law. Under the Indian Passport Act, local governments could direct the removal from British India of any undesirable person entering by sea into British India of through Afghanistan. But the law did not cover entry via French possessions.

From France Horniman was headed not to Pondicherry, but to British Ceylon. He had booked himself a second-class berth on the SS *D'Artagnan*, from Marseilles to Colombo. The ship's list laconically described the passenger as 'B. G. Horniman, Sans profession, Nationalité Anglaise'.[54]

The carrier was splendidly named for the ruse that the musketeer temporarily without a profession was attempting. The SS *D'Artagnan*, and Horniman with it, arrived at Colombo in the first week of January 1926. When the news reached Delhi, the new capital of British India, the authorities were taken aback. The Viceroy was informed that the Indian passport rules 'do not admit of preventing his entry into British India if he proceeds from a port in Ceylon'. Writing to the Imperial Government in London on 7 January, the Viceroy said he was considering the 'question of advisability of amending the rules, if time permits'.

The next day Horniman landed on the shores of British India, sailing across the Palk Strait to the small port town of Rameswaram. He made his way from here to Madras; and from there by train to his adopted hometown, Bombay.

The Madras Government had to permit Horniman to land, as the as-yet-unamended Indian Passport Act did not allow them to prohibit it. The Viceroy, realizing that he had been tricked, wrote ruefully that 'amendment cannot now be made applicable in this case. No action can therefore be taken against him unless he otherwise offends against the law.'[55]

The Viceroy was angry that the renegade had found a way to return; the Governor of Bombay, absolutely livid. The Government of India's Home Department, he complained, should have instructed the authorities in Madras not to let Horniman land, since an amendment to the law was being moved. Now, however, that the man was back, 'any prosecution would probably only make things worse than they are once he has arrived in Bombay'.

Horniman's return had made the Bombay Governor very angry

indeed. The journalist, he told the Viceroy, 'is going to be a terrible embarrassment to me, and particularly arriving, as he does, just before my budget session, with a Bye-election in Bombay caused by [the Liberal leader M. R.] Jayakar's resignation, which I felt certain of winning with a moderate man . . .' The Governor could 'only hope that I have exaggerated the importance of his coming; but, having read all the files concerning this gentleman, and knowing of his past relations with Governors and Government, I am certainly in for a great deal of trouble'.

Having expended his outrage, the Governor ended his letter in tones of sullen resentment. He would now have Horniman 'very carefully watched, and every word he utters recorded; but he is clever enough to keep within the law, and at the same time use his tongue and pen to the detriment of peace and order'.[56]

Horniman landed on the southern coast of India on 8 January 1926. The next day, Gandhi sent this message for publication in the *Bombay Chronicle*: 'My hearty greetings to Mr. Horniman. The Government deserves congratulations on redressing the grave wrong done to this brave Englishman and us. May his work prosper! India needs at the present moment all the assistance that her friends can give.'[57]

Gandhi did not know that the return of the renegade was owed entirely to his own bravery and desperation. Far from facilitating his re-entry, the Government had done all they could do to stop it. Their failure led to a lot of anger and recrimination within the colonial State, with Bombay blaming New Delhi (for not amending the rules in advance), and New Delhi in turn blaming Ceylon, for allowing the journalist to enter there, even though his passport did not specifically carry an endorsement for that colony, and although the Ceylon Government had previously been warned of Horniman's 'antecedents and his defective passport'. Chastised by the Government of India, Colombo answered that they had allowed the renegade to land because 'they had no quarrel with Mr. Horniman and because they understood at the time that [the Government of India] would be able to stop his entry into India from Ceylon'.[58]

It was now too late to do anything about it. Six and a half years after the British Raj had (so they thought) deported B. G. Horniman from India for ever, they had him back on their hands.

CHAPTER 4

Anti-Colonial American

I

Our third renegade, Samuel Evans Stokes, was born in 1882, into a well-known Quaker family in North America. His ancestor Thomas Stokes had joined the Society of Friends not long after it was founded in the seventeenth century, and knew the great pioneering Quaker George Fox. After moving to the New World, the family was based in rural New Jersey, living in a home called Harmony Hall, built in the second half of the eighteenth century. Here, wrote Samuel Stokes in a history that he later compiled,

> the family lived the plain and healthy life of the period, patriarchal in its simplicity and bountiful in its hospitality. The tradition still lingers of friendly intercourse with the [American] Indians, and I have heard how often in the early mornings our forefathers upon coming down would find a number of them wrapped in their blankets and asleep on the floor towards the fire on the great flagstones in the centre of the kitchen midden.[1]

Stokes grew up in the city of Philadelphia. His father was an engineer who designed elevators. The son, however, early on showed a spiritual rather than technical bent of mind. He joined Cornell University, but dropped out before graduating, to join the Young Men's Christian Association.

Shortly after Samuel Stokes had turned twenty, he met an American doctor, Dr Carleton, visiting from India, who ran a colony for lepers in the Himalaya, close to the imperial summer capital, Simla. The young Christian was fascinated by Dr Carleton's stories about life in the subcontinent, and decided to join him. 'Over the strong objections of his parents, he sailed for India in January 1904.'[2]

After he reached the Himalaya, Stokes worked on the alleviation of smallpox, also helping with relief after a devastating earthquake struck the district of Kangra in 1905. He went from village to village, documenting the losses that the people had suffered, and the food, clothes and financial help they required to rebuild their lives. In a letter to his mother (to whom he was devoted), Stokes wrote:

> This is a work in which you can satisfy no one except the Government. The people either curse you behind your back for not giving them as much as they want, or else for not considering them to be in need of help. If they [the donors] could only give Rs 100,000 more, I could have got along much better. However, where I have myself done the work, the people seem satisfied.[3]

His parents in America were worried about their son far away. Two years after he arrived in India, Stokes wrote to his mother:

> I know that you both (esp. Papa) consider me unwilling to be guided, unstable in my purpose, extreme in my views. Be it so; I am not willing to be guided by <u>any</u> man. I try, as much in me lies, to have no purpose of my own but to wait constantly on Him that he may reveal His purpose to me and then to do it with all my might.[4]

Stokes's social work in the Simla Hills focused on medical relief and education. He began a school for village children. He shed Western dress for the robes of an Indian mendicant, though he would not go so far as to adopt the celibacy that such *sadhus* normally practised. In 1907, Stokes was visited in his new home in Kotgarh by the compassionate Christian missionary C. F. Andrews, a close friend of Rabindranath Tagore and later on a friend of Mahatma Gandhi too. Andrews wrote admiringly of the American and his flock of hill children: 'Every one of them was a waif and stray of humanity. Stokes had fathered and mothered them all and taken them like a hen under his wing. But a merrier company you would hardly meet in the world. They hardly knew what sorrow was.'[5]

Although Stokes was a member of the Church Missionary Society, he converted very few people, and these by force of example, not through material inducements. He was disgusted by the luxurious lifestyles of European priests in India. As he wrote to one such, 'if we live lives of ascetic self-denial and service we will be loved and respected . . . If we govern righteously and well, we shall win the gratitude and admiration of many. But if we desire that our Indian brothers should think us one with themselves, we must be truly prepared to become one with them.'[6]

In an article recalling his early years as a Christian in India, Stokes wrote of the contempt for Indians and Indian culture that his fellow missionaries displayed. Studying the Upanishads and the Puranas, he discovered that 'these works contained the intellectual efforts of those who were seeking to grapple in the boldest and noblest manner with the deeper problems of life, its meaning and its purpose'. These studies, however, 'in no sense diminished his faith in Christ'; rather 'the light from the Hindu scriptures had come to fill the gaps in Christianity as he had known it, and to make of it a connected whole'.

Stokes said of himself that 'he came to teach and stayed to learn'. From his personal experience he drew this broader conclusion:

Christianity and Hinduism need each other. The best in each is incomplete without the other. The truths of each remain but half truths without the light which each can shed upon the other. As men have learned to see with eyes unblinded by the age-old prejudices and preconceptions that shackle them today, they will come to understand that when the divine synthesis has been affected a true Christian will be able to call himself a Hindu, and a true and perfect Hindu will be able to say, 'I also am a Christian.'[7]

II

In December 1910 Stokes's father died, and he went to America to spend some time with his mother. On his return to India, he resolved to abandon the ascetic life and find a partner to marry. In September 1912 he wed a Christian woman of Rajput origins, named Agnes Benjamin. He built a large wooden home with a tiled roof overlooking a valley through which the River Sutlej ran. As the building was being erected he wrote his mother a series of letters describing with pride the process of its construction. He spoke of the solid stone walls that he had built, of the quality of the timber (from Himalayan cedar), which went into the sloping roof, of the hollow cavity near the entrance where he had placed a long written account of his American ancestors. He named the new building Harmony Hall, after the family home in America.

Stokes's letters to his mother are redolent with love for his Indian wife. 'I can only say that she is always in my thoughts and I am never so happy as when sitting and watching her at work or playing with her little niece', he said in one letter. In another he wrote:

> I have found in my little wife a trust and a love which have not been ashamed to let themselves be seen after the first embarrassment was over, and even from the first the simple manner in which she has given herself to me has been a joy which has filled me with gratitude to the Lord who has given her to me as my wife.[8]

By now, although he still thought of himself as a Christian, Stokes had sundered his formal association with the Church. In his new house of wood and stone, Stokes raised a family with Agnes, and paid attention to nurturing the land he had bought. In his homestead he grew peas, pumpkin and cabbage. He much enjoyed gardening. 'There is a quiet helpfulness in the sweet earth', he wrote to his mother, 'and the fresh green shoots and the pea leaves creeping up through the soil seem like little children, and make us feel very tender. They seem to say to me – now we have come and you must take care of us.'[9]

The peasants of Kotgarh had tiny plots on which they eked out a living, growing potatoes for the townsfolk in Simla. Stokes wanted them to shift to more productive crops. So he got strains of good wheat from the plains and began to experiment with them on his farm. It occurred to him that the temperate climate of the middle Himalaya might be suitable for apple cultivation. In February 1914 Stokes took his wife and children for a year-long visit to America. While his mother got to know her daughter-in-law and her grand-children, Stokes spent time in the flourishing apple orchards of rural Pennsylvania, studying how their owners planted and tended trees. Convinced that apple cultivation would suit the Himalayan peasants, he took seeds and saplings back with him to India. He planted them on his own land, and when they seemed to flourish ordered more seeds from America, which he distributed to the peasants in his locality.[10]

In 1913, by which time he had been eight years in the country, Stokes wrote an essay entitled 'India of the Future'. This argued that the country he had now made his own 'can become truly great by quiet internal development, and by reforming, building up and perfecting its ancient civilization'. Stokes thought that India should strive for 'an economic prosperity which does not imply ability to compete industrially with the West in the markets of the world, but which will find its expression in the quiet prosperity of her children in the towns and villages'.[11]

In between raising a family and working on his farm, Stokes was also reading the poetry (in translation) of the newly crowned Nobel Laureate from Bengal, Rabindranath Tagore. The collection *The Crescent Moon* sparked a long, meditative letter to his mother in January 1914, where he remarked: 'Surely those who have read the poems of Tagore even in English must, whether they will or not, come to see that the general feeling in the West of vast superiority over the East is at certain points open to question.' This Westerner turning into an Easterner continued: 'Though the East, as a whole, still lacks much that the West make for character, there are, generally speaking, elements lacking in the atmosphere of the West which make themselves felt here, and on account of which I have come to love my land of adoption.'

After praising Tagore, Stokes went on to speak of South Africa, where Indians were battling, non-violently, for rights to property, livelihood and free movement that the white regime had denied them. This struggle was led by a lawyer turned protester named Mohandas K. Gandhi. In his letter, Stokes did not mention Gandhi himself; yet he showed a keen understanding of what Gandhi and his comrades were fighting for. After describing the contours of the conflict, he told his mother: 'The white man is welcomed everywhere and the various colonies advertise and offer all sorts of concessions to those who will come to them. But the Indian is excluded and treated with insults in every country governed by white people.'[12]

III

In July 1914, war broke out between England and Germany. Despite his Quaker roots, Stokes wanted to enlist on the side of the former, believing (at this stage) that the interests of the Indians and of the British were intertwined. 'The awakening and growth of the land of my adoption', he told his mother, 'is closely bound up with the success of the Allies.' For 'if we are to enjoy all the benefits and blessings of the Pax Britannica in normal times it is up to us to play the game in such times as these . . .'[13]

The British Army, however, were not sure they wanted an American at the front. In June 1916 Stokes went to Simla to enlist, but his application was rejected. Stokes thought that this was because 'we Americans are more or less under suspicion, I think, on account of the various German spies who have sailed under our colours'.[14] He persisted, applying again. The British still wouldn't allow him to take up a uniform; however, they permitted him to do recruiting duties instead. The fact that he was now fluent in Hindi as well as the local hill dialect certainly helped.

In April 1917 the United States entered the war on the side of the Allies. Stokes was both pleased and relieved, writing to his mother: 'We have long thought about it but I thank God that we are at last doing our duty. I have no enmity against Germany or the Germans . . . [But] we would have been traitors to the cause of individual freedom and personal responsibility had we not helped to destroy the German Government. It is pleasant to hold one's head up again.'[15]

A letter written a few weeks later spoke of how Germany had undermined her great history of cultural achievement by greed and military ambitions. He remarked:

A nation's true conquests must [run] along the line of higher achievement [than] that of arms – in arts and letters and religion and science and industrial progress . . . I venture to predict that a few centuries hence the 'scope for political activity' which she [Germany] so desires – the opportunity to rule over alien peoples – will be looked at as one of the departed aspects of ancient barbarism.

Stokes now hoped that, once the war was won, the British would also see sense and give up their colonial possessions. The support for self-determination for smaller nations by the American President, Woodrow Wilson, reinforced these hopes. As he wrote to his mother: 'It is only for as long as we remain partly civilised that one nation will consider it has a right to acquire the country of another and rule over it.'[16]

Through 1917 and 1918 Stokes travelled through the Himalaya, recruiting men for the war. Sometimes he stayed in the palaces of hill chiefs, at other times in Government rest houses. Or he slept in a tent on open ground. He enjoyed the work, but missed his wife and children (Agnes and he now had two boys and a girl, and more were to follow). In November 1918 the war in Europe finally ended, with Germany being defeated. Stokes now wrote to his mother with relief and in expectation:

God grant that as we have fought well we may make peace well and nobly, and that racial pride and selfishness may not mar what has been so well begun. We have fought the good fight; it now only remains for us to keep the faith and keeping the welfare of mankind before us, not degenerate into 'vulgar dividers of the spoils'. God grant that our several governments may prove worthy of their great responsibility.[17]

IV

Samuel Stokes spent the winter of 1918–19 at his home, Harmony Hall, attending to his farm and catching up with his family. As the snows melted and spring appeared, he felt a sense of renewal and hope. With his pretty wife and their boisterous kids around him, he exulted: 'This is the life I love. I have no use for the striving competitive restlessness of the West. God made us, it seems to me, to live simply – close to the good Mother Earth, who teaches us to look daily to Him, the Giver of all good gifts . . .'[18]

As summer appeared and advanced his mood dipped. He was supremely happy at home, but the world was not turning out as he had thought it might. The League of Nations had revealed itself to be a closed club of arrogant and self-satisfied Westerners. It wanted ancient civilizations such as India and China to give up their history and ethos and become pale imitations of Europe instead. In their racial conceit, the Americans and the British had proved themselves to be the equal of the Germans. 'Just as the Germans believed in the "Kultur"', wrote Stokes disgustedly, 'and their mission to force it upon the rest of the world, so we believe in our Western civilization. It is our "kultur", and the world must accept it whether they want to or not . . .'[19]

Many soldiers from the Himalaya fought in and helped win the First World War. They had expected gratitude; what they got instead were harsher laws, among them the Rowlatt Act. Stokes saw this Act as an outrageous betrayal, which would stoke nationalist sentiment within India. In June 1919 he wrote to his mother in prophetic terms:

The time will come – though not until my old age – when the smouldering resentment of the East will rise into a flame, and her nations will demand of the West a justification of her attitude. They will say, 'We refuse to allow your claim to interfere with us and exploit us,' and if the West refuses to admit her mistakes there will be a world conflagration beside which the recent war was a child's-play. And the West will be to blame. God grant that before that time Europe and America may wake up to the real nature of their attitude and change

it. The thought of my sons ranged against the West harrows me, but
if for such a cause such a war should break out, I should wish them
to be on the side of the East.[20]

In Stokes's mind the Rowlatt Act had 'started a train of thought
which ended in a strong conviction of the necessity for the non-
European peoples to get out of the clutches of the West'.[21]

At this time, the province of British India nearest to the Simla Hills,
Punjab, was seething with anger and resentment. Protests around land
rights had been brutally crushed; and then in April 1919 came the
Jallianwala Bagh massacre, about which the colonial regime was
entirely unapologetic. By the summer of 1920, Stokes had more or
less lost faith in the Empire. As he wrote to his mother, while he had
sympathized with Indian nationalist aspirations for many years he
had always identified with the Moderate wing of the movement. Now,
however, post Rowlatt, post Jallianwala Bagh, it was harder to resist
the call towards the Extremist side. 'Indeed it takes a real patriot
among Indians to be a "moderate" these days', he remarked.[22]

As Stokes became more radical in his politics, as he threw in his
lot more thoroughly with Gandhi and the Indian national movement,
he justified this deeper immersion in terms of his ancestral faith. 'We
are descendants of the Quakers', he wrote to his mother in August
1920, 'and have a right to be proud of our inheritance. Our fathers
founded their faith upon the equality of men and consequently of
races. We only of all the founders of the American commonwealth
can claim a clean record in our dealings with non-whites. Now, for
the sake of the world, we should prove true to our spiritual ancestry.'[23]

The dealings that the British had with non-whites in India were
anything but clean. Stokes deeply deplored the arrogant condescen-
sion with which the officials of the Raj treated their subjects. He
had resolved that in his own work with Indians he would treat them
as equals. Nonetheless, it pained his conscience that other whites in
India would not do likewise. In the hills, a particularly egregious
form of racial exploitation was the provision of free labour and
services by village folk to touring officials. To be fair, the British did
not invent this practice; they inherited it from the Rajput chiefs,
under whose feudal order the ruler could order his subjects any

which way he wanted. One of the 'privileges' of the Raja was that when he went on a hunting expedition, his subjects had to carry his loads, and provide his entourage with food and milk.[24]

This practice of forced labour was known as *begar*. The British both inherited and expanded it. With Simla as their summer capital, the high officials of the Raj took their families on treks and tours, forcing the villagers to carry their loads and supply stuff for their meals too. Meagre wages were paid for these services; and sometimes nothing at all. As one who lived with (and for) these hillmen, Stokes was appalled at the continuation of this practice. In April 1919 he wrote to the Deputy Commissioner of the Hills about 'the hardships endured by the coolies in the hills on account of the present rates per stage, and the injustice of them'. When no remedial action was taken, he wrote again, saying: 'In strict justice no demand can be made upon them to carry the luggage of such people against their will. It is a form of helotism which would have to go absolutely, in British territory at any rate, if its legality is called into question.'[25]

Having failed with personal appeals, Stokes tried the route of collective action. He drafted a petition which asked that such services be restricted only for government officials (hitherto all sorts of white men had availed of them), and that villagers be properly paid for them. The petition was endorsed by more than two hundred peasants of the Kotgarh *ilaqa*, some via signatures, most through thumb impressions. This representation was sent to the Deputy Commissioner's boss, the Commissioner of the Ambala Division. Once again, the request went unheeded.[26]

Stokes now decided to go public with his concerns. In the late summer of 1920, the Viceroy, visiting Simla as usual in the hot weather, went on a hunting expedition to a forest thirty miles away from the imperial summer capital. He was accompanied by a large contingent of European officials and their wives. To carry their loads, to cut grass for their horses, to fetch wood for their fires, and to provide milk for their morning tea, hundreds of men from villages along the way were forced to abandon their farms and service the ruling race instead. The work would have been irksome anyway; it was particularly so at this moment, since the summer crop had just been harvested and the fields had to be prepared for the autumn ploughing.

Stokes was now prompted to write two articles in the press about the pernicious practice of *begar*. One article he published in Gandhi's magazine *Young India* (in its issue dated 13 October 1920); the other in a Delhi newspaper read by Government officials. He hoped thus to reach both Indian nationalist and British imperialist. Both articles were careful not to put the blame on the Viceroy directly. Stokes suggested – whether sincerely or strategically one cannot say – that the most powerful white man in India may not have known himself of the suffering inflicted on the peasants. But his officials certainly did. Stokes quoted a farmer as telling him: *'Kya karen! Sarkar ka na dharma na daya.'* (What can we do? The Government has neither righteousness nor humanity.)

Through the system of *begar*, said Stokes in these essays, 'ignorant and inarticulate people of the hills are being exploited and wronged in every direction'. He was clear that the system 'must go and go at once. It is responsible for thousands of poor people being forced to minister to the comforts and pleasure of those who are supposed to serve them and to whom their interests have been entrusted.'[27]

V

On 22 October 1920, Stokes met Gandhi for the first time. The Mahatma was touring the plains of the Punjab, and Stokes went down to see him in the town of Bhiwani. He was also to spend several days in Gandhi's ashram in Ahmedabad, where he and C. Rajagopalachari had a long argument about whether there were times when absolute non-violence could not be practised.[28]

In December 1920 Stokes made the long trip across India to attend the Nagpur Congress. It was the first Christmas since his marriage when he would be away from his wife. But this was a crucially important meeting of the Congress – where Gandhi would announce his campaign of Non-Cooperation – and Stokes felt compelled to be present, to show his solidarity with the country he had made his own. As he told his mother: 'Feelings are running so high at this time that there are few non-Indians who would obtain a hearing from Indians. Andrews is one and I am another. I know of no others in exactly the same position. Indians know we are absolutely <u>with</u> India.'[29]

Early in 1921, Stokes published a fifty-six-page pamphlet with the telling title 'The Failure of European Civilization as a World Culture'. It had an introduction by C. F. Andrews, which, speaking of the author's ancestry, remarked: 'The Quaker blood in Mr. Stokes is strong today, making him a friend of humanity, and not of one nation alone.' Andrews recalled how Stokes and he came out to India at around the same time, how they both immersed themselves in the lives of ordinary folk, the American with the peasants of the Simla Hills and the Englishman with the indentured labourers of the colonies, each witnessing the 'treatment meted out' to Indians 'by the ruling white race', each having 'shared in the humiliation'.

Andrews wrote that he had 'visited him [Stokes] many times in earlier days and [had] stayed with him'. Now, having outlined their parallel lives, he said: 'It is surely no light matter, when, at the end of the last years of both our lives, we compare notes together, after long absence from each other, we find that we have come to the same conclusion as to the impossibility of India remaining with self-respect within the British Empire as it now stands.'[30]

Stokes's own pamphlet began with a brief history of Western civilization. The best among the Greeks had advocated a 'feeling of unity between all men', and early Christianity likewise embodied (according to Stokes) 'the antithesis of race-feeling'. It was modern Europe, through its colonization of territories in Asia and Africa, that had promoted 'a definite cleavage of the human race upon a permanent basis'. It erected a colour bar between the whites and the rest, with the former in a position of economic, political and cultural superiority.[31]

Stokes quoted copiously from works such as *Cambridge Modern History* to show how Western statesmen and scholars partook of such feelings of racial superiority. Not only did they think brown and black people inferior; they wished to stop them from coming into territories they had themselves violently occupied. Tracing the global expansion of Europe and the settling of the New World by Europeans, he concluded that both 'the British Empire and the United States are completely committed to the policy of shutting up the

peoples of Asia and Africa within their borders, while they populate at their leisure all vacant habitable areas with their own people'.[32]

Modern European colonialism, wrote Stokes, 'has been a sorrowful tale', the 'betrayal of humanity for its own ends by a race which had inherited the broadening and human culture of the Greeks ennobled and spiritualized by the teachings of Jesus of Nazareth'. Now, as India sought to find itself, he warned against a reverse racism, of Indians setting themselves up as superior to those they were fighting against. Inspired by Tagore and by Gandhi, but in words that were unmistakably his own, Stokes wrote: 'No culture is worth striving for which is grounded in selfishness. No nationalism is worth straining for that does not stretch beyond the interests of one's race so as to include the interests of all humanity.'[33]

In May 1921 Gandhi went up to Simla to meet the Viceroy. He spent several days in the hills. During this visit Stokes and Gandhi must surely have met and spoken. While there is no record of their conversation, we know that at a public meeting in Simla Gandhi remarked:

> I assure all religions that we want to be united at heart. Are we not already of one heart with the Christians? Do we not accept the help that men like Andrews and Stokes give us? We never want to make any one our enemy. . . . If the Englishman wishes to remain here as India's servant, as a brother to the Indians, if he wishes to live here on condition of giving up his imperious manners, he is welcome to stay; otherwise he must pack up his baggage and go.[34]

In August, Stokes and Gandhi both attended a meeting of the Congress in Allahabad, the town where the Ganga meets the Jamuna, the home of the Nehrus and a hotbed of nationalist agitation. There was a public meeting, where Stokes spoke just before Gandhi. A member of the Mahatma's ashram, who was present, later wrote: 'What was my surprise when I heard him give his speech in such good Hindi and with so much ease!'[35]

From Allahabad, Stokes went to Lahore to meet the leading Congress workers of the Punjab. By now, he had 'been gradually forced from a position of approval of British rule to that of moderate

Nationalist and from that to a thoroughgoing Nationalist'. He wrote to his mother in admiring tones about the movement he had joined, and of the leader he had chosen to follow. He observed:

> To Gandhi and the best of his followers this is not, at bottom, a political but a spiritual and moral movement. It is a fight to raise up the dying manhood of the Indian people. It aims at freeing India – and Indians – by a process of self-purification through suffering. We are invited to stand fearlessly but injure no one, to brave death but kill no one, to resist evil and injustice 'even unto death' but to be angry with no one.

It had been a year since Stokes had first met Gandhi. During this time he had long talks with him, in private, attended party meetings with him and mass rallies with him too. He had observed Gandhi in action, and studied his writings rather closely as well. He was convinced of the greatness of Gandhi, writing:

> He stands for the noblest in our nature – and the Scribes and the Pharisees and Herodians are aghast. I don't wonder at it; he sometimes makes one's hair stand on end – but so did Christ. Indeed it seems to me that just as Jesus attacked the strongholds of selfishness and sin in the personal and social life, so Gandhi is continuing the operation in the economic, national and international life of our race.[36]

This adoration of Gandhi was offered by Stokes to his mother, in private; meanwhile, Gandhi was praising Stokes in public. In July 1921, the Mahatma published an article in *Young India* which began:

> If proof were needed that the movement of non-co-operation is neither anti-British nor anti-Christian, we have the instance of Mr. Stokes, a nationalized British subject and staunch Christian, devoting his all to the eradication of the evil of *begar*. Mr. Stokes is a convinced non-co-operator and Congressman. I think I am right in saying that he has come to it by slow degrees. No Indian is giving such battle to the Government as Mr. Stokes. He has veritably become the guide, philosopher and friend of the hillmen.

'Why this persistence in exacting *begar*?' asked Gandhi, before supplying this answer: 'For the authority, the influence and the comfort of the officials and officers depend upon the continuance of *begar*.' He particularly deplored the use of hill labour and free provisions on hunting expeditions. 'For the doubtful pleasure of shooting tigers and innocent "game"', wrote Gandhi, 'a way had to be cut by impressing the labour of thousands of unwilling villagers. If the beasts had intelligent speech at their command, they would state a case against man that would stagger humanity.'

Gandhi quoted a letter that he had received from the Simla Hills. This narrated how a peasant leader named Kapur Singh, who was protesting against *begar*, had been arrested and his followers harassed. 'People were subjected to a reign of terror', said this letter-writer to Gandhi: 'The Simla police were brought, a number of them arrested [and] all the people scared by threats of machine guns and Kala-pani. . . . It was in such an atmosphere that the evidence for the prosecution was collected.'

This description 'reminds one of the Punjab martial law days', wrote Gandhi. Because of such oppression, he continued,

> naturally the hillmen feel sore about this persecution of their trusted leader [Kapur Singh]. I hope that under Mr. Stokes' inspiration, they will resolutely refuse to do any *begar* at all even for full value until their leader is discharged. They must not weaken, but must invite upon their devoted heads the wrath of the authorities and face imprisonment even as they did.[37]

In the first week of August Gandhi was campaigning against foreign cloth in North India. Stokes came down from the hills to meet him. He spent several days with Gandhi's party, travelling through the United Provinces. In his published notes on the tour, the Indian patriot introduced the American renegade more fully to the readers of *Young India*. After praising his involvement in the campaign against forced labour, Gandhi remarked:

> Mr. Stokes is married to an Indian Christian lady and has six children. He has not, to this day, taught his children a single word of English.

They only know two languages – Pahadi and Hindi. He too threw his clothes into the sacrificial fire on July 31 and now dresses himself in a dhoti, shirt and cap, all made of khadi. As he has some time to spare now, he is accompanying us on this journey in order to get some experience. For many years now Mr. Stokes has been living in purely Indian style.[38]

On 15 August, Gandhi issued a public 'Appeal to Residents of Simla Hill States'. So long as their leader Kapur Singh and his associates were in jail, he told them,

you will, in pursuance of Mr. Stokes' advice, refuse to give *begar* to the British Government and the State. Do not allow any excess on your part; remove anger from your minds during the time your brothers are under custody. It is much better for you to undergo hardships and be ready to fill jails for the sake of your faith (dharma) than to give *begar* to any official. . . . In your efforts I am with you all my heart and soul.[39]

VI

Through 1921, Stokes wrote prolifically in the press, publishing in *The Tribune* of Lahore for a Punjab audience and in the *Bombay Chronicle* for a wider, all-India readership. His articles on *begar* he reserved for the former paper; writing, for example, of how army officers savagely beat up mule drivers on the India–Tibet road who had asked to be paid for their services, and of the oppressive policies of the feudatory chiefs, who levied harsh taxes on their peasants and exploited them even more than the British did.[40] In the *Bombay Chronicle*, then the leading English-language paper identified with the nationalist movement, Stokes wrote expressing his own identity with Indian aspirations. It was here that Stokes published a polemic against (unnamed) liberals and Moderates who opposed Gandhi and Non-Cooperation, in the naive belief that freedom could be had through polite petitioning, rather than through struggle and sacrifice.

Thus Stokes wrote: 'I can well understand that an Indian [such as Gandhi] with the mental outlook of a free man, must be an altogether disconcerting phenomenon to the [colonial British] bureaucracy. . . . But if the spectacle is as disconcerting to Mahatmaji's cultured and educated [compatriots] it is an ominous sign, and should lead to anxious reflection.'

Stokes remarked of these Moderate, genteel, Indian critics of Gandhi that they would 'trust to lawyers and legislation to win them a place among the free and self-respecting nations of the world. They would have Swarajya [freedom], but have it comfortably and without undue inconvenience. . . . Yet by no such timorous road has any nation ever achieved Swarajya since the dawn of history.' This American-turned-Indian was himself convinced that

> the greatest value to a people of Swarajya, is the soul-experience of the nation while attaining it. You [the Moderates] would obtain Swarajya for slaves and then teach them to be free-spirited, but freedom has never come in this way to a people. It cannot be given from without; its advent is like child-birth. Mother India must bring it forth as her child, and travail in anguish for it as a mother. . . . India will attain Swarajya if her sons are prepared to suffer and sacrifice for their country – not otherwise.[41]

Another essay in the *Bombay Chronicle* expressed his fervent personal loyalty to the leader of the moment. Stokes had met, in Simla, the Bengal nationalist Bipan Chandra Pal, one of the troika, known as 'Lal/Bal/Pal', who had led the Swadeshi movement of 1905–7 (the others were Lala Lajpat Rai and Bal Gangadhar Tilak). Now, fifteen years after his own greatest triumphs in Indian politics, Pal grumbled that 'democratic principles were being sacrificed to the enthusiasm for, and adherence to, the view point of certain great Nationalist leaders'. Stokes disagreed with him, saying that at times of great crisis, it was important to trust and put one's faith in a single leader. The First World War was won because after 'several years of loss and weakness, the Allies forces throughout the western front came under the supreme command of that individual who was deemed most worthy of the great responsibility'. Now, said Stokes, in India too

in an altogether wonderful way we have been granted the presence
of a great and unique personality, altogether devoted to the voicing
of the national aspiration. . . . There are some men who can appeal
to many, and many men who can appeal to a few, but only Mahatmaji
has gripped the hearts of all India. He is, as it were, the very incarnate
expression of India's aspiration. His utter sincerity, his absolute fearlessness, his profound simplicity, his unflinching loyalty to our noblest
longings, mark him as the one man to whom the masses and the
classes can give their allegiance at a time of supreme crisis.

Stokes told the readers of the *Chronicle* that he himself had dis-
agreements with Gandhi about specific aspects of his programme.
But at this critical time it was the duty of all Congressmen to 'give
our loyal allegiance to Mahatmaji and strengthen his hands by our
implicit obedience till Swaraj is attained. . . . The road in which he
leads us cannot be followed half-heartedly. It is a question of *all* or
nothing. India must choose.'[42]

In the Simla Hills, the struggle against *begar* continued. With the
peasant leader Munshi Kapur Singh in jail, Stokes contemplated
organizing a strike whose aim was 'to alleviate the monotony of our
comrades' existence in Keonthal jail by furnishing them with a large
number of companions there'. However, when he consulted the
educationist Madan Mohan Malaviya ('whom, next to Mahatmaji,
I respect and honour'), Malaviya told him not to court arrest yet
but give the authorities more time 'to do justice themselves'. In
pursuance of this course, Stokes met the relevant officials and even
the Governor of Punjab who 'heard me most patiently and gave me
to understand that the affair would receive due consideration'.[43]

In September 1921 the Government announced that the *begar*
system would end in the Simla Hills. Stokes thought this 'a vindication of my trust that one determined man can fight a government
and make it give in if the cause is a just one'.[44] The pride was
understandable, and largely deserved. But perhaps not wholly so.
The Government's decision was surely also influenced by a major
popular movement against *begar* in other parts of the Himalaya,
such as Kumaon, also a territory from where many soldiers in the
British Indian Army came.[45]

In early October, Gandhi convened a special meeting of the Congress Working Committee in Bombay. To this meeting Gandhi invited his closest colleagues – Jawaharlal Nehru, Vallabhbhai Patel, Maulana Azad, Rajendra Prasad, etc. – and a few others whose advice he valued. Stokes was one of them. The meeting ended with a manifesto affirming that 'it is the duty of every Indian soldier and civilian to sever his connection with the Government and find some other means of livelihood'. Gandhi was the first of forty-seven signatories; Stokes was the only foreign-born person in the list.[46]

Stokes spent much of October travelling the Punjab, preaching the gospel of Non-Cooperation. His limbs were tired and his voice hoarse, but his spirits remained high. His wife's love and support had been unwavering. Nonetheless, he was sensible of the risks he ran for his family through his wholehearted support for the freedom movement. He wrote:

> In my efforts for India I shall never heedlessly run into danger. On the other hand, I shall not try to avoid it, if by doing so I have to sacrifice anything which justice demands for India. I do not hate the English; many of those whom I am struggling against are my old friends. All I can do is fight them cleanly and as a gentleman.[47]

In October 1921, Stokes published a pamphlet entitled 'The Spirit of Swadeshi'. It carried a (brief) foreword by Gandhi; which was appropriate, since the pamphlet was written in support of the Mahatma's campaign to promote hand-spinning. Stokes characterized the objectives of Gandhi's 'khadi movement' as two-fold: 'First, to save India from economic ruin by removing the drain on her resources involved in the purchase of foreign-made cloth; second, to secure the possibility of Indian-made cloth so cheap that none of India's poor will have to go naked.'[48]

VII

In the first week of December, *The Tribune* of Lahore carried a three-part series of articles by Stokes entitled 'The Acid Test of

Loyalty'. These took issue with an editorial in *The Pioneer* of Lucknow, a solidly pro-imperialist paper. The Prince of Wales was visiting India that winter, and the Gandhian nationalists had called for a boycott of his visit as part of their Non-Cooperation movement. *The Pioneer* urged Indians not to heed this call; to pay proper respect to the Prince and the throne was, it wrote, 'an acid test of loyalty'. Stokes remarked that while it was entirely natural for every Englishman to feel a sentimental, historical attachment to the Royal House of Windsor, that House could not have the same meaning to Indians. He conceded that the King and the Prince were themselves good men, who may have had the welfare of Indians at heart. Nonetheless, Englishmen could not 'demand from Indians loyalty to the King merely on the grounds of his being the symbol of world-wide British domination'.

The second part of the article documented the economic conse-quences of British rule in India. Stokes spoke here of the early exploitation of Bengal by the East India Company, and of the destruction of indigenous industries under colonial rule. Then, moving to his own province, Punjab, he narrated how British land policies had created poverty and indebtedness. The economic history of India since the British took over, remarked Stokes, 'furnishes us with no material on the basis of which anyone has a right to demand an exhibition of loyalty'.

The third and concluding part of the article began by remarking that 'so far as the past is concerned, if gratitude needs expression, it is for the British Nation to express it to India, because it was from the exploited millions of the early Company Days, that those aggregates of Capital came into being in England which made possible the Mechanical Revolution and subsequent British great-ness'. The real question, however, concerned the conditions under which loyalty could be asked for and given in the present. In a climate of economic oppression and racial division it was 'unrea-sonable' to expect blind loyalty to the British monarchy. The 'plain issue' identified by Stokes was: 'Either the Empire stands for equality of opportunity between its subjects, irrespective of race and colour, or it stands for nothing to which any fair-minded Englishman can demand the enthusiastic loyalty of Indians. Which is it?'[49]

On 2 December, the day the second article appeared, Stokes travelled to Lahore to attend a meeting of the Punjab Provincial Congress Committee. 'What the month will bring forth no one can say', he wrote to his mother: 'We have done our best but the whole affair is in the hands of God. My own feeling is that we leaders will be soon arrested. I am ready for it and so are the rest.'[50] His prescience was uncanny; for the next morning he was arrested, and taken straight off the train to Lahore Central Jail. In his first letter after his arrest, he said: 'I am very happy and proud to be allowed to take my share of the suffering which the Nationalists will have to undergo so that India may have her rights. We all gladly go; our women folk send [us] with loyalty to the cause and in the spirit of true devotion.'[51]

Stokes had been charged with 'breaching the peace' on account of articles he had published on the oppression of peasants in the Simla Hills and in defence of the Congress credo. His article 'The Acid Test of Loyalty' was the lead exhibit for the prosecution. Stokes wrote a long and eloquent statement of defence, whose object, he made clear, was 'not [to] evade imprisonment, for which as a non-co-operator I am prepared'. Rather, it was made 'in order to categorically deny the charge that I have ever given a lecture or written an article that tended to provoke hatred upon the part of the hearer or reader'.

In his writings and speeches, said Stokes,

> I have not shrunk from telling the truth as I see it; I have used every effort of late to persuade the people of this land to strengthen by their support and obedience the great leader who has been granted to India at this time of crisis. And yet I have lost no opportunity of making the people feel that their most sacred duty was to start the work of reformation in their own hearts by cleansing them of hatred and violence.

Stokes ended his statement in court with recalling how he had himself served on the side of the British Empire in the First World War, as had so many others now active in the nationalist cause. These erstwhile loyalists had become Non-Cooperators because they had come to feel 'that the Government's only idea of co-operation is that the people of India should submit to its decisions'. Had the authorities even come to meet the dissenters halfway, remarked Stokes, 'had they said, "Help us to devise a method by which India can attain to a position in the Empire consistent with her interests and her self-respect" . . . can we imagine that there would have been any non-cooperation movement in India today? I do not think so.'[52]

Stokes's statement was a brilliant defence of the Gandhian credo, of its commitment to non-violence and to social reform, and of the passionate spirit of patriotism that underlay it. The British magistrate dismissed the renegade's defence, and sentenced him to six months in prison. For someone accustomed to roaming where he wished to, the confinement was at first irksome; the barred windows and enclosed quarters a striking change from the views from his own bedroom window in Harmony Hall of the snow peaks above and of the River Sutlej down in the valley below. But he gradually got used to his new home, keeping himself busy by writing a diary and reading about Indian history.[53]

In jail, while he missed his family, Stokes took great solace in having followed his Quaker forebears in standing up for his convictions. 'I am', he told his mother, 'only [doing what] my own Stokes and Spencer ancestors did for conscience sake. Thomas Stokes was in the White Lion prison in Surrey with George Fox for a considerable period. Surely we have not gone so soft that we can no longer do the same for our ideals.'[54]

Stokes was visited in Lahore Central Jail by C. F. Andrews. Andrews sent an account of his meeting both to the prisoner's wife, in Kotgarh, and to the prisoner's mother, in Philadelphia. In an article in Gandhi's magazine *Young India*, Andrews quoted from their replies. Stokes's wife wrote back saying: 'I know well that when my husband is in jail with many other sons of India suffering from righteousness, he is sure to be happy.' Stokes's mother wrote back saying that 'here, in America, there is, I think, among the educated, thoughtful people a great sympathy with India's effort for Self-Government; but few, I believe, grasp Mr. Gandhi's idealism, and most people feel that India is so huge and is made up of so many races and religions that Non-violence appears hopeless.'[55]

When Stokes was arrested, his mother had at first kept the news from her friends and neighbours in Pennsylvania, fearing that they would not comprehend why a white American would go to prison on behalf of Indians. The news got into the local press anyway, and, contrary to what the mother had feared, was received well. One friend told Florence Stokes that she should be proud to have a son like Samuel; another wrote saying: 'Bully for Sam Stokes! If more of us went to jail for what we believed, the world would soon be a better place.'[56]

Reassured by how her friends saw her son's transgression, Florence Stokes agreed to being interviewed by the *New York Times*. The paper later published a short report entitled 'BRITISH ARREST MINISTER: Former Philadelphian Accused of Being a Gandhi Supporter', the headline accurate in all except one telling detail – although he had been ordained as a priest, Stokes had no church of his own in which he 'ministered' to souls. The report quoted the prisoner's mother as saying that her son had 'conceived a strong admiration' for Gandhi and gave him 'his unqualified support'. His support, said Mrs Stokes, 'was a result of his general attitude rather than any specific act, although an attempt was made to fasten certain seditious utterances on him'.[57]

Meanwhile, back in Lahore Central Jail, with the onset of summer the heat and the mosquitoes bothered Stokes a great deal. His term was approaching its end, leading to a sense of anticipation at being reunited with his wife and children. 'The hardship of jail life', he wrote to his mother in the last week of May 1922, 'is not prison-life, but the nameless fears which enforced absences from one's dear ones begets. The thought comes: "Suppose I should die here, unable to see them." It is the horror of such thoughts, increased by one's surroundings and sense of helplessness, that the hardship of being a prisoner is most felt.'[58]

Three days later Stokes was freed from prison. But while he was himself out of jail, his leader, Gandhi, was still incarcerated. Stokes returned to Kotgarh to be reunited with his family and resume his work of agricultural renewal. Stokes remained in sympathy with the Congress, but now thought it should adopt a less confrontational approach, and work within the Legislative Councils that the colonial Government had set up.[59]

Through 1922 and 1923 Stokes was mostly in and around Kotgarh. He watched his children grow, and his apple trees grow too. He built a school for the village children, in which, apart from the three Rs, he also had them learn the elements of carpentry and masonry, to allow them to get productive jobs in Simla once they had matriculated.[60]

In February 1924 Gandhi fell seriously ill in prison. He was released – the British did not want his death on their hands – and went off to the seaside near Bombay to recover. Knowing his leader's dietary tastes, Stokes had five pounds of Himalayan honey shipped to him.[61] Stokes also sent Gandhi a loving letter asking him not to abort his recovery and return prematurely to political work. He wrote:

If you are suffering from weakness and nervousness as a result of taking too active an interest in the problems before the country before you have gained sufficient strength I feel very strongly that it is in the interests of India for you to relax. In this, of course, I can only give my personal opinion with diffidence and humility, as I certainly do with deep affection. 'Brother body' as St. Francis used to call it, must be considered if it is to do the work for which it was given to us.[62]

He knew that the Mahatma was well looked after by his disciples on the seafront. But, said Stokes to Gandhi, 'some day I hope to share the beauty of this quiet hilltop with you. I am certain that I shall do so.'[63]

While Gandhi was in jail, a debate had broken out within the Congress, between those committed to achieving political independence through non-violent Non-Cooperation, and those advocating that nationalists enter the Legislative Councils created by the British, and seek there to influence Government policies by incremental means. After his own release from prison in June 1922, Stokes had come round to the view that Council entry was a worthy aim. He thought legislators could press for education and employment opportunities for the hill peasants. In March 1924, after Gandhi had come out of jail, Stokes wrote to him about his support for Council entry. Gandhi wrote back affirming his own faith in absolute Non-Cooperation with colonial institutions.[64]

Gandhi was a fervent advocate of hand-spinning. Stokes appreciated the need for nationalists to do manual labour, and was (in Gandhi's own words) 'himself an enthusiastic spinner'.[65] However, he opposed Gandhi's desire to make spinning mandatory for membership of the Congress. In November 1924 Stokes wrote Gandhi a long letter expressing his dissent. He thought the imposition of a particular practice on every member of a political party a violation of democratic principle. Would it not send a dangerous precedent for when India became independent? Stokes alerted Gandhi to the arrogation of supreme power by the Bolsheviks in Soviet Russia, and the suppression of individualism that a party's monopoly over decision-making had led to. As Stokes wrote:

> The first step is 'You must work if you are to have a voice in the affairs of the nation'; the next is, 'It is the right of the Government to define what constituted <u>work</u>.' The last is 'You will lose your citizen's right if you do not do the sort of work that appeals to the party in political power.'

In offering his dissent, Stokes did so with utmost affection and respect. 'Dear Mahatmaji, forgive this long letter', he wrote: 'To tell the truth it does me good to pour out my heart to you. I have been fated to love you for your truthfulness and fearlessness – and also to differ from you in so many things. Accept the love and pardon the other things.'[66]

When confronted with disagreement by a colleague on a major point of principle, Gandhi's practice was to respond to it in public. So he printed his friend's arguments in his newspaper *Young India*, and set out to refute them. Stokes's 'excessive regard for liberty of the individual', he wrote, 'has disabled him from distinguishing between voluntary acceptance and compulsion'. For

> when a man joins a voluntary association such as the Congress he does so willingly and tacitly or explicitly undertakes to obey its rules.

These rules generally include submission of the minority to the wishes of the majority. The voluntary nature of every act of every member is clear from the fact that he can secede whenever the majority pass a rule which is in conflict with his conscience.[67]

The exchange in both public and private was conducted with grace and courtesy. Stokes then did what his leader had advocated; he seceded from the Congress. He would now focus on his family, his school, and his farming.

In the last week of December 1924 the annual session of the Indian National Congress was held in the southern town of Belgaum. Mahatma Gandhi was elected President of the Congress. There were thousands of delegates to cheer him on. Stokes was not one of them. He had chosen to spend Christmas at home with wife and children. In letters to his mother he sketched the scene at his home as the year ended; with snow falling, and the children drawing pictures, and he himself reading works of religion and philosophy, having, as he said, 'again launched upon my "Oriental mysticism"'.[68] Five years of intense political activity had come to an end.

CHAPTER 5

Daughtering Gandhi

I

On 28 May 1923, the classified columns of *The Times* of London carried, in minutely small print, the notice of a piano concert by a certain Madeleine Slade. This was to be held the following Saturday, at the Queen's Hall in Westminster. The notice said the pianist would play Beethoven's last five sonatas.

In May 1923 Madeleine Slade was thirty, and leading a rather humdrum life in the middle reaches of the English upper classes. She was born in 1892, the daughter of a homemaker and a naval officer who was often posted abroad. Madeleine was brought up in her maternal grandfather's country house in Surrey, with fine views of the North Downs. The young girl developed a love of horses, and of riding them. When the weather forced her indoors, she spent her time on the piano instead. At the age of fifteen she heard the music of Beethoven for the first time, and, as she later recalled, 'my spirit within was awakened to a living sense of the Divine Power . . .'[1]

When Madeleine was in her teens, her father was posted to Bombay, and took the family with him. Here, the girl improved her riding and piano skills, while encountering Indians only as gardeners, bearers, cooks and sepoys. After the family returned to England, several young men of her social class pursued her, seeking her hand – she refused them all. Instead, she became a (not very successful) concert pianist, performing mostly Beethoven, braving the hostility to German music in England that came in the wake of the First World War.

Madeleine's knowledge of the composer was greatly enhanced by reading books about him by the French writer Romain Rolland. Winner of the Nobel Prize for Literature in 1915, and best known for his ten-part novel *Jean-Christophe*, Rolland was a considerable scholar of classical music and the life and work of Beethoven in particular. (He taught the subject to students at the Sorbonne.)

At the time of her London concert in May 1923, Madeleine was busy learning French, in preparation for going to meet Romain Rolland. By the next spring she had acquired enough confidence in her command of the language to write to Rolland at his home in Villeneuve, on the Swiss side of the border with France. He invited her to visit him. So she went. They had several long conversations. Writing about them years later, Madeleine recalled:

> He sat opposite me at the table and we talked on and on. It seemed as if we had always known one another. His thoughts flowed forth as if he were thinking aloud. He advised me to travel, and spoke of Austria and other places. Then he mentioned India, not with any suggestion that my travels should take me there but in connection with a small book he said he had just written, and which was in the press, called *Mahatma Gandhi*. I looked blank.
>
> 'You have not heard about him?' he asked.
>
> 'No,' I replied.
>
> So he told me, and added, 'He is another Christ.'[2]

At this stage Rolland had not met Gandhi. However, he had heard of him through Indian friends, and read works by him and about him.[3] The novelist was deeply impressed by the politician-cum-reformer and his mission; and wrote a book celebrating his ideas, which was published in French in September 1924. Madeleine was passing through Paris when Rolland's *Mahatma Gandhi* hit the stores. She bought the book, and took it back to her lodgings. As she later remembered:

> I could not put it down. I read and read, and as I read the dawn in my heart glowed brighter and brighter, and by the time I had finished, the Sun of Truth was pouring his rays into my soul. From that moment

I knew that my life was dedicated to [Gandhi]. That for which I had been waiting had come, and it was this.[4]

Madeleine's first impulse was to go to India straightaway. She even went to the P&O shipping company to book a ticket to Bombay. But then she thought she'd better prepare herself properly for this radical change of career, climate and country. She obtained materials on the Sabarmati Ashram, and studied them attentively. She practised how to sit cross-legged on the floor, and adopted a vegetarian diet.

In India, Gandhi was embarking on a long fast for Hindu–Muslim harmony. Madeleine read about the fast – which was conducted in Delhi in September 1924 – and was further impressed. She wrote to Gandhi of her wish to join him, enclosing, as a token of her love and appreciation, a cheque for twenty pounds (then not an insubstantial sum) for his work. Gandhi wrote thanking her for the gift, remarking: 'I am glad indeed that instead of obeying your first impulse you decided to fit yourself for the life here and to take time. If a year's rest still impels you to come, you will probably be right in coming to India.'[5]

Madeleine wrote back saying that

the first impulse has never faded – but on the contrary my desire to serve you has grown ever more & more fervent. It is impossible to express in words the greatness of the inspiration which impels me but I pray God with all my heart that I may be able to give expression to my life in work – in acts. However humble they may be they will at least be utterly sincere.

She now put before Gandhi 'my <u>most earnest request</u> – May I come to your Ashram to study spinning and weaving – to learn to live your ideals & principles in daily life, & indeed to learn in what way I may hope to serve you in the future?'

Madeleine told Gandhi that she was continuing her preparation 'as best I can'. She had 'given up the drinking of all wines beers or spirits', and no longer ate meat of any kind. She was learning to spin and weave, but with wool, since 'nobody seems to know much about the management of cotton in France or England'. With the help of 'many kind Indian friends', she was learning Hindi, and reading books on the country and its culture. 'The more I enter into Indian thought', she wrote, 'the more I feel as if I were reaching at last, a long lost home.'

Madeleine confessed to Gandhi that 'my being is filled with a great joy & a great anguish. The joy of giving all I have to you & to your people – & the anguish of being able to give so little.' She planned to reach Bombay in November 1925, and take the train from there to Ahmedabad. 'Dear Master – may I come?' she asked, before signing off as 'ever your humble & most devoted servant'.[6]

Gandhi wrote back saying Madeleine's letter had touched him 'deeply'. Besides, the samples of wool she had enclosed with it were 'excellent'. She was welcome to join the ashram, and if she intimated her travel details in advance would be met off the boat. Gandhi added: 'Only please remember that the life at the Ashram is not all rosy. It is strenuous. Bodily labour is given by every inmate. The climate of this country is also not a small consideration. I mention these things not to frighten you but merely to warn you.'[7]

Madeleine wrote back thanking Gandhi for having 'permitted me to enter the Ashram'. She hoped to sail for Bombay from Marseilles in late October. 'It is most kind of you to arrange for someone to meet me at the steamer,' she said, adding: 'I deeply appreciate your warnings with regard to the life and the climate. For a strenuous and severely simple life I am fully prepared. Bodily labour I am familiar with, and indeed am never happy without.'[8]

II

When Madeleine Slade took the dramatic step of leaving England for India she was a month short of her thirty-third birthday. The ship she was on docked at Bombay on 6 November 1925. She was met at the quayside by sympathizers of Gandhi. That evening the Mahatma's youngest son, Devadas, who was in town, dropped in to see her. Madeleine was asked whether she wanted to spend some days seeing the sights of India's *urbs prima*; she answered that she would rather get to Ahmedabad straightaway.[9]

Devadas now booked Madeleine on a night train from Bombay to Ahmedabad. She was met at the station by two of Gandhi's closest associates, Vallabhbhai Patel and Mahadev Desai. Patel got into a car with her, while Mahadev waited to collect her luggage and bring it separately. In a later remembrance, the Englishwoman-becoming-an-Indian vividly described her physical entry into the world of the ashram and of Gandhi, already 'Bapu' (Father) to her:

> Suddenly my companion [Patel] remarked, 'You see those trees and some buildings beyond? That is the Ashram.' In a moment the car drew up under a big tamarind tree, and I found myself walking down a little paved garden path. We passed through a small gate, then up two steps to a verandah and through a door into a room. As I entered, I became conscious of a little spare figure rising up from a white *gaddi* [mattress] and stepping towards me. I knew it was Bapu, but, so completely overcome was I with reverence and joy, that I could see and feel nothing but a heavenly light. I fell on my knees at Bapu's feet. He lifted me up and taking me in his arms said, 'You shall be my daughter.'[10]

Gandhi chose to call his adopted daughter 'Mira', a name that was easy to pronounce, but in this case also a mild – or perhaps not so mild – act of conceit, since it was also the name of a medieval mystic who had turned her back on her aristocratic background to devote herself, in song and verse, to the worship of Lord Krishna. This twentieth-century English Mira settled in to the ashram fairly quickly, her preparation in London allowing her to adjust to the routine. The diet and physical regimen were easy to handle; and the company was kind and loving too. The main difficulty she had was with regard to language; the Devanagari script she found difficult, and she was too shy to speak Hindustani. But otherwise she was content, conveying her happiness in a series of letters to Romain Rolland in Switzerland. These letters are lost; but we do have a reply of Rolland's where he expresses his pleasure at Madeleine/Mira's great joy: 'joy to have found the Master of goodness, of love & of truth, – joy to have entered at last on the good and just way for which you have hunted so long, & where your energies will best deploy themselves'. The French writer however urged his former disciple not to disavow her roots. 'Do not forget the light of Europe upon the roads of Asia!' said Rolland: 'Make those around you enjoy it! Take and give!'[11]

In early December, Madeleine, now Mira, accompanied Gandhi to an ashram in central India run by the ascetic scholar Vinoba Bhave. From here she wrote to Devadas who was now a sort of sibling to her: 'This beautiful and quiet little Ashram has proved a perfect place for Bapu to rest in, and it is a joy to see how quickly he is recovering' (from a purificatory fast he had recently undertaken). Then, turning to herself, she proudly proclaimed: 'I have learned two new kinds of labour – corn-grinding (splendid exercise!) and cotton gathering.'[12]

The annual meeting of the Indian National Congress was being held that year in the industrial town of Kanpur, in the United Provinces. Gandhi took Mira with him to the meeting. So far, she had seen the Mahatma only in the company of his disciples in the ashram. Now, travelling with him by train, she wrote that

> a new and amazing realization burst upon me, and that was the peculiar hold Bapu had upon the masses. At every station, pressing, surging crowds thronged the platform, and the air throbbed with the cry 'Mahatma Gandhi ki jai' (Victory to Mahatma Gandhi). The faces did not reflect the excitement of people out to catch a glimpse of a celebrity, but the eager, thirsting look of devotees seeking to set eyes on some holy person, a saviour on whom they had pinned all their hopes with a faith which they would not have been able to explain or express in so many words but which drew them irresistibly.[13]

From the Congress, Mira wrote to Devadas that 'the terrible strain of work here, the noise, the dust and the crowds of people have worn poor Bapu to a shadow, and he looks as thin again as he did at the end of the fast. He is right down to the bottom of his strength.'[14] In Kanpur, Gandhi was examined by the celebrated doctor (and nationalist) M. A. Ansari, who recommended several weeks of rest on his return to Sabarmati, and a change of diet, including the eating of white bread. Mira wrote to Devadas: 'How glad we shall be to get back to Sabarmati! And you have heard, no doubt, that Bapu has decided to stay at the Ashram for a whole <u>year</u>! Is that not the best of news!'[15]

Through much of 1926, Mira was in Sabarmati, with Gandhi in his year of rest from travel and political work. She spun and wove, cleaned and cooked. In December she travelled alone to Delhi, where she stayed in a women's hostel. Gandhi wrote making sure she was keeping to the regimen he had prescribed for her. 'You should give me your day's doings', he told her,

> and describe the prayers, the studies and the meals. Tell me what you are eating. How are your bowels acting? What is the quantity of milk you are taking? What are the times of your meals? Are there mosquitoes there? Do you take your walks regularly? Do you write any Hindi? Does anyone teach you? What fruit are you getting?[16]

Mira spent the winter of 1926–7 visiting ashrams across North India, writing of what she saw and did to Gandhi. He wrote back asking her – as always – to be careful about her diet, and about her accounts. He had also given her a special task: to correct the grammar and language of the English version of his autobiography, being translated from the Gujarati by Mahadev Desai. She was posted chapters while on the road; these she sent back to Ahmedabad with her corrections.[17]

When she returned to Sabarmati after her travels, Mira decided that she must discard European dress. She learned to wear a sari, but found it cumbersome, so adopted the *ghaghra*, the long skirt, worn with a loose shirt, that Gujarati peasant women wore. Mira also came to the conclusion that she must shave her head and take a vow of celibacy. The ladies in the ashram urged her not to discard her long locks, but she was determined to do so; and in the end it was Gandhi himself who cut her hair with his own hands.[18]

His sabbatical year now over, Gandhi had resumed his travels across India. On most trips outside Ahmedabad he could not take Mira with him. She missed Gandhi terribly, sometimes writing to him four or five times a day. When separated from her Bapu, she was prone to despondency and abrupt changes of mood, as their correspondence reveals. Thus Gandhi wrote to her from South India in May 1927:

> I observe from your wire that in spite of your previous letter of attainment of peace, the pendulum has swung back and that you are again perturbed. This does not surprise me. If our lucid moments were lasting, nothing further will remain to be done. Unfortunately or fortunately, we have to pass through many an ebb and flow before we settle down to real peace.[19]

When Gandhi was in Sabarmati, Mira yearned to be at his side all the time. She wanted to be the one to take out his spinning wheel, the one to peel his fruit and pour his goats' milk into a tumbler, the one to keep track of his blood pressure and his bowel movements. Gandhi resisted this possessiveness. Thus, as Mira wrote to Gandhi's disciple Jamnalal Bajaj, 'Bapu is very strict with me.' He 'will not let me do anything for him personally, except look after his spinning wheel. He says, I must get on as fast as I can with my own work, and I shall not be allowed to help him any more until I know Hindi, spinning, cooking, etc. thoroughly well.'[20]

III

In March 1928, Gandhi told Mira he hoped to visit Europe in the summer, telling her that 'the chief reason for going will be to spend some time with Romain Rolland'. Gandhi had asked Motilal Nehru to apply for a passport on his behalf. If he went, he planned to take three companions with him – his secretaries Mahadev Desai and Pyarelal Nayar, and his adopted daughter Mira.[21] Mira wrote to Rolland to ask for suitable dates from his side. When no reply came, she became very anxious, as she really looked forward to the meeting of her two mentors.[22]

In the event, the trip to Europe in the summer did not take place. In June 1928, Devadas Gandhi wrote to Mira of his desire to marry Lakshmi, daughter of Gandhi's 'Southern Commander' C. Rajagopalachari. They had fallen in love in Bangalore, while their fathers were doing khadi work in South India. Mira, who had determinedly taken the Gandhian vow of celibacy, wrote to Devadas that the revelation that he wanted to marry came to her

> as a heart-rending blow. . . . I had always looked on you as a sure brahmachari [celibate] on whom we could count in the Ashram. And still I insist on looking upon this condition as a passing stage. We nearly all have to go through it sooner or later. I went through it myself in the dark days of my past life, and I now never cease to thank God that I got through it without becoming permanently entangled in this deadly snare. That is my feeling – and I pray to God that he may safely bring you through to freedom![23]

In September 1928, Gandhi sent Mira on an 'all India khadi tour'. She was to travel alone, with her carding bows, through north, south, and east India. Gandhi hoped that the tour would equip her to start a centre to train students in spinning and weaving when she returned to Sabarmati.

It was in the course of this tour that Mira visited the Himalaya for the first time. From the town of Almora, once capital of a medieval kingdom, she wrote to a friend that she was very happy to be in these 'marvellous mountains', which 'surpass anything I could have imagined – hundreds and hundreds of miles of unbroken snow!'.[24]

After a week's break in the mountains, Mira came down to the plains and resumed her educational tour. She travelled through the towns and villages of the United Provinces, studying spinning and weaving techniques. In early November she arrived at the town of Madhubani in Bihar, a famous centre of folk art. From here she wrote to Devadas Gandhi of the lessons learned thus far:

> Never gin without first cleaning the caps.
> When carding keep the gut spotlessly clean.
> Treasure your implements with loving care.
> Well cared for instruments last long and render good service.
> Badly kept instruments soon wear out and always give trouble.
> Make it a point of honour never to use any other slivers but
>   those of your own carding.[25]

Mira now proceeded to the town of Muzaffarpur, on the Gandak river, and famous for its lychees. She wrote Devadas a long letter on how invigorating her travels had been. 'I feel', she said, 'much nearer to Bapu's true spirit when I am out in the villages or in little simple local Institutions like this Sevashram.' By contrast, the Sabarmati Ashram in Ahmedabad was too large, too structured, with too many visitors coming and going. 'I feel more and more', Mira told Devadas, 'that we must have a real Ashram, no matter how small, where those who want to strive to lead the real life can live and vindicate, to the best of their power, Bapu's great idealism . . .'[26]

In December Mira rejoined her master at Wardha, where he had come to Vinoba's ashram for his annual period of rest and recuperation before the Congress. She found Gandhi well, and taking long walks, but 'again making a drastic food experiment. No milk, no fruit, no almonds – simply boiled wheat flour and oil as a milk substitute, and vegetables with oil.' Mira persuaded him to resume eating almonds and fruit.[27]

In the new year Mira resumed her travels. She visited Santiniketan, the university founded in rural Bengal by the poet Rabindranath Tagore, and spoke to the students there, reporting to Gandhi that 'of course I told them without hesitation of the overwhelming veneration & faith with which you inspire me, & of my absolute belief in the spinning wheel, & how it was that inspiration which drew me out of my former life into a new birth'.[28]

Mira also had long conversations with Tagore himself. She told Devadas Gandhi that she had been 'deeply impressed by his simple sincerity and real beauty of inner nature'.[29] To Devadas's father, she wrote that 'from the first moment I was struck by the wonderful freshness of his countenance, the grandeur of his head, & above all the liquid beauty of his eyes'.[30] Later, Tagore wrote to her explaining the difference (and complementarity) between himself and Gandhi: 'According to the Upanishads the reconciliation of the contradiction of the contradiction between tapasya [austerities] and ananda [bliss] is at the root of creation and Mahatmaji is the prophet of tapasya and I am the poet of ananda.'[31]

From Santiniketan, Mira returned to the eastern province of Bihar. She suffered a severe intestinal infection, which took her weeks to recover from. Once she had, she established a khadi centre in a village called Chattwan, in the Darbhanga district. The women took to spinning 'with remarkable enthusiasm'. Mira spent several hours a day with them, teaching, guiding, supervising. 'It is intensely interesting and sympathetic work', she wrote to Devadas: 'The joy of working with these poor peasants is something one cannot describe. Their happiness over the new carding is one's continual inspiration and support.' She was delighted when the leading Gandhian of Bihar, Rajendra Prasad, came to visit her in rural Darbhanga.[32]

Soon afterwards Mira fell ill again, this time with malaria. Gandhi had asked her to always sleep under a mosquito net; this she had neglected to do. Hearing of her illness, which had led among other things to an alarming loss of weight, he wrote to her saying: 'I constantly think of you. This leanness of body won't do. You must have enough flesh on you to support your big frame.'[33] He now asked her to return to the drier and healthier climate of Ahmedabad. She did so, reluctantly, keeping alive the hope that she might soon go back to Darbhanga. Her time in rural Bihar, she wrote, 'has been an experience of priceless value'. It had given her 'new confidence and an infinite inspiration'. She now thought she knew how to 'really reach the hearts of the peasants, and help and save them'.[34]

On her return to Sabarmati, Mira wrote a short pamphlet on the connection between the khadi campaign and the movement for political freedom. This rehearsed the nationalist argument that the Indian economy had flourished before British rule, and that colonial policies had deliberately destroyed indigenous manufacturing and enterprise. The promotion of homespun cloth would, she argued, generate income and employment, alleviate poverty, and foster self-reliance. The pamphlet ended with this stirring invocation:

> **To wear Khadi** is to save the starving millions.
> **To wear Khadi** is to remove England's chief economic exploitation of India.
> **To wear Khadi** is to bring back the strength and independence of our land.[35]

In Sabarmati, Mira pressed Gandhi afresh to allow her to attend to his needs large and small. Gandhi gave Mira one specific task: to observe, and minutely record, his bowel movements. Thus, on 18 August 1929, she recorded that

> Bapu is a little better today. The extreme weakness of yesterday has gone. His bowels have also become quieter. There have been motions at 5 a.m., 6.40 a.m., 2.40 p.m., and now there has just been one at 3.40. There is still much mucous and signs of blood, but no pain, and the last motion has been the best to-day. Every hour and a half he is taking 1/2 tola of gur [jaggery] dissolved in 6 oz. of water . . .[36]

In November, Mira accompanied Gandhi on a village tour through the United Provinces. The party took a day off to visit the abandoned Mughal capital, Fatehpur Sikri, built by the Emperor Akbar in the latter part of the sixteenth century. A large group of curious villagers followed them inside. After walking for several hours around the 'beautiful harmonious verandahs and palaces which surrounded the court', Gandhi sat down for a little rest. The sun was about to set; of the sight in front of her, Mira wrote:

> There where the mighty Mogul once sat in royal glory, was a sheet gleaming white in the twilight, and on the sheet a little dark brown figure, clad in loin-cloth, sitting silent and thoughtful, while, on every side, in spite of the authorities' efforts to separate them, were to be seen his brother rustics peeping in at all the gateways, doors and outer windows.
> The contrast between the old and the new was unforgettable.[37]

IV

In December 1929, the Congress held its annual meeting in the city of Lahore, in the Punjab, a seat of political and military power for the British and before them for the Sikhs and Mughals too. Here, at a tented conference centre on the banks of the River Ravi, the charismatic Jawaharlal Nehru became President of his party for the first time. The Congress declared it stood for 'Purna Swaraj', full independence. There was now a growing clamour for a fresh round of countrywide civil disobedience.

In the new year, Gandhi, back in Ahmedabad, thought deeply about what form this movement should take. He finally decided that it should involve the breaking of the salt laws. In the first months of 1930, as Gandhi prepared for what was to become known as the Salt March, the Sabarmati Ashram, wrote Mira, 'reached its zenith in physical energy and moral strength. Every morning and evening Bapu spoke in the prayers, and an atmosphere of uplifting inspiration filled the air.' The march was to begin on the morning of 12 March; while the rest of the ashram was abuzz with nervousness and excitement, 'Bapu was the only person who slept that night, and he rested in that sweet sleep which never failed him.'[38]

The march to the sea was an all-male affair. Mira stayed in the ashram while Gandhi walked for three weeks to the village of Dandi, where he scooped a fistful of salt from the sea to challenge the colonial state's monopoly over a commodity so vital to the diet of every poor Indian. Gandhi was soon arrested, and taken off to Yerwada Jail, on the outskirts of the city of Poona. Now Mira and the Mahatma experienced their longest separation yet. From prison Gandhi wrote to her of weaving, diet and other such (non-political) matters.

Mira spent the rest of 1930 partly in Sabarmati, and partly in the villages, promoting khadi. Gandhi was released in the last week of January 1931. In March, when he had a series of meetings with the Viceroy in Delhi, Mira accompanied him. Every day, when the meeting broke for lunch, the high officials for the Raj would repair for a lavish meal, while this adopted daughter of Gandhi's would walk up the steps of the Viceregal Palace carrying his modest repast of dates and goat-milk.

Later in the year, Gandhi proceeded for a Round Table Conference in London, convened to discuss India's political future. He chose to take four people with him. The daughter of the English admiral was one of them. Of their departure in late August, Mira wrote:

In an atmosphere of intense excitement and enthusiasm, Bombay bade farewell to Bapu that morning. The ship steamed out into the Arabian sea and we (Bapu, Mahadev, Devadas, Pyarelal and myself) at last had time to breathe. Bapu now began to make inquiries about how much luggage we had got. This was a disturbing question. We told him the number of trunks, suit cases, etc., and explained why the number was rather large. Bapu was not satisfied and told us that we must open up all the boxes, sort out everything and whatever could possibly be done without, we should send back from Aden.[39]

In London, Gandhi and his party lived in a Quaker home in the East End. They were to spend almost two and a half months in England, with Gandhi closeted in the Conference in the day and taking trips outside London over the weekend. Mira accompanied him to the textile towns of Lancashire, her presence captured in photographs that have since become iconic.

The presence of an aristocratic Englishwoman in Gandhi's entourage attracted the attention of the *New York Times*, which printed a half-page profile, with the tell-all title: 'MIRABAI: GANDHI'S ENGLISH DISCIPLE: The Daughter of an Admiral, Miss Slade Keeps Her Stern Vows of Service'. The article presented the facts of Mira's family background, her comfortable if not luxurious upbringing, her discovery of Romain Rolland and through him of Gandhi. The reporter then quoted a cousin of Mira's, Marie Slade, as saying: 'Madeleine always had a sort of "crush" for first one thing and then another. She was a charming girl, very good-looking, and had her share of admiration. She took up things violently and would drop them as suddenly.'

The profile in the *New York Times* paid special attention to all that this Englishwoman did for Gandhi: prepared his meals, washed his clothes, etc. The correspondent was impressed that 'Mira should have been able to adapt herself so completely to her new surroundings'. That, in this case, the boundaries of race, class, religion and nationality had been comprehensively transgressed was underlined in the concluding paragraph, which read:

It is rarely that a tree can be transplanted with such success in an entirely different soil. And the question inevitably presents itself, 'Has the tree taken root now?' Such a question to Mirabai is not feasible, but let us hear what Mahadev Desai, for fourteen years personal secretary to Mahatma Gandhi, has to say. 'I am quite confident that Mirabai will remain a member of the Ashram', he says, 'while yielding to no one in my desire to live out the ideas and principles of Mahatmaji, I know the weakness of my flesh whereas I think that Mirabai has better self-control.'[40]

V

The Round Table Conference in London ended in failure. Gandhi and his party now returned to India via Europe, where Gandhi met Romain Rolland, with Mira acting as the interpreter. There was now a new Viceroy in place, the absolutely authoritarian Lord Willingdon having replaced the relatively liberal Lord Irwin. On landing in Bombay, Gandhi was arrested almost immediately, and taken off to Yerwada Jail. The civil disobedience movement now bestirred itself again. Mira was tasked with preparing weekly reports of who had courted arrest, where, and why. This angered the authorities, and soon she was arrested herself, and sentenced to three months in prison.

Mira was incarcerated in Bombay's Arthur Road Jail. With her in the same prison were two other remarkable women followers of Gandhi, the poet Sarojini Naidu and the socialist Kamaladevi Chattopadhyay. Mrs Naidu entertained them with jokes and poems, while the variously gifted Kamaladevi taught Mira how to skip and sing *bhajans*.

Mira was released in May, and almost immediately wrote up a note on the awful treatment of women prisoners in the jails of British India. They were subjected to 'endless pin-pricks, insults, and harassments. There are not often things which can be called, brutal and so forth. But the sum total of the treatment is thoroughly bad, and obviously designed to try and crush our spirit.' The women prisoner was 'denuded of all her clothing and made to wear only a heavy coarse sari and a loose bodice, no under bodice, drawers or petticoats are allowed, nor is a sheet of any kind allowed for the bedding, which consists of a straw mat and a harsh woollen rug'. There were curbs on correspondence, and on meetings – with only one interview permitted every three months, and these conducted 'through the bars of a gate, even little children and babies not being allowed to reach their mothers'.

Mira remarked that 'the Government may think that it is crushing our spirit by their policy, but what it is actually doing is to rouse a spirit of burning indignation in the people and to widen the gulf day by day which divides it from the sympathy of the masses'.[41]

Mira was now out of prison but Gandhi was not. She applied for permission to see him in Yerwada, and was refused. While disappointed she wore the refusal as a badge of honour. Willingdon had put strict curbs on whom Gandhi could see – no Congressmen or Congresswomen were allowed to visit him. Being treated on par with Patel, Nehru, Sarojini and Kamaladevi, pleased Mira; as she wrote to a friend: 'I don't feel upset – in fact I am happy to feel I get my full share – as an Indian!'[42]

Mira returned to Ahmedabad, but was soon re-arrested, for entering Bombay without permission. Another and longer term in jail followed. She adopted a saltless diet and took regular walks in the prison compound, without which, she told Gandhi, 'I should never have kept my health at all in this jail.' She was reading the Koran, and hoped to turn next to the Mahabharata. Having already read the Upanishads, she would then be finished with the year-long course in spiritual reading that Gandhi had laid out for her.

Even in jail, Mira retained her interest in and love for Nature. 'The spirit of Spring', she wrote to Gandhi,

has even touched the crows with its softening influence. There is one now, which sits in the papaya [tree] outside and utters soft croaks and would-be sweet warbles. Little singing birds now and then pass through the yard, and on their way they alight for a minute or two and tell us that Spring is there alright, outside – and my thoughts go to the river bank at the Ashram. How the little birds and squirrels must be busy all day in the grass and trees – how the water birds must be calling as they fly home in the evening to their roosting place by the well – and then, when the night has closed all in sable-stillness, how the glorious full moon will rise over the river spreading a path of gold across the water to the Ashram bank.[43]

Later in the spring Mira was shifted to the Sabarmati Jail in Ahmedabad, where she shared a cell with Gandhi's wife Kasturba. Her health remained good, and she keenly observed the birds and animals in these new surroundings. From the prison yard, Mira could see the trees on the road leading to the Sabarmati Ashram. Before embarking on the Salt March, Gandhi had said he would not return permanently to Ahmedabad. Mira approved of the decision; notwithstanding the beauty and 'sacred associations' of the ashram by the river, she felt that once they were all released from jail, the Mahatma and his inner circle should relocate away from the city. 'I feel so strongly', she told Gandhi, 'the need of contact with the real country.'[44]

On the morning of 22 August 1933 Mira was released from Sabarmati Jail, her one-year term having ended. From the jail she went straight to the Ahmedabad railway station, and caught a train to Bombay at 7 a.m., en route to Poona where her master was. After his return from the Round Table Conference, Gandhi had decided to devote himself to the abolition of Untouchability. The challenge to his authority of the brilliant and greatly gifted leader of the depressed castes, Dr B. R. Ambedkar, had affected him greatly. In prison in Poona, he had undertaken several long fasts to shame his fellow Hindus into doing more, much more, than they had so far done to abolish the pernicious practice of Untouchability.[45]

When Mira was released, Gandhi had just embarked on yet another fast. In the train to Bombay from Ahmedabad she got the news that the fasting Gandhi had been removed from Yerwada Jail to the Sassoon Hospital, but was still technically a prisoner. The other women in the carriage train soon recognized Mira and began to talk to her, the conversation thus recorded by her: ' "How terrible this is! The Mahatma is dying! Has the Government altogether lost its senses?" and so on – the day dragged on – and the train seemed to crawl.'

After they reached Bombay, Mira went to a friend's house for a wash and then took the night train to Poona. She tried to see Gandhi at the Sassoon Hospital but was denied permission. She waited anxiously at 'Parnakuti' (the bungalow of Gandhi's admirer Lady Thackersey) with C. F. Andrews, while Kasturba (who had been allowed to see her husband) was away at the hospital. Kasturba came back at 2 p.m. and told them that 'Gandhiji had a very bad attack of vomiting in the night, and he was now unable even to drink water – it appeared that he was already preparing for death'.

Sensing the gravity of the situation, the Government released Gandhi. He was brought to Parnakuti in an ambulance and carried out in a stretcher. As he did, Mira 'could see that he had sunken eyes and hollow cheeks – but his face was still lit with love and patience and above all shone the light of his indomitable will'.[46]

VI

In November 1933, now free and with his health restored, Gandhi set off on an all-India tour to campaign against Untouchability. He took Mira with him. Before they left Wardha, Mira wrote to Devadas that 'we will do our utmost to save Bapu as much strain as possible, but you know how much Bapu will give and give of himself'.[47]

Gandhi began his tour in the Central Provinces. He walked from village to village, addressing public meetings as he went. While Gandhi spoke at these meetings, Mira stayed in their camp, attending to various chores. Reports of how Gandhi was met and greeted reached her nonetheless. Based on these inputs she wrote that 'as to the enthusiasm of the masses, it is greater than ever and the tour is a wonderful procession through the country. I have not attended the meetings (no time) but I am told that they are tremendous, 30–50 thousand sometimes running up to one lakh. Money too is pouring in. All this lifts and gladdens Bapu's heart.'[48]

In the winter of 1933–4, Gandhi's anti-Untouchability tour traversed through South India. In March 1934 the tour reached the north-eastern province of Bihar, which had just witnessed a massive earthquake. Mira was deeply depressed to 'see Bihar that I know

and love so well devastated in this way'.[49] But as the pilgrimage moved on to the adjoining state of Orissa, her depression lifted. Gandhi was 'in a highly inspired mood', she reported, 'and I have utmost faith in the possibilities of the Great Pilgrimage if it is enabled to fully develop'.[50]

In the summer of 1934, Mira told Gandhi that she wished to tour the West to promote the message of the Indian freedom struggle. Gandhi thought it a good idea too, writing to Vallabhbhai Patel that he had consented to her going as 'her personality had become suppressed under me. I hope she will regain her former independence of character.'[51]

The Mahatma's friend and patron in Ahmedabad, the mill-owner Ambalal Sarabhai, agreed to underwrite the costs of Mira's trip. So she booked a second-class berth on a P&O steamer, landing at Marseilles, from where she took a short detour to see Romain Rolland in Villeneuve before proceeding to England.[52]

One of Mira's first talks in London was to a group of Quakers at Friends House. As a reporter on the spot noted,

> in a touching speech, Miraben made a pointed contrast to the one-time wealthy villages of India before the advent of the British with the present-day India where the villages were nothing but poverty-stricken. The audience gasped, as she reminded it of the grim fact that one-fifth of the human race was in starvation in India. She was ashamed that such a state of things should exist side by side with a wealthy British Empire which was aiming at still greater prosperity for the British people.[53]

In London Mira found 'a touching amount of sympathy amongst the people, especially amongst the working classes'. She planned to take the message of Gandhi and India's freedom to the mining areas of Wales, the textile towns of Lancashire, and the Midlands before returning to the capital city.[54]

Mira first proceeded to Wales, stopping en route at the country home in Somerset of her sister. This lady lived with her husband and two children in proper aristocratic fashion. Their home was a former royal hunting lodge, with a splendid view of unspoilt countryside. Her sister had done it up, Mira reported to Gandhi, 'in

perfect English taste, just as Mother would have done. All the pictures, books, furniture, ornaments, and old family silver look their best in the setting of that ancient house.'

In Wales Mira spoke first at a Unitarian Church and then to members of the Independent Labour Party. She had sought, she told Gandhi, to take this group of socialists 'into the spiritual aspect of things. I had to talk to them of God – though I told them they could give Him any name they liked – "humanity", "brotherhood", or the like.'[55]

Mira now carried on to Lancashire, which she had last visited with Gandhi back in 1931. Here she had 'practically packed halls every night', the meetings extending for two hours and longer. In the factory town of Darwen she spoke in the same room that the Mahatma had.

While on the road Mira wrote to a British friend:

I am having a most wonderful experience in Lancashire. Somehow the very thing I most long for has come. I have come face to face – heart to heart – with the People. Last night I had a weaver as chairman and another weaver and his tailoress wife as hosts. And, at Oldham and Wigan too, the chairmen were working-class people and they spoke in glowing terms of Mr Gandeye.[56]

Mira had been instructed by Gandhi's great and wise secretary Mahadev Desai to speak to the British people not just about the Mahatma alone. She must also tell them that, as and when the British left, the Indians were perfectly capable of running the country on their own. Mahadev told Mira to explain how, even under British rule, when Congressmen had got the chance to run local bodies such as Municipalities, 'they gave a very good account of themselves and were the recipients of reluctant praise even from Government'. He instructed her to give specific examples, of how, as President of the Bombay Municipal Corporation, Vithalbhai Patel was

said to have been more efficient than any European I.C.S. [man] could have been. He worked like a machine. He was exceedingly popular . . . The same can be said of Vallabhbhai Patel as the Chairman of the Municipality of Ahmedabad. Pandit Jawaharlal [Nehru] set an

excellent example as the Chairman of the Allahabad Municipality and broke many records of hard work and administrative ability.[57]

Among the places Mira spoke in were Nelson, Newcastle, Nottingham, Warwick, Maidstone and Ashford. In Warwick she had spoken at the Unitarian Church. A reporter 'found Miss Slade startlingly Indian in appearance. Her eyes had an Eastern brilliance, her eyebrows were black, and her skin was pale brown. She was dressed in a white garment and a brown cloak, reaching to her feet. They were both of Indian cotton and had been made by herself . . .'

Mira also spoke of British colonialism's destruction of rural industry and the high taxes it imposed on the peasantry. 'The Government was only known through its police and tax collectors', she proclaimed. In resisting these exactions, non-violently, Gandhi's movement had 'made India a country of spirit and determination instead of a country of submission'. She had herself come on this tour to tell the ignorant British public the truth about India; in the hope that 'it would prefer to sacrifice something rather than buy material comfort at the price of blood'.[58]

After criss-crossing the country, Mira returned to London, where – having already met ordinary British people – she sought appointments with politicians. She had a good meeting with the former British Prime Minister, David Lloyd George, who spoke very warmly of Gandhi.[59] She also wrote to Winston Churchill requesting an appointment; he wrote back saying that while he would 'have much appreciated the pleasure of a conversation with you', he was going abroad for a month. Churchill told the Mahatma's British disciple that while he was 'strongly opposed, as you probably know, to Mr Gandhi's politics, I am a sincere admirer of the heroic efforts he is making to improve the position of the depressed classes in India'.[60]

VII

Mira had been in touch with the radical New York priest John Haynes Holmes, a great admirer of Gandhi's, whom she had met (with the Mahatma) when the American came to London in 1931.

Holmes now urged her to come to the United States after England. He would arrange for a guide and typist for her, and get a professional lecture bureau in New York to set up speaking engagements.[61] Gandhi approved of the plan; having never been to the United States himself, he told Mira that 'it was an experience you certainly needed'.[62]

When the India Office heard that Gandhi's English disciple was to tour America they were slightly alarmed. A British mandarin in London wrote to a colleague posted in New York that

> if the visitor had been Gandhi himself I would not have much cared. But here is a most picturesque woman . . . an Englishwoman of good family gently reared who lives the simple life as an Eastern ascetic and the disciple of one whom some of your silly people regard as a Second Christ. She may well impress the womenfolk at least over on your side without getting the bird as she would at ordinary meetings in this country.[63]

Mira sailed for New York in the first week of October 1934. Travelling on the Cunard liner *Majestic* with her were the American tennis champion Bill Tilden and the President of the Philippine Senate, though it is unlikely that she spoke to or with either.[64] A large press contingent, doubtless primed by John Haynes Holmes, had come to meet Mira's ship when it docked. A dozen reporters, male and female, came on board. After answering their questions she was led up to an upper deck where a bevy of photographers awaited her. 'New York photographers beat all others by pace and persistence', she wrote later: 'They all began shouting "Look right this way please!" "Now please look this way!" and so on.'

After the photo shoot, Mira was taken by Holmes to the ship's lounge, 'where there was a movie-talkie apparatus set up and there we had to go through a regular ceremony of reception and speeches'. In the following week she spoke at the Town Hall, to an audience of over 1,500 people, and at the International House, to 600 students of fifty different nationalities. She also spoke at the synagogue of a Rabbi Wise, 'a famous Rabbi and a remarkable man', and had several meals with Holmes himself.

In a letter to friends, Mira gave her impressions of New York, pro and con. The climate was 'fine and surrounding', with blue skies and sunshine. The people were 'most charming, frank, kind-hearted and natural'. And yet:

> There is one detail which has taken me quite by surprise and that is that in its streets it is the dirtiest town I have seen in the West. I had always imagined that it would be spotlessly clean. The rich hotels, shops, etc., are clean enough inside, but the streets, pavements, buses, taxis, all have a shabby appearance. The traffic goes at the most appalling rate – the motor cars have a way of starting off with a jerk, tearing off at some thirty or forty miles a hour, and pulling up at a moment's notice with another sharp jerk. There are no refuges in the middle of the streets, even on the biggest, and pedestrians at the risk of their lives go dodging in and out amongst this whirl-wind of motor traffic.[65]

In two weeks in the United States Mira addressed twenty-two gatherings and gave five radio broadcasts. In America, she wrote, the

> meetings were much bigger than in England, and everywhere extraordinary interest was shown in Bapu as a person. Every sort of question was asked about him, while the political aspect, so much to the fore in England, was of secondary importance to these American audiences. Gandhi the man, the Teacher, the Apostle of Truth, was what they sought, and with such thirst and earnestness![66]

An American lady who heard Mira speak in Holmes's church in New York wrote saying that her talk 'inspired me, lifting my thought high above our so-called civilization; and I am grateful to you. . . . Your coming to the West has brought a light which we so need in our present chaos and darkness. May God protect you and the great Mahatma, that his shining principles will continue to illumine the thought of mankind.' This was a charming, and manifestly sincere, letter of praise; enclosed with which was a long and maudlin poem about the greatness of Gandhi that I need not reproduce here.[67]

In 1931, when Mira was in London with Gandhi, the *New York Times* had run a profile of her. Now, three years later, when she was in America, the paper published an even longer, and even more earnestly breathless, story about this Englishwoman who had become an Indian. The report began: 'Ten years ago an English woman turned to the Orient in search of happiness; recently – an ardent disciple of Mahatma Gandhi – she came back on a visit to the Occident, more firmly convinced than ever that the ways of the West are wrong.'

Mira was staying in the Lower East Side, in the dormitory of a social welfare organization known as the Henry Street Settlement. This is where the reporter met her, sitting on the floor, her legs crossed, her head shaven, looking as though 'she might have been a nun instead of a devotee of Brahma and Vishnu'. Mira spoke to the journalist of the trajectory of her life, of how she found Romain Rolland and through him Gandhi, of her life in the Sabarmati Ashram and of her journeys through the Indian countryside. She contrasted the contemplative East with the impetuous West, prompting the reporter to ask if ever the twain could meet. Mira answered: 'The East and West have met before. To say they have not met is to deny Christianity, for Christianity came from the East.'[68]

Mira also spent several days in Washington, where she stayed at the Mayflower Hotel, her homespun clothes and leather sandals in stark contrast to the high heels and evening gowns of the women in the hotel's foyer. She spoke at Howard University, addressing an audience of African Americans on 'Gandhi's spiritual message'.[69] While in the American capital, Mira met the First Lady, Eleanor Roosevelt, being struck by the simplicity and lack of ostentation in the home of the President of the United States. 'I was immensely delighted with the democratic atmosphere', she told a reporter later: 'No pomp and ceremony. You could just walk up to the White House as to any homely establishment.' Mira 'found Mrs. Roosevelt so charming. I enjoyed talking to her like I enjoy talking to a dear friend.'[70]

On her way back to India, Mira stopped again in London. She met several senior Conservative politicians, among them Sir Samuel Hoare, the Secretary of State for India. Parliament was then discussing a proposed 'Government of India' Act, which would partially, modestly, involve Indians in the running of their own country. Mira told Hoare he should invite Gandhi to London and discuss the legislation with him one-on-one before finalizing it. The Tory grandee replied: 'You speak as if Mr. Gandhi were the only Indian who counted, but I assure you I know some Indians who foam at the mouth at the very mention of his name.'[71]

Mira also met Winston Churchill, who was opposed even to the meagre devolution of powers the new Act proposed. Churchill told her emphatically: 'The Indian nation does not exist. There is no such thing.'[72] Mira, of course, entirely disagreed, and came back to her new homeland to try to prove Churchill wrong. When her ship docked in Bombay in late November, she was met by the prominent Congressmen Vallabhbhai Patel, Bhulabhai Desai, and K. F. Nariman. While they naturally greeted her very warmly, her baggage was subjected to 'severe scrutiny' by Customs, who confiscated many of her letters, documents and newspaper clippings.

Also on the dockside were representatives of the Indian press. Asked how her trip went, Mira said that she had addressed sixty-seven meetings in the United Kingdom alone. 'We had questions and answers after practically every meeting,' she said: 'In this way, I was able to come nearer to the people.' Of her visit to America, where she had addressed twenty-five meetings, she singled out one person, the First Lady, Eleanor Roosevelt, who 'was most friendly and asked her many questions concerning Mahatma Gandhi and India'.[73]

That same evening, Mira took the overnight train to Ahmedabad, to rejoin her master and to devote herself afresh to him and his cause.

CHAPTER 6

Blowing Up India

I

In January 1927, the Viceroy wrote to his boss, the Secretary of State for India, about 'an Englishman calling himself P. Spratt', who had landed in Bombay on the last day of the previous year. Spratt claimed to be a publisher's representative, but he had spent his first weeks in Bombay entirely in the company of local Communists. This alarmed the Viceroy, who now asked London to send across 'available particulars regarding Spratt whose description is given as: somewhat tall and stout, grey eyes, wears grey suit and gold rimmed spectacles'.

The India Office in turn contacted Scotland Yard to provide some information. The Yard reported back that Spratt was a graduate of Downing College, Cambridge, whose home address was 8 Wallis Road, New Cross, London. From around 1925 he had been involved with 'the extreme Left movement in Great Britain'. Spratt was travelling to India on behalf of Birrell and Garnett, a firm of new and second-hand booksellers in London 'run by a group of young intellectuals, at least one of whom, Graham Pollard, is a known Communist'.[1]

The India Office then asked for a report from the Master of Downing College. He wrote back saying:

I am sorry that I cannot remember Mr. Philip Spratt clearly enough to say anything about him from my own knowledge. He was a scholar; but obtained only a third class in Part I of the Mathematical Tripos – a poor performance – and on part II of the Natural Science Tripos was allowed the B.A. degree – also a very poor performance.

The Master continued: 'The Tutor and the Dean tell me that during the latter part of his College course he seemed to be unbalanced and abnormal. It is clear from the examination result that he did not live up to the standards of a scholar.'[2]

This characterization from the colonial archives must be fleshed out by the subject's own testimony. In his own (brief and incomplete) memoir, published decades after he came to India, Philip Spratt tells us that he was the son of a schoolmaster, who moved around England, teaching at several different schools while his children were growing up. Spratt's father 'was brought up as a Baptist, and there was something of the old straitlaced Nonconformist about him'. The household was hostile to art, and indifferent to politics. The boy Philip, however, read voraciously, and would take long walks where, as he recalled, 'I argued with myself about science and religion. I decided quite early that the religious theory of things was unsound.'[3]

Spratt went up to Cambridge on a scholarship in 1921. He was at a somewhat unfashionable college, Downing, but the university as a whole was awash with intellectual fervour and ferment. He read the poetry of T. S. Eliot and W. B. Yeats, and the philosophy of Bertrand Russell and G. E. Moore. He joined the Labour Club, soon gravitating further leftwards to the Communists, of whom there were quite a few in Cambridge at the time. The Russian Revolution was just a few years old, and it seemed to these idealistic young Englishmen to herald a new dawn across the world.

As Spratt wrote about his own conversion, years later, 'various lines of thought can lead a young man to espouse social revolution. I felt most acutely a dislike of social inequality. That Lenin treated everybody as of equal consequence was his great attraction.' Reading Lenin's political writings, recently translated into English, Spratt experienced 'a sudden enlightenment and tough exhilaration when I grasped the idea of the party: whole-time, professional, dedicated, under solitary discipline, but with one goal – power'.[4]

By the time Philip Spratt left Cambridge in 1924, he was a full-time activist of the Communist Party of Great Britain (CPGB). He sold the party paper in working-class neighbourhoods, attended meetings and organized study circles. His devotion to the cause attracted the attention of a party leader, Clemens Palme Dutt, older brother of the CPGB ideologue Rajni Palme Dutt. The father of the Dutts was Bengali (their mother was Swedish), and they had a familial interest in fomenting revolution in India. Clemens Dutt now asked Spratt if he would go to India as a messenger for the party. The plan was for him to stay for perhaps six months, and come back with a report for the CPGB (and their Soviet masters) to act upon as they chose.

Clemens Dutt told the young man not to say 'yes' to this proposal in a hurry. He warned him that there was a risk of his being arrested; and that even if he wasn't, 'under imperialism sanitation [in India] was terrible'. He gave Spratt a few days to think it over. But, as the man recalled in ripe middle age, 'it did not take me long to decide. I was 24, with no ties, and in the full flood of enthusiasm for the cause. I jumped at it.'[5]

II

In India, Spratt was supposed merely to study and document, but he couldn't stop himself from writing for the press. Not long after he landed, he sent a Bombay newspaper a series of articles advocating the need for 'reviving the great mass movement of 1919–21, as a counter-measure against the action of Government in sending Indian troops to China'.[6] He followed this up with another series on politics in China, which, he told the newspaper, was 'sufficiently tactful on the question of violence'[7] (so as not to attract undue attention from the authorities). These articles appeared not under his own name but as from a 'Special Correspondent'.

The first record of a speech on Indian soil by Spratt is from 24 April 1927, when he spoke to the Students Brotherhood in Bombay, telling them that to 'make a revolution in India possible it was first necessary to free the country from capitalistic leadership'. Spratt 'regretted the loose condition of the Congress organisation in India and emphasised the need for a sound organisation of the people on an international basis if any useful result was to be achieved'. These words come from the report of a plainclothesman in the audience, who himself found the speech 'very objectionable'.[8]

The next week, on May Day, Spratt participated in a march of workers and their leaders. This started from the Municipal Gardens at 3 p.m. The *Bombay Chronicle* reported that 'the unmistakeable feature of the procession was that it was thoroughly cosmopolitan. Hindus, Mahomedans, Parsis and Christians and even an Englishman (Mr. Spratt) had all alike congregated together in a common comradeship.'

Winding its way through the city, the procession stopped at the maidan near De Lisle Road, and the speeches began. The main talks were by D. R. Thengdi and N. M. Joshi (both liberal reformists) and S. S. Mirajkar and S. H. Jhabwalla (both Communists). Speaking after them,

> Mr. Spratt paid a glowing tribute to those labour leaders who organised the May Day celebration and made it a success. The task before the workers of the world, he continued, was very arduous and they had to face it with courage and perseverance. It was the bounden duty of every labourer to join the Trade Union and make it stronger. In his opinion, there should be one big and representative Union instead of several disjointed petty unions. He was sure that if 150,000 workmen engaged in cotton mills of Bombay united, there was no power that would resist their Union. That was the chief lesson that the May Day had to teach.[9]

III

In June 1927, Spratt travelled to the Punjab, where the Communists were building a base. He met with left-wing activists in Lahore; when he asked them why they hadn't found it possible to organize a trade union, they pleaded lack of funds. From the Punjab, Spratt travelled to Kanpur, where the trade union movement was well established, before returning to Bombay.[10]

In August, Spratt published a pamphlet entitled 'India and China'. It was read by the Intelligence Bureau (IB), which provided this summary of its contents:

The argument in brief is that India and China are engaged in substantially the same struggle against the same enemy; that the object of both is to throw off the domination of the British; that China is well on the road to accomplishing this; and that India should follow her example and use the same methods including the organisation of force.

The Bombay Government now proceeded to take action against Spratt. The Advocate General of Bombay, J. B. Kanga, observed that the pamphlet had condemned Gandhian non-violence, arguing that 'no fundamental social change takes place without use or threat of violence'. On his advice, the pamphlet was proscribed, and charges brought against Spratt for preaching disaffection against the Government. He was arrested on 15 September under Section 124 of the Indian Penal Code.

Spratt's comrades in Bombay immediately formed a defence fund for him. They got on board two famous Bombay lawyers, F. S. Talyarkhan, and the future founder of Pakistan, M. A. Jinnah. One report claimed that Jinnah agreed to appear after he had been assured 'that his fee of Rs. 1,500 a day would be duly paid'. A junior on the case was B. R. Ambedkar, in the fullness of time to become the first Law Minister of independent India and the Chairman of the Drafting Committee of the Indian Constitution.

In his statement to the court, Spratt disingenuously claimed that he was a Labour Party man rather than a Communist. He was sent to India, he said, by the Labour Research Department, to collect information on the working class. He said that in writing this pamphlet on India and China, he

did not intend to create feelings of disaffection or disloyalty towards the Government established by Law in India. The intention was from the point of view of one who desires 'Swaraj' for India to discuss the conditions prevailing in China and in India, to criticise the conduct of the Nationalist leaders, to analyse as far as possible the economic conditions and to point out the feasibility of organising the working classes and peasants. The criticism is against the policy of Imperialism followed by the British Government and there was no intention of attacking the British Rule.

There were several hearings of the case through October and November. On 23 November, in his concluding remarks to the jury, the judge noted that the pamphlet focused on China, and in so far as it was critical of British colonialism, it was of its operations in that country, which meant that it was His Majesty's Government in London, not the Viceroy in New Delhi, who could legitimately take offence. He further observed that the India sections of Spratt's pamphlet were far more critical of Congress leaders and the capitalist class than they were of the Raj itself. 'The *main* object of the accused', therefore concluded the judge, 'was not to excite feelings of hatred against the Government of India.' He urged members of the jury to read the offending pamphlet 'in a generous spirit, and not merely in a niggardly spirit'. Thus guided, the jury voted 8 to 1 in favour of acquittal.[11]

By this time, Spratt had been two months in jail. When the judge finally pronounced him not guilty, this was met by loud cheers from the crowd in the courtroom. A representative of the Workers and Peasants Party (a front for the now banned Communist Party of India) presented Spratt with a large bouquet of flowers as he walked out of the dock, a free man.[12]

Spratt's arrest, trial, and release had made him a minor celebrity in Bombay. He met this new-found fame with ambivalence, for he was an intensely private man, notwithstanding his ideological commitment to revolution. He didn't mind attending or speaking at meetings, but equally cherished his time alone, reading and writing. Now this became increasingly difficult. So, as he wrote to his London mentor Clemens Palme Dutt,

> I have the misfortune to be something like a public man. Constantly people in the street rush up and say 'Ah Mr. Spratt I must have a *long* talk with you' – and many of them try to carry out the threat. If you are staying alone you can be rude to them and send them away, but if with friends it is more difficult, at any rate with their acquaintances.[13]

Among the duties of a newly minted revolutionary hero was to endorse the works of other revolutionaries. In December 1927, Philip Spratt wrote an introduction to a memoir by Shaukat Usmani, a

Communist who had travelled from India to the Soviet Union via Afghanistan, before returning to his homeland to rejoin the struggle against imperialism. Spratt particularly commended what his Indian comrade had to say about the Socialist Fatherland. 'Information about Soviet Russia, other than that supplied by the official news-agencies', he remarked, 'is scanty anywhere, but especially so in this country. And India has much to learn, as comrade Usmani points out, from a country whose conditions are in many respects similar to our own.'[14]

IV

Clemens Dutt had sent Philip Spratt to India for six months; but now the CPGB told him to stay on. He went to attend a trade union congress in Kanpur, where he broke his glasses. He could not afford to pay for a new pair; so the leading local Congressman, Ganesh Shankar Vidyarthi, paid for a pair from his pocket. A bourgeois reformist had, in a manner of speaking, allowed the Communist revolutionary to see more clearly.[15]

In the last week of December 1927, Spratt went to attend the annual meeting of the Indian National Congress, held that year in Madras. He lodged at the home of Singaravelu Chettiar, a lawyer and trade unionist and a pioneer of the Communist movement in South India.[16] Staying with Singaravelu was his widowed niece, Sivakami, and her daughter, Seetha. The latter was a precocious teenager with a keen interest in literature and nature. The young Tamil girl and the radical Englishman got talking. After the latter left to recommence his revolutionary travels, they embarked on a long and intense correspondence. Of this exchange of letters we have only one side, Spratt's, but it is revealing enough. The first letter, sent from Bombay in January 1928, has Spratt recommending some novels to Seetha, as well as an anthology of modern verse published by Oxford University Press. He commented that 'the English language became in some way exhausted by the middle of the XIX century', and that 'poetry as a whole after that time is rather decadent'. He however allowed that 'one or two American poets have produced work of a new type which is very good, and may lead to "fresh woods and pastures new"'.

The letter then turned from literary to political matters. 'The mill-strike here [in Bombay] seems to be going on fairly well', wrote Spratt to Seetha, adding: 'I am rather busy because of it, and I shall probably not leave for Calcutta until it is over. And I have been made a member of the committee to organise a one-day strike of the Municipal Workers when the [Simon] Commission lands. This should be a pleasant job.'[17] The letter ended with Spratt saying to Seetha: 'I hope I shall see you again before I leave India. And I hope that you will redeem your promise to teach me "Bande Mataram".'[18]

Three weeks later, Spratt wrote to Seetha that he had

been extremely busy, mainly in helping to arrange the hartal [strike] in Bombay. We had to go round every day, addressing public meetings, Trade Unions, and college students, as well as preparing handbills and posters and so on. Fortunately it was a great success, though it was partly spoiled by the evening meeting, where, owing to the tactics of Mrs [Sarojini] Naidu, only the most reactionary bourgeois speakers addressed the enormous crowd, of a lakh or more, which assembled. The workers' procession was fine; we had quite 30,000 men on strike, and the students also demonstrated in large numbers, I am told. We had banners with slogans: Down with Imperialism . . . Votes for All. 8 hour Day etc. . . .

Despite his ideological commitment to proletarian revolution, Spratt was in his personal demeanour anything but fiery. He told Seetha:

You express surprise that I should turn giddy at the sight of blood and what not. It is not a case of weakness in a general sense, I imagine, but of some special mental affliction. Nearly all people have it in some degree, but I more than most. Nevertheless I am weak . . . In this connection I must repeat an insulting remark made in a letter I received recently from a friend in London. She says that when people heard of my arrest they said: 'Why that poor harmless creature? He wouldn't hurt a fly' (etc). That, I fear, expresses the common opinion about me. I will not discuss its correctness.

The letter then turned to matters of culture. 'I also went to a cinema on Saturday', he wrote:

> It was fair – a 'farce-comedy', I think they call it. Previously I had been so busy that I had not seen anything since I left Madras. I even missed hearing Zimbalist, who was playing in Bombay a week or so ago. He has the reputation of being one of the best violinists in the world. I am keen on music, especially instrumental or orchestral. I like the 'veena' or whatever it is called, that you play, though it is unlike any European instrument. . . . When you make your promised visit to London, I hope you will bring yours with you and play it to us. . . . One of the reasons why I want to return to England is so that I can hear music whenever I want to.[19]

At this stage, Spratt was not sure how long he would be in India. In the spring of 1928, he travelled to Calcutta, where his guide and host was Muzaffar Ahmad, one of the most zealous and hard-working Communists in India.[20] The Englishman found the weather trying, and had frequent bouts of fever. Ahmad nursed him when he was ill, and when he was well, took him on tours of jute factories along the Hooghly.

Inspired by Ahmad, Spratt had – as a colonial intelligence report described it – 'completely identified himself with the Indian Communists, and seems quite prepared to share in their social life and customs. His meals consist ordinarily of pulse and rice, but it is doubtful whether he is doing this from choice or because he cannot afford a more suitable diet.'

The report continued: 'The Bengal Communist group, assisted by Philip Spratt, is taking an active part in fomenting labour agitation in Calcutta and elsewhere in Bengal.' Spratt was trying to organize a scavengers' union in Howrah, and also visiting various railway stations and loco-sheds with a view to 'bringing about sympathetic strikes among the workers'.

Spratt spent the summer and monsoon in and around Calcutta.

His only pair of shoes had worn thin. 'I hop around in flimsy and ridiculous rubbers', he wrote to a Communist friend in Bombay, while asking him to send a spare shirt.[21] Despite the scanty dress and ill health, he worked furiously for the cause. 'Though Philip Spratt has been very busy organising and encouraging railway and mill strikes in Bengal', ran one intelligence report, 'he has nevertheless found time to write a number of Communistic articles for the Indian and foreign press.' An article entitled 'Russia and India', intended for a paper in Poona, was intercepted by the police. Of its contents the IB remarked:

> The excellent style in which it is written, and the ingenuity with which Spratt develops his arguments, are sufficient evidence of the ability of the writer and of the evil influence which it is in his power to exercise over the group of Indian Communists who have accepted him as their leader. It will be seen that Spratt unequivocally asserts that India's only hope of salvation is 'to follow the Moscow road'. The conditions in India at present are, he says, very similar to those which obtained in Russia before the revolution, and he contends that Swaraj will only be attained by copying the Russian model.

Courtesy of the records of the IB, we have verbatim accounts of many of Spratt's speeches in Bengal. He spoke in English, with a party comrade translating. From Calcutta, Spratt ventured further east, visiting cotton mills in Dacca in the company of Muzaffar Ahmad. He 'then left for Mymensingh, where he delivered a speech to an audience consisting mostly of boys. His dogmatic form of delivery quickly reduced the attendance from 300 to less than 40, and his later speeches were equally ineffective. His lukewarm reception and the unfavourable climatic conditions caused him to abandon his intended visit to the Atia forest area.' Apparently, Spratt's speech at Mymensingh 'dealt with such recondite subjects as "surplus value" and "concentration of capital", and was far above the heads of those to whom it was delivered'.[22]

The IB records tell us that, on 24 April 1928, the Englishman instructed a group of striking jute mill workers in Changail to form an army of the Union wearing [the] union badge, thoroughly drilled and disciplined, who were to carry on to picket peacefully at important places so that the men of the contractors might not go in. He also instructed them to form a Strike Committee including the female members who would by all means make the strike a success.

A week later, on May Day, Spratt addressed a large meeting on the Calcutta Maidan, where he contrasted the timidity of the British Labour Party with the radicalism of the Bolsheviks in Russia. A later speech gave the credit for this contrast to one man, Lenin, who 'brought up Marxism from the slough of "reformism" into which it had sunk and remodelled it with the revolutionary spirit which it has originally held'. The Englishman praised his Russian icon with having 'brought Marxism, as it were, up to date', and for having enabled 'the seizure of power by the working class'. In another speech, Spratt affirmed the superiority of Bolshevism to Gandhism, arguing that 'the principle of non-violence weakens the power of self-determination' – therefore, India needed 'the spirit of violent action' to become independent of British rule.[23]

In October 1928, Spratt wrote to Seetha that he hoped to visit Madras once more before he left India. He wanted to go south for two weeks, so that he could 'see all the places worth visiting'. He told her: 'I also want to learn "Vande Mataram". Your music to it is the best version I have heard. I hope you have kept up your practice with the Bina or Sitar or whatever it is.'

Spratt told Seetha that he expected to return to his homeland in March. 'People often ask me if I shall be pleased to go back to England', he said:

I don't know actually; in some ways I shall be pleased, to be in a cold climate again, and so on. But I shall be very sorry to leave also. Perhaps the worst part of going back will be that I shall be asked to write a book about what I have seen here. I am striving to collect materials, but I fear it will be a very poor book. But I shall avoid doing it at all if I can. I hate writing, like all lazy people.

The letter ended by conveying regards to her sisters and her 'Thatha' (grandfather), this being his fellow Communist, Singaravelu Chettiar.[24]

V

In the first weeks of 1929, the Governor of Bombay wrote to the Viceroy about the increasing Communist influence on the mill workers of the city. He said the existing laws didn't provide the State with sufficient powers to deal with Communists; besides, they exempted British subjects. The Viceroy replied that a new Public Safety Act removing these exemptions was on the anvil; once it was passed, then the fact that 'we possessed such powers would lead the Manchester or Sheffield Communist to think twice before he embarked on an Indian trip'. The Viceroy offered the Governor 'reasonably good hopes of being able to run a comprehensive conspiracy case' against the Communists, which would deal a 'severe blow' to their movement.[25]

In the third week of March 1929, in pursuit of this policy of repression, some thirty Communists were picked up from different parts of India and sent to prison in the town of Meerut. Spratt, who was then in Calcutta, was one of them.[26] He was put in solitary confinement. As he recalled, 'for some weeks I was unable to read, write or talk. Beyond that the only real hardship was lice. My convict warder hung his clothes on a peg which held some of mine, and the creatures migrated. I had never come across lice before, and I endured many days of itching before I discovered its cause.' After some weeks of solitude Spratt was placed in a communal barracks with his comrades. Here they read and argued, and played chess and volleyball.[27]

The Communist prisoners at Meerut had been charged with 'conspiring to deprive the King Emperor of his sovereignty of British India'. The Crown Counsel in the case described Spratt as 'the chief actor in the conspiracy'.[28] In keeping with this exalted status, the case was listed as 'King-Emperor versus P. Spratt & Others'. These 'others' included the leading Communist activists Muzaffar Ahmad of Bengal, P. C. Joshi of the United Provinces, Sohan Singh Josh of Punjab, and S. A. Dange of Bombay – as well as Spratt's fellow Englishmen Benjamin Bradley and Lester Hutchinson, who had been sent out by the CPGB to help catalyse a revolution in India.

Among those who came forward to defend the accused was the radical Congressman Ranjit Pandit. Himself a considerable scholar, and a man of compassion and courage, Pandit also happened to be the son-in-law of Motilal Nehru, at the time the most famous barrister in North India. Pandit successfully urged Motilal Nehru to raise funds for the defence and to contribute the first cheque of Rs. 500 himself. He also got his brother-in-law, the rising star of nationalist politics, Jawaharlal Nehru, interested in the matter.

Congressmen like the Nehrus and Ranjit Pandit got involved in the case as the thirty-one arrested were mostly union activists, and mostly young Indians. Although not Communists themselves, they saw trade unions and rights of workers as important. As an appeal for funds drafted by Pandit said:

> We desire to make it clear that this appeal is not made in the inter-ests of communism or in that of any class of communists. We do not ourselves subscribe to the doctrines of the Communist International and no subscriber to this fund will in any way be committed to them or any particular view in matters social or political. It is an appeal in the sole interest of humanity and justice to help our young men in distress to defend themselves.[29]

Spratt's best friend in jail was P. C. Joshi. A scholar from the hills of Kumaon, Joshi had a warm personality and a gentle wit. Like Spratt, he had been attracted to the Party out of a sense of idealism and empathy with the poor. In jail, Joshi introduced the Englishman to classical Indian philosophy, and also sought to teach him Hindi.[30]

In the boiling month of June, Spratt had to spend several days in court listening to the State Prosecutor, Langford James, speaking at length about how he was central to the case. Mr James was not without a certain sense of humour; in distinguishing between an Old Testament of Communism, associated with Marx, and a New Testament, associated with Lenin, he placed our renegade squarely in the second camp. He emphasized the fact, that in training camps in Bombay, Spratt had 'selected for the education of the youth' Lenin's *State and Revolution*, a tract which argued that 'the substitution of the proletarian state for the existing state is absolutely impossible without a violent bloody revolution'. That was Exhibit A for the damning of Spratt; Exhibit B a syllabus that Spratt had prepared for the Workers and Peasants Party, which defined politics in terms of class struggle; Exhibit C the text of a speech he gave on 1 May 1927, in which (said the Prosecutor) 'Mr. Spratt is putting forward May Day as being a festival which is almost comparable with the anniversary of the Russian revolution and is pointing to China, which at that time was in a state of revolutionary ferment, with the intention that India should go and do likewise.'[31]

The accused, led by Muzaffar Ahmad, had decided to use the case to bring their revolutionary doctrine to the wider public. They refused therefore to engage a full-time lawyer, but to offer their own defence, which they did in terms of an extended statement of objects, reasons, and purposes, which – when published in book form many years later – ran to more than three hundred pages in print. This began with a summary of Marx's analysis of capitalism, carried on via the success of the Russian Revolution and the building of the world's first socialist state in an Indian context, where the Gandhi-led national movement was disparaged as bourgeois reformism, bound to be replaced and supplanted by a revolutionary upheaval on the Russian model. In seeking to hasten this transformation, said the defendants,

> We openly declare that we shall have to use violence, the violence of the mass revolutionary movement. But in contrast to Imperialist violence, an ocean which has engulfed the whole world for generations, our violence can be but a drop. As opposed to Imperialist violence, which, while Imperialism lasts, is permanent, our violence is temporary. As opposed to Imperialist violence, which is used to maintain an obsolete, barbarous, exploiting system, our violence is progressive and will be used to attain the next great step forward in the march of the human race.[32]

Spratt had some part in the drafting of this manifesto. The main burden, however, fell on the shoulders of his co-accused G. Adhikari, who with a doctorate from Germany, was better versed in the Marxist catechism.

As the case dragged on, Spratt's thoughts turned to his family in England, who had not seen him in the last four years. 'They are very worried about me', he wrote to Seetha, adding: 'But they must be getting used to it by now. We were arrested more than nine months ago.'

'We are expecting to get the magistrate's orders on our case in a day or two,' he continued: 'You will read of it in the press, no doubt. Then the Sessions will begin in two weeks or so. I shall be very pleased when the whole case is over, even if I am sentenced, for it has become a terrible bore.'

Seetha had asked Philip what books he was reading. He answered that he had finished almost all the English books in the barrack, and was now on to stuff in other languages. 'I read German rather badly', he remarked self-deprecatingly, 'and so do not gain much pleasure from it, but it is good practice.' He ended his letter by asking Seetha to 'please accept my apology for not writing to you before. One becomes demoralised in jail, though to be truthful, I was always lacking in morals in this respect.'[33]

In the last week of October 1929, the accused in the Meerut Conspiracy Case had an unexpected visitor – Mahatma Gandhi. Gandhi was then on a tour promoting khadi in the United Provinces, and, finding himself in Meerut, chose to visit his left-wing critics in jail. When the Communists expressed surprise at his coming to see them, Gandhi said he hoped it was not a 'painful surprise'. The militant Bombay trade unionist S. A. Dange told Gandhi that he had heard that landlords in UP were extracting money from their peasants to contribute to the Mahatma's khadi fund. Gandhi asked him to supply names, which however Dange declined to do.

The conversation between Gandhi and the Communists was mostly amicable. They urged him to look beyond Dominion Status to the achievement of complete independence. For his part, he told them to eschew violence in favour of non-violence, insisting that it was far more effective as a political weapon, offering to 'retire from politics if it was proved otherwise'.[34]

VI

In jail, Spratt had begun to read more books about India than he had ever done before. He 'found it a little disturbing. It was clear that the history of India has been very different from that of Europe. India has substantially no slavery and no feudalism, and in the mediaeval period the merchant class appear to have put up no struggle for power such as their confréres in Europe conducted.' What he read puzzled and confused him, since Marxism maintained 'that all civilizations follow the same course of evolution'. The first seeds of doubt about the Communist ideology were being planted.[35]

In April 1930, a year after he was first incarcerated, Spratt called the court an 'infernal institution which we have to visit each weekday. The rest of the time we are either preparing to go to court, or else recovering from the effects of it.'[36] The case dragged on, and on. Meanwhile, back in Madras, Seetha had completed her matriculation, and joined the university, choosing chemistry, biology and geography as her special subjects. While confessing his ignorance of these subjects, Spratt speculated that biology and geography 'might conceivably supplement each other very successfully, in ecology, it is called?, and in paleontology and what not'. He was himself 'always sorry personally that I never made any study of a biological subject'. He was now reading mathematics and logic to amuse himself, in between the daily trips to the court which are 'totally unnecessary'.

A letter of December 1931 contrasted life in and out of jail for the book-loving Englishman. 'Outside you can use libraries, consult periodicals, and sift the useful from the useless and so on. Here you have to buy (or beg) everything you want, and a mistake costs you a lot.' Because of this, he could not make any 'serious effort to "keep up" with modern literature'. He wistfully remarked that 'if one may judge from the reviews an enormous number of absolutely first class novels are appearing now'. Thus 'Mrs [Virginia] Woolf's "The Waves" must be very good, I should think.' He told Seetha of novels he had previously read by Virginia Woolf, E. M. Forster, Rebecca West and V. Sackville-West, which he had liked, although they were sometimes 'too refined and sophisticated'. In meditative mood, Spratt observed that the Russians call this [the Bloomsbury novel] decadence (probably they are right) but such of their efforts at correcting things as I have seen do not succeed at all. But then no Russian literature pleases me much, except Chekhov. The post revolutionary Russian literature, naturally, goes to the other extreme, and becomes clumsy (it is called 'elemental') and of course 'crudely propagandist' as the bourgeois critics say. I must admit that being an English petty bourgeois, I cannot help agreeing. Propaganda if it is to be not offensive, must be very unobtrusive and subtle.

The letter went on to offer Spratt's theories about art. He believed that 'art must be (1) simple; and (2) either (a) spontaneous and unaffected . . . or (b) if it consciously aims at . . . propaganda, etc., must be hidden, or at least subordinate'. He classified different artists and art forms under these heads (saying, for example, that George Bernard Shaw fell in category 2 (b)), before going on to admit that 'my theory seems disproved by such work as that of T. S. Eliot, for which I confess I have a great weakness'.

After having written eight pages of such stuff Spratt became somewhat guilty, telling Seetha: 'I am afraid this letter has become very introspective, as well as long and dull. One gets like that in jail. We shall all go mad fairly soon I think.' Spratt ended by referring to what had placed him in jail in the first place. 'The case is still going on regularly,' he said: 'The press don't report it, because, I imagine, the sub-editors are all tired of it. They are not as tired as the accused, though, I may say. It will finish sometime towards next June or so.'[37]

The Meerut Conspiracy Case was being heard by the Additional Sessions Judge of Meerut, R. L. Yorke of the Indian Civil Service. The case dragged on for three and a half years. As many as 320 witnesses were examined, and more than 5,000 exhibits – letters, books, pamphlets – entered as evidence by the prosecution.[38] In January 1933, after dozens of hearings spread over four years, R. L. Yorke delivered his verdict. Twelve closely printed pages of his judgement dealt with the activities of the principal accused. Yorke argued that Spratt had been sent out from England with the explicit purpose of 'bringing about a revolution in India', and, further, that he was 'the moving spirit or perhaps I might better say the inspiration of the Workers' and Peasants' Parties, so much so that in everything important throughout this period except possibly the inauguration of the Punjab Party and the direction of the Textile Strike in Bombay his hand is traceable'.[39]

Here the judge seems to have exaggerated Spratt's influence, for home-grown Communists like S. A. Dange and Muzaffar Ahmad, rooted in the country and speaking the people's language, were far more important in the revolutionary movement. In fact, the sentences handed out by Yorke confirmed that Muzaffar Ahmad was, as it were, the ringleader. Ahmad was convicted to imprisonment for life, while five others, including Spratt and Dange, were each sentenced to twelve years in prison.

VII

In the trial at the Sessions Court, the Communists had chosen to defend themselves. But after having been handed these extremely harsh sentences they decided to get a professional lawyer to appeal on their behalf to the High Court in Allahabad. Ranjit Pandit – remembered by Muzaffar Ahmad as 'a man of large and liberal sympathies' – suggested that they engage the celebrated barrister Dr Kailas Nath Katju. They did, and Katju was able to get the sentences drastically reduced, from life to three years in the case of Ahmad, and from twelve years to two in the case of Spratt and others.[40]

While the case was being heard in the High Court, the undertrials were shifted from Meerut to Naini Jail, on the outskirts of Allahabad. From here Spratt wrote to Seetha in June 1934 explaining why he had not sent any letters in recent months (she seems to have complained about this). 'Your question is an awkward one,' he began:

> One of the Meerut people once charged me with being a Victorian. I was annoyed, but had to agree. On the admittedly few occasions I have thought of writing to you, I felt restrained by the reflection that you are no longer the very junior schoolgirl you were when I saw you in 1927 . . . My reasons for not writing to you were: (1) that

just described; (2) my people, if they do not demand, at least expect, a letter from me each month, and having a thoroughly Victorian sense of my duty towards them, I supply it; (3) I feel doubtful whether you would not look with a cold eye upon one of my usual essays in the psychopathology of jail life. For the same reasons, (2) and (3), I have written to no one else since my conviction.

After asking Seetha about her family, Spratt requested a favour. Since his letters were rationed, he wanted her to write to his bookseller, the Book Company, College Street, Calcutta, asking them to send, to the jail, the complete translation (in three volumes) of the Mahabharata from the Bengali, by Kali Prasanna Sinha. He expected to be released in September or October. 'I shall have to go home fairly soon of course. But before that I hope to be able to see you.'

Spratt wanted to visit Seetha before he left for England, and some other places too. They included the old Mughal capital, Fatehpur Sikri, the Buddhist sites of Ellora and Ajanta, and the Hindu temples of the Madras Presidency. 'But to do all that would be expensive, and would take too long, also,' he wrote.

As his jail term approached its end, Spratt had begun reading a lot of philosophy. One of his brothers, who had converted to Roman Catholicism, sent him books on Aquinas and Augustine. 'Perhaps he judges from my parenthetical letters that I am promising,' he remarked to Seetha. Characteristically, he ended with an apology: 'I see that I have just given you at least an outline of one of my usual essays after all. Jail life makes one self-centred . . . What a terrible bore I shall be when I get out!'[41]

Spratt was finally released in the first week of September 1934. He spent his first few days as a free man in the home of Ranjit Pandit in Allahabad. He wrote to Seetha that 'I have been out for dinner once or twice, but apart from that I have done nothing – just sloping around in a state of semi-consciousness.' He said he would like to visit her in Madras. Then he asked her to 'please forgive my very short and abrupt letter. Long letters can be written only in jail.'[42]

From Allahabad, Spratt proceeded to Calcutta, catching up with his comrades. An IB agent who eavesdropped on some of his conversations claimed he said that 'imperialism had taken a brutal and drastic attitude against the working class movement'. He was reported to have met and spoken with the left-wing Congressman Ram Manohar Lohia. From Calcutta Spratt went to Jhansi, where he told railway workers that capitalism 'should be given a speedy burial in India'. In October he was in Bombay, where he attended a session of the newly formed Socialist wing of the Congress.

In the second week of October, Spratt wrote to Seetha about how after his release, in both Calcutta and Bombay, he had been feted at public meetings, and treated like a hero, by working-class organizations. He feared he would now be 'asked for my "views" on subjects of which I know nothing, and for my "advice" to people about how to do things of which I do not approve, and to people who would not do what I should want, even if I were to suggest it'. Of the excitement around him in left-wing circles he said:

> What a contrast to the placidity – of course somewhat bored placidity – of jail! There is a lot in monasticism. A friend of mine was predicting that I should take to sanyas within five years. I am strongly inclined to agree . . . The only thing is complete retirement from the world. I shall take a vow of silence, too, like the Trappists. And then you will be free from persecution by angry letters from me.

Seetha had wanted him to come from Bombay straight to Madras. Spratt said that was not possible, adding, 'but be sure that I shall come to see you before I go. I am very keen on that, and even if I have to defy these people here, I shall do it.'[43] One supposed those 'people' were his comrades, who frowned on romantic attachments taking precedence over party work.

The IB report on his first travels as a free man claimed that Spratt was collecting information on revolutionary prospects in India, 'with a view to reporting to his masters at the 7th International Conference of the Comintern which is to be held at Moscow early in the coming year'.[44] The Raj's spies were out of date. For his experiences and readings in jail were curing Spratt of Communism. He was now moving away from the revolutionary left. By the time of his release he saw himself as a democratic socialist – thus his meetings with Ranjit Pandit and Ram Manohar Lohia, thus his interest in the

Congress Socialist Party, thus also his keen desire to meet with Mahatma Gandhi.

Spratt seems to have spent at least a month in and around Bombay. In the second week of November he left for Wardha, where he met Gandhi by prior appointment, and had several conversations with him. Of these talks he wrote to Seetha:

> Many of my friends were surprised when I announced my design of writing to the Mahatma. I was a bit doubtful about it at first, but several Congress people encouraged me to come, and it turns out that they were right. The Mahatma received me very kindly, and wasted a lot of time in answering my questions. He is extemely impressive, no doubt. I shall not tell you here what he has said. I have to write an account of it to my brother, and two letters on the same topic would be impossible. I shall tell you when I see you.[45]

From Wardha Spratt took the train to Madras. He and Seetha spent several days together; and feelings suppressed for so long finally found free expression. They decided they would get married; leaving open the question as to whether they would afterwards live in India or in England.

From Madras, Spratt returned to Bombay. Here he attended a few meetings and gave a few speeches. On 18 December 1934, the police arrested him for acting 'in a manner prejudicial to the public peace'. He was at first sent to Yerwada Jail, near Poona, and kept there for two months, before being told that he could either leave for England at any time of his choosing, or, if he chose to stay, live under certain restrictions governed by the Special Powers Act. He chose the latter. So he was sent to Belgaum, in the Deccan, and housed in the town's medieval fort. He was allowed to take a one-hour walk inside the fort's grounds twice a day, and could leave for an excursion into the town only with special permission, returning by sunset. But he could 'in no case visit any education institutions, student hostels, factories or localities inhabited by factory or railway workers or municipal menials'. All letters written or received by him were first to be submitted to the District Magistrate. This house arrest was effected because the Home Department believed, still, that 'Spratt is a very dangerous communist organiser'.[46]

As compared to Meerut and Naini, Spratt's new 'jail' premises were actually quite spacious. He had been allotted a cottage in Belgaum Fort, which had a bedroom, a sitting room, and a kitchen. In February 1935, Spratt wrote from here to Seetha about his and their future:

> The question now is what choice am I to make. I can stay here till Government pleases to release me or until the Act lapses – if it ever does. Or I can go home: I am free, I gather, to do that at any time. As you know, I had good reasons for not going home even before I went to Madras, and I still think that my prospects here would be better than in England. (It is not that the chances in India are great, but that those in England are small.) But now, after visiting you, I have, it seems to me, overwhelming reasons for trying to stay here by all possible means.

Spratt told Seetha that he had received letters from his parents and his brothers. 'They are of course unanimous and vehement that I should return immediately, but they all argue on the assumption that I want to stay in India for political reasons. I told them in reply what the facts were, including my most important reason' (namely, the desire to marry Seetha).

The letter then turned to matters of literature. He had been reading Byron. 'It is school-boy stuff, or almost all of it', he wrote: 'But I envy his power of hatred. In spite of the Mahatma, I sometimes feel one ought to hate, but I can't.'[47]

Spratt signed off this letter as 'Your Phil'. Previously he had merely ended by saying 'PS'. After that meeting in Madras in November 1934 the two were no longer merely friends. The Englishman was now becoming a renegade in much more than a political sense.

VIII

When Spratt was sent to Belgaum Fort, Seetha seems to have suggested to him that, as a compromise, after they got married, she could move with him to England. Spratt demurred, replying: 'When we discussed the matter, my impression is, you were not keen on England. It was acceptable only as the worse alternative, I thought. I still think there is no need, and no justification, for me to inflict it on you, though the other thing [i.e. an inter-racial marriage in British India] is awkward enough, I know.'[48]

Spratt wanted Seetha to come to Belgaum to discuss their future. He had applied to the authorities for permission for him to receive her in jail. 'You need not spend much time – a day or two here would be enough – and I can provide the money,' he wrote. He thought that it was important that they met soon, since 'there are many subtleties which we could not discuss by correspondence . . .'[49]

The permission for Seetha to visit Spratt in Belgaum was granted. However, Spratt was having second thoughts. He wrote to Seetha that while he 'was full of enthusiasm about the scheme at first', slowly 'the other aspect, that is your view of it, began to occur to me'. He now realized that she would have a long journey on 'a rather inferior railway', that it would be hot, and most of all, that 'there may be difficulties with your people'. So 'if such difficulties arise', he said, 'please don't insist. It is better not to create opposition now.'[50]

In the event Seetha did not make the hot and dusty journey from Madras to Belgaum and back. Her family may have been against it. Then, in April 1935, the Government said to Spratt that they would release him if he left immediately for England. Spratt told them, in writing, that this was unacceptable to him, for three reasons:

First, that he was engaged to an Indian lady, who had lived all her life in Madras City, and had 'no relatives or friends in England, and is not accustomed to a European mode of life'. If she 'were compelled to reside in England', said Spratt to the Government, 'she would be put to great inconvenience, and would be exposed, by reason of the cold climate, to the certainty of serious discomfort, and to a grave risk of ill health and danger. On this account alone, therefore, I feel that I am precluded from returning to England, except for the most weighty reasons';

Second, that he had lived outside England for eight years and was now thirty-two years old. Given the depressed labour market in his home country, he would find 'very little prospect of obtaining satis-factory employment, or indeed any employment';

Third, that having been resident for so long in India, he had become 'acclimatised and accustomed' to life in this country, 'and correspondingly unfitted to live in England'. The Government had made to him what was, he said, 'in effect an offer of exile; and exile is generally and rightly regarded as a drastic punishment to be inflicted only in case of serious crime'.

For these reasons, Spratt asked that he may be released from prison and allowed to remain in India.[51]

The plea was rejected. The Bombay Government told the Government of India that 'there is no reliable evidence at all that Mr. Spratt has abandoned his Communistic views'. It further noted that 'his fiancée is of Communist environment in Madras, being the daughter or niece of Mylapore Singaravelu Chettiar (vide Madras page 12, Volume I (Second Edition) 1923, of the Madras Political "Who's Who"), and she herself is reported to hold Communistic views and to correspond with Communist leaders outside the Madras Presidency'. Even if 'he were released full of good intentions', thought the Government, 'pressure would be brought on Mr. Spratt to take part in organising Communist activities once more in Bombay'. Therefore, it concluded, it would be 'most undesirable to release him except on condition that he goes back to England at once'.[52]

Resigned now to spending more time in jail, Spratt wrote to Seetha asking her to order some books for him, among them *Raja Ram Mohan Roy: His Life, Writings and Speeches*, *Mahatma Gandhi's Ideas* by C. F. Andrews, and pamphlets by Gandhi about women, health, and ethical religion (*Niti Dharma*). He wrote:

> You will see that I have become rather interested in the Mahatma especially since I saw him at Wardha. What I want at the moment is to find out whether he has an ethical system or not. I fancy not, but one is tempted always to underestimate his intellectual resources. . . . I do not intend, at present at least, to follow his guidelines in regard to food; though I suppose one could do worse.[53]

Seetha sent Spratt the stuff he wanted, and then he wrote back with his views on them. He says:

'Niti Dharma' is very disappointing . . . He [Gandhi] makes no attempt
at all to systematise his teachings, and that is the main point of interest.
He is hardly even consistent, though that is not an uncommon fault
in ethics. 'A Guide to Health' is much better. I get the impression that
he really knows something about it, but that may be due only to his
dogmatism. I should like to get medical opinions . . . on some of his
statements, though. I regret to say that he is a little over-emphatic.

Spratt then listed, for Seetha's information, the various food restrictions and prohibitions recommended by Gandhi. 'I am surprised to
find how many of my fads agree with his,' he said. He was thinking
of giving up tea, and eating more fruit. Gandhi's 'Guide to Heath',
he concluded, was 'interesting', and 'helps to illuminate its author's
mind, a subject I have been concerning myself with'.[54]

While reading Gandhi intensively in jail, after having met him in
the flesh, Spratt found that 'his ideas and personality strongly
attracted the puritan in me and I was inclined to think that in
internal Indian affairs he might be partly right'.[55] He had now begun
writing a book on Gandhi's life and thought, from a Marxist point
of view.

In July 1935 the Government once more offered to release Spratt
if he went off to England. He told Seetha:

I have decided to stay . . . I think that they cannot continue to keep
me here much longer. I am really not guilty, I believe . . . Unfortunately
they don't know me, or they would realise that I have no desire
whatever to upset the public peace, and what is more, could not do
so even if I wanted to. The whole thing is laughable, but also very
annoying. Some day, I suppose, I shall write my autobiography, and
it will be a tragi-farce – if I may invent a new literary category – of
inappropriateness.[56]

A letter written a little later contained some fascinating reflections
about relations between the races. So Spratt wrote to Seetha:

You are right about race-prejudice. I think there are two racial feelings, pride and prejudice, so to speak. Everyone probably has

prejudice – you just dislike other races. But everyone has not, I imagine, racial pride in the sense of a conviction that his own race is superior to all others. My own feelings in the matter, which I suppose are those of English people generally, are that every other people is inferior to us, except perhaps the Germans. The French are hopelessly inferior of course. They are vicious, and gourmets (or gourmands or something) and 'mercurial', and all sorts of things. Even the Americans we consider, rather uneasily, to be inferior. They mispronounce our language, invent incomprehensible expressions, and are unscrupulous in business. I don't know why we like, or fail to disapprove of, the Germans. Because they drink beer, I think. Of course colour makes it worse. In fact only the colour prejudice is really serious, I think. I should like you to go to England, at least for some time. I fancy you would not find it very annoying, on this account at least. For we are fairly polite. But almost everybody would behave artificially towards you, and in the end you would find it intolerable.[57]

To keep his spirits up, Seetha sent Spratt sketches she had done of birds and plants. A portrait of the paradise flycatcher made him want to see that gorgeous bird 'in the flesh'. He sent some sketches back in return, of the characters of the Tamil alphabet. In jail, with time on his hands, he was trying to learn Seetha's language. He was, he told her, having trouble with the complicated grammar. 'I have always looked upon law as the deadliest and dullest of subjects, but it must be bright and fascinating compared to grammar.'[58] Of his ongoing difficulties with the Tamil language, he commented: 'I wonder how you got on when you began learning English. You must have thought it frightfully mysterious.'[59]

Spratt wrote to Seetha once a week, which is all that the prison rules permitted. He was desperate to see her. He applied for permission to visit Madras; to his surprise, and pleasure, it was granted.[60] He was told he had to go and return within a week. With half that allotment being taken up by the tedious train journeys to and fro, he was able to spend four days with Seetha in Madras in December 1935. What they spoke of can only be guessed at. But we do have the letter that he wrote after he was back in Belgaum Fort. 'My gloom consequent upon returning here has gone', he said here, 'and

I am feeling much better, mentally at least, for my visit to Madras. I am no longer worried or undecided, and those anxiety dreams I spoke of have apparently ceased. I expect my physical health will improve as a result. So you can be quite at ease about me.'[61]

IX

In the 1930s Belgaum was a quiet backwater, a town in the interior Deccan not known as a centre of commerce or a hub of politics. The British officials posted there had time on their hands, some of which they spent speaking to their compatriot, kept under house arrest in the fort. It thus came about that in May 1936, the Commissioner of Belgaum wrote to his boss, the Home Secretary of the Bombay Presidency: 'I am personally convinced both from my conversations with him and from what I have heard from others, e.g., Mr. Mills, the Dy. Supdt. of Police, who lives within 25 yards of him, that Spratt's political views have really changed and that he would be *most* unwilling to be drawn into politics again.' The Commissioner recommended that Spratt be released, and allowed to remain in India, 'on the understanding that he would be immediately re-incarcerated if he made himself objectionable'.

To this letter the Commissioner attached notes of the conversations between himself and Philip Spratt. On 27 April Spratt told the Commissioner that if released he would first try to find employment in Madras. When asked if he would promise in writing not to engage in political activities, Spratt answered that while he did not now intend to engage in political propaganda, he objected in principle to giving an undertaking. Two days later they met again. When the Commissioner suggested that he return to England, Spratt said he could not do this. He then added that 'he would like to consult Gandhi as to his giving an undertaking, but does not know him well enough to write [to him]'.

On 1 May, Spratt handed over a written statement to the Commissioner. This noted that the Government had already dealt 'severely enough' with him, and should now not, as a condition of release, impose a 'humiliating' undertaking. Spratt wrote: 'If I were

to give a promise of a general character, I would ever after feel ashamed of myself, and I should be degraded in the opinion of those whose regard I value.' He understood that the Government was worried that as a free man he would spread Communist propaganda; however, his own intention now was not to be a political propagandist, 'but to seek employment, or establish business, whereby I might support myself, and to marry'. In any case his views on political subjects were 'not the same as they were seven years ago, or even as they were eighteen months ago'. However, he said he 'does not know what they will be in future, and I cannot undertake to say that they shall not be of any particular character'. If released, he would not 'take part in any political activity or propaganda; except by means of writing for the press or publication, which may have some political reference, and for which I realise that I should be liable under the ordinary law'.[62]

By the summer of 1936 the political climate was propitious for Spratt's release. The Government of India Act had come into effect, and there would be elections held under it, in which the Congress and other political parties would participate. In these circumstances it made little sense to keep a lapsed Communist in prison. The Bombay Government therefore accepted the recommendation of the Commissioner of Belgaum and ordered that Philip Spratt be set free without either having to return to England or give an undertaking that he would abstain from politics altogether.

In the second week of June 1936, Spratt wrote to Seetha what was by his – or their – standards a very short letter. It began: 'I have only one thing to say in this letter, but that is a matter of some importance. I have received an order of release.' He would leave for Madras as soon as he sorted out loose ends, but he could not specify an exact date. 'Anyway, don't go to the station to meet me, or you will be disappointed,' he told his expectant lover: 'When I come I shall find you out, wherever you are . . . That is what I have to say. I think I need not elaborate it. I shall see you within a week I hope, and elaboration can be left till then.'[63]

Spratt's life in India after his release will be taken up in later chapters. Let me end this one with a series of articles he wrote immediately on being freed. Published in the respected Calcutta

journal *Modern Review* – for which Tagore, Gandhi and Nehru
(among others) had also written – these dealt with the psychology
of prison life in India. Spratt wrote of how incarceration led to a
repression of sexuality, with male prisoners tending to fall in love
with every lady visitor. He spoke of how when alone prisoners
craved for company, but when they had too much of chatter longed
to get back to the privacy of their cell. Based on six years of intense
experience, he offered this maxim, to be followed in jail and out
of it: 'A reasonable combination of association and solitude is of
course best.'

Spratt spoke of the mood swings he and his fellow prisoners were
prone to: moving from sullenness to anger, from bouts of joy to
bouts of weeping. He observed that for some in jail, religion provided
consolation; for others, tobacco did. 'The strongest and most constant
desire of the prisoner', he remarked, 'is of course for release.' Of his
own final release, after the second of his two terms in prison, he
observed that immediately the worst physical symptoms disappeared.

> Some psychological effects however remain. Shyness and the feeling
> of incapacity are more pronounced. I am more introverted, more
> self-centred, and solitary, less emotionally tied to external things,
> whether personal or general, more pessimistic, and more timid, and
> I have nightmares or similar dreams more frequently. I have no doubt
> that I am less able than before to face life and to adapt myself to the
> world. My state can now be considered, I fancy, in some respects like
> that of a man prepared for conversion, but whom the positive achieve-
> ment, the new conviction, is denied.[64]

Of the new conviction – or convictions – that this once fanatical,
now wavering, Communist was to adopt, there will be plenty to tell.

CHAPTER 7

Retreat of the Matriarch

I

It is time now to return to our first renegade. We left Annie Besant in the spring of 1919, on the cusp of being displaced as the charismatic face of Indian politics by Mohandas K. Gandhi.

Gandhi had intended the satyagraha against the Rowlatt Act to be wholly non-violent. It turned out to be otherwise, in part because the Government prevented him from travelling to the Punjab in early April. News of this disbarment spread far and wide, provoking protests and attacks on public property. Annie Besant was in Simla at the time, and heard these stories with horror and a certain sense of vindication. In the letter to the *Times of India*, she attributed the violence to the methods of Gandhi. She had, she said, repeatedly written about 'the vital importance of respect for law', but it was 'a matter of deep regret that no one in Madras cared to protest with me against the *Satyagraha* movement, so great was the magic of Mr. Gandhi's name and so great the influence of the large crowds he addressed'.[1]

The reversion of Mrs Besant from militant to Moderate prompted some sarcastic commentary in the nationalist press. In an article entitled 'Mrs. Besant's somersault', a newspaper in Calicut commented that 'Mrs. Besant has entirely revised her political views, thrown Mr. Gandhi overboard, divested Mr. Tilak of the title she had conferred upon him, diverted her artillery from the Secretariat to her erstwhile friends and followers, and now she is at the very congenial game of slinging mud at her adversaries. She is now more moderate than the Moderates . . .'[2]

Gandhi's Rowlatt Satyagraha of 1919 was in some ways an extension of Mrs Besant's own Home Rule Movement of 1916–17. Like the latter, it had a newspaper as a vehicle for propaganda, brought young people into the campaign, and charged the British with betraying their own sense of justice. However, since Gandhi was much younger, he was able to travel far more intensively across India, taking his ideas into the mofussil and the countryside, whereas Besant knew only the major towns. Besides, as a home-grown Indian, speaking in the vernacular, Gandhi appealed to a far wider spectrum of public opinion than would (or had) an English-speaking foreign-born Indian.

Through their Home Rule Leagues, Tilak and Besant built the base of popular nationalism; on this base Gandhi was now erecting more (and ever more impressive) storeys. Sensing her own marginalization within India, Mrs Besant now reached out overseas. In August 1919 she issued a printed appeal, which she sent to many individuals in England. Addressing them as 'My Dear Fellow-Worker', Mrs Besant said that she planned to start a weekly newspaper in London, called *United India*, which would dispel 'the lamentable ignorance of India among the British people'. Subscribers and patrons to this paper would, she proclaimed, help the 'Great Cause of India's Uplift and Freedom'.[3,4]

On 1 October 1919, Mrs Besant turned seventy-two. Her newspaper *New India* asked Gandhi for a message, and he gladly complied. Beginning with his early admiration for her and the impression her speeches had made on him as a student in London, he went on to note that in recent times there had been 'sharp differences of opinion' between them. But, he added, 'in the midst of all my doubts I have never wavered in my belief in her great devotion to India'. Gandhi ended his message by saying: 'I have no doubt that she has popularized Home Rule in a manner no other person has. May she be spared for many a long year to serve the country she had made her own.'[5]

By this time the Home Rule League had become a total Cult of Mother Besant. Even the pamphlets written by her were printed at 'The Besant Press, Second Line Beach, Madras'. However, her band of devotees was shrinking rapidly; it now consisted largely of Brahmins educated in English. Yet she still tended to speak as if she was the Voice of India (and Indians). This irritated the other founder of a Home Rule League, the charismatic Poona-based nationalist Bal Gangadhar Tilak. In April 1920 Tilak criticized her in public for her sense of self-importance. While acknowledging her 'high intelligence, unflagging capacity for work, her great learning [and] her rousing eloquence', he called Mrs Besant an 'ambitious self-willed lady', who desired always to dominate – 'She must lead, she must boss every movement she joins.' Tilak recalled how out of pique she formed her own Home Rule League 'with only a few dozen members, almost all her followers'. Now she wished to use her position as an ex-President of the Congress 'to mislead ignorant men and women in England', where she thwarted an official Congress Deputation (which had visited England in 1920) only to promote herself, 'evidently intending to show that it was she who alone awakened the sense of political freedom in India'.

Tilak sarcastically remarked that by 'believing that all her actions and thoughts are dictated by [imaginary] Mahatmas [in the Himalaya]', Mrs Besant 'claims for herself [a] supernatural position which tolerates no opposition'. He himself believed that 'in democratic politics we must go by the decisions of the majority, even if they are unpalatable to us. Mrs Besant quarrelled with the majority at [the] Delhi [Congress of 1918], and has been trying ever since by fair or unfair means to force her importance on the Congress.'[6]

By this time Tilak himself was ailing. He died on 1 August 1920, leaving the field clear for Gandhi to become the unquestioned leader of the freedom struggle. Gandhi was now planning a movement of non-cooperation against British rule, advocating the boycott of courts and colleges and the burning of foreign goods. This appalled Mrs Besant, who, in a signed article in her own journal, *The Theosophist*, wrote:

> Mr. Gandhi lives in a world of his own, quite different from the world of human beings, with their crude ideas, their easily aroused passions, and their sudden bursts of activity. He is dangerous, well-meaning man as he is, because his imaginary human beings whom he arranges so nicely are not the human beings who live in our world, and do not dance to his piping, as he expects them to.[7]

These words were printed in August 1920. The next month, Mrs Besant attended a special session of the Congress, held in Calcutta. During a discussion on Non-Cooperation, she argued that the Government of India did not merely comprise the Viceroy or his Executive Council, but was a complex social organization built up through hundreds of years of social evolution. If Non-Cooperation was carried out as per Gandhi's programme, and Government officials of all classes were to resign, said Mrs Besant, 'you will not be able to find a court to go to if you have been struck or robbed in the street'. You would not be able to send a letter or post a telegram, or catch a train. Thus Mrs Besant concluded that Non-Cooperation 'is a war cry against government and a war cry alike against society. Mr. Gandhi does not, I know, think it is a war cry, it is only soul force. Is it soul force to gather together thousands and thousands of people in order to paralyse the Government? I submit it is physical force in another form . . .' Gandhi's movement, warned Mrs Besant, would lead to 'social chaos, anarchy, a mass of solitary individuals united by no social bond'.[8]

Mrs Besant's speech was met by jeers and catcalls from Gandhi's supporters. Gandhi personally intervened to calm the crowd, urging them to listen to her; while he didn't agree with Mrs Besant's views, he said her services to the country demanded respect. As one news report noted: 'In the name of the country, in the name of the great cause on which they were about to embark Mr. Gandhi asked them kindly and prayerfully to give Mrs. Besant and every one of those they might consider to be their opponents a respectful hearing.'[9] This was, as it were, a reversal of the Banaras incident of 1916. Then, Mrs Besant stopped Gandhi from speaking when she didn't like what she heard; here, Gandhi asked her to continue with her public criticisms of him and his work.

In the last months of 1920, as the Non-Cooperation movement grew, Mrs Besant visited its epicentre, the Bombay Presidency, and gave speeches against Gandhi and his methods. In the new year, she set up an informal group of Moderates in Madras who opposed Gandhi's takeover of the Congress. Called the '1921 Club', its members included C. P. Ramaswamy Aiyar and V. S. Srinivasa Sastri. The club's stated aims were to work towards attaining India's 'rightful position as a Free Nation in the British Commonwealth'. It aimed to 'forward the progress of India on all lines in a social and co-operative spirit'. It met once a week at the Theosophical Society to discuss current events, while also forging links with like-minded Moderates in other provinces.[10]

In April 1921, Lord Reading took over as the new Viceroy of India. Mrs Besant attended his inauguration, and shortly afterwards gave a public speech in Malabar praising the Viceroy for having reconstituted his Executive Council, and for having promoted a more progressive attitude amongst his Governors. She thought these reforms from above represented the victory of 'the common sense constitutional Briton'. She went so far as to proclaim: 'Now the autocrats are gone, never to return, and our rulers are constitutional.'

After praising the new set of apparently liberal-minded rulers, Mrs Besant launched into a fresh attack on Gandhian Non-Cooperation. She complained that the Congress Party, of which she had once been President, had become totally 'submissive' to Gandhi. She claimed that Gandhi's 'influence on students has been unhappy, breaking up discipline, and substituting nothing in its place; for they utterly disregard him where he commands them not to break up meetings, use violence, or the like'. The 'preposterous propaganda' of Non-Cooperation, she insisted, had 'done an untold amount of mischief' to India.[11]

Through 1921, as the Non-Cooperation movement gathered pace, Mrs Besant's attacks on Gandhi intensified. In a speech in Bombay, she spoke with dismay of 'Mr Gandhi's undisciplined followers, whose general tendency is towards mob-tyranny in enforcing the orders of their dictator, now advanced by many to the rank of an Avatara'.[12] In a book-length polemic published by the Theosophical Society, and distributed both in England and in India, she vented her anger on the leader who had displaced her at the head of the freedom struggle, taking so many of her erstwhile followers with him. 'Under the Gandhi Raj', she fulminated,

there is no Free Speech, no Open Meeting, unless for Non-Co-Operators. Social and Religious boycott, threats of personal violence, spitting, insults in the streets, are the method of suppression. Mob support is obtained by wild promises, such as the immediate coming of Swaraj, when there will be no rents, no taxes, by giving to Mr. Gandhi high religious names, such as Mahatma and Avatara, assigning to him supernatural powers, and the like.[13]

Mrs Besant's alarm was expressed in public, and in private. In February 1922 she wrote to her London solicitor, David Graham Pole: 'Gandhi is now planning barefaced revolution'. On 9 March she told Pole that 'the spirit of general lawlessness is spreading and has to be faced sooner or later; and it will only get worse the longer it lasts'.[14] The next day Gandhi was arrested in Ahmedabad, and sentenced to six years in prison.

II

With Gandhi in jail, and the Non-Cooperation movement having been withdrawn, Mrs Besant sought to revive her Home Rule League. She sought the assistance of prominent Moderates across India, such as Tej Bahadur Sapru of the United Provinces, Hari Singh Gour of the Central Provinces, and N. M. Joshi, Bhulabhai Desai, and M. R. Jayakar of the Bombay Presidency. These nationalists who did not follow Gandhi held meetings in Delhi, Bombay and Madras, discussing the prospects of provincial autonomy, the Indianization of the top jobs in the Army and civil service, etc.[15]

Early in 1923, Mrs Besant asked an astrologer to predict what might happen to her career in general, and to an all-India conference she proposed to hold in Delhi in 1924 in particular. The astrologer made his calculations based on her personal data, and predicted the Delhi conference would succeed. Of Mrs Besant's astrological chart the soothsayer wrote:

It is a strong map, full of possibilities for rapid advance, though, of course, there will also be much opposition to be overcome first, and some delay in consequence at the very beginning. However, one thing is certain, both open and secret enemies will have to declare themselves as such before long and many wobblers (with N[on].C[o].O[peration] tendencies) who might have become secret enemies and concealed their intentions (had the planets fallen in other houses) will probably find themselves merged in time into the Moderate Party (Neptune sextile Saturn) . . .[16]

This astrologer was fallible – as astrologers will be. The Delhi meeting of February 1924 was well attended, but, before the month was out, Gandhi was released prematurely from prison, and naturally all the attention of India and Indians was once more centred on him. Mrs Besant now chose to travel to London to state her case before the British public. Moderates in other provinces, seeing how the wind was blowing, declined to accompany her, but her loyal Madras associates Srinivasa Sastri and R. K. Shanmukham Chetty came along. The Labour Party had just come to power for the first time in the United Kingdom, and this made these Moderates hopeful that they might succeed in wresting some serious concessions from the Raj.

On 17 June 1924, the delegation met with the Secretary of State for India. Mrs Besant spoke first, and at length. She and her colleagues were working out a scheme for dominion status for India, and wanted to put it before the Prime Minister when it was finalized. The scheme would cover, among other things, the relations of the Centre and the Provinces; taxes and finance; the constitution of legislatures; protection of minorities, etc. 'India is not willing to wait any longer' for dominion status, said Mrs Besant. She however added that the British connection must stay, since (in her view) the people of India wanted it.[17]

The Secretary of State made polite noises, but no promises. After the meeting, when asked by a reporter whether she was 'hopeful about the results of her mission', Mrs Besant answered:

I should not use the word hopeful. I am *confident* about its success. I feel sure that the Labour Government, when it has a majority of lovers of British traditions and of liberty in the House of Commons will meet and satisfy India's aspirations. No battle for liberty carried on by reasonable and thoughtful men and women can fail to win success. Above all, I rely on that Power that makes for righteousness, which keeps nations alive, if they follow its dictates, and breaks them, if they deny to a subject nation its birthright of liberty.[18]

In July 1924, Mrs Besant's friends and admirers organized a huge celebration in London to mark her completing fifty years in public life. For it was back in 1874 that she had given her first public lecture, on 'The Political Status of Women'. Now, the Queen's Hall in London was booked for her Jubilee, with Mrs Besant sitting garlanded on stage while messages of praise were read out from the British Prime Minister and the Chancellor of the Exchequer, from the writer George Bernard Shaw and the politician George Lansbury. There was even a message from Gandhi, which read: 'I wish to express my deep admiration for this long record of service and the amazing energy and courage that lay behind it. I cannot forget, though it is many years ago, the inspiration I drew from her in my boyhood and then again in my expression of political activity.'[19]

This was slightly mingy, suggesting that while Gandhi had admired Annie Besant when he was young, he had now outgrown her and her brand of politics. Nonetheless, the fact that he had sent a public message of congratulation pleased Mrs Besant, and on her return to India she reached out to Gandhi, seeking a reconciliation. In the last week of August they were both in Bombay, and met, arguing about the boycott of Councils and the need for Congressmen to spin khadi, both of which he supported and she opposed. They disagreed without being disagreeable, at least according to Gandhi's account, with him saying in a speech the day after their meeting that 'in view of her hoary age and mature experience, I placed my views before her like a son pleading before his mother'.[20]

The next month, Mrs Besant wrote to a man she was now addressing as 'Dear Gandhiji', this a mark of her desire for rapprochement, a significant advance from the cold and impersonal 'Mr. Gandhi' she had once chosen to use. She was trying to arrange a meeting of leading members of different political parties in November, 'to discuss the outlines of a Swaraj Constitution for India'. She asked Gandhi to attend. If a draft constitution was agreed upon, said Mrs Besant, the Congress and the Muslim League, as well as other 'bodies which have grown up separately during these years of division', could come together and prepare a common draft, which could then 'be presented to Parliament as the demand of United India, to be passed by Parliament, not changed by it, as were the constitutions of Australia and South Africa. Then India would never again have to go to Parliament for any internal changes that she required; she would make them herself.'

After having presented her new scheme, Mrs Besant said to Gandhi: 'It would be a splendid thing if this were accomplished in the Congress presided over by yourself, with a United India behind you.'

Gandhi sent a brief and utterly non-committal reply to this long proposal. 'Regarding the Congress passing the Constitution' as suggested by Mrs Besant, he said, there were 'many difficulties but I am keeping an open mind. We shall discuss it when we can meet.'[21]

Gandhi had by now prevailed upon the Congress to adopt the so-called 'spinning franchise', whereby every party member had to spin a certain amount of yarn himself (or herself). Mrs Besant bravely said she was willing to try her hand at this new game. So Gandhi dispatched his son Devadas, to Madras, where he gave the seventy-year-old lady and her Theosophical disciples lessons in how to operate a spinning wheel. From Devadas's account, published in *Young India*, it appeared that although Mrs Besant tried hard, her poor eyesight and ageing limbs went against her.[22]

Hoping still to rejoin the Congress and work within it, Mrs Besant attended the annual meeting of the party, held that December in the southern town of Belgaum. Gandhi was elected President, and even without that honorific he would have dominated the proceedings. And so he did. Mrs Besant now sought to separate herself from him once more. After her return to Madras from Belgaum, she sent a letter to those she thought might still be sympathetic to her and her ideas. She wanted help from them in reviving the 'Old Congress', which would be separate and distinct from the 'New Congress' led by Gandhi and his men. She even had a name for this proposed party of anti-Gandhi-ites: 'All-India Political Congress'.[23]

The response to Mrs Besant's proposal was distinctly lukewarm. C. Y. Chintamani, the Moderate journalist from Allahabad, reminded her that there was already in existence a National Liberal Federation 'as the continuation organisation of the old Congress and its doors are open to every one who stands for the attainment of constitutional ends by constitutional means'. He added: 'I have no reason to think that the new organisation which you suggest will, merely because of a different name, be a stronger body or will attract larger numbers.'[24]

There was to be no new Party, but this was not to stop Mrs Besant from drafting and offering new proposals. In June 1925, she sent a four-page memorandum to the British Parliament. Among the other signatories were V. S. Srinivasa Sastri, M. R. Jayakar, M. C. Rajah and N. C. Kelkar, all likewise bitterly opposed to Gandhi and his new, remodelled, mass-based Congress. The memorandum urged that a Bill be passed in the House of Commons to grant India Dominion Status on par with countries such as Canada. Back in 1918, said Mrs Besant and her colleagues, the old (pre Gandhi) Congress had passed a resolution claiming the right to self-determination, which had got the approval of the then Prime Minister, David Lloyd George. Seven years had passed, but no action had been taken by the British Parliament. Hence this fresh appeal, which insisted:

> For India, freedom is a matter of life or death; the appalling poverty of her masses, the neglect of their education, shown by the disgracefully low figure of the percentage of school attendance, the short life-period . . . [T]hese and many other signs, such as the death-rate being twice lately higher than the birth-rate, show that, as a Nation, she is on the down-grade under British rule.

This latest Besant-inspired memorandum continued:

> There is only one cure for the admitted 'restlessness' of India, and that is her freedom. Her irritability finds vent in domestic quarrels, because she is denied self-expression as a Nation. If this continues and Britain is obdurate in her refusal to agree to her demand for Dominion Status – on which all political parties are agreed – Government will become increasingly difficult and ere long impossible. We do not say this as a threat, for we seek an honourable agreement, such as Britain refused to her American Colonies and created a

Republic but made with her other Colonies and created peace and amity. We also desire peace and amity, and therefore, before it is too late, we state the danger as an approaching fact.[25]

Once more, the British Government would not be moved. But we must nonetheless admire Mrs Besant for her dogged tenacity, for her desire to struggle on with her vision for her adopted country. She still hoped, against the odds and against the stars, to recreate the glory days of 1916–18, when she stood at the head of the fight for India's freedom.

III

In Annie Besant's papers, which are housed at the Theosophical Society in Adyar, is a copy of a passport issued to her in 1924. This 'British Indian Passport' says its holder was five feet two inches tall (or short), and had hazel eyes and white hair. An early page of the passport listed the countries she was travelling to in 1924 and 1925, these being thirteen in all, including Switzerland, Poland, Portugal, Hungary and the United States.

Increasingly marginalized by Gandhi, the Congress, and Indian politics, Mrs Besant consoled herself by her still active Theosophy. She experimented with new forms of dress, such as a purple cassock. She travelled across the oceans and back, seeking and getting new converts.[26] When she gave a series of lectures in London, among those in attendance were her old socialist comrade George Lansbury and his wife. Afterwards, Lansbury wrote to Mrs Besant: 'Though we do not understand as you do, we both know lots more about "Theosophy" than we ever did before.'[27]

Mrs Besant's restless and combative temperament could not, however, allow a total retreat from politics. In the first week of April 1926, Tej Bahadur Sapru and she convened a conference in Bombay to form a 'National Federation' of people working for Dominion Status in a spirit of what they called 'Responsive Co-operation' (with the Raj). The usual Liberal/Moderate suspects were in attendance: Srinivasa Sastri, R. P. Paranjype, M. R. Jayakar, Hridayanath Kunzru, and C. Y. Chintamani, but also the ageing Congress veterans B. C. Pal and M. M. Malaviya.[28]

The year 1927 was relatively quiet politically speaking, for Mrs Besant and for India. But when in 1928 a boycott of the all-white Simon Commission was proposed, she attended an All Party Conference held in Delhi in November, alongside the leading Congressmen Motilal Nehru, Maulana Azad, and Lala Lajpat Rai. The first-named had just finished his job as chairman of a committee charged with drafting a statement of Indian aims and aspirations, known as the 'Nehru Report'. This asked for, or demanded, an independent nation with democracy based on universal adult franchise, and the protection of the rights of minorities. To this report Mrs Besant had also given her endorsement. This pleased Gandhi, who wrote thanking her for her support, adding that 'having at last got a document with the *imprimatur* of all parties, it will be a great national tragedy if the report is not acclaimed by the public'.[29]

In December 1928 there was a reconciliation of another sort, when Mrs Besant was invited to deliver the Convocation Address at Banaras Hindu University, an institution she had helped found but from whose workings she had since been excluded. Her address began:

> When a gardener plants a seed in a new garden, even if he knows the kind of flower which the seed will yield, yet he does not know the circumstances as to the welfare and the nourishment of that seed. And so it is well for us to understand in the first place what kind of soil is needed if we wish that the seed we plant bring forth the desired yield. The same analogy can be applied to the nursery of [the] human race, and it is our duty to ensure the success of seeds left to us by our forefathers. But in regard to this matter the soil is not the same earthly soil as in the garden of flowers but it is in the soil which can be described in two words 'Love and Sacrifice'. Let us then today look at this heritage covering a large number of our younger brothers and sisters who are sent from this place, this temple of learning full of youthful enthusiasm and high ambitions to surround the motherland.

There is a strong element of self-projection here. Mrs Besant saw herself as the gardener of the university in Banaras, whilst Love and Sacrifice were the motifs of her life in and for India. [30]

IV

Mrs Besant spent the summer of 1929 in England. On the last day of May, she gave a talk at Caxton Hall in London. She titled it 'Nehru Report, India's Last Gesture'. She began by telling the audience that India, in the sixteenth century the wealthiest country in the world, was now one of the poorest. She continued: 'You are responsible for the condition of India. . . . You have no right to own a country when you do not know its condition and force on it the rulers of your little land.'

Mrs Besant recalled her 1917 Presidential address to the Congress, where she spoke of the three great awakenings in India – of the Women, the Masses, and the Merchants. 'India awakened, would no longer tolerate domination. She demanded her freedom.' She then came to the Motilal Nehru Report, which was based on all party consultations, and hence very representative. The report had outlined the process of the constitutional transition to self-government. Mrs Besant ended her ninety-minute talk with these words: 'Friends, my last word to you is this: that this Report is the last gesture – the last friendly gesture that India will offer to Britain. If you reject it – if you scorn it – if you refuse India the liberty she demands, then she will appeal to God and her right and she will win.'[31]

As it turned out, the Nehru Report was not to be India's last gesture. But this speech urging its acceptance on the British public was to be Annie Besant's final appeal on behalf of her new homeland to her old.

V

In August 1929 – not long after she returned from London – J. Krishnamurti walked out on Mrs Besant and the Theosophical

Society. He wanted to escape from her shadow – or clutches. He no longer saw himself as the Anointed One, the Messiah. He said he was just an ordinary teacher, although his lectures continued to attract large crowds, especially in California, where he now had a base.

Mrs Besant was estranged from her spiritual heir, and isolated in the world of Indian politics. The mood in nationalist circles was now increasingly combative, with young Congressmen itching for another direct confrontation with the Raj. In November 1929 some militant hotheads picketed a meeting addressed by Mrs Besant in Madras. When Jawaharlal Nehru wrote to apologize on their behalf, he got this reply:

> Dear Panditji,
>   It is very nice of you to express regret about the handbills given away at my lecture. Believe me, it in no way pained me. I am always so glad when our youths take an active interest in public affairs, whether they agree with me or not. Also I am too old a politician to mind what people say!
>   With always kind regards
>   Annie Besant[32]

The next month, Jawaharlal Nehru was elected President of the Congress at its Lahore session, which committed the party to fighting for 'Purna Swaraj', complete independence, implying a total severance of the British connection (unlike the 'Dominion Status' preferred by Mrs Besant). Early in the new year, Gandhi announced that there would be a fresh round of civil disobedience. Mrs Besant termed Gandhi's decision 'regrettable', claiming that it 'must, for all his precautions, result sooner or later in outbursts of violence'. The Congress's new policies, she said, had put an end 'to the unity of all parties, achieved first, on the boycott of the Simon Commission and then over the Nehru Report'. She bitterly wrote that 'Gandhiji has no use now for that unity, built up amidst difficulties and after much toil'.[33]

In early March, Gandhi set off for the sea to break the salt laws. His campaign aroused widespread interest in India and around the world. Many were impressed, but not Mrs Besant. After the Mahatma reached the coast and broke the law, she wrote that

> Mr. Gandhi had been acknowledged by a number of people as a dictator, whose opinion is to be accepted as supreme. He is hailed as 'Commander', as 'General', and we are all bidden to obey him, on pain of being denounced as unpatriotic, as enemies of the Motherland. Despite the fact that some of his ideas have proved to be impracticable and others to be mischievous, the mass slave mentality marches triumphantly along, denouncing and persecuting all who resist its sway.[34]

In May Gandhi was arrested, and sent off to Yerwada Jail, outside Poona. In his absence the movement continued, with men and women breaking the salt laws in many locations across India. In October, Mrs Besant wrote to the Government seeking permission to see Gandhi in jail. The Home Member was lukewarm about the request, writing on file that it might lead to 'probable further applications for interview as for example by [the socialist journalist H. N.] Brailsford which in my opinion there would be no good ground for permitting'. He continued: 'I would suggest that the following line be taken. Ghandi [sic] was doubtless allowed to receive personal visitors at intervals in ordinary way. If he desires to see Besant in ordinary way as personal friend, this might be permitted on the condition that there was no publicity.'[35]

The meeting did not take place. Gandhi was perhaps not very keen to meet Annie Besant, who was by no means a 'personal friend'; she was probably not very keen on a visit *sans* publicity. Meanwhile, Mrs Besant issued an interestingly equivocal statement on the ongoing protests. She was, she said, 'very much distressed to learn of the numerous arrests that have been made of members of the Working Committee of the Congress, including many of the leading men in India. I have spoken very strongly about this in England.' Then she added:

> But I am and always have been against Civil Disobedience. I can understand people who disapprove of any specific law and conscientiously refuse to obey that law or who break that law knowing what

the consequences are and being prepared to take the consequences. But that is a very different thing from a wholesale condemnation of laws in general.

I am not prepared to urge young men to a general breaking of laws, and possibly to going to their death, when I disapprove of this as a method of political propaganda and am not prepared to follow it myself.[36]

This was the last public statement of any significance Mrs Besant was to make. She was now old and ailing, and increasingly confined to her rooms at the Theosophical Society at Adyar. Through 1931 and 1932, with Gandhi in and out of jail, travelling to London for the Round Table Conference and campaigning for the abolition of Untouchability, Mrs Besant 'no longer cared to go out, but preferred to sit quietly in her room or on the verandah. She tried to read, but she could not concentrate. She especially avoided newspapers recording events in the outside world.'[37]

Through 1933 Mrs Besant's health continued to decline. In late August, a letter arrived in Adyar asking her to contribute to a volume in memory of the founder of the Arya Samaj, Swami Dayanand Saraswati. In normal times she would surely have written an essay, perhaps juxtaposing personal homage with philosophical reflection, exploring the links between Hinduism and Theosophy, India and the world. But now her secretary wrote back that 'Dr Besant is in a very weak physical condition'. 'If she had been in her normal health and strength', the secretary continued, 'I have no doubt she would gladly have seized the opportunity to pay her tribute to the Swamiji's greatness and services to India.'[38]

Annie Besant died on 20 September 1933, at her home in Madras, a full forty years after she first came out to India. The next day her body was taken for public viewing in the Main Hall of the Theosophical Society. The flags of the fifty-four countries in which the society had branches were displayed. Prayers from all religions were recited, and then the body was taken to be cremated on the banks of the Adyar river. The following day, the ashes were collected in an urn, and taken by her disciple, the philosopher Bhagavan Das, to be immersed in the Ganga at Banaras.

I owe this description of Mrs Besant's last days to her most dogged and devoted biographer, Arthur Nethercot. Of the range of tributes that poured into the mailbox of the Theosophical Society, Nethercot writes:

> Telegrams and letters came from everywhere: municipal boards, bar associations, journalists' associations, colleges and schools, Boy Scouts, Young Men's Indian Associations, Moslem Associations, Buddhist Associations, Women's Associations, Round Tables, Humanitarian Leagues, Social Service Leagues, Trade Unions, and of course Co-Masonry and Theosophical groups. Tributes were received from Sir P. S. Sivaswamy Iyer, Rangaswami Iyengar and Viceroy Willingdon in India; from Subhas Chandra Bose in Geneva; from Wedgwood, Esther Bright, Mrs Josephine Ransom, Ben Tillet, Graham Pole, George Lansbury, Krishna Menon, and, briefly, Krishnamurti in London. Mahatma Gandhi, ever forgiving, sent an immediate dispatch of sorrow and praise.[39]

Nethercot does not give us Gandhi's own last words on Annie Besant, so I shall:

> Whilst the people will thank the Almighty for relieving Dr. Besant from lingering illness by sending to her the Angel of Death, thousands will, at the same time, mourn the event. So long as India lives, the memory of the magnificent services rendered by Dr. Besant will also live. She had endeared herself to India by making it the country of her adoption and dedicating her all to her.[40]

CHAPTER 8

Seekers North and South

I

In 1934, Mahatma Gandhi moved base from Ahmedabad to the Central Provinces. His friend and follower, the entrepreneur Jamnalal Bajaj, owned several tracts of land in and around the town of Wardha, which he happily handed over to Gandhi. One of these tracts was in a village called Segaon (later renamed Sevagram), where Gandhi based himself.

Once Gandhi shifted to central India, Sevagram replaced Sabarmati as the mother ashram of the Indian freedom movement. Now, political activists and constructive workers seeking the Mahatma's counsel took trains to Wardha, rather than to Ahmedabad. Wardha was located in the very centre of the Indian peninsula; whether one was coming from Delhi or Madras, Calcutta or Bombay, it took about twenty-four hours to get there.

Sometime in the mid-thirties, two foreign admirers of Gandhi came independently to see him. One, an American male originally from rural Minnesota, arrived from South India, where he was based. The other, a British female, originally from the great city of London, came from North India, where she was based. Somehow, they found themselves seated opposite one another during a dinner at the Mahila (women's) Ashram. They spoke, among other things, of the layout of houses in warm tropical climes and how these differed from homes constructed in the cold countries from which they came. 'How I love these Indian courtyards,' said the American. The Englishwoman said she loved them too.[1]

II

The seeker who came to see Gandhi from the south was named Ralph Richard Keithahn. All his grandparents had moved to the United States from Germany. His mother's family settled near New Hampton in Iowa, and his father's family near Fairmont, in Minnesota. The eldest of seven children, Dick Keithahn grew up on the family farm, in a home of devoted (though not dogmatic) Lutherans. He studied in a rural school and then in Carleton College, where he helped pay his fees by milking the cows at the college dairy. He went on to study theology in Chicago and at Yale. Here too he paid his fees by working in the students' kitchen.

Dick Keithahn was deeply influenced by his college teachers. His principal at Carleton, Dr Donald G. Cowling, taught a transformative course on 'Philosophy of Life'. Professor J. M. P. Smith of the Chicago Divinity School introduced him to the Old Testament Prophets; ever since, he later recalled, 'I have always tried to make my own Christianity prophetic.'[2]

On completing his education, the young idealist chose not to join the priesthood at home but to work in a poorer part of the world instead. He considered both China and India, eventually choosing the latter. In the summer of 1925 he took a boat across the Atlantic. He saw the Lake District and Paris, before jumping onto another ship in Marseilles bound for Colombo. Here he took another (and smaller) boat for the southern tip of India, and from there a train to his eventual destination, Madurai, where an American mission was based. The monsoon had just ended, and from his train window he saw 'the irrigation "tanks" were full of water. Palm trees were scattered everywhere over the landscape. What a beautiful, unusual sight it was! I was to realise, however, that normally there was little or no water in these tanks. Most of the Ramnad District area is almost like a desert during most of the year.'[3]

The American Mission in Madurai had some eighty members. They lived in a large compound, away from the servants who served them and away from the villagers they sought to take the Gospel to. Dick Keithahn's first conversations with his colleagues were replete with warnings; he was not to go out into the sun without a large and wide-brimmed *topi*, he was to beware of snakes, he was to drink only boiled water.

Keithahn was dismayed by the casual racism of his colleagues. 'For example, Indians normally stood when they came into the missionaries' office. Seldom were Indians invited to a meal in the missionary bungalow.'[4] Enjoying an evening walk in the countryside, Keithahn was told by a colleague that if he passed through a village he should use a horse-carriage or at the very least a bullock-cart, since on no account must a white missionary be seen walking on a street on the same level as natives. He was appalled by the acceptance of caste distinctions, so that while high-caste converts listened to a white priest's sermon from inside the church, low-caste converts stood outside, on the verandah.

Wishing to immerse himself in his surroundings, Keithahn took Tamil lessons with a teacher in Madurai, and then went for a year to the Language School in the hill station of Kodaikanal. He fell in love with the hills, returning whenever he could. However, he was increasingly uncomfortable with the luxury of the mission life, these feelings deepening when Gandhi entered his mental and moral universe. As he recalled half a century later: 'In these early years I remember reading one evening in *Young India*, Gandhiji's words at one of his regular prayer meetings, "If you have two chairs in your home and need only one and your neighbour has none, you are a robber!"' Thus the young missionary, coming to convert Hindu India, found himself challenged by India's outstanding Hindu leader. And 'the more I read about Jesus, the more he thought about him "who has no place to lay his head", it seemed to me that Gandhi was right. Thus, I started the simplification of my life.'[5]

The Mission Board expected its members to own and wear a dinner suit; Keithahn now discarded his, and wore a pair of trousers and a bush-shirt instead. (Eventually he was to wear only khadi.) Travelling in South India, he found other Christians more congenial to his views and temperament. He visited the Christian Ashram at Tirupattur, where the Englishman Ernest Paton and the Indian S. Jesudason were seeking to indigenize their faith. He went to Madras, and was impressed with the zest and energy of the activists of the

Student Christian Movement. These institutions both stood for full racial equality, and had Indian and Western Christians working side-by-side in an equal partnership.

In the year 1929, Keithahn visited Mahatma Gandhi at Sabarmati as well as Rabindranath Tagore at Santiniketan. Conversations with both 'left no doubt' in his mind that if he was to live in India he 'must identify with the Indian people'; something that was impossible 'in Missions as organised today'.[6]

Having been to Sabarmati and Santiniketan, he chose now to visit a modern place of pilgrimage closer to him; the ashram of the saint Ramana Maharishi, outside Tiruvannamalai, a town merely a couple of hundred miles from Madurai. He was deeply impressed, writing that while he had often experienced

> the same fellowship with devout Hindus that I have had with Christians, with Ramana there was something unique. As soon as I came into the hall of meditation, where some forty devout seekers were gathered that afternoon, I felt a fellowship of the spirit that I had not experienced with another until then. There was a remarkable communication which seemed to lead to a full understanding.

It was from Ramana that Keithahn learned that the 'number one enemy' of the social worker was not the poverty that he wished to eradicate, but his own ego, which got in the way of disinterested service.[7]

Sometime in the first half of 1930, Keithahn was visited by another like-minded Westerner, the English Quaker Reginald Reynolds. Reynolds had spent time with Gandhi, and was chosen by the Mahatma as his emissary to carry letters to the Viceroy prior to the launching of the Salt March.

Keithahn's hosting of the dissident Quaker upset his colleagues in Madurai, and enraged the District Collector, a man named Hall. His Mission warned him that his staying on would jeopardize their funds and their movement. He was told that he would have to choose between being non-political and leaving India. He chose the latter, as by now he was absolutely unsympathetic to the ways in which missionary work was being conducted in the subcontinent.

Keithahn left India on 16 July 1930, returning to his homeland via China. His deportation was noticed by the American press, with a Chicago newspaper carrying a report headlined: 'Britain Orders U. S. Pastor to Quit India Over Gandhi Revolt'.[8]

III

On his return to the United States Dick Keithahn first spent some months in New York City, taking classes at the Union Theological Seminary. In February 1931 he married Mildred McKie, a young doctor from Iowa he had known from his days in Chicago. They moved to South Dakota, joining a mission that allowed Dick to preach and Mildred to attend to patients. In the 'grass-hopper, dust-ridden' county where they lived, she was the only doctor, he the only priest. Some of his parishioners would say: 'Keithahn preaches; his wife practises!'[9]

Keithahn persuaded his wife that their real mission lay overseas. The Great Depression temporarily put paid to that idea. However, by 1934 the situation in India (and the world) was congenial to his return. All Congressmen were out of jail, and would soon participate in elections under a new Act guaranteeing provincial autonomy. In his time in the Tamil country Keithahn had got to know Gandhi's close associate Chakravarti Rajagopalachari. 'Rajaji' persuaded the British authorities to allow the renegade American to return. However, as a condition to his re-entry they made him sign an undertaking that he would abstain 'from participation in public affairs'.

So in December 1934, Dick Keithahn sailed for India, with Mildred and their two little children. While glad to be back, he wished to keep a distance between himself and his former missionary colleagues. The Keithahns first based themselves at Devakottai, sixty miles from Madurai, where they worked with village labourers and artisans. After two years here they moved to the cosmopolitan city of Bangalore, where the climate was milder, and where Mildred would find it easier to adjust.[10] Shortly after relocating Dick called on Gandhi in Sevagram. In the course of their conversation, the Hindu

Indian told the Christian American that 'there is an essential equality in our nakedness. God is not going to think of me as Gandhi and you as Keithahn. . . . The differences of race and skin and of mind and body and of climate and nation are transitory. In the same way essentially all religions are equal.'[11]

At first in Bangalore, Dick and Mildred stayed in a working-class area named Shrirampur. Here, the pioneering social reformer R. Gopalaswamy Iyer had established a students' home for those from Harijan (or 'Untouchable') backgrounds. The Keithahns lived in this Harijan hostel, with Dick organizing labourers and Mildred opening a free clinic.

When he could Keithahn went to see Ramana Maharishi, in his ashram on a hilltop outside the town of Tiruvannamalai. Once, when he was with Ramana, a man came and asked aggressively for the seer's blessings. An eyewitness to the encounter was a professor of English from Madras, who later wrote:

A young man from Andhra walked into the Hall, folded his palms, and almost demanded Bhagavan [Ramana]'s *anugraha* (approval) for his starting a social service centre in his town. Silence prevailed and the youngster was disappointed. Keithahn looked for a nod from the god on the couch and proceeded to explain why the *anugraha* was not so readily forthcoming. He questioned the young man: 'Are you sure you love the poor as you love your brother or sister? Do you form a society when you take your sister to the doctor as soon as she falls ill? Do you want to be an office-bearer, read the annual report and feel big? Are you really concerned over the plight of your poor neighbour?' Thus Keithahn brought out (as Bhagavan smiled His blessing) the paramount importance of loving and 'identifying' with people in trouble and the ever-present danger of ego-boosting when service is undertaken not as *sadhana* for self-improvement but as a means of self-aggrandisement.[12]

In 1940, the Keithahns set up an ashram of their own, in the village of Kengeri, on the western outskirts of Bangalore. They were now a family of five, with a girl born in India joining the boy and girl born in South Dakota. Among the first to join this new Christian ashram were two young men from Kerala, M. M. Thomas and A. K. Thamby. Keithahn guided them in their studies; both went on to become major figures in progressive Christianity in India. A third protégé, A. K. Tharien, whom the Keithahns met through the Student Christian movement, became a pioneer of low-cost, affordable, health care.

M. M. Thomas was to later write of his time with Keithahn that 'the year I spent with him in Bangalore was one of the most creative periods of my life. It was not an easy life. We lived on about Rs. 10 a month per person. I remember rendering strict accounts for the monthly pocket money of one rupee! Keithahn was strict with us, but he was even more strict with the members of his family and strictest of all with himself – in true Gandhian tradition.'[13]

In Europe, the Second World War had broken out. Bangalore was a major hub of the British Indian Army; and the comings and goings of soldiers, and the imposition of censorship and of food rationing, must have affected the Keithahns, with their three small children to care for.

But their work carried on regardless. In August 1941, Keithahn wrote to Gandhi about a South India Rural Workers Conference, to be held at the Vinaya Ashram in Guntur District in December. This was the fourth such conference; and the Mahatma had sent messages for the previous three. Therefore Keithahn wanted a message for this one too. 'Of course I need not say that these are very important days for constructive work,' he wrote:

In fact I can see no other hope for world harmony than the basis of sacrificial constructive work among the masses of our people. Thus such a fellowship and conference as this is extremely important at this time and I know we have your blessings. But if it is not too much to ask, I would very much appreciate also any suggestions you may have: (1) As to leadership, (2) as to subjects, (3) as to whether at this time it would not be well to invite some of our brother workers from central and north India.

The letter ended with news of his own work:

We are having our own labour problems in Bangalore just now but I am convinced that we are moving ahead. It is difficult for labour and labour sympathisers to be patient; on the other hand it is difficult for those who are running industries to understand the terrific problems of their workers and to realise that tremendous changes and advances are needed. Again I know your prayers are with us when we try to move ahead more rapidly.

The letter was answered on behalf of Gandhi by one of his secretaries. While Gandhi had no objection to the organizers inviting constructive workers from north and central India, these should be a select few rather than very many. The letter from Sevagram added: 'Bapu has been kept informed of the labour troubles at Bangalore. I hope Mrs Keithahn has completely recovered from her illness, and you and your family are doing well. You may receive during the next week some non-violent pamphlets.'[14]

The war in Europe was ostensibly being fought in defence of freedom, but the British refused to countenance freedom for their own subject peoples. From September 1939 Gandhi and the Congress had repeatedly pointed out this anomaly, this hypocrisy rather. They told the Viceroy they would support the Allies wholeheartedly in the war if the Raj gave an assurance that India would get its independence once victory came. For this, Gandhi was even willing to suspend his doctrinal commitment to non-violence. Sadly, the Viceroy at the time, Lord Linlithgow, was an unreconstructed imperialist, and he refused to concede any ground whatsoever.

In August 1942, despairing of the Raj's intransigence, Gandhi launched his 'Quit India' movement from Bombay. He was immediately arrested and taken off to prison. All other Congress leaders were also quickly detained, but then the movement took off on its own, with students showing the way. Through the second half of 1942 and all through 1943, there were protest demonstrations all over India, defying prohibitory orders. Tens of thousands of arrests were made, yet the protests continued.

Unlike previous struggles initiated by Gandhi, this movement was not restricted to British India but also penetrated the princely states. Nationalists in the state of Mysore, whose borders came close to

Bangalore, were particularly active. Here (as elsewhere) the movement was led and largely staffed by students. Keithahn was in touch
with some of them; telling them 'they should be working along
"constructive" lines instead of blowing up bridges and trains, etc.!'
Nonetheless, his work attracted the attention of the British Resident
of Mysore State, who called Keithahn in for a meeting. As the
American-turned-Indian later wrote: 'When the Resident asked me
why I should not be sent out of India, I replied, "You ought to be
grateful that I am guiding the students into constructive service when
they might be destroying your efforts." He could not appreciate
this!'[15]

All this while Gandhi himself was in prison in Poona. His seventy-
fifth birthday was due to fall in October 1944. In anticipation, some
of his admirers in Bombay began planning a volume of tributes.
Keithahn was asked to contribute. Based on his recent work in
Bangalore, he sent an essay on what students, 'the hope of the future',
could learn from Gandhi's life and example. Young men who wished
to serve the nation, said Keithahn, should be inspired by the Mahatma
to make the village the centre of their work, to 'always live in the
open and in truth', to 'cultivate the spirit of true humility and reverence', to 'rid yourselves of all caste and class feeling and actions',
to 'learn the dignity of labour', to 'look upon every woman as your
equal', and to 'Give Mother India your all in times of crises'.[16]

Mildred, meanwhile, was doing some writing of her own. In
between attending to patients and bringing up three children, she
was working on a short book bearing the title *Indian Foods and
Nutrition*. That book is now unavailable (at least in Indian libraries)
but we do have an article that draws on it, entitled 'Our Village
Health'. This appeared under both their names in the *Indian Journal
of Social Work* in 1944.

The Keithahns advised Indians not to be over-dependent on
modern medicine, which 'all too often tends to enslave man . . .
enslave him to drugs, to wrong habits, to wrong ideas of living, to
bad habits of eating, sleeping, etc'. Folk medicine, they thought,
offered great possibilities. Individual households could maintain their
own kitchen gardens, plant trees for food and fuel, eschew sugar
for jaggery, etc. Village councils should provide community facilities

for sanitation, with a common compost pit for human waste, located at a distance from homes and dwellings. They did not discount the value of modern medicine, but urged that it be 'reoriented and integrated with the potential life of India'.[17]

As these essays showed, the Keithahns were deeply committed to India, and wished to spend the rest of their lives in the subcontinent. The British Raj, however, had other ideas. In February 1944, the Government of India expressed concern that Dick Keithahn had not observed the terms of his undertaking to stay away from political activities. They noted that in 1943 he had addressed several student conferences where patriotic slogans were raised, and where he had himself 'characterized Mr Gandhi as the world's greatest Leader, and declared that Indian students wanted freedom to think, act and live like free men'. The Raj wanted him deported, but were willing to give him a hearing before taking final action. Keithahn wrote a long defence of his work, arguing that he had not in fact violated the undertaking, and had merely sought to 'work for reconciliation wherever there was misunderstanding' between Hindus, Muslims and Christians, and between Indians and Englishmen. 'My position', he said, 'has always been that Indian and British, for their mutual welfare, must work out their problems together. And that together they might demonstrate to the world how East and West could co-operate constructively.'

In May 1944, while the Government was contemplating the deportation of the American renegade, Gandhi was released from prison. In July, Keithahn wrote to the Mahatma asking for a message for a meeting of social workers in South India that he was organizing. 'Dear Friend', Gandhi wrote back, 'I hope you will have a successful gathering. Twenty real votaries of Truth and Love are equal to or rather more than a match for a number of indifferent persons raised to Nth power.'[18]

It is not clear whether this meeting was held, for in the first week of August the Government issued an order deporting Dick Keithahn from India. He was given three months to sort out his arrangements. The only saving grace was that the Government would pay for the cost of the passage back to the United States of Keithahn and his family.[19]

The Government's order was the subject of a long editorial in the Madras-based newspaper, the *Indian Express*. This asked the question as to why 'such a life-long and devout American servant of the Indian village has had to suddenly and compulsorily leave India'. The editorial helpfully provided a summary of Keithahn's career in India, in Madurai, Bangalore and Kengeri. It spoke of how he had chosen to leave missionary work and 'cast in his lot as a free man with the people of the Indian villages and to serve them in all their bitter needs'. For many years he and his wife had 'literally buried themselves in village work'.

After describing what Keithahn had done for and in India, the newspaper commented:

> It is such a man, an American, a devout village worker and friend of India's common people who is to-day to be chucked out of the country unceremoniously at the arbitrary dictate of the British Government. It is curious how Mr. Keithahn did not get any protection from the American Consuls in Delhi or Madras. Are the American Consuls in India unable to protect an innocent American citizen from the anger of the British, for the reason that he has become too good and intimate a friend of the Indian people?

Keithahn, wrote the *Indian Express*, was one of those rare foreigners, such as C. F. Andrews, who had come to India 'with the single purpose of serving India without the slightest ulterior motive'. The American had gone further than Andrews, 'in identifying himself with the common people of India. Latterly he had even begun to dress like an Indian peasant and to eat only such simple food as was obtainable in the village itself. He had reduced his life to such utter simplicity that even his Indian friends found it difficult to conform to it when they visited him.' Now, as he was being sent back to America, said the newspaper, 'India will never forget that the cross Mr. Keithahn has to bear to-day is only part of the cross that India bears in her subjection to British rule.'[20]

But of course (and especially during wartime) the British Raj could not be moved by editorials in Indian newspapers. The order of deportation would stay. In September, the Mysore police escorted the Keithahns in a train that took them to the border of the Bombay Presidency. Here they were placed under the supervision of the Bombay police, who took them in another train to the island city, from where they would board the ship that returned them to their (original) homeland. Also in Bombay at this time was Gandhi, who had just finished a long and inconclusive round of meetings with his great rival, the Muslim League leader M. A. Jinnah. Gandhi gave his American admirer a brief audience, where he joked: 'Keithahn, you are a very clever fellow: when you want to go home, you know how to do it!'[21] (This was a reference to the fact that the Raj paid the family's passage to America.)

IV

The Keithahns reached the United States towards the end of 1944. A year later, they sent a circular letter to friends bearing the title 'Keithahns of India Send Greetings', signed by Dick, Mildred and their three children. It was sent from Merom, Indiana, where they were now based. The town boasted of a Merom Institute, which called itself 'A Regional Centre of Christian influence'.

The letter first gave news of the children. The son, Richard, was 'going American over basketball', and played guard on the 8th grade team. The older daughter Mearl Marie, 'having learned the art of Indian cooking, now is at American cooking', and made a fruit cake at Thanksgiving. All three kids were taking piano lessons. The family as a whole were helping on a small farm which has 'three good milk cows. How Kengeri would rejoice to have them!'

From this circular letter we learn that since his involuntary return to America, Dick Keithahn had travelled 26,000 miles, and spoken at 150 different venues, while Mildred and the kids had been rooted in the small town of Merom. The letter drew attention to Mildred's difficulties with her husband on the road: 'To manage a homeless family, with the Father gone months at a time, taxed her ability. It could be done in India with the security of the Ashram, but without the help of sister and friends it would have been impossible here. All of us long to return to India's simplicity . . .'

The pamphlet ended with this statement, surely written mostly or wholly by Dick himself:

One year in the U. S. A. leads us to the following conclusions:
1. The American Church is a chaplaincy to a pagan civilization.
2. There has been a deterioration of the moral and spiritual life of America in the last 10 years.
3. There are many hopeful evidences of vital life.
4. Christians are comparatively well-informed but have no effective form of action.
5. Unless the creative forces formulate a united, nation-wide program of action immediately, America will grow in her economic imperialism and will be the greatest source of evil in the world.
6. American youth, although potentially good and strong, are jittery, dominated by American paganism.
7. The schools serve business interests rather than creative community-wide interests.
8. Much has been done for the Negroes during the past 10 years. Anti-Semitism has increased.
9. America is wasting her tremendous sexual potentialities.
10. America is drugging herself with drink and the Church seems content to have it so.
11. America is still a land of hope; but evil has become so dominating, one fears seriously for the future.[22]

On his trips to Sevagram, Keithahn had befriended the Gandhian economist J. C. Kumarappa, both a Christian and a Tamil, and a pioneer of rural reconstruction besides. With so much in common they became friends; now, back in America, Keithahn tried hard to have Kumarappa's book on Jesus as seen through an Indian lens published. He sought the help of, among others, the pacifist and civil rights leader A. J. Muste. Muste wrote to Keithahn that though it was 'a sound and interesting piece of work', it was not 'sufficiently new and distinctive to get a publisher in the United States. Of course, if it were done by Gandhi himself, it would be different; but I doubt whether J. C. Kumarappa is well enough known for the name to carry the book.' Passing on this letter to Kumarappa,

Keithahn said he had also approached several other friends, 'but with no results'.[23]

Back in Keithahn's adopted homeland, some momentous political developments were taking shape. The war had ended, the Labour Party was in power in the United Kingdom, and had committed itself to independence for India. In early 1946 fresh elections were held, and in September of that year, an Interim Government headed by Jawaharlal Nehru was sworn in. A prominent member of this Government was C. Rajagopalachari. Keithahn wrote to him, and Rajaji arranged for his deportation order to be rescinded by a Raj now absolutely on its last legs.

In the summer of 1947 the Keithahns packed their bags and prepared to leave Merom, Indiana, for somewhere in South India. From the ship, Dick Keithahn sent J. C. Kumarappa a letter asking for advice on what he might do when back. 'I assume you are still at Maganwadi and Sec[retary] of the A[ll]. I[ndia]. V[illage]. I[ndustries]. A[ssociation]', he wrote: 'What is the present situation? I would like to continue to co-operate with the village industries work. . . . You may address me at Kodaikanal, So[uth] India where we shall make our h[ea]dq[uarte]rs. until we find our place in some village.'

This letter, Keithahn told Kumarappa, was being written

as we 'plough' thru the Gulf of Aden but we shall be in Karachi Friday and in Bombay next Monday or Tuesday we hope. The family will go on to Kodai by train. I shall follow with the 'Jeep'. We have had a good trip and look forward to a new period of work in India that ought to be with much less tension than heretofore.

There was also this postscript, combining anxiety with hope: 'Have you any suggestions as to our future work in India? We are free to do as we think best.'

Kumarappa sent back an encouraging reply: 'I am so glad to see you are back in India again. Yes, I am still at my post though it may seem a burning deck. . . . As soon as you settle down somewhere we shall see how best to utilise you.'[24]

India was soon to be free of British rule, and this American who was now Indian had come back to serve his adopted country.

V

It is time now to introduce the last of our renegades, the woman whom Dick Keithahn met at Gandhi's ashram in the 1930s. Her name was Catherine Mary Heilemann. Born in London in April 1901, she studied history, English, geography, French and German at school. At the age of fifteen, she left her studies prematurely to take a job as a clerk at a firm of merchants, Terry and Co., which imported goods from Australia.[25]

This Englishwoman came from a rather different class background than her compatriot Madeleine Slade/Mira Behn. Her father was a goldsmith, whereas Mira's was an admiral. Because his own parentage was German, Catherine's father was briefly detained during the First World War. This experience shaped the daughter decisively, and made her sceptical of British claims to moral superiority.[26]

After she began working, Catherine moved out of her parents' home into rented accommodation. The landlord was a broad-minded fellow, who also took in some Indian students. They told Catherine about Gandhi and his movement. Her exposure to the subcontinent deepened when, in 1927, she met an Indian named Mohan Singh Mehta. Mehta was a senior civil servant in the princely state of Udaipur. However, he had been educated in British India, and in his travels had met many nationalists and social reformers. He was particularly influenced by the work of the Servants of India Society, which had been founded by Gandhi's own mentor, Gopal Krishna Gokhale.

Speaking to Catherine, Mehta was impressed by her intelligence and determination, and told her that she needed a more fulfilling outlet for her abilities than merely being a clerk in a London firm. Since she was already interested in India, the idea of going there to work was planted in her mind.[27] In his travels through Europe, Mehta was greatly impressed by the Boy Scout movement, and thought of starting a school in Udaipur 'which would generally follow Baden-Powell's methods for developing children's character, self-reliance, knowledge, initiative, physical fitness and social outlook'.

In 1930, with some like-minded colleagues, Mohan Singh Mehta set up a school on the outskirts of Udaipur. It was called 'Vidya Bhavan', the Home of Knowledge. The school was co-educational from the start, which in the feudal surroundings of Rajasthan was 'indeed a bold and rather radical measure'. Outside the classroom, the school emphasized sports and the arts, and also physical labour, with a small farm and dairy on which students were encouraged to work.[28]

Once the school was up and running, Mehta asked Catherine Heilemann to join it. She sailed from Liverpool in January 1932. Landing at Bombay, she then travelled overland by train to Udaipur. Her first task at Vidya Bhavan was to set the accounts in order; after this was done, she began teaching English to the children. She liked the kids and her colleagues, and admired Mohan Singh Mehta. However, she found the social atmosphere in Udaipur depressing. The Maharaja and his retainers were treated with utter obsequiousness. The women were mostly in purdah. In her spare time she read more about Gandhi, and his work in education and for ending Untouchability. In the school holidays she toured the United Provinces, spending time in cities such as Banaras and Allahabad. As she later recalled: 'Escaping from the narrow-minded environment of the princely state and travelling in other parts of north India, it seemed as if I was at last breathing in fresh air, in the sense that there was a clearly visible restlessness for independence.'[29]

VI

In 1935, after three years at Vidya Bhavan, Catherine travelled across India to Gandhi's new headquarters in Wardha. She stayed a week, having several conversations with the Mahatma, and with his colleagues, such as Vinoba Bhave, who impressed her with his saintly asceticism, and the economist J. C. Kumarappa, who impressed her with his pragmatism. Altogether, she saw enough to judge that she must move from Udaipur into the ambit of the Mahatma and his world. Mohan Singh Mehta, sensing that the change of direction was inevitable, graciously did not stand in her way.

Her time in Udaipur had given Catherine invaluable experience of life in India, and also an alternate name, 'Sarala', Hindi for a person who is steadfast, resolute. From about 1936 she decided that she would henceforth only be known by her Indian name. By now, she had also acquired proficiency in reading and speaking Hindi.

In Wardha, Sarala worked under the guidance of a remarkable Gandhian couple, the Aryanayakams. The husband was a Tamil from Ceylon who had gone to Tagore's Santiniketan, where he fell in love with Asha Devi, daughter of a Bengali professor of philosophy. This couple then moved to Wardha, where Gandhi put them in charge of his education programmes. This renegade Englishwoman was assigned to work with them and the schools they helped run.

Sarala liked the work and adored the Aryanayakams, with whom she shared a hut in Sevagram. However, the hot climate of central India did not suit her. She had frequent bouts of dysentery and malaria. Gandhi sent her to recuperate at Poona, where his natur-opath friend Dinshaw Mehta ran a clinic. Mehta was able to cure her of dysentery, but the malaria kept recurring. Gandhi told her that she was welcome to return to Udaipur if she wished; but the idea did not appeal to her.

The kindly Asha Devi suggested that Sarala stop working for a year and simply rest in Sevagram. She needn't go to the schools, or do any household work either. 'We can give you plenty of milk, butter and vegetables and oranges', wrote Asha Devi to Sarala. For the sake of her health, they would even abandon the Gandhian practice of fending for themselves and hire a cook at Rs 10 a month. With that, wrote Asha Devi, there would be 'no longer the same strain'.[30]

In September 1939 war broke out in Europe. Sarala's father wrote to her from England, to ask how the 'present situation' was affecting her 'thought and work'. He worried that 'perhaps Russia has designs on India', but hoped 'the leading thought in India is towards democracy rather than dictatorship, or domination of any kind'. After speaking of how the air raids were affecting London, this letter by Sarala's father suddenly became very personal, saying:

It is nearly November – can you remember the climate of England in November, I know how this affects one's outlook? – mists and

darkness, though truly we have had some glorious days, and the sea
has been extraordinarily beautiful lately . . .

I had a very vivid dream this week that you were back in England.
How I came to dream this, right out of the blue, I don't know, but
I was terribly pleased and excited about it, and it seemed to be so
real that I've had it with me all week. It is so long ago now, but I
would dearly love to see you again. I wonder when? And where?[31]

Sarala's reply is unavailable. She must have reciprocated the love
and the sentiment, though she knew she might never see her father
again. She missed her family, but not, any longer, the country in
which she was born and raised. Her father still called her 'Katie',
but Sarala was now Indian, wholly Indian.

By the summer of 1941, by which time she had been five years
in Wardha, Gandhi, the Aryanayakams and Sarala all understood
that she must, if only for the sake of her health, find some other
place in India to live and work. But where? She sought the counsel
of one of the Mahatma's closest associates, Acharya Kripalani. A
professor of history turned patriot, Kripalani had taken Gandhi's
message of khadi across northern India. From his base in Meerut,
a town forty miles north of Delhi, he had helped establish spinning
and weaving centres in the United Provinces. One of these centres
was located in a village named Chanauda in the Kumaon hills.

Kripalani had never visited the ashram at Chanauda. But he knew
its founder, a Gujarati named Shantilal Trivedi; and thought the
bracing climate of the Himalaya would aid Sarala's recovery. Gandhi's
permission was sought, and granted. Sarala would take a year's
sabbatical from the plains to regain her health in the hills.[32]

Sarala reached the Chanauda Ashram in September 1941. At first
she merely observed what its members were doing, but as her health
improved she started taking part in its activities, particularly spinning
and weaving. When she felt fully recovered she accompanied Trivedi
on trips to the interior hills, studying traditional crafts and sourcing
wool. She loved the beauty of the mountains and warmed to the
people, and decided that this was where she would settle for good.[33]

Sarala liked Trivedi and his colleagues, but she strongly wished
for an ashram of her own. In her travels in Kumaon she discovered

Kausani, a village with glorious views of the snow-capped peaks. Gandhi himself had spent a fortnight in Kausani in 1929, revising his interpretations of the Gita. The views and the associations encouraged Sarala to base herself here. She had made the acquaintance of a Government official named Poornanand Sanwal, who was sympathetic to the nationalist cause. Sanwal had an unoccupied house on a hill outside Kausani, where he wanted to start a school in memory of his recently deceased wife. He offered its use to Sarala, and told her she could do what she wished with it. He had already renamed the premises Lakshmi Ashram after his late wife.

On 5 August 1942, Sarala wrote Sanwal a long letter in English. 'Since you have been kind enough to allow me the use of your house to live and work in', she said, 'I feel that it is only fair that you should know something of me and of the work which I feel it will be possible to do here, especially in these unsettled times.' She told her benefactor of her experiences in Udaipur and Wardha, and why because of her ill health she had to come to the hills. Her recent travels through Kumaon with Shantilal Trivedi, she said, had convinced her that 'I should stay fixed and concentrate on work in one place, not dissipate my energies by various activities.'

She went on:

I feel that the best return for effort expended can be drawn from work among the young, for they are more easily influenced and their impressions are more lasting. I therefore wish to create an atmosphere here in which the children of the surrounding villages will come to me freely and feel at home. I was trying at Chanauda to get in touch with the children through the primary schools, where I played games with them and gave them talks. They also came to me to learn knitting, which I am trying to introduce as a subsidiary industry. I hope to continue these activities here. Local workers are pressing me to open a girls' school, but my knowledge of Hindi and my deficiency in the background of Indian culture prevent me – also the fact that this would be a full-time job, preventing me from undertaking more general activities. I have suggested that if six girls of suitable age are ready, they may live with me from next session, and attend the upper or high schools here. I would try to supplement the deficiencies of official education – this little hostel would be self-supporting in the sense that the girls would do all their own work – they would learn to work cooperatively, to organise their time. I would contribute to the joint family in kind and not in cash. When one or two of these girls have passed at least to class VII, we may open a basic school with agriculture and housecraft as the basic crafts.

Sarala's letter to Sanwal continued:

Your garden I believe opens the way for agricultural experiments . . . I should like to experiment with the making of jams and marmalades, and the drying of fruits, and to explore markets. If this proves profitable, it might be organised on a cooperative basis. . . . In course of time, if this developed, cooperative marketing might be applied to other produce also, ensuring a fair deal to producer and consumer, and eliminating middle[man] profits.

Work in the garden and amongst the children should bring me into contact with the local women, for whose hard lot I feel a burning sympathy, although I cannot yet see clearly whether, or how, I can help them. I have sometimes spent nights in the villages here, and it has been indeed a humbling experience.

So far as expenses are concerned, I have a small income of £14 per annum which, so long as it arrives regularly, is sufficient for my personal needs. The Gandhi Ashram are kindly placing at my disposal for the present year Rs.100/- for the purchase of a little equipment for fruit processing, a small dispensary, a children's library and reading room, and incidental expenditure. I feel however, that in the long run [the ashram] must be self-supporting or, failing that, must depend on local support, and that every effort should be made in this direction. . . .

I feel that there is nothing in the above suggestions which can be found fault with by the officials, or which can compromise you as the owner of the house. It has always been Gandhiji's wish that constructive workers, and more especially Europeans, should not take part in direct political activities. I should naturally wish to follow his wishes, and continue quietly with constructive work, as long as self-respect allows me to do so. Only if the situation became intolerable,

as once was the case with Mira Ben, should I deliberately court arrest
– or if asked to take active part in any direct war effort.[34]

Three days later, in distant Bombay, Gandhi called for the British
to Quit India, and the last line of Sarala's letter to Sanwal turned
out to be prophetic.

VII

As earlier noted, the arrest of Gandhi and other major Congress
leaders in August 1942 spurred protests in many parts of India. In
Almora district, militant satyagrahis attacked state forest offices, and
damaged a bridge. The Commissioner of Kumaon convinced himself
that the Gandhi Ashram in Chanauda was behind the troubles. On
20 August, the Commissioner came to the ashram with sixty
European soldiers, and demanded that the premises be shut down.
Seven khadi workers were arrested, as was the veteran Gandhian
Shantilal Trivedi. The popular protests continued regardless. On the
night of the 30th, a resin depot at Totashiling was burned. In early
September, two forest bungalows were destroyed. Now the police
came down hard, arresting anyone with the remotest connection to
the Congress.[35]

With hundreds of their men in jail, the village economy of Almora
came to a standstill. Sarala had stayed aloof from the protests, while
going around giving succour to the families of freedom fighters. She
helped with food, medicines, litigation, and jail visits. The District
Magistrate did not arrest her, because she was a lone Englishwoman
perhaps, but deputed a revenue official to keep a watch on her
movements. He sat all day in a shop at the bottom of the hill on
which the Lakshmi Ashram lay. Sarala trekked at night from village
to village, carrying messages and money, returning before daybreak
to escape the official's attention.[36]

Eventually, exasperated by her movements and angered by her
sympathies, in December 1943 the District Magistrate issued a notice
to 'Miss C. M. Heilemann' asking her to return at once to the
Lakshmi Ashram from wherever she was. The order confined her

henceforth to within a two-mile radius of the ashram and forbade her from any communication with 'absconding persons' (i.e. protesters still at large) or with those who had been released from prison. To this restraining order Sarala wrote a spirited reply:

Dear Friend,

I have received your signed notice restricting my movements under Section 26 of the Defence of India Rules. . . .

My friend, to me humanity is one, regardless of colour, creed or politics. If the government wishes to punish, and punish heavily, those who have been justly convicted of rebellion, I have nothing to say. Those who rebel in time of crisis must be prepared to face the consequences. I cannot, however, sit still in comfort in Lakshmi Ashram while suffering, sickness and poverty abound in the neighbourhood. In this matter, I must obey the dictates of conscience and not of the British Government.

I returned yesterday to Kausani in accordance with your instructions. During the course of the next few days, I shall obey the first call which comes to me to attend the sick and suffering or the destitute, whatever may be the distance from Lakshmi Ashram. You may take such action as you choose in the matter. What meaning has restricted freedom to enjoy the beauty and peace of the hills when suffering abounds? Better enforced confinement within the walls of jail. Please rest assured that I shall bear no grudge or ill-will in any way, whatever may be the action you decide to take. We must all do our duty as we see it, loyally and honestly, to the cause which conscience dictates.[37]

Three weeks later, Sarala wrote once more to the District Magistrate, informing him that

in the circumstance, I do not feel justified in sitting indefinitely in Lakshmi Ashram with my goods and chattels up, and normal work at a standstill, but propose to carry out the programme of winter touring which I had previously planned. Limited freedom preventing one from carrying out that what according to one's conception is one's duty is useless, and as I said before, in this matter I must 'render unto Caesar that which is Caesar's and unto God that which is God's'.

Having, in proper Gandhian style, stated her intention to break the law in advance, Sarala told the District Magistrate: 'May you be guided rightly in these treacherous days, [and] not become the innocent means of exciting further injustice, mistrust and ill-feeling.' This last prayer was not about herself, but about the hill people as a whole. The British Gandhian was urging the British Raj to treat its subjects with compassion and in the spirit of service.[38]

Thus provoked, the District Magistrate had Sarala arrested, and sent her off to Almora Jail. She was charged with breaching the peace. Produced in court, Sarala issued a statement that recounted her early life, how she came to India, and worked in Udaipur and Wardha before moving to the hills. In her decade in this country, she told the court, 'I have always scrupulously obeyed Mahatma Gandhi's instructions to his fellow workers from overseas to refrain from political activities and to cooperate only in work of social reform (seva) and village industry (khadi and gramudyog).'

But then in September 1942 all the workers of the Gandhi ashram in Chanauda were arrested. So were many others. Touring the villages, Sarala was

> touched to the heart by the condition in the homes of men in jail. With the breadwinner gone, in many cases the land to be auctioned, women and children [were] half demented with fear and anxiety, their health rapidly deteriorating due to semi-starvation and anxiety, no-one to care for them in illness or arrange for medicines or treatment. It was obvious, whether the men were guilty or innocent, the women and children were bearing the real punishment.

This, said Sarala, was the context in which she began raising money for food and supplies, and for medicines, while also helping with drafting appeals for prisoners. Sarala believed that none of these activities were 'illegal or subversive'. As she laconically put it, 'I have never heard that it is contrary to the law of the land to arrange for the supply of simple and harmless medicines in villages.' So, when the order restraining her to the Lakshmi Ashram came, she chose to defy it. As she told the court, 'the only alternative left to me as a self-respecting citizen of a free country which claims at present to be waging war for right and liberty against the forces of oppression, was to commit civil disobedience and contravene the order.'

Sarala's statement ended: 'It appears that in this country at present, the price of spiritual liberty is physical bondage. I prefer the path of physical bondage and therefore pray the court to sentence me to the maximum punishment on this charge.'[39]

The judge hearing the case was a kindly hillman, who gave her the minimum possible sentence; three months in prison.

VIII

While Sarala was in jail, the district authorities warned Poornanand Sanwal of dire consequences if he were to continue to host the anti-colonial Englishwoman on his premises. After she was released in May, Sarala heard of the intimidation of Sanwal, and at once wrote a combative letter to the District Magistrate, berating him for seeking 'to apply critical pressure' on a good man seeking to honour his wife's memory. She also told the official that 'you may, by dint of these indirect methods, succeed in making me a homeless wanderer in these hills, but you will not coerce me into desisting from any activities which my conscience dictates to me'.[40]

By the time Sarala was released, Gandhi was out of jail too. He was in ill health, and devastated by the recent death of his wife Kasturba. Sarala now decided to devote her energies to raising money for the newly established Kasturba Gandhi Memorial Fund. She travelled all over Kumaon, while staying away from Kausani, so as to protect Sanwal from harassment.

Writing to Gandhi in August 1944, Sarala remarked that there was 'great demoralization among Congress workers in the district', because of state intimidation and the absence of their leader Shantilal Trivedi who was in prison. She continued:

The further one comes into the interior of the hill districts, the more
one is confronted with this general feeling of frustration & helplessness, which importantly is not confined to the general public, but is
only too prevalent amongst Congress workers & leaders. I am firmly
convinced that the only way to combat this is by bringing sincere
reforms, on however small a scale, into our own daily lives, in accordance with the constructive programme, as the basis of further building,
but mine is a lone voice in the wilderness. I miss Shanti[lal Trivedi]'s
support and companionship. Now is the time for sincere & honest
workers with unwavering faith in non-violence & the constructive
programme, & it is a great pity that a combination of circumstances
prevent his immediate return to the district, to which he has given
so many years of devoted service, & in which his whole heart lies.
His sincerity & whole heartedness have earned him real love &
respect, and he has a great influence here.

In a postscript to this letter, Sarala wrote that the Indian magistrate
who had given her a far less stiff sentence than what the British
officials wanted, was 'fairly promptly (and vindictively?) transferred
to Lucknow for the heat!'. Also, Poornanand Sanwal, who gave her
a house to live in, had been called by the authorities and 'been firmly
asked to give me orders to quit'. Sanwal had planned to start a trust
called the Kasturba Mahila Seva Mandal and make Sarala the secretary. The trust hoped to run a residential school for girls. With these
threats from the state, it was not clear if this project would get off
the ground.

Sarala told Gandhi of her own immediate plans, now that she
was out of prison. These were

to wander in the villages with a pack, until I am stopped. It is incred-
ible to what underhand means [the officials] will resort, when they
have the sweeping powers of the ordinances in their hands, in order
to see that the last ounce of suffering & loneliness will be extracted
from innocent women & children. My recent tour in the villages
around Kausani [before her arrest] was a very depressing experience,
but now that the 'second round' has opened, the feeling of frustration
is gone, & I can again hold up my head as a self-respecting citizen.[41]

For a whole year Sarala roamed the hills, a pack with her meagre belongings on her back. She stayed in the homes of poor peasants and rich merchants, being treated with warmth and affection everywhere. And with generosity too – with most people she asked contributing to the Kasturba Gandhi Memorial Fund, the individual donations ranging from a few annas to a few thousand rupees.

IX

In her fundraising in memory of Gandhi's wife, Sarala was greatly aided by a patriotic merchant in Kumaon, Mohan Lal Sah. He gave generously from his own pocket, while introducing her to other possible donors. By September 1944, Sarala had collected Rs 45,000 for the Kasturba Gandhi Memorial Fund, a very impressive sum. But then she ran afoul again of the Raj. An elderly ascetic she knew jokingly said to her, 'You ought to be ashamed of yourself. Just think how badly that British district judge must be feeling, that everyone in his district was obeying him except one white woman!'[42] The District Magistrate soon issued an order to arrest her. This time she was produced before a British judge, and sentenced to a full year in prison. In Almora Jail, she was visited by the DM, who said he would have her released and sent back to Mr Sanwal's charming house in Kausani, on condition that she stopped her travels. She refused to these terms. Angered by the rebuff, the official then had her transferred to the burning plains, to a jail in Lucknow.

In this, her second term in prison, Sarala read works of Hindi literature to her illiterate fellow prisoners. Intellectual companionship was provided by Sucheta, wife of Acharya Kripalani, who was also in Lucknow Jail. Sucheta 'used to continually talk of all her experiences while she was underground, and used to describe just how easy it was to deceive the police'.[43]

On her release in September 1945, Sarala decided she must first see Gandhi before deciding what to do next. The Mahatma was then in Dinshaw Mehta's Nature Cure Clinic, outside Poona. Sarala changed several trains to get there, and on seeing Gandhi immediately touched his feet. He responded by affectionately thumping her on the back. She accompanied Gandhi on his walks, and during the day used the intervals between his other commitments to seek his counsel about her future plans.[44]

Also in Poona with Gandhi at this time were the Kripalanis. When Sarala told her former jail-mate that she was thinking of starting a school for girls in Kausani, Sucheta asked how much money she thought she required. Rs 3,000 answered Sarala. Now Kripalani came into the conversation, and said a public-spirited Parsi had started a fund in memory of his recently deceased sister, and had offered Kripalani Rs 10,000 from that. Both the Kripalanis were of the view that 'Sarala Behn is the most suitable person to see good use is made of this money'.[45]

From Poona, Gandhi went back to Sevagram. Sarala followed him, and spent a few weeks intensively studying the teaching methods of the ashram school. When it was time for her to leave, she called on the Mahatma, and placed in front of him a photograph of himself with Kasturba. Sarala said she wanted him to sign it, and then she would take it back to Kausani, to be displayed in the school she planned to start. Gandhi agreed to sign the photo, adding however that it should act not as inspiration but caution, for he had made many mistakes himself when he was young. She then stepped down to touch his feet, to receive once more that friendly thump on the back.[46]

When they met in Poona, Acharya Kripalani had teased Sarala for going to Sevagram immediately on being released from prison, an arduous cross-country journey of more than two days. Could not, he asked, Sarala have first come to see him at Meerut, which was just a few hours away from Lucknow by train, and in the same province besides? It was a tease, not a scold; but it made Sarala feel bad, since it was Kripalani who had been instrumental in sending her to Kumaon, and who had now raised money for her new school-in-the-making. When she was back in Kausani she wrote Kripalani a letter of contrition which is lost. But we do have Kripalani's quite wonderful reply:

My Dear Sarla,

It was a delight to have your letter. Of course I was disappointed that you did not come immediately to see me. And that is because I was led to understand that by you when I met you in jail. Unfortunately Sucheta too had the same impression. . . . But you exaggerate the importance of my complaint. By this time I must have grown used to the neglect of your tribe. It is nothing unusual. And then the old man you see attracts everybody of your tribe. Naturally every prophet has done so in the past. One cannot afford to compete with him. Anyway that is past history. If you want to meet me the best time will be immediately. The whole executive committee of the ashram will be here from the 21st to the 23rd. If you can reach that time by any chance it will be nice for then we can check out the woollen work too. You can meet everybody. I suppose that you have already met everybody who counts in my ashram. . . .

. . . I can offer no guidance to people beyond telling them to be in particular places. The rest they have to do themselves. You have found your way into the hearts of the Paharis [hillfolk]. You could not have succeeded better if you had done even more tangible work, and more tangible work is easy for you.[47]

X

A decade after their first meeting in Wardha, Sarala Behn and Dick Keithahn met for dinner in late 1947, in Delhi, at the home of a mutual friend. As Sarala later recalled, Keithahn 'had recently returned from his exile in America, now much aged, and I should not have recognised this white-haired friend, looking taller and leaner than ever in his *khadi loongi*. He enquired "How was it that they did not send you out?" and was highly tickled by my reply, "Because they put me in".'[48]

PART II
SEEING OUT THE RAJ

CHAPTER 9

The Second Innings of
B. G. Horniman

In January 1926, Benjamin Guy Horniman returned to India after almost seven years spent unwillingly in England. His friends and admirers in Bombay planned a grand welcome for him. He was taken in open procession from the Victoria Terminus to the city headquarters of the Congress in Girgaum, via Crawford Market and Bhuleshwar. At Congress Hall a large public meeting was held, presided over by his fellow writer and fellow Indian patriot, the poet Sarojini Naidu.[1]

In Horniman's absence, the *Bombay Chronicle* newspaper had first been edited by another Englishman, Marmaduke Pickthall, who was more interested in religion than in journalism. A scholar of Arabic, he converted to Islam and eventually left the paper for the life of a wandering mystic and scholar. A brilliant and effervescent young Indian, S. A. Brelvi, stepped into his place. However, now that Horniman was back, the board chose to make him the editor once more, with Brelvi gracefully accepting to work under him.

On resuming the editor's chair at the *Chronicle*, Horniman declared, 'I am not changed. I am not aged.' In the first editorial he wrote in this, his second stint in the job, he assured readers that the newspaper would remain the 'voice of the National Spirit of India'.[2] To further demonstrate that his political commitment to the Congress was resolutely intact, Horniman agreed to stand for election to the City Corporation. In a campaign speech he is reported to have said,

'I am a man of many weaknesses but remember my good points.' The electors did, and he won his seat comfortably.[3]

On 2 March, Horniman was due to preside over a Congress meeting in the central Bombay locality of Matunga. He did not come, the reason conveyed by another speaker, who said the editor had just been sacked by the management of the *Bombay Chronicle*. Cries of 'shame, shame' rent the air. Two days later Horniman gave an interview to the Associated Press, where he said that, when he had recently resumed the job he had been forced to vacate seven years previously, he had urged the management to accept two conditions: that he would have full freedom to hire and fire members of the editorial staff, and that he would himself serve on the board of directors. He had insisted on the latter as he had 'such a long and varied experience in the conduct of newspapers both on the editorial and management sides'. Horniman noted that it was he who, in his first stint as editor, had succeeded in having the *Chronicle* 'firmly established as the leading nationalist organ'.

The management said they would consider these requests. When Horniman pressed the point in correspondence, they terminated his services. Asked what he would do next, Horniman said that while he had offers to edit papers elsewhere in India, he had no intention of leaving the city he had made his own. 'I believe the people of Bombay have confidence in me', he said, 'and I should be betraying their trust if I were not to make every possible effort to establish a new organ of opinion here through which I can resume my relations with the Bombay public.'[4]

On 11 March there was a meeting held at the Gaiety Theatre to protest against the dismissal of B. G. Horniman from the editorship of the *Bombay Chronicle*. The meeting was chaired by B. T. Desai, who spoke briefly, whereupon Horniman took the stage. He began by speaking of the *Chronicle* not as a mere newspaper but as a public institution, which it had been 'so regarded on account of the warm enthusiasm with which the public received it in the early days, on account of the warm enthusiasm with which the public supported it all through its life, at any rate, I can say, up to the time that I had to leave India'. Now, so soon after his return, he had to leave the newspaper. Horniman said:

When I arrived here a month ago and was received with such generosity and affection I never expected that I should have so soon to stand on a public platform in this city and explain to a public audience that I had severed my connection with this journal to which, I assure you, I have always been as devoted as I could possibly be.

At this meeting, Horniman said that

when I left India, not of my own free will, I left the 'Bombay Chronicle' in a supreme position, among the organs of public opinion in this country. I left it as a journal whose name was known not only widely over the whole of India as a champion of Indian interests, but a journal that was known in other countries all over the world.

He meaningfully added that in 1919 the paper had shown a substantial profit of Rs 60,000.

On 16 January 1926 – less than a week after taking over as editor of the *Bombay Chronicle* once more – Horniman met with the newspaper's board of directors. The meeting was held at the city's grandest establishment, the Taj Mahal Hotel. Here they agreed to terms, which included that 'the policy of the paper to be as heretofore a strong nationalist policy in accordance with the resolutions of the Indian National Congress'; a salary for the editor of Rs 18,000 per annum; appointments and dismissals of editorial staff to be in the hands of the editor; and the editor to be on the board of directors.

Horniman joined on these terms, but without there being a formal agreement signed by both sides. As soon as he resumed his duties as editor, however, the Managing Director (MD) of the holding company, Indian Newspapers Co., N. H. Belgaumwalla, told Horniman that it was better they waited for a month or two to see 'how we were going to pull along together', before inviting the editor to join the board. The MD sent Horniman a letter asking him to confirm terms previously agreed on, except a seat on the board. He refused. Several letters were exchanged between Horniman and Belgaumwalla on the subject, with no ground being yielded by either party.

Now, in this public meeting of his supporters, Horniman charged
Belgaumwalla of displaying 'very great rudeness' towards him. Then
he spoke of his future plans. He was, he said, 'wedded to this City
of Bombay', since he had 'always been shown so much splendid
support by the people of Bombay and have always been shown so
much generosity and affection by them'. So, out of a sense of duty
to them he wished to start a new newspaper for the city, 'a people's
paper, a paper to be devoted to the interests of the people and
nothing else'.

Horniman was clearly consumed by anger and bitterness. So, after
speaking briefly of his plans, he returned to the matter of his departure from his beloved *Chronicle*. He asked his crowd of fans:

> Why, I ask you, are these men of whom none perhaps with one
> exception has any professional knowledge of newspaper work and
> who know nothing about newspaper machinery afraid of me? Why
> should they be afraid of one man with 30 years' experience of news-
> paper management and newspaper editorship? Why should they be
> afraid of his coming and sitting on the Board of Directors with them
> and putting in his poor little voice as to what should or should not
> be done?

Horniman did not answer these questions directly, speaking darkly
of people on the *Chronicle*'s board who were 'only representative
of capitalist interests'. He now wanted to start

> a paper that will work for the people of India, for the people of
> Bombay, shall work to redress every kind of grievance, shall work to
> see that the people, the poorer people, of this City shall be raised
> from their miserable conditions and allowed to lead healthy respect-
> able and happy lives, a paper which will work for that and for that
> alone . . .[5]

At this meeting at the Gaiety Theatre there was no one to tell the
other, or management's, side of the story. This was that with the
collapse of Gandhi's Non-Cooperation movement, Bombay's influential Moderates were once more reasserting themselves over the

newspaper. The *Chronicle* had been started by Moderates, among them the great Sir Pherozeshah Mehta. Gandhi's advent and rise to prominence had swayed the paper (and its editor above all) to the Extremist side of the national movement. But now that Gandhi had come out of jail, chastened, and had retreated to his ashram in Sabarmati, the 'swaraj' (freedom) he had promised in one year nowhere in sight, those who sought political reform by incremental means were once more coming to the fore. The prominent Moderate M. R. Jayakar was a director of the board that ran the *Bombay Chronicle*, and people like him wanted the paper to return to the old, non-adversarial relationship with the Raj with which it had originally begun, and which the militancy of Gandhi had disrupted. In this endeavour B. G. Horniman was evidently a stumbling block. For Horniman's deportation and enforced (as well as unbearably long) exile had only confirmed him in his radicalism. To have him back as editor was to acknowledge the force of public pressure and Horniman's own stature; but to have him on the board of directors was evidently a step too far.

II

In the third week of April 1926, B. G. Horniman announced that a new company, the National Newspapers India Co. Ltd, had been registered for the purpose of publishing a new 'nationalist daily paper' in Bombay. The paid-up capital of the firm was Rs 300,000. On its board of directors sat, apart from Horniman himself, the prominent nationalists Sarojini Naidu, K. F. Nariman, and Umar Sobhani, and the gifted young journalist Pothan Joseph, who had chosen to depart the *Chronicle* when his mentor did.[6]

The paper was called the *Indian National Herald*. In October 1926, Horniman wrote to Gandhi asking for a message for the inaugural issue. He told the Mahatma that his new paper 'will be strongly nationalist and in support of the Indian National Congress'. Gandhi wrote back saying that he couldn't send a message, since 'the increasing bitterness [between different groups of nationalists] has made me sad. Multiplication of newspapers multiplies bitterness.

Of late, therefore, I have ceased to send messages to newspapers, especially new ones.' He told Horniman that he had recently refused to send messages for new newspapers in the Punjab and in the UP, adding: 'If I could I would dissuade you from your enterprise at this juncture and feel I had done a true friend's duty.'[7]

Horniman was committed to going ahead, with or without the Mahatma's approval. The first issue of the *Indian National Herald* appeared on Saturday 23 October. The paper announced that it would 'advocate the cause of Indian freedom and the equitable distribution of the wealth of the country among the people producing it'. While deeply committed to the nationalist cause, Horniman's new organ stood more to the left than the *Chronicle*, opening its columns more readily to Communists such as Philip Spratt, several of whose essays it published.

In November, elections were held for the Bombay Legislative Council. Horniman was one of the star campaigners for the Congress. A reporter present at one of his talks remarked that 'the burden of his song was: "Vote for the Congress candidate even though the Congress nominee happens to be a lamp-post. Don't vote for the Responsivist [i.e. the Moderate] – however cultured and intellectual he may be, he is sure to betray the cause of the country."' Horniman then launched into a sharp attack on the Responsivist leader M. R. Jayakar, a director of the *Chronicle* who had played a part in his dismissal.[8]

Horniman brought to the *Indian National Herald* some of the techniques of the tabloid press in Great Britain. Thus, towards the end of 1926, the editor asked readers to choose the ten greatest living Indians. The readers sent back postcards listing ten compatriots each of them greatly admired. On 21 December 1926, Horniman's paper reported the consolidated results. Gandhi had by far the most votes (19,308), followed by Rabindranath Tagore (7,391), Jagadish Chandra Bose (5,954), Motilal Nehru (4,035), Aurobindo Ghose (3,907), P. C. Ray (3,524), Sarojini Naidu (3,519), Madan Mohan Malaviya (2,618), Lala Lajpat Rai (2,568), and V. S. Srinivasa Sastri (1,516).

Accompanying the results of the poll were some paragraphs of text, written possibly by Horniman (or perhaps by his colleague

Pothan Joseph). This offered short biographies of these 'ten greatest living Indians': Tagore the poet, philosopher and interpreter of the East; Aurobindo the patriot and mystic; Sarojini Naidu the Nightingale of India; Ray and Bose the country's leading scientists; and the rest politicians of various persuasions, Congress, Swarajists, liberals. The article concluded by saying that 'every sphere of life has received its meed'.

This last line was excessively self-congratulatory. For one thing, the ten 'greatest Indians' were all upper-caste Hindus, of whom at least five were Brahmins. There was only one woman. There was no Muslim, and no Christian, Sikh or Parsi either. It is also striking that there were as many as five Bengalis in the list, a reflection of the prominence in national life that the province then enjoyed. It was notable that Aurobindo Ghose ranked so high. He had been out of public life for more than a decade, living quietly in exile in Pondicherry. Yet many middle-class Indians apparently yearned for him to abandon spirituality and return to politics.[9]

Such exercises are now very nearly ubiquitous, but this was almost certainly the first such poll ever conducted in India. It was a mark of the editor's flair and daring, but unfortunately market trends as a whole did not favour his new venture. The *Times of India* and the *Bombay Chronicle* were already well established; and there was, it seems, no room for a third daily English newspaper in a city where a small minority read or spoke the language.

From the time of its founding, the *Indian National Herald* struggled to find a readership. Unlike in the *Chronicle*, here the editor had also to double up as finance manager, and keeping regular and scrupulous accounts was never Horniman's forte.[10] In 1928 the paper folded up. Soon afterwards Horniman started a new paper, a weekly this time, called, in fact, the *Weekly Herald*. It was funded by a Punjabi named Dewan Singh Maftoon who was active in the All India States Peoples' Conference, a body floated by the Congress to canvass for greater rights for the subjects of princely states. The paper was headquartered in Delhi; loath to leave Bombay, Horniman commuted to and fro between the political capital of India and its financial (and cultural, and sporting) capital.

In August 1930 the *Weekly Herald* published a summary of a

report of a committee of the All India States Peoples' Conference, chaired by the liberal journalist C. Y. Chintamani, and including the industrialist L. R. Tairsee and the social worker A. V. Thakkar among its members. The report severely indicted the Maharaja of Patiala for his misrule, speaking of, among other things, 'inhuman tortures, illegal arrest and confinement and high-handed confiscation of property', the 'ruinous consequences of [the] Maharaja's Shikars', the 'tyranny of *begar* or forced labour' and 'revenue and irrigation grievances'. It further alleged that the Agent to the Governor General for the Punjab States, J. A. O. FitzPatrick, had whitewashed the Maharaja's misdemeanours in a report to the Government.

The Maharaja of Patiala was then Chancellor of the Chamber of Princes, and in that capacity was due to travel to the first Round Table Conference to be held in London. In its issue of 16 August 1930, along with a summary of the All India States Peoples' Conference indictment, the *Weekly Herald* printed a cartoon entitled 'Patiala Gets a New Coat for his Trip to London', which insinuated that the Maharaja had paid FitzPatrick Rs 25 lakhs for the report that exonerated him of misrule. FitzPatrick thereupon wrote an angry letter to the Government urging that legal action be taken against Horniman and Dewan Singh Maftoon. The Government advised against it, and the matter was dropped. Meanwhile, the *Weekly Herald* folded up.[11]

Once more out of a job, once again Horniman found one. The editor's prestige was so high that a series of well-heeled Indians hoping that a newspaper would further their ambitions were happy to recruit him. The next patron (whose name and business has not come down to us) was based in Lahore, the capital of Punjab. He began, with Horniman's help, a paper called the *Daily Herald*, with the editor popping in and out of the head office from his own home in Bombay.

In July 1931, Horniman was travelling in a train from Bombay to Delhi, en route to Lahore. When he entered the second-class compartment for which he had a valid ticket, he found that it was chock-full with ladies in purdah. So as not to embarrass them, he moved to the next compartment, which, as it turned out, was reserved for first-class passengers. A ticket inspector (of what race or religion is not recorded) accosted him, and demanded a penalty of Rs 48. Horniman said he would pay the difference between the first-class and second-class fare, which was a few rupees, not as many as 48. The case went to court, where the British judge (named Barlee) agreed with the inspector, ruling that 'there is nothing in the Act to show that he can, in any circumstances, travel by first class on a second class ticket'. So Horniman had to pay up.[12]

III

As B. G. Horniman was editing a succession of newspapers whose names all ended with the suffix *Herald*, the *Bombay Chronicle* was once more shuffling off its Moderate coils and becoming militantly anti-British. For Gandhi had now come out of his ashram retreat and re-entered the field of anti-colonial politics. In 1928 the Congress led demonstrations against the Simon Commission, in 1929 the Congress promised Indians *Purna Swaraj*, full independence, and in 1930 the Congress inspired by Gandhi organized breaches of the Salt Laws all over the country.

From 1928 onwards, the *Bombay Chronicle* lined itself solidly behind Gandhi. It supported and endorsed whatever Gandhi said, whatever Gandhi did. The paper's editor since Horniman's departure had been Syed Abdullah Brelvi, of whom it was said that he 'was monogamous in his loyalties and it was always the Congress for him'.[13] Brelvi revered Gandhi, going so far as to call him 'the truest nation-builder since [the Mughal Emperor] Akbar's time', and adding, 'of the two [he] will prove to be the greater'.[14]

A thoroughgoing nationalist, with an abiding commitment to Hindu–Muslim unity, Brelvi admired Gandhi and the Congress so much that he was even prepared to go to jail on their behalf. In early 1932, the editor of the *Bombay Chronicle* was arrested in the Civil Disobedience Movement and sentenced to a long term in prison. By now, the *Daily Herald* of Lahore had folded up, and Horniman was once more without a job. The directors of the *Bombay Chronicle* now wisely let bygones be bygones and asked him to step into the breach left by Brelvi's arrest. At this stage, the paper needed an experienced hand to guide it, and who better than the editor who had made the paper so famous?

In July 1932, Horniman wrote a long article in the *Chronicle* on the prospects for Indian freedom. He launched an excoriating attack on the Secretary of State for India, Sir Samuel Hoare, accusing him of being 'politically dishonest', of 'abandoning principle' and 'breaking pledges', of having 'a mission to crush the Indian National Congress, the most influential and representative political body in the country'. At the same time, Horniman added that 'India must look to herself for her salvation, and the first step to be taken is one towards a reconciliation of the differences between Nationalists and the dissident Mussalmans'. The Congress, he wrote, should take the lead in forging a compact between Hindus and Muslims, which was the most pressing issue facing the country.[15]

Through most of 1932 and 1933 S. A. Brelvi was in prison, and so was Mahatma Gandhi. We don't know what the former was doing – reading, and teaching fellow prisoners, most probably – but the latter's activities in jail have been minutely recorded for posterity. Through 1932 and 1933, Gandhi was obsessed with the question of Untouchability. During the Second Round Table Conference in London in 1931, Gandhi had been strongly challenged by the emerging leader of the Depressed Classes, B. R. Ambedkar. Gandhi wanted to afford special reservation to the Depressed Classes within the Hindu fold; Ambedkar wanted them to vote in separate electorates altogether.

The British sided with Ambedkar. They announced that in elections to Indian Legislatures, a certain number of seats would be reserved for the Depressed Classes; and that voting for these seats would not be open to caste Hindus. Gandhi saw this as a malign effort to separate one category of Hindus from another, and went on a fast-unto-death in prison in protest. The fast compelled Ambedkar to yield, and a 'Poona Pact' was signed, whereby many more seats were allocated to the Depressed Classes, as part of a joint electorate with other Hindus.

The debate about separate versus combined electorates in general, and between Gandhi and Ambedkar in particular, has spawned a vast and ever proliferating literature, to which this writer has contributed

more than his fair share.[16] What remains of relevance to this book
are the views at the time of B. G. Horniman. The stand-in editor of
the *Bombay Chronicle*, while not unsympathetic to Ambedkar, was
more on Gandhi's side. So much so that the Mahatma, in jail, is
reported in July 1932 as telling his secretary Mahadev Desai that
'Horniman was nowadays writing very well indeed'.[17]

In September 1932, shortly before Gandhi commenced his fast,
Horniman wrote that the British Prime Minister's 'Communal
Award' was 'designed to inspire the minds of "untouchables" with
a spirit of antagonism and hostility to their brethren of the Hindu
community and petrify the sense of separation with which they
now be obsessed into a perpetual phenomenon in India's future
polity'.[18] Ten days later, after the fast had been concluded, Horniman
argued that the agreement between Gandhi and Ambedkar did not
mean that the battle to end caste prejudice had ended. To the
contrary, it had just begun. A pact had been signed, but, as the
editor remarked,

> for those who work in the field of social and religious reform there
> is still a stupendous task to be attacked and completed, in the eman-
> cipation of the untouchables from their outcaste status from birth to
> death – their right to take water from the wells, to enter the temples
> of their faith, for their children to sit in the schools with those of
> other castes and communities, and the right to live and move and
> have their being on equal terms with their fellow-men. All this will
> not be the work of a day or a year. The battle against orthodoxy will
> still be a hard one, and it will be prolonged.[19]

In the same month, September 1932, Horniman spoke with equal
insight (and greater authority) on a very different topic altogether,
the freedom of the press. Addressing an audience of students in
Bombay, Horniman proclaimed that 'an ideal newspaper' would be
one 'that is absolutely independent of all business considerations in
the way of advertisements or anything of that kind'. In the West ads
had become more and more important, resulting 'in daily newspapers
being practically at the mercy of advertisers'. He hoped things would
never come to such a pass in India.

Horniman told the students that he would 'not recommend journalism as a career to anybody who was anxious to advance himself materially in life'. On the other hand, 'for a man who had ideals in life, especially for any young man in India who wanted to serve national interests', he would strongly recommend journalism, 'because it was through the public press more than anything else that the interests of the country were protected and the national cause was ably advanced towards the goal which India desired'.[20]

IV

In October 1933, S. A. Brelvi was released from prison. B. G. Horniman graciously vacated the editor's seat for him. While the Indian was to resume editing the flagship newspaper, the *Bombay Chronicle*, the management now decided to start an evening tabloid and ask the renegade Englishman to edit that instead. The city had expanded rapidly northwards, and every day tens of thousands of people commuted in from the suburbs by train to work in the offices and factories in the heart of the city. There was, for the first time, a market for an evening paper on the model of London and other European cities, and this new paper, to be called the *Bombay Sentinel*, would meet it.

The paper was launched in 1934. The masthead on the front page had 'All The News' on top, followed by, in much bigger type 'The Bombay Sentinel'. Between the 'Bombay' and the 'Sentinel' was the paper's logo, which was of a man with a turban on a horse, his left hand shading his head for a better view. Below the paper's name came a line reading, 'Edited by B. G. Horniman'.

The format of the paper was innovative. The first page carried an editorial, unsigned but written on most days by Horniman; followed by chatty and gossipy pieces of news, including on viceregal and gubernatorial engagements. The rest of the front page had a sprinkling of British 'Home' news, as in a news item headlined 'Sergeant Fined for Keeping Private Gun', about a soldier in Surrey who bought a gun and did not obtain a licence (thinking that as a soldier he didn't need to).

Pages two and three were devoted to sports news, radio programmes and film information. Later pages judiciously mixed political news (of interviews given by the rising star of nationalist politics, Jawaharlal Nehru, for example) with non-political news (e.g. a story headlined 'City Gets Good Supply of Mangoes'). On other pages were book reviews, business and market news, and some stuff on science. There was also half a page devoted to letters to the editor, and much coverage of races in Bombay and Poona.

The paper was clearly aimed at a mixed audience, at European residents of Bombay, as well as English-speaking Indian nationalists. It ran to ten pages every day, with no issue on Sundays. A line at the bottom of the last page ran: 'Printed and Published on behalf of the Proprietors, The Bombay Associated Newspapers, Ltd., by BENJAMIN GUY HORNIMAN, at the "Bombay Chronicle" Press, Red House, Parsi Bazaar, Fort, Bombay'.

The great American editor H. L. Mencken once said that a journal is a despotism or it is nothing at all. A successful periodical could not be run as a collective; it had to have the stamp and the authority of a single person, its editor. The *Bombay Sentinel* followed his maxim in good part, for Horniman's imprint was all over it. The editor's name was prominently displayed on the first and the last page. But it was a benevolent despotism nonetheless. A journalist who worked with Horniman at the *Sentinel* recalled the man he called 'Governor' as having an eye for good clothes, who 'even in the midst of busy editorial work would find time to appreciate and question either the quality or fit of the apparel' a colleague was wearing; as a lover of operatic music who was often to be found humming an aria from *Il trovatore* or *La traviata*; as a betting man who was often at the horse-races; and as someone who, unlike other Indian editors, showed 'perfect comraderie [sic] and affection even to the most junior member of the staff'.[21]

Another younger colleague, likewise an Indian, recalled that every day, at lunch, Horniman would take a walk from his office at the *Sentinel* to the public gardens that lay in front of the great building of the Asiatic Society of Bombay. He would take with him two brown paper bags; one with breadcrumbs for birds, the other with small change for the urchins at street corners.[22]

One of the many Indian journalists whom he mentored wrote of Horniman that 'he was a great chief. In a few words he would give instructions that illumined the subeditor's or the reporter's path. Sitting in his room he gathered Bombay's political strings in his hands and knew all that was happening politically, noble as well as ignoble.'[23]

Sometimes, what he gathered in his chambers moved (or provoked) Horniman to get out into the field himself and become a reporter once more. Shortly after he became editor of the *Bombay Sentinel*, he started a vigorous campaign against illegal gambling, which was known locally as *satta khel*. On the night of 28 April 1934, Horniman went into a notorious den with his secretary, when a posse of policemen swooped in and charged him as being one of the gamblers. There were 124 accused in all, and of course Horniman was the most prominent.

In his testimony in court, Horniman told the magistrate that he had gone with his secretary to Shumshet Street, where he found 'open gambling was going on'. A man sitting there told the editor that 'they had nothing to fear as the police were their "partners"'. From here Horniman walked on to other nearby dens, and, when they entered the aptly named 'Old Satta Gully', Horniman was 'seized violently from behind by three men'. They were dressed in ordinary clothes, but Horniman at once understood that they must be policemen. When he asked why he had been arrested, one of them answered, 'for being found in a crowd where gaming was going on'.

Horniman and his secretary were taken to the police station. He was not allowed to phone his lawyer, nor was he given any food or water. However, by now news of his detention had reached the office of the *Sentinel*, and some of his colleagues rushed to the police station. At 2.30 a.m., he was given bail on payment of Rs 500 in cash.

When the case came to court, Horniman chose to conduct his own defence. The newspaper reports reveal the editor closely cross-examining the witnesses produced by the police, while presenting his own case, which was that he had gone to the gambling den in pursuit of his professional duties. He told the court that he had been writing and publishing articles on the evils of *satta khel* since February, 'strongly urging the need for greater vigilance on the part of the police in its suppression'. He added that he had, 'in the course of his investigations, frequently visited the locality where satta gambling was most rife, and satisfied himself that it is often carried out openly, without police interference'.

After a prolonged trial, extending over three months, the case ended in the triumphal acquittal of Horniman and his secretary. The Magistrate, Sir Hormuzdiar Dastur, chastised the police severely, both for arresting Horniman in the way they did, and for demanding bail surety of Rs 500 when normally a mere Rs 5 would do in cases like this. This was 'a journalist of repute' who did not warrant such harsh treatment by the police. More importantly, the Magistrate had, after examining the evidence, satisfied himself that 'so far as Mr. Horniman and his secretary were concerned, there was no doubt that they were there for a legitimate purpose'.[24]

The *satta khel* case was merely one of dozens of occasions on which B. G. Horniman had appeared in a Bombay court. Over the past two decades, as the editor of the *Chronicle*, the *Herald*, and now the *Sentinel*, he had to face an array of civil and criminal suits filed by those offended by what he or his paper had written. A lawyer who had occasion to defend the editor in court wrote that

Horniman is the last man to run away from a bad case by just resorting to a small technical trick. He would stand four-square and go the whole hog in his defence and fight every inch of the ground. His guts to face the worst criminal trials arising out of his editorial duties are something not found anywhere. He can boldly face the worst situations even when counsel lose their nerve. There were the cases of half a dozen city newspaper editors who were hauled up for the technical violation of an offence. They made a quick job of it all by tendering an 'explanation' which was virtually an apology: but Horniman was a tough guy. He offered no apology and was even determined to teach a little law to the Magistrate! . . . As a client he is a proud possession; but he can provide you with the most exacting job.[25]

V

All this while, in political terms, Horniman remained strongly allied to the Congress. He was particularly attracted to its socialist wing, led by Jawaharlal Nehru, Minoo Masani, and Kamaladevi Chattopadhyay. The editor was harsh on the conservative faction of the party with whom Nehru and company were battling, telling a political meeting in November 1935 that 'until the Congress became truly representative of the whole country, and until its policy and programme were dictated and carried out by an organization representing the masses as a whole, it would be impossible for it to achieve independence, or even Dominion Status'. In particular, argued Horniman, the Congress must get 'the strength of the peasants behind it'.[26]

Given these inclinations, it was not surprising that the *Bombay Sentinel* was sharply critical of the lavish lifestyle of India's princes, many of whom had large homes in Bombay. In the summer of 1938, the paper launched a campaign against Ganga Singh, Maharaja of Bikaner, who was soon to celebrate the Golden Jubilee of his ascension to the throne. The Maharaja was one of the most prominent of all the 500-odd princes. In 1919 he had signed the Treaty of Versailles on behalf of India. He had served several terms as Chancellor of the Chamber of Princes. Yet, far from being enlightened and progressive as one would expect a prince of such responsibilities to be, the Maharaja of Bikaner, commented Horniman in an unsigned editorial, had become 'one of the most dangerously reactionary and consciously Fascist princes in India'. One-fifth of the State's finances were spent on the Maharaja and his household; 'as for social relief, solution of peasant indebtedness, rural uplift – these ideas find no practical expression anywhere in the State'. Now, a fresh Jubilee Tax was to be imposed on every resident of the State to further gratify the Maharaja's luxurious lifestyle. There were reports of the brutal treatment of prisoners, with some even being beaten to death.

The *Sentinel*'s editorial ended with this exhortation: 'It is the duty of the Congress to declare a boycott of the jubilee celebrations backed up with such propaganda and agitation that, either the Ruler will be forced to end this ruthless exploitation, or the Government of India will be compelled to intervene and rescue the people of the State from such oppression.'[27]

This commentary was carried on the front page, while the inside pages carried a long report on oppression in Bikaner, sent by an anonymous reporter on the spot. In subsequent weeks there were more reports on peasant distress in Bikaner, with the paper urging Jawaharlal Nehru, now President of the Congress, to intervene.

The tone of the *Bombay Sentinel* was consciously more conversational than that of the *Bombay Chronicle*. Apart from serious editorials, the paper also carried a lighter, more satirical, column also written on most days by Horniman. It was called 'Twilight Twitters'. Yet the *Bombay Sentinel* was certainly not apolitical, using satire and whimsy, and sometimes straightforward polemic, to make its arguments about the pre-eminent public figures of the day.

In 1938, thirty-five years after B. G. Horniman first moved to Bombay to edit the newly established *Bombay Chronicle*, Jawaharlal Nehru – by now second only to Gandhi in importance in Indian politics – decided to start a newspaper of his own. It was based in Lucknow, capital of India's United Provinces, incidentally also the home state of the promoter. Nehru chose to call his new paper the *National Herald*. This was surely a nod to the *Indian National Herald* that now no longer existed. That Nehru would name a newspaper after one of Horniman's was a remarkable tribute offered by a great native-born Indian to a once famous, now sadly forgotten, foreign-born one.

VI

On 3 September 1939, England declared war on Germany. The next evening's 'Twilight Twitters' column began:

YOU WILL HARDLY BELIEVE
That Chamberlain is determined to finish the war, and even
Hitler, whose dear friend he once was. . . .
That the British always fight against brute force, bad faith, justice,
oppression and persecution – when practised by others.

The same day, an unsigned editorial on an inner page, most likely written by Horniman, said unequivocally that Nazism must be crushed, that 'the sympathy of the greater part of the world will be with Britain and France in the struggle . . . to rescue Europe from the fate which awaits, if the cause of the brutal despotism, which Hitlerism represents, is allowed to triumph'. But then, drawing no doubt on the writer's own bitter personal experience, it warned that steps must be taken to 'avoid the treacherous betrayal of democracy that characterised the settlement after the last Great War'. In a clear reference to Lord Linlithgow, the Viceroy, taking India into this war without the consent of Indians, the editorial continued:

> What is astonishing at this critical juncture in Britain's history is the crass ineptitude of British statesmanship in not utilising the opportunity to secure India's active support and co-operation by a sincere and honest attempt to meet the demand for India's freedom while expecting Indians to fight and sacrifice their resources a second time for the freedom of Europe.[28]

Gandhi and the Congress told the Viceroy that they would support the war effort in exchange for a commitment that India would get freedom from British rule after the conflict ended. Horniman entirely agreed with this position. India, he wrote, 'fully sympathises with the victims of German aggression and is ready to help the British Government to the fullest extent, if it is made possible'. At the same time,

> Indians have a duty to themselves and that is to secure their own freedom first. That is the first duty of every patriotic Indian and cannot be put aside on any account. They could no longer rely on vague promises: Indians must know whether their liberty is also included in the abstract principles for which the Tory politicians tell us they are fighting.[29]

On 17 October, the Viceroy finally issued a statement on what might happen to India after the war. This was mealy-mouthed, merely saying that after Germany had been defeated, the British Government would be 'very willing to enter into consultations with representatives of the several communities, parties and interests, in India, and with the Indian Princes, with a view to securing their aid and co-operation in the framing of such modifications [of the 1935 Government of India Act] as may seem desirable'.

Linlithgow's statement prompted Horniman to write a signed article which began: 'After a prolonged period of gestation the Viceroy has produced a very small mouse the insignificance of which cannot be disguised by his long-winded and redundant statement, which reveals that British statesmanship stands exactly where it did in 1935, and before that.' Calling the Viceroy's statement 'a sheer denial of Self-Government', Horniman said:

> it is an insulting and contemptuous answer to the demand of the Congress for a clear statement by Britain here and now, that if India is to pour out her money and resources in a war for democracy in Europe, she should have an uncompromising undertaking that, at least, when the war is over, the principle of democracy will be applied unconditionally to India.

He added that while 'the country, as a whole, is behind the demand for Swaraj without dilution', through this Viceroy's speech 'once more we have to listen to all this pitiable stuff about the claims of the minorities, safeguards, gradual stages and what not, that British statesmen have exploited for the last fifty years or more to preserve British dominion over the people of India'.[30]

Most Congressmen, and Jawaharlal Nehru in particular, were bitterly opposed to Nazism, and wanted the British to win the war. At the same time, having fought for so long for their own freedom, they thought it extremely hypocritical that while claiming to be fighting for democracy against authoritarianism, the British did not recognize the need to finally award freedom to their own colonies.

Between 1939 and 1942 the Congress and the Raj played a game of cat and mouse. The Congress organized an 'individual satyagraha' campaign to put pressure on the Viceroy and his advisers. Gandhi's secretary, Mahadev Desai, travelled to Delhi to have long conversations with Linlithgow's secretary Gilbert Laithwaite. But the Viceroy remained as pigheaded as ever, backed up in his obstinacy by the British Prime Minister, Winston Churchill, himself an unreconstructed imperialist.

The National Government that Churchill now headed however had several important Ministers from a party, Labour, that had long been committed to independence for India. In March 1942, one of these Ministers, Stafford Cripps, came out to the subcontinent to seek to break the deadlock. Gandhi travelled to Delhi from Wardha to meet him. Cripps, like the Mahatma, was a man of God as well as an ascetic vegetarian. Of their meeting, Horniman, in his jokey 'Twilight Twitters' mode, commented:

YOU WILL HARDLY BELIEVE
That Gandhiji did not discuss politics with Sir Stafford
but talked about his latest food fads . . .
That Gandhiji refused to open his mouth, when he
left Cripps except to emphasise that he was silent for
the day by speaking a few words.
That M[ahadev] D[esai], however, is already sharpening
his pencil to write a brilliant verbatim account of
what Gandhiji said and did at New Delhi.[31]

At the same time, in an unsigned editorial, Horniman wrote in more serious vein that while the Cripps proposals represented an 'honest and sincere attempt' to break the deadlock, 'the one defect in the scheme' was that it 'refuses to hand over to Indians the defence of their country'.[32]

Horniman hoped that this defect could be modified or removed. It wasn't, with the Viceroy insisting that the Defence Member of a new Executive Council had to be a white official of the Raj. The Cripps Mission had failed, prompting an editorial written by Horniman with anguish and feeling, expressing manifest love for both countries, Britain and India. 'Who could be more anxious for the defence of the country against foreign aggressors than Indians?' Horniman wrote: 'Yet Sir Stafford contends that the defence of India will be weakened if Indians are placed in charge of it. . . . The responsibility for the failure [of the Mission] is, therefore, that of the British Government.' Horniman continued:

> Britain has suffered many grave losses but the gravest is this failure to grasp the golden opportunity of gaining the whole-hearted, enthusiastic co-operation of the Indian people.
>
> It is a greater disaster than any that has yet befallen her, and it was so easy to avoid it.[33]

Now Gandhi and the Congress had no option but to resort to collective satyagraha and demand that the British 'Quit India'. In the first week of August 1942, as the leaders of the Congress arrived in Bombay for a crucial meeting of the All India Congress Committee, Horniman still hoped for a last-minute reconciliation. In an editorial he asked: 'If it is proper for European nations to resort to every measure to win back their freedom from Hitler and his Nazis, is it unreasonable for Indians to resort to Civil Disobedience in a non-violent manner, when it is blandly refused to them.' He insisted that 'the Congress is not at all anxious to seize power for itself'; its leaders had 'stated publicly that, so far as the Congress is concerned, they would not have the least objection if the Government hands over power even to the Muslim League'. This, remarked Horniman, 'proves the "bona fides" of those who are in the forefront of the demand for freedom. Can we hope that the British are equally anxious to prove their "bona fides" by divesting themselves of power over India, by exchanging it for a friendly alliance.'[34]

These words (and warnings) are unlikely to have been read by the Viceroy in Delhi, and even if they were he was in no mood to heed them. Gandhi and his colleagues were arrested and packed off to prison. Horniman was deeply upset, writing that when Gandhi had clearly indicated that he was writing to the Viceroy to explore 'all avenues of peaceful settlement', the Government ignored the offer and instead 'chose to act and arrested the Mahatma and all the leaders'. The Englishman who had become an Indian now worried about the consequences of this ill-advised act. As he wrote:

The point is now – WHITHER?

People might become violent because their beloved apostle of non-violence has been taken away from them. People might become rowdy and uncontrollable because those who could have controlled them are taken away from them.

People might become panicky and panic might do anything. Students might forsake studies; presses might suspend publications; civil servants might sever their connections; the police might become peevish and irritable; the war effort might become worsened.

Is this what anyone wants? We do not think any patriotic Indian wants it.[35]

Horniman was prescient. For the arrest of Gandhi did anger his supporters, especially the young among them. Writing in the *Bombay Sentinel*, Horniman deplored the arson and hooliganism in Bombay that followed the arrest of the Congress leaders. He was dismayed that not one of the Congressmen still free had condemned it. The violence and the failure to stem it had, he noted sadly, harmed the cause of Swaraj.[36]

War had brought other kinds of problems for the editor of a newspaper in India – shortages of paper and printing ink, and censorship by the authorities. In the third week of October 1942, Horniman addressed the last issue in a lecture on the freedom of the press in Bombay. He accepted that censorship of military news was justified in wartime, for one did not wish to convey 'news that might be of value to the enemy'. But such censorship, he contended, should 'not extend to the ordinary political field'. That would 'only result in "doping" the reading public with one-sided news'. The editor sharply criticized the Raj and its press censor for failing to recognize this distinction.[37]

With Gandhi and all his colleagues in jail, the political front was quiet. But, as ever, Horniman could not, would not, stay out of controversy. In May 1943, he criticized a judgement of the Allahabad High Court in one of his columns. The judges of Allahabad, enraged, ordered the police of the United Provinces to travel to Bombay and arrest Horniman for contempt of court. The police did as ordered. When they reached the editor in Bombay and issued summons, he at once approached the Bombay High Court for redressal. Appearing for him was the celebrated lawyer K. M. Munshi. The judges in Bombay chastised their colleagues in Allahabad for so hastily ordering the editor's arrest. They then examined the paragraph Horniman had written, and deemed it to be not in contempt of court. The editor was released from police custody, the case burnishing his public standing even further.[38]

VII

In July 1944, a Horniman Golden Jubilee Fund was started to mark fifty years of his entry into journalism. Money was raised through public subscription, and through music and dance performances (including one by the great dancer Ram Gopal). The chairman of the fund was the distinguished jurist Sir Chimanlal Setalvad, who issued an appeal 'to the people of all communities in the country to unite in raising adequate funds'. Setalvad spoke of how, 'during his long stay in India, Mr. Horniman had fought many a successful battle for the freedom of the Indian people and the Indian Press'.[39]

Towards the end of 1944 Horniman was sacked as editor of the *Bombay Sentinel*. He was now in his seventies; and with negotiations for Indian independence now taking a more concrete turn, perhaps the management wanted a younger person at the helm. He was given three months' notice and asked to go. He went, but later was advised to fight this latest (or last) dismissal, and, given his litigious nature, did so. Horniman approached the Bombay High Court for redressal, telling them that he had never ever availed of the one month's annual paid leave that he was due according to his contract. So, at the very minimum, he should have got an additional twelve months' salary when he was sacked. The paper disputed this, saying that he had agreed to a settlement that had been paid to him in full.[40]

Horniman now had no job, and no pension. But he did have with him the Rs 35,000 collected by his admirers for his Jubilee Fund. For the first time in many years he had no office to go to. Little is known of his life after he exited the *Bombay Sentinel*, of how he saw out the years 1945 and 1946, of how he welcomed the independence of

India in August 1947. His old newspapers, the *Bombay Chronicle* and the *Bombay Sentinel*, however record that on Monday 11 October 1948 he was admitted to Marina Sanatorium with acute diarrhoea. He had a heart attack on the Thursday, lost consciousness and died at 4.30 a.m. on Saturday the 16th.

Since Horniman died in the early hours of the morning, the *Chronicle* could not carry the news of their founding editor's death the same day. But the *Sentinel*, being an evening paper, did. The front page of its issue of 16 October 1948 was devoted entirely to Horniman, with these banner headlines: 'HORNIMAN DEAD/VALIANT FIGHTER WHOM INDIA WILL NEVER FORGET/FOUGHT LIFE-LONG BATTLE AGAINST TYRANNY AND INJUSTICE/CITY RECEIVES DEATH NEWS WITH ACHING HEART'.

The front page carried statements of praise and condolence from, among others, the Mayor of Bombay and the strongman of the Bombay Congress, S. K. Patil. Inside was a long editorial, which began with Horniman's bold act of racial and national transgression, as one of 'that gallant band of few Britishers in India, who identified themselves completely and whole-heartedly with Indians in their right for Swaraj'. The *Sentinel* then praised their founding editor's 'incisive, bold and uncompromising writings', his 'heart of gold' (and his purse 'invariably at the disposal of the needy'), his knowledge of the law and his love of animals, his 'debonair charming personality'.[41]

On the evening of 16 October, as the paper with these words was being distributed on railway platforms, the funeral procession was wending its way from Marina Sanatorium to Sewri Cemetery. Walking alongside the coffin was Horniman's great and fearless successor as editor of the *Bombay Chronicle*, Syed Abdullah Brelvi. After the coffin was lowered into the ground, Brelvi made an impromptu speech, where he said 'nothing would have pleased Mr. Horniman more than he should have been laid to rest in Indian soil for the freedom of which he had fought'. He continued: 'Benjamin Guy Horniman loved India with a love that was greater than the love of many Indians for their country.'[42]

The next morning's *Bombay Chronicle* reproduced what it called 'a rare portrait of Mr. Horniman dressed in Khaddar', a white Gandhi cap on his head, a white khadi shawl draped over his shoulder. The newspaper carried a sheaf of tributes, including one from the veteran nationalist Jamnadas Dwarkadas, who said that only two other Westerners, Annie Besant and C. F. Andrews, matched Horniman in their contributions to the Indian freedom struggle. The following day, the *Chronicle* carried a long editorial on his work, entitled 'A GREAT JOURNALIST'. Though unsigned it was surely written by Brelvi himself. This recalled with feeling Horniman's first stint as editor of the newspaper, from 1913 to 1919: 'To no small extent the success of the paper and of Mr. Horniman was, of course, due to his own unrivalled qualities as an Editor, his remarkable courage, and the fact that he, as a Briton, was carrying on a relentless fight against fellow-Britons for the emancipation of the country from their political and economic strangle-hold.' Horniman, said Brelvi, 'loved Indians with a love that was not artificial, but deep and genuine. He served her and her people with a devotion and ability not surpassed by many of her own sons.'[43]

There were obituaries for Horniman in *The Hindu* of Madras, and in the *Hindustan Standard* and the *Amrita Bazaar Patrika* of Calcutta. And there was a lead editorial in the *Hindustan Times* of Delhi, which began: 'In the death of Benjamin Guy Horniman, at the age of 75, India loses one of the few Britishers to whom she was a land of adoption, Bombay its sleepless sentinel, and journalism in India its doyen.' After speaking of his coming to India 'for the wrong paper' (the pro-Raj *The Statesman*), his immersion in Indian nationalism and his move to Bombay, his deportation and return, the court cases he had to fight etc., the paper remarked that although 'Horniman's purse was ever notoriously empty', 'his spirit was always gaily defiant', and 'never had he compromised his sense of independence'. The appreciation in the *Hindustan Times* (almost certainly written by Gandhi's son Devadas, then the editor of that paper) ended with these words:

> Horniman was a vigorous writer. The pen in his hand was 'no aesthetic instrument' but a 'mode of action'. In his crusading zeal and reckless courage, and in the vibrant tone of his writings, he was much like W. T. Stead. He was not only a great journalist in himself, but he was a considerable figure in rallying round him several ardent young men

and in fashioning them after his own pattern. To Bombay he is, and will be, an unforgettable memory. India will remember him with gratitude for having dedicated his brilliant gifts to the cause of her freedom, and more particularly to the cause of the freedom of the press.[44]

Never before had the death of an editor of an Indian newspaper occasioned such widespread and appreciative commentary in papers that he had not worked for himself. And never since.

VIII

I cannot end this account of Benjamin Guy Horniman without some mention of his private life, since it was as unusual as his public career. Horniman was a homosexual; a fact known to his close friends and colleagues, and perhaps to a few others. As early as 1916, Annie Besant wrote an article about him that seems to have alluded to this. Here she spoke of a conspiracy in Bombay, where an Anglo-Indian newspaper 'was found to bring against Mr. Horniman the filthiest accusations', which were now being given credence by the police and the bureaucracy. Of this campaign Mrs Besant said:

> Mr. Horniman is one of those rare Englishmen who feel keenly the dishonour thrown on the good name of Britain by the un-British methods of Government followed in India, and his name is therefore anathema to the Bombay Anglo-Indians. His journal is a constant annoyance to them, for it is bold and outspoken. Hence the need to destroy him.[45]

Let us juxtapose Mrs Besant's remarks of 1916 with some lines in a 'biographical sketch' published after his death in 1948:

> The late Mr. Horniman loved life, enjoyed life and lived like a prince in his best days. He would not miss any good picture or dance. Few are aware that Mr. Horniman was one of the finest art critics in the

East. When Madame Pavlova, the well-known Russian dancer, came to India, he gave a review of her dance. It was considered a masterpiece.

The sketch ended with this line: 'Mr. Horniman was a bachelor, a vegetarian and a teetotaller.'[46]

These allusions were delicate and discreet. An Indian journalist was to matter-of-factly write, many years after his death, that 'there was a belief that he [Horniman] was a gay'.[47] And he was, though we know little more than that. Did he have one partner, or several? Were these all Indians? Was this unusual sensitivity to art and aesthetics in an otherwise deeply political man a mark of his sexuality? When he asked voters in 1926 to remember his 'good points' and forget his 'weaknesses' did this have any bearing on his life outside politics? Was his desperate desire to return to India all through the early 1920s merely a product of his political views and journalistic ambitions? Or was there a lover he had left behind in Bombay with whom he wished to be reunited?

To these questions we have alas, only speculations, no answers. But as regards Horniman the public man we are on surer ground. Here, we can say with some certainty that in his lifetime Horniman was at once the most loved Englishman in Bombay and the most respected editor in India.

Shortly after B. G. Horniman died, an admirer proposed that in his memory a housing colony for working journalists be built, and named after him.[48] In the event, the lovely park outside the Asiatic Society, abundant in trees, shrubs and benches to sit on, was renamed the 'Horniman Circle'. Although – unlike when he was alive – few citizens know what he did for their city, his name lives on in a famous landmark in one of the oldest parts of Bombay, once the place where the city's first stockbrokers traded (under an old banyan tree), now a meeting place for friends and lovers, a park through which Horniman himself roamed, feeding breadcrumbs to birds while he composed in his head the editorial he was about to write.

CHAPTER 10

Going Solo

I

In November 1934, Gandhi's adopted daughter Mira Behn returned from her trip to England and the United States. Gandhi was now based in Wardha, in central India, the hometown of his disciple, the patriotic entrepreneur Jamnalal Bajaj. The Mahatma's temporary home was in a building gifted by Bajaj to the All India Village Industries Association. Mira, on moving in here, found

> a few of the old Sabarmati Ashramites were still there, but a strange medley of various kinds of cranky people had gathered around Bapu, and since we were all cheek by jowl in one building, there was no peace and no escape. Even at night the disturbances went on, for one of the inmates was a somnambulist, and when he walked in his sleep another inmate, who had St. Vitus's dance, always got up and tried to catch him, with the result that in the dead of night blood-curdling shrieks would rend the air. In spite of all this Bapu carried on with a prodigious amount of work.[1]

Mira did not like these cramped quarters, so she spent her time touring the countryside, promoting sanitation among the villagers. Rather than rely on bullock-carts, she got herself a local pony, smaller and far less thoroughbred than the horses she had once ridden in the English countryside, but serviceable nonetheless. Gandhi was in search of a suitable location for a new ashram, and Mira promised to help in finding one. On her rides, she told a friend, she found 'fine air, good water, hills, woods, little villages – but it is difficult to get <u>just</u> the right place'.[2]

A suitable site was finally found; in a village named Segaon where Bajaj owned land and an orchard he was happy to gift to Gandhi. A cottage was soon built for Gandhi, but not one, to begin with, for Mira. This was both because he found her possessiveness trying, and because he wanted Mira to become more independent herself. So she moved to a nearby village called Varoda; she could come once a week to see her beloved Bapu, but otherwise was on her own.

Mira wrote Gandhi a series of beseeching letters asking him to allow her to be at his side, permanently. 'My true self expression, and therefore, happiness and peace of mind', she said, 'I can only find in your service.'[3] She urged Gandhi's secretary Mahadev Desai to intercede on her behalf. They asked her to cultivate self-reliance; but then she had a bad attack of malaria, whereupon Gandhi came to get her in a bullock-cart. She recovered from malaria, but shortly afterwards fell ill with typhoid. This was an even more debilitating illness. It laid her low for more than a month. When she was finally able to move around, Gandhi, taking pity on her, allowed her to set up residence in his village, albeit in a separate cottage from his.[4]

In 1937 Mira fell sick again. This time Gandhi sent her to the Himalaya to recover. She spent a month with a friend near the town of Dalhousie, in present-day Himachal Pradesh, where she met shepherds who traded with Tibet. 'Now that we are approaching some sort of self-government', she wrote to Devadas, 'I feel we ought to study and get in touch with this mountain world and the countries beyond.' She read with interest the travelogue of a Hindu sadhu named Satyadev who had made a pilgrimage on foot to the holy mountain of Kailas.[5]

After Gandhi moved to Segaon, the place was renamed Sevagram, the village of service. In the summer of 1938, a tall, well-built, bearded man walked into the Sevagram Ashram, asked to meet Gandhi, and told him his life story. His name was Prithvi Singh. In his youth he had emigrated from the Punjab to Canada, and, inspired by Indian revolutionaries in exile, returned home to carry out their mission. He was arrested in 1915 as part of what was known as the 'First Lahore Conspiracy Case', and awarded a life sentence. He spent some time in the notorious Cellular Jail in the Andamans, and was then transferred to the mainland. In 1922, he escaped from Rajahmundry Prison, and had succeeded in eluding the police ever since. He had travelled through Central Asia and on to the Soviet Union, and then came back to India, always using an assumed name. After his return he lived mostly in Gujarat, where he taught physical culture in schools, and learned to speak Gujarati fluently.[6]

Prithvi Singh told Gandhi he now believed entirely in non-violence, and said he would be guided by him as to what to do next. Gandhi advised him to surrender to the police. So he did. Gandhi then wrote an article in *Harijan* about his visitor, and said he would strive 'for the early discharge of Sardar Prithvwisingh', who, given his inspiring story, and his conversion to the creed of *ahimsa*, he saw as a 'fellow pilgrim' in 'the pilgrimage to the temple of freedom'.[7]

Mira was in the ashram when Prithvi Singh came, and was deeply impressed by him – by his manner, his bearing, and his extraordinary and moving tale of courage and recantation. She would have wanted to know more, to talk to him at length, but he had been told by Gandhi to give himself up to the authorities.

In the autumn of 1938, Gandhi visited the North West Frontier Province, and that winter he sent Mira there as well. She enjoyed the views and the clear mountain air, the fresh fruits and the honey. She was tempted to base herself there, but in the end decided against it, for the Pathan men were uncomfortable with the idea of a single Englishwoman moving around from village to village, while the Pathan women were unenthusiastic about spinning and weaving. 'I became worn out, both body and nerves', wrote Mira to Devadas: 'After six months of trying, one seemed to have got nowhere!'[8]

II

On his surrender to the police, the lapsed revolutionary Prithvi Singh was sent to a jail in Rawalpindi. Mahadev Desai visited him there, and found him productively occupied. He had spun eighty pounds of wool, was teaching gymnastics to his fellow prisoners and also reading and writing (among other things, his autobiography). He made a great impression on the prison warder, who told Mahadev that in his thirty years of dealing 'with numerous political prisoners, distinguished and ordinary', he had 'not come across one who can approach Sardar Prithwising'.[9]

With Gandhi's intervention, Prithvi Singh was released within a year. He came at once to Sevagram, where he spent time with the Mahatma, and also with Mira. After a few weeks in the ashram Prithvi became restless, and resumed his travels around India. He promised Gandhi he would be back soon. When he didn't come back as quickly as he had said he would, Mira wrote him a letter redolent with affection – and love. It began with a flirtatious complaint: 'So the week is up and instead of yourself there comes only a letter! Well – something is better than nothing.' Mira then spoke of how her 'dream has always been that Bapu's [Sevagram] Ashram should be the nerve centre of India, giving birth to few but best of workers. But my dream has remained a dream for want of the man to take command. You, I believe, could fulfil that dream.' The letter ended with Mira telling her new friend: 'Remember, when you come, to bring with you a good lantern, a strong pair of sandals which will protect you from the thorns, and two warm rugs. It will be quite cold in December and January even for a Punjabi!'[10]

It is clear that Mira was deeply attracted to Prithvi Singh. Madeleine may (or may not) have had romantic attachments when she was a young lady in London, but from the time she became Mira she had been scrupulously and wholly celibate in mind and in deed. Now this was changing. That seems abundantly clear from the letters she wrote to Prithvi (we have none of his to her).

The first letter from Mira to Prithvi that we know of, and which is quoted above, was dated 26 October 1939. On 1 November she wrote to him again: 'You can understand how much I have been longing for your quick return! Of course it may all end in smoke but there is a feeling that it is serious. I have no one to turn to who is sensible and organised in his mind as to what we should do.'

Prithvi had written an autobiography, and had asked Mira to edit it for him. She took to the task energetically. Reading the early chapters, she told him that 'because of the language difficulty you have even given a wrong impression of yourself at times. But it is a precious and remarkable book which must see the light of day. When you come we must go through it together and if I can help you to the full expression of thoughts, the joy will be fine.'[11]

In November 1939 Prithvi came to Sevagram, and spent a whole week. The attachment, at least on Mira's side, grew exponentially. She went and told Gandhi of her feelings, and Gandhi, to her surprise, said she could marry Prithvi if she wished.[12] But there turned out to be a problem; Prithvi did not want to marry her. What sort of romantic relationships the revolutionary had in his youth we do not know. But now that he was in his late forties, he had got pretty used to being on his own. Mira was the same age as him; he was certainly flattered by her attentions, and appreciated her comments on his manuscript. He was willing to have her as a friend, not as a life companion.[13]

On 10 November, Prithvi left Sevagram again. No sooner had he departed than a letter from Mira followed him. Addressing him for the first time as 'Dear Prithvi' (rather than 'Dear Brother'), she wrote: 'Yesterday I was overwhelmed. You were to go away and at the same moment I realized for the first time that perhaps in the future we may not see very much of one another. I had not time to gather myself together, and if I clung to you for a moment, it was because the pain was unbearable. That is past.'[14]

A week later Mira wrote again to Prithvi, this time about his manuscript, which she was editing. 'You do realize yourself the great value of what you have written', she remarked, continuing:

That is the beauty of it – all straight from the heart and absolutely natural. The first time I read it through I was too much disturbed emotionally. To read all that about one whom one loves from the bottom of one's heart is an ordeal, and [a] fever was running in my body the whole time. Now on second reading I can see the book as a whole. And it is a great impression. All those long and weary years of suffering, which seemed to you to have gone to waste, will fructify in the great influence that this book will have on the minds and emotions of others.[15]

Prithvi Singh was travelling furiously across India. He was in Gujarat and Maharashtra, and sought to enter Punjab, but the authorities, fearful of his presence in his home state, wouldn't let him in. Now he chose to move east, going via Calcutta to Rangoon, where one of his brothers lived. Letters from Mira followed him everywhere. They appear to have made him feel guilty; did he in those first days with Mira in Sevagram give the impression that her love was reciprocated? He seems to have written to Mira expressing some sort of remorse, to get a letter in reply, which most likely made him feel worse. Here Mira wrote:

> Do not speak of having wronged me. It is not that you should wrong me, but that you should wrong yourself that pained me so much. God cast you in purest gold, and I cannot bear that anything should dim its brilliance. Be your true self, and trust me as part of your own being. I would no more like to harm you, than you would like to harm yourself. What room is there, then, for misunderstanding and complications? Only tell us what you feel and think, that I might understand your wishes. I know that you were innocent of all hard intentions. You meant everything for the best – so did I. But somehow everything went wrong. And I have paid for it with my heart's blood. May God, in His mercy, make things right.[16]

The letters that Prithvi wrote Mira are lost. One supposes they would have been shorter as well as less sentimental. His side of the story is briefly told in his autobiography, which was published many years after the events I have just narrated. Here he writes:

> The writers of love stories often manipulate imaginative tales of love letters, but her story beats them completely. In search of true love, the seekers would have to take their hats off to Mira, when they read her letters and come to know what efforts and sacrifices she made to win me over. The sentiment of love uplifts even a mean person from the dust of the earth to the level of a god. This is what Miraben made of me. She was a romantic lady of great devotion. She overflowed with emotion, but I was a political sportsman. The struggle which I had to wage in life made me critical of whatever was offered to me.

Confronted with Mira's love, Prithvi would not surrender to it,
yet he did not know how to escape it either. As he recalled,

> I had not yet taken a vow in regard to truth and non-violence. I could
> not consequently place the whole truth before the Mahatma and say
> that Mira loved me and that I could not reciprocate her love. . . . I
> was on the horns of a dilemma. At last, like a coward I sneaked out
> of the Ashram under the pretext of seeing my brother and his family.[17]

III

After her love for Prithvi went unrequited, Mira looked for other
sorts of consolation. She had for some time thought of setting up
an independent ashram of her own. In the autumn of 1940 she went
to Kangra, in the foothills of Himachal Pradesh, staying for several
months in an ashram set up by Gandhians. She liked the countryside
and the climate, and would have stayed longer, except that the
political situation was hotting up in the plains. So she returned to
Sevagram. But she hadn't really got over Prithvi, and being in the
place where she had fallen in love with him made her moody and
anxious. She tried to calm herself by reading Hindu religious texts,
and by furiously spinning. She took no part in the ashram activities,
and hardly talked to anyone.[18]

Months passed and Mira would not come out of her semi-seclusion.
She was drawn out of it by Gandhi's compassionate Bengali disciple,
Asha Devi Aryanayakam, who took her into her own cottage and
urged her to translate into English the Vedic hymns she was reading.[19]

Towards the end of 1941, Prithvi Singh came to visit Gandhi in
Sevagram, and seeing him brought forth all sorts of conflicting
emotions within Mira. In early 1942, she wrote to him, addressing
him now as 'Dear Comrade' (rather than 'Brother' or 'Prithvi'). Mira
told Prithvi that her seventeen years with Gandhi was

> a great disciplining and training out of which I learned a tremendous
> amount, but it also undermined my self-reliance and self-expression,

and I became unable to do any sustained or independent work. Before I came to Bapu I was a person of free energy, enterprise and self-reliance. All this I somehow lost. Only when you came into my life did my natural strength re-awaken.

But, the letter continued, since Prithvi would not agree to making a life with her, Mira went into a long period of seclusion. From these '15 months of silent prayers and reading, I gained spiritual riches which were unknown to me before,' she wrote. She now knew that to fulfil herself she had to work away from Gandhi, and Gandhi himself had come to see it that way too. Now, in the new life she hoped to begin outside Sevagram, she wanted, desperately, the companionship of the man she loved.

Mira told Prithvi that her plan was to start a centre for training women somewhere in North India. 'I am anxious to find a fine and healthy site in U. P. towards the Himalayas, if possible on the bank of one of the great rivers, within a hundred miles or so of Delhi.' She was looking for funds and co-workers. She enclosed a note on her proposed scheme, asking:

If you have any suggestions or ideas, how glad I shall be to have them. The same inspiration drew us both from our homes and sent us out into the unknown – the same ideal for India's freedom fills our hearts to-day. The only difference of opinion between us is that I believe with all my heart and soul that our strength for fullest service lies in our union, and you believe otherwise. So long as you feel like that I will accept without further argument your wish and I will strive with all the strength in me, to serve alone. But if, in my solitary service, I can have your comradeship of heart, it will enrich my work as nothing else could. To know that he in whom and through I live and find my strength, is there in my life, a friend, a comrade – Oh how that will sustain and strengthen me![20]

In March 1942, Prithvi Singh appears to have written to Mira asking her to forget him and the fact of their friendship. This brought forth an unbearably sad cry of anguish. So she wrote:

You ask me to renounce my love, as if it were some sort of self-indulgence, harmful to the furtherment of India's service. You do not realize that <u>real love</u>, love that rises from the depths of the soul, increases the power of service and is as sacred as religion. In woman love and faith become one. To ask me to renounce my love is asking me to renounce my faith in God and my strength to serve. What good can that do to you or India? Why should you think that my love for you is impure or selfish? How much I wish you could realize that my love can be all turned by you into service of the Nation! A woman's fullest strength comes to her only after she has found her beloved. From that day she becomes a new being, with redoubled strength, patience and understanding. But if her beloved turns on her and says, 'renounce your love for my sake', he stabs to death the new being and all the sources of endurance and service that had sprung to life in her are dried up.

Mira continued:

Prithvi! Why do you turn from me as if my love were poison? Nobody in the world can long more ardently than I do that your great ideals should be fulfilled. From the first days of our coming together I have been conscious of the feeling that my ambitions for you are even greater than your own. I long that your heart should turn towards me and fill me with unfettered strength for work, instead of being left as I am at present, to struggle under the heart-breaking load of your cold aloofness. You have no need to fear what would happen if you were kind to me. I am not urging you all of a sudden to marry me. I am only asking you, in the beginning, to accept the truth of my love and faith, and not to shun me because I am honest with you. Let us be generous and fearless in our dealings with one another – the rest is in God's hands.[21]

Reading these letters, one feels desperately sad for Mira – a lady now close to fifty, experiencing the first great passion of her life, a passion that was wholly unrequited. But one feels some sympathy for Prithvi Singh too. After all that he had gone through, in jail and on the run, he must have hoped that with the remission of his prison sentence he could now focus on constructive work in the villages. Whereas he had to contend with these letters declaring undying love, which followed him around from place to place. It is noteworthy, though, that he kept them for posterity, depositing them with his papers in a public archive, to be discovered after both Mira and he were long dead.

IV

In May 1942, seeking perhaps to divert her attention from Prithvi Singh, Gandhi asked Mira to tour the eastern province of Orissa. The Japanese were advancing rapidly through South East Asia. The British territories of Malaya and Singapore had been conquered, and Burma was soon to fall into their hands. If the Japanese now decided to invade the east coast of India, how should Indians respond?

It was to seek an answer to this question that Mira went to Orissa at Gandhi's behest. After travelling around the coastal villages she wrote Gandhi a long letter describing the likely scenario if the Japanese invaded India. In Orissa, she found that, for the most part,

> the villagers ready to take up the position of neutrality. That is to say they would leave the Japanese to pass over their fields and villages, and try as far as possible not to come into contact with them. They would hide their foodstuffs and their money, and decline to serve the Japanese. But even that much resistance would be difficult to obtain in some parts, the dislike of the British Raj being so great, that anything anti-British will be welcomed with open arms.

Although by now Indian in spirit, Mira was British by birth. She certainly did not want the Japanese to conquer India. So Mira suggested that the Congress in Orissa advise the villagers to:

1. To resist formally, mostly non-violently, the commandeering by the Japanese of any land, houses, or movable property.
2. To render no forced labour to the Japanese.
3. Not to take up any sort of administrative service under the

Japanese. (This may be hard to control in connection with some type of city people, Government opportunists, and Indians brought in from other parts.)

4. To buy nothing from the Japanese.
5. To refuse their currency and any efforts on their part at setting up a Raj.

After outlining a plan for resistance, Mira came to the problems in executing it. What if the Japanese paid for labour, food and materials in British currency, and offered a decent price? What if the Japanese asked for assistance in rebuilding canals/bridges blown up by a retreating British Army? What if the Japanese came accompanied by Indian soldiers they had taken prisoner in Singapore and Burma? 'Should we treat them [these Indian soldiers] with the same aloofness as we are to show the Japanese', asked Mira, 'or should we not try to win them over to our way of thinking?' And what to do with the dead and wounded in battle? Regardless of their nationality, Mira thought 'it will be our sacred duty to attend to them', by giving them a decent burial or cremation as the case may be.[22]

While bracing themselves for a possible Japanese invasion, some villagers in Orissa were deeply resentful of the foreigners who currently colonized them. The British were building an aerodrome in the hinterland of the province, seizing fields and farms to do so. Mira visited the villages that were facing evacuation because of the aerodrome. She wrote to Gandhi:

The villagers themselves say they would rather die of the bombing that is likely to come, than leave their homes. I explained to them the dangers to which they were exposed by having the military camps and the aerodrome in their midst, but again and again they said 'No, we would rather stay . . . If we leave our wells and tanks where shall we find others ready made except in villages which are already short of water as it is being taken away daily for the building of the aerodrome. And if we are sent far away from our lands we shall not be able to cultivate them and then how are we possibly to live?'[23]

Mira also met the Chief Secretary of Orissa, and told him about the rounding up of boats and bicycles for the war effort and the evacuation of villagers from the vicinity of planned aerodromes, without providing land elsewhere. She assured him that 'we' (meaning the Congress), 'are most anxious to avoid friction in this purely humanitarian work, where the well-being of thousands of poor villagers is concerned'. She hoped that the Government and the Congress 'might be able to co-operate in finding out and alleviating the villagers' hardship at this time'.[24]

The Orissa Government, for its part, distrusted this Englishwoman who had so visibly identified with the other side. They wanted her deported from the province, and asked Delhi for permission to do so. The Home Secretary of the Government of India, R. M. Maxwell, warned them that this would be counter-productive. If Mira was served with an externment order, he said, then 'Gandhi will merely send another woman to take her place, and by repetition of this process he will gain his object of exciting public sympathy and working up the usual sort of hysteria. My own view is that we are now in so much stronger a propaganda position that we can hope to defeat Gandhi by his own methods.' The Communist Party of India (CPI) was now solidly supporting the Raj (since Hitler's invasion of their Fatherland, Soviet Russia, had miraculously transformed an Imperialist War into a People's War), and Maxwell was hopeful that the CPI's student wing, the All India Students' Federation, would be useful in counteracting Mira and the Congress. Maxwell asked the Viceroy to agree to his proposal, as he 'should like to set the All India Students' Federation going as soon as possible. We should, of course, pay their expenses. But we should have no other obligations as they would undertake this work of their own accord.'[25]

Mira had spent more than a month in Orissa, whereupon Gandhi wrote to her to take up another mission on his behalf. He wanted her to travel to Delhi to meet the Viceroy. Back in 1930, before he started the Salt Satyagraha, Gandhi had sent a young Englishman, Reginald Reynolds, as his emissary to meet Lord Irwin in a last-ditch effort at reconciliation. Now, as he was contemplating a 'Quit India' movement, he was seeking to do the same with Lord Linlithgow, using an Englishwoman as an intermediary this time. Both aspects of this move were characteristic; that Gandhi wanted to explore all possible options to avoid conflict, and that he would do so by sending a white renegade to the rulers as his emissary.

Mira went to Delhi in July, hoping to meet the Viceroy. Linlithgow palmed her off to his Private Secretary instead. This was Gilbert Laithwaite, a former army officer. At first Mira was cross at being downgraded, telling Laithwaite that Gandhi would 'take the Viceroy's refusal to see her ill, as also would Nehru'. Then she calmed down and the two had a very long conversation, extending for more than an hour, with Laithwaite jotting down a detailed note as soon as it had concluded.

Mira began by saying her experiences in Orissa had been an 'eye-opener', exposing her to the depth of anti-British sentiment among the common people. Then she complained afresh about not being able to see the Viceroy, saying 'Mr Gandhi would be greatly disgusted if knowing the need for understanding between the two sides he found she had not been able to make her observations direct.' Laithwaite said that at a time when Congress had used 'very hard words' about the Government, and Gandhi himself had referred to 'open rebellion', it was impossible for the head of the Government to agree to a meeting with her directly, but he assured Mira that any message conveyed to him would be passed on to the Viceroy.

Laithwaite's notes on the meeting continue:

Mira Ben replied that she was very close to Mr Gandhi who was indeed for her her father and mother. Two people could not understand one another better: yet she had a more independent identity than most of the others around him. She had her own views. She led her own life, harmonizing her existence with his: but she was in no sense a mere reflection, and she tried to interpret.

Then, of Gandhi's latest challenge to the Government, Mira said:

Gandhi was doing what he was doing in the fullness of his sense of friendship for the English. The gesture of friendship was strongest in his heart, and his solution was the only way to save the situation. It was like a wife and husband who could not get on together in the same family. One of them might have to leave. A drastic and terrible cure would have to be taken in for England and for India, because, though we did not know it, this country was slipping out of the control of Great Britain. Up to 6 or 8 months ago there had been strong anti-British feelings throughout the country but nothing more than that. Now the feeling of the masses was (in her own phrase) pro-anything-anti-British to a degree that we could not believe. They would wish to garland the Japanese and the Congress could not stop them because they had been so tortured by the present Government.

Laithwaite gently disagreed with Mira's assessment of the situation. Recruiting for the war was going well, he said, and even if there was anti-British feeling here or there, 'it was not anything like so general as she had described'. Mira answered that 'the success of recruiting was entirely artificial. People were poor; their existence was miserable; the thought of a little money attracted them into the army.' Mira then made a heartfelt plea to the British to immediately grant Swaraj (independence) to India, saying:

> The aim of Congress was to see that, rather than let the country throw itself into the hands of any other Raj, they should rouse her to win for herself through her own non-violence real independence. She begged me to try to understand that that was the only real war effort that both of us could make to-day. Once Congress could say to the people that England had opened her heart and had given independence, that would remedy the situation and would put an end to all the dangerous propaganda which was now going about in favour of Subhas Bose [and his pro-Japanese Indian National Army].

Mira added that if independence was granted, British troops could stay on, and defend India against the Japanese, while acting under the orders of a civil administration run by Indians themselves.

Laithwaite now said that the Congress did not represent the Muslims and other groups. The party claimed to speak for all India, but it had no justification for this claim. 'I said that I had no doubt that Mr. Jinnah carried the Muslims with him; that equally I had been struck by seeing the photograph of Dr. Ambedkar in a Mahar's [Untouchable's] house in the Central Provinces, 20 miles from

Nagpur.' He added that the Princes had also stayed aloof from the Congress. Mira answered that the Congress would work to make the minorities feel secure. And the people of the princely states were 'the slaves of slaves. No such disgrace as the Indian States could exist in the world had it not been for the existence of the British rule.' Once independence was granted, the Princes 'would come to their senses', and their subjects would become free men.

Mira made a final appeal, saying 'she had in conclusion a very terrible observation to make, but one which it was necessary for the Viceroy to realise'. She warned that this movement would be more militant than the previous ones.

> In the last civil disobedience movement, though sent to jail Congress followers had behaved well there. They had been non-violent. But on this occasion they would not follow the rules of the jail. It would be a case of Swaraj or death. We should have to take on more than we had ever tried to cope with before once a movement began inspired by that idea. The more we tried to suppress Gandhi the greater his power would become.

Laithwaite concluded his account of his talks with Mira as follows:

> The conversation, which lasted an hour and a quarter, was very friendly. Neither side yielded any ground. Mira Ben struck me as entirely wedded to the full Gandhian demand for immediate independence, and as quite unimpressed by the practical and political issues which this concession involved. I gave her no justification for thinking or hoping that any acceptance of the demand, or any move towards yielding to the Congress claims, should be looked for.[26]

V

The outreach to the Viceroy having failed, in August 1942 Gandhi announced at a meeting of the All India Congress Committee in Bombay that a non-violent struggle to compel the British to 'Quit

India' would be launched. The British swooped down hard, arresting Gandhi and all the major (and many minor) Congress leaders. The Mahatma was incarcerated in a large house owned by the Aga Khan in Poona. With him were his wife Kasturba, and a handful of his close disciples, including Mira.

A week after their incarceration Gandhi's remarkable and indispensable secretary Mahadev Desai died of a heart attack. He was only fifty. Gandhi was devastated. In the grounds of their prison, Mira made a small memorial to Mahadev of stone and mud plaster, placed over the ground where his ashes were. On the flat top of this structure she carved the letter 'OM' in Devanagari, and at Gandhi's suggestion added a cross next to it, with the star and crescent of Islam on the corners. Every morning Gandhi would visit this small shrine, place flowers on it, and read verses from the Gita.[27]

In her memoirs, Mira had much praise for their jailer, a man named Kateley. He was always very solicitous about the health of Gandhi and Kasturba, and, for the younger members of their entourage, arranged for an impromptu badminton court in the garden, and a table-tennis table in the building itself. In these games, the athletic Englishwoman usually defeated the bookish Indians.

The Aga Khan's house was set in many acres of parkland, around which the prisoners could roam. Mira walked four or five miles a day. She read a great deal, including (perhaps for the first time) some Communist literature. From an anthology of writings by Marx, Engels, Lenin and Stalin, she turned to the worshipful accounts of Chinese Communists by Edgar Snow and Agnes Smedley. Then she read a book by Ella Winter, called *Red Virtue*, a glowing portrait of Soviet Russia. After reading these contemporary works Mira went back to the New Testament, to discover 'the wonderful similarity of object', between Communists and Jesus. She wrote to a friend: 'The Communists deny God, but they do His work. The Christian world takes the name of God, but leaves His work undone.'

She added:

Of course, there are many things in which one does not see eye to eye with them [Communists], but the spirit is most inspiring. Though they believe in violence for certain purposes, yet in social matters they do their best to avoid violence or coercion. Children are not whipped in schools, prisons are places of education and reform. . . . The worship of the machine is the thing I find most difficult to appreciate, but I believe they will modify the idea as time goes on.[28]

This sort of naivety about Soviet Russia was of course quite common among upper-class English people, and among some Indian nationalists (notably Jawaharlal Nehru), though Gandhi did not share it.

After a year in jail, Mira began to experience sharp pain in her left arm and shoulder. As she wrote to the prison doctor, a helpful Indian named Bhandari, 'there is something vitally wrong with my arm. A fear haunts me that if it is not radically cured there may be permanent disablement.' Bhandari called in a specialist, Lieutenant Colonel H. K. Shah of the Indian Medical Service. Shah examined Mira, and in a report dated 1 December 1943, wrote that 'she requires further treatment. This could best be done in a hospital. The ordinary remedies as tried at the Palace have not been very successful. She requires long and special treatment.'[29]

Gandhi was very worried about Mira's health. He told the Government of India's Additional Home Secretary, R. Tottenham, that he felt a 'special responsibility' for Mira, who, 'forsaking the easy life of her English home came to me 19 years ago in search of things of the spirit for which her heart had been yearning'. He appealed to the British to either grant her parole or allow her to see an outside specialist. 'I am sure the Government would not wish her to be permanently damaged,' he said.[30]

The appeal fell on deaf ears. Tottenham was an old-style colonialist. He detested Gandhi, and always suspected his motives, often, as in this case, without reason. He told his superiors that it seemed 'quite possible that Gandhi, having failed to get anything out of us by direct correspondence, was now trying indirect methods of getting his propaganda across by engineering the release of one or more or his companions'.[31]

The Home Secretary of the Bombay Government was an Indian, H. V. R. Iengar, and he viewed the matter more sympathetically. He could not get Mira released, but he could at least arrange for another specialist to see her in prison. Thus a Dr Simcox came to see Mira

in jail, and his treatment provided her some relief. Simcox told Iengar that Mira 'is a very good patient and most anxious to cooperate with him and to get better. He also said Gandhi came out of his room to tell him how much he appreciated his coming to treat Miss Slade.'[32]

In February 1944 Kasturba Gandhi fell seriously ill, and died. Gandhi sat for hours alone with her body. 'He seemed to be in silent commune with her', wrote Mira: 'At one moment Sushila [Nayar] even heard a murmured soliloquy, as if he were talking to Ba.' Gandhi wanted their sons to come and collect the body and have it cremated outside the prison, with family and friends in attendance, but the Government refused. So she was cremated inside the grounds of the prison, and her ashes placed next to where Mahadev's were.[33]

In March, H. V. R. Iengar urged the Government of India to release from prison the women who remained with Gandhi. The Home Secretary, R. M. Maxwell, said that while that both Gandhi's niece Manu and Sushila Nayar could be set free,

> Miss Slade cannot be released unconditionally. . . . This woman is as dangerous as any member of the [Congress] Working Committee and would use any opportunity that presented itself of carrying on propaganda against Govt. and in favour of the Congress. . . . A desirable thing would be to deport her but we have no power, I understand, to do so, and it is therefore necessary if she is to be released to restrict her activities severely in this country.[34]

The hostility was astonishing, and can only be explained by one thing – racial and national pride, combined perhaps with a strong dose of patriarchy. It was all right in British eyes for Indian women to follow and admire Gandhi, but for a British woman, never.

In the event, Gandhi himself was released in May 1944, and all his companions came out of jail with him.

VI

In the Aga Khan Palace, Mira had once more been thinking of starting an ashram of her own when they were freed. Now Gandhi

agreed to let her go, and offered to raise a sum of money to get her started. Her previous trips to the Himalaya had greatly attracted Mira to the mountains. In November 1944, she found a plot of land near the holy town of Haridwar, where the Ganges descends into the plains. The place had a fine view of the snows. The surrounding villages had a mixed population of Hindus and Muslims, among whom were several hundred weavers. The area was appealing socially as well as visually.[35] When she wrote to Gandhi about where she planned to settle, he sent his blessings, albeit briefly: 'So you have the land of your choice. May all your dreams be fulfilled.'[36]

Mira started a Kisan (Farmers) Ashram, with two younger Indian males, a young Gandhian who had also just come out of jail named Dharampal, and an ayurvedic doctor. The local villagers constructed a house and a cattle shed, where Mira placed their first cow, named Jamuna. She was soon joined by four other cows and two bullocks. Slowly, a shed for khadi work also came up. A dispensary was then added on, supplying some basic medicines for common ailments.[37]

The year 1945 gave way to 1946, and as Mira and her team continued with their work at the Kisan Ashram, the political situation in India was becoming intensely charged. The Muslim League did remarkably well in the elections held in early 1946, consolidating the case for Pakistan. In August bloody riots broke out in Calcutta, spilling over into the countryside. Gandhi left Sevagram for a pilgrimage of peace in rural Bengal. Had this been a few years earlier Mira would have been at his side. But now she was in her own ashram, at the foot of the Himalaya, the other side of the subcontinent from eastern Bengal. But of course she thought of him all the time.

At 7.45 a.m. on 7 November 1946 Mira wrote to Gandhi: 'At this very hour 21 years ago I came to your blessed feet, and again this morning I am there in thanks & prayer.'[38]

Mira's work was gathering shape; the Government of UP, now led by her old Congress comrade Govind Ballabh Pant, was keen to involve her in their agricultural extension programmes. They asked her to take charge of a larger cattle farm, a couple of miles upstream on the Ganges from her Kisan Ashram, close to hills clothed densely with forests. On moving there, wrote Mira, 'the wild beauty of those great forests, and their wealth of animals and birds, stirred

in me great strength. There is a vast vitality in untrammelled Nature which communicates itself to those who live with her.'[39]

In this new settlement, which she named 'Pashulok' (The Abode of Animals), Mira acquired a horse, a present from a departing British official. She named the animal Draupadi, and on its back made trips into the hills. A correspondent of the *Hindustan Times*, a newspaper edited by her old friend Devadas Gandhi, travelled from Delhi by train and bus to see Mira at work. When the reporter got there she was out on her pony, somewhere in the countryside. He found the dispensary run by an ayurvedic doctor humming with activity, with patients from the surrounding villages coming in. When Mira returned to the ashram, she took the reporter around the premises, showing him the cows, the weaving shed, and the manure pits, which she regarded 'as the most important experimental activity in the Ashram'. Mira told the visitor that 'it is clear as daylight that if we can organize the use of our village materials, we can more than double the fertility of India's soil without the assistance of any foreign experts or machinery'.[40]

In the third week of November 1946, word reached Mira that Gandhi, in Noakhali, was 'on an extremely low diet', and that he threatened to reduce it further by dropping glucose. Mira wrote to Gandhi urging him to 'start taking milk again. Without it your health will become seriously undermined, and that is a bad thing to contemplate at this crisis in the Nation's development!'

Mira then turned to her own difficulties, which were that 'no reliable workers have turned up during these two years except Dharampal', who now wished to leave to devote himself to political work. The ayurvedic doctor wanted to return to his family in Delhi. What would remain were two khadi workers, a typist, and a 'second-rate man' from the Agriculture Department. Her work in and for the surrounding villages had grown, she told Gandhi, but the ashram itself languished, because she hadn't been able to find 'the right type of co-workers'.

Mira asked Gandhi whether an experienced worker could be sent from Sevagram to take over day-to-day operations, while she focused on her work in the villages. She would retain her little hut, around which she had planted banyan, peepul, neem and sheesham, 'so that it may become a tiny forest'.

Mira ended by complaining that Gandhi's promised visit to her ashram had been indefinitely postponed: 'This was the very season where we were thinking Bapu would be here – now all has changed and everything is full of uncertainty! When will my Bapu come now? In the spring? Who can answer? Only God, and He ever keeps His purpose secret.'[41]

Gandhi replied saying no one could be spared from Sevagram to work with her. 'The Ashram is purely your own original idea', he said: 'If the present site is not suitable for you, you should make what use you can of it. Personally, I would say, give up the idea of Ashram life except for your own person. Then you won't feel cramped and you can expand as high or as broad as the universe.'[42]

In the third week of December 1946, Mira wrote to Gandhi that

I feel, most of all, that I would like to dedicate the Ashram to the service of the cow and her progeny. You know how I love the animal, & feel perfectly at home in their society. One good Animal Husbandry man assisted by a veterinary surgeon could take up the work. Three or four of the buildings can be turned into family quarters for them, & I will have my hut in the jungly field amongst my baby trees.[43]

In another letter to Gandhi, Mira spoke of how, while being on the banks of the Ganga and seeing the snows every day cheered her, there remained a loneliness within. She said:

I am at peace with myself & feel infinite joy in Nature's glory but there is always the instinct to share the joy with another who knows & understands. Joy is only complete when shared with that other. But where is that other – God is there, but it is the very joy of God's presence that one seems to want to share. And so it is that a deep down loneliness rises to the surface from time to time. Not a sadness, but a loneliness. Commune of the spirit is so precious & so rare.[44]

Mira evidently still yearned for Prithvi; still wished that she had him at her side as her co-worker and partner in building this ashram in the hills.

On the plains below, 1946 had passed into 1947, with no sign of the communal troubles abating. On the contrary, they had intensified, and it was now clear that Partition was unavoidable. On the night of 14/15 August, the independent countries of Pakistan and India were carved out of the British Raj. But the violence continued, with Gandhi fasting first in Calcutta and then in Delhi to try to prevent it.

In these years of intense activity for Gandhi, he had not forgotten his adopted daughter entirely. In May 1947 he wrote to her saying that he had just received a book called *Inspiring Songs and Kirtans* by Swami Sivananda of the Divine Life Society, which was located at Rishikesh, up the river from where Mira was. Gandhi asked her to trace the place and 'tell me all about the Ashram and its activities'.[45] Gandhi periodically sent Mira advice on how to run her own ashram, writing to her in August 1946 of the importance of preparing compost manure, and in December of the same year not to fret too much if she did not get the right kinds of men to work with her. When she fell ill in the monsoon of 1947, he said she might consider joining him afresh to regain her health. She went down to Delhi, where Gandhi was, and spent three months around him and in his circle. In the third week of December she returned to her ashram in the hills.[46]

On 30 January 1948, Mira was having her evening meal in Pashulok when a Government officer came in with the news of Gandhi's assassination. The official, who had never seen or met the Mahatma, was sobbing, but Mira herself was calm on receiving the news. She knew that 'Bapu's spirit [was] released and at peace'; coming out of the house, and looking at the trees and the stars above them, she thought of how 'the long-drawn-out crucifixion of Bapu's spirit was over, completed and consummated in the crucifixion of the flesh. It might take years, it might take centuries, but this last sacrifice, willingly given for the love of humanity, would conquer where all else might fail.'[47]

CHAPTER 11

Recovering Revolutionary

I

When Philip Spratt came out of jail in June 1936, he moved to Madras to be near Seetha, the Tamil girl he had been courting. Her family, being of a Communist bent of mind themselves, were not as averse to an interracial marriage as other Indian households might have been. However, they wanted the couple to wait; because Philip had as yet no job, and Seetha was still in college, studying Botany, where one of her classmates (and close friends) was the future naturalist M. Krishnan. Krishnan admired Seetha's artistic skills (her plant drawings especially), and her independence of mind. A story he liked to tell in later years was of Seetha and him in conversation, when he saw a scorpion climb up her leg. 'And you know what happened after the scorpion bit Seetha – it curled up and died.'[1]

Having moved away from the Communist Party, Spratt was consumed by two things: his love for Seetha, and his desire to write a book on Gandhi. He rented a shack on the beach at Thiruvanmiyur, on Madras's southern periphery, cycling into town to see Seetha several times a week. Otherwise he spent his time reading all that he could find by Gandhi, and about Gandhi. He was keen that the book he was writing be published in England, and prepared a synopsis for his family to show around. His brother Bert passed this on to the celebrated Professor Harold Laski of the London School of Economics, 'who was quite impressed by it, and prophesies a good sale for it'.[2]

The synopsis was also sent to publishers. Writing to Seetha in January 1937, Spratt's mother said that 'Fisher and Unwin have had it for just over a month now, so we are getting hopeful that they are considering it.'[3] The doting mother did not realize that, in these matters, no news was not good news at all. If a publisher had sat on a book proposal for more than a month, they were very unlikely to want to publish it.

To pay the bills, Spratt worked with a firm called Viswanathan and Co., producing guides for high school students in mathematics and physics.[4] Otherwise, he laboured away on his Gandhi book, which grew longer and longer. In the cold weather he took a trip around the temples of the Tamil country, writing of the great shrine at Tanjore that it 'gives one a thrill, and an insight, and other odd things'.[5]

Spratt and Seetha got married on 23 January 1939. There was no religious ceremony, the formalities being conducted by the Registrar of Marriages. Seetha had completed her degree and got a job as a schoolteacher. Her husband had finished his book on Gandhi; unsuccessful in finding a British publisher, he had handed the manuscript over to a Madras firm called the Huxley Press to print and distribute.

Spratt had been without a regular job since coming out of jail. However, shortly after his marriage he was asked to join the staff of a new English weekly published from Bangalore called *MysIndia*. Carrying a mix of news, profiles and photo features, this sought to do for southern India what the widely circulated *Illustrated Weekly of India* was doing for the north and west of the country. Spratt took the job, in the hope that Seetha could come and join him once he had found a home for them to live in.

Bangalore in 1939 was a mid-sized cantonment town with a population of less than half a million, not the bustling megalopolis of 10 million and more people that it has since become. Situated on a plateau, at 3,000 feet, the weather was much more pleasant than in Madras. The distance between the cities was 220 miles; a journey of a few hours by train. Once or twice a month Spratt travelled to Madras to spend the weekend with his wife.

Spratt's first letters from Bangalore exhibit mixed feelings. He liked the climate, and had found a decent public library 'pleasantly situated in the middle of a park, and you will like going there', as he told Seetha. But, he added, 'I am more and more dissatisfied with my work. At the beginning the paper tried to be semi-serious at least, and there was some pleasure in writing. Now it is trying to imitate the "Sunday Times" (of Madras, not London) and all interest has gone.'[6]

II

In the summer of 1939 Philip Spratt's book on India's most famous man finally appeared under the title *Gandhism: An Analysis*. It was published not by a reputed London firm (as he and his family had once hoped), but by an obscure press in Madras. Reading the book today, one can understand why it failed to find a British publisher. For it is intellectually very promiscuous. The empirical account of Gandhi's life and career is juxtaposed with theoretical digressions inspired by Marxism, but also by psychoanalysis (as in the references to Freud, Jung, Adler), and by Western political philosophy (Kant, Hegel, etc.). At the same time, there is an excess of detail on Indian politics.

In his preface, Spratt says that his book was written 'from a point of view which can be called a qualified Marxism'. The existing Marxist studies of Gandhi suffered, he said, from two defects, that they viewed the subject only from without and not from within, and that they sought to advance party propaganda. The latter required that 'for simplicity, the subject must be painted either white or black, with no half-shades . . .' Spratt added: 'I have attempted to correct this mistake, and in doing so very possibly put on too much white.'

For all its faults, the book has many arresting insights. Spratt did not view satyagraha (as other Marxists had done) as a clever bourgeois device to dim or stem the revolutionary instincts of the masses, but as a praiseworthy attempt to develop resilience, courage and self-reliance in a colonized people. He also took Gandhi's religious development far more seriously than an orthodox Marxist would, writing that 'his social teaching, with its democratic and equalitarian character, must be considered foreign to the practice, and to most of the theory, of Hinduism . . .' Spratt concluded that in this sphere, Gandhi was 'attempting a religious synthesis of Europe and India: he is a Christianised Hindu'.[7]

Spratt wrote of Gandhi that he was 'the first man in Indian history to make a serious attempt to induce the masses to take part in deciding their own destiny'. Unlike Marxists, who hailed the industrial proletariat as the class that would bring about the revolution, Gandhi had concentrated his attention on the peasantry. 'But the Gandhian scheme', argued Spratt, 'would not depend solely upon the interests of a class. It could probably mobilise both nationalistic and revolutionary idealism, and idealism is no less important than class-interest.'[8]

In his preface, Spratt insisted that a biographer must study his subject from within as well as without. By the same token, one must view this book itself from without and from within; for what it says about Gandhi, and what it says about Spratt. The narrative is testimony to the author's own intellectual and political evolution, his move away from party dogma. Spratt thus writes that 'the characteristic which most forcibly strikes a reader of Mr. Gandhi's account of his childhood and youth is the sensitiveness of his conscience'.[9]

To speak of a person's 'conscience' like this, unmoored from class and class analysis, was decidedly unMarxist; and later on Spratt guiltily remembers this, writing that through his readings in England and South Africa,

> Mr. Gandhi had been developing a set of principles or ideals which it is not inappropriate to call bourgeois, individualist or even non conformist. Such are his dependence upon the voice of his conscience, and his respect for the conscience of others; his acceptance of traditional religion, subject to such amendments as will satisfy himself – his conscience here also is the ultimate authority; his emphasis upon self-reliance, self-respect, independence, energy, thrift, fearlessness and other such virtues.[10]

This is a *very* qualified Marxism indeed. Through his readings and experiences in jail, Spratt had been developing his own conscience, his own individuality. Writing about the incident in South Africa when Gandhi was evicted from a train, Spratt said that after this humiliating experience, Gandhi 'had sloughed off his slave-mentality'.[11] The person who wrote this had by now himself sloughed off his slave mentality with regard to the Communist Party. No longer would he dutifully follow its dictates. Henceforth, he would take from Marx and Lenin only that which satisfied his individual conscience.

Not long after his volume on Gandhi went to press, Spratt was asked by the peasant leader N. G. Ranga to write a foreword to a book that Ranga had put together on the village economy. Here, Spratt urged educated Indians living in the cities to bridge the vast gulf between themselves and their compatriots in the countryside. He asked them to get 'into close contact with the villagers, not only to learn the bare, external, economic and legalistic facts about the agrarian problem, but also to understand the villagers' minds'. Spratt continued: 'Lenin and Gandhiji "approached the poor with the mind of the poor", and it is by doing this rather than by their knowledge of economic facts that these great popular leaders were able to perform their remarkable feats.'[12]

That he praised Lenin and Gandhi in the same breath, and that he even used the respectful suffix 'ji' for the latter, showed how far along the road from his once dogmatic Marxism Philip Spratt had travelled. He was to move much further yet.

III

When Spratt moved to Bangalore to join *MysIndia*, the plan was that Seetha would follow soon afterwards, and look for a job as a schoolteacher in the same city. But when in April 1939 Seetha became pregnant, the plan had to be rethought. For with her mother and other relatives around her, it would be far easier to raise the baby in Madras. The husband would come by train whenever he could to see both wife and child.

In the second trimester of her pregnancy, when it was safe to travel, Seetha spent several weeks with Philip in Bangalore. After she left he wrote her a sad note: 'The room is lonely and empty without you here. I shall get used to it, but for the present I feel it. It is raining too, and cold. Good night. I must go to bed.' A letter written ten days later had him saying: 'I hope to be paid next week. How much money do you want? Please tell me before it is all spent.' And one sent soon after runs: 'I hope you are not too inconvenienced by the failure of the cash supply. We have not been paid yet, and there seems no immediate prospect of payment. As soon as we get anything I will send you whatever I can.'[13]

MysIndia was owned by an Indian named Hosali, and managed by an Englishman named Hawes. Spratt wrote most of the unsigned edits, rewrote signed articles by others, and corrected the proofs. How much the weekly relied on him is revealed in a letter he wrote to Seetha a fortnight before her baby was due. Here he said:

> You are so anxious that I should stay in Madras for a bit when I come. I hope I shall be able to. But it won't be easy. This paper is dependent on me to a very great extent. This week I had to do the leaders: Mahadevan didn't send anything, presumably because he has not been paid. Or he may be ill. Anyway it looks as if I shall have to go on doing them. (Hawes said something about paying me what would otherwise be paid to Mahadevan. I hope it comes off.) There is nobody else who can write at all, or even knows English well enough to correct the stuff. So it is essential for me to be here on Thursday and Friday, and really for two days more. It would be possible for me to manage one week if I left on Friday night, or even midday, and got back again on Tuesday. I shall speak to Hawes about it.[14]

The baby (a boy, to be called Herbert, but also carrying an Indian name, Mohan) was born in December 1939. Spratt rushed to Madras to see him, and on his return wrote to the mother saying: 'You must tell me how your offspring is. Are his charms as compelling as at first, or are they fading away? Are you starving him, dropping him over the side of the bed, drowning him in his bath, or rolling on him and suffocating him? I suspect the worst. I wish I had brought him here with me.'

The letter continued: 'I met [his old Communist comrade S. V.]

Ghate at the station. He was arguing on [the Soviet invasion of] Finland, in the same away as Thatha [Seetha's grand-uncle the Communist Singaravelu Chettiar] but more rationally. But I am not convinced. It is sheer barbarism, I think. There is no excuse.'[15]

Through 1940 and 1941, Seetha applied for jobs in Bangalore schools, but failed to find one. Her husband would send her money when he could, and come to see her and their child when he could too. In October 1940, hoping that Seetha could join him, Spratt found a house for them to live near Richards Town. Drawing a map of the house, he told her it was 'open and airy', adding: 'The trains may annoy you, but Bertie will like them.' He asked her to bring some of his books – such as Gertrude Stein's *Picasso*, books by Virginia Woolf and Ezra Pound, and Thompson and Garratt's *Rise and Fulfilment of British Rule in India*.[16]

The war in Europe was becoming more savage by the day. His parents wrote to Philip saying they had temporarily moved out of the London suburb of Croydon to Ripley in Derbyshire, since air raids were now a daily occurrence. One Sunday, German planes 'crossed right across our once peaceful valley and dropped three bombs on the ground next to ours . . .'[17]

Back in India, or in Madras rather, Bertie came down with bronchitis, so Seetha decided not to risk a journey with him to Bangalore. Philip travelled to see them, and, on his return to his desk in *MysIndia*, wrote:

> I arrived here duly, after an awful journey. The train was so full that I had to stand up in the carriage up to Katpadi. After that I got a seat, but jammed tight. My luggage was then at one end of the carriage, used as a foot-rest by two or three people, and I was at the other end, and it was taken out by somebody else at the station. Fortunately somebody noticed it, and I got it back.[18]

Seetha was doing a teachers training course, hoping it would increase her chances of getting a job in Bangalore. In March 1941, in anticipation of a visit by wife and son, Spratt wrote the latter a letter that I must reproduce in full:

Dear Bertie,

I am sending you a nightie in a parcel. I hope you will be comfy in it. Don't wet it, and don't tear it to pieces, or I shall ask Mummy to spank you.

Tell Mummy to pass her exam., or if she fails you will sit for it in her place next time. If neither of your parents can pass an L[icentiate in]. T[eaching]. exam., surely they are not fit to bring you up. So you must encourage her, and not be naughty and waste her time if she wants to read things up. (But she ought to have finished that by now.)

So you are coming here on the 15th. Uncle John [Spiers; the person Spratt shared the house with] has gone away to Coonoor, so the house will be empty for you. And Daddy's pockets will be empty by that time too, unless a certain fat man named Hawes puts some more cash into them. So tell Mummy to hang on to that money tight.

This is a nice house, with plenty of steps for you to fall down, and windows to bang your head on, and little rickety tables to pull down on top of yourself, and trains passing every half hour or so to keep you awake when you ought to be asleep, and books for you to tear to bits, and so on. And there is nobody to look after you when Mummy is out or asleep, so you can do as much mischief as you like. And there is nobody for you to play with, so you will want to do mischief. You had better bring Auntie with you, I think. Or Lakshmi, or someone.

I trust your liver is in order.

Your
Daddy[19]

At this stage, Bertie was less than a year and a half old. He probably knew a few words, but of Tamil. This jokey, satirical letter therefore was written for Seetha, and also for Spratt's own amusement, bored and lonely as he was in Bangalore.

IV

Through 1941 and 1942 the Spratts maintained their commuter marriage, Philip in Bangalore and Seetha in Madras, each going to see the other when they could. In August 1942 they had a second child, a boy called Aju. Now they found the separation even more difficult than before. In January 1943, after Seetha had applied unsuccessfully for several teaching jobs in Bangalore, Philip wrote to her:

> Another brainwave has occurred to me. You come here, and if you can't get a school job, join the WAC (I) [Women's Auxiliary Corps (India)]. They are advertising all over the place for women, and I am sure they would have you. They pay 100 [rupees a month], I believe, unless you are promoted, as you probably would be. I know quite a decent woman from the Maharani's College who is in it. She is Junior Commander and is probably getting 3 or 400 [rupees a month]. She just sits in an office and writes stories, some of which have been published in *MysIndia*.[20]

So Seetha came, with her two kids, and her mother Sivakami too. She got a job at the WAC, the grandmother looking after the children while the parents were at work. Sivakami also ran the kitchen, cooking on an open firewood hearth. While the rest of the family had Chettiar non-vegetarian food – plenty of meat spiced up – Spratt mostly ate bread, boiled eggs, and porridge. For he had a British stomach; further messed up by jail. Occasionally Seetha made him a simple, bland mutton stew as a treat.

Spratt's children remember their father as a man of few words. Residues of his own non-conformist upbringing remained; thus he did not smoke or drink. He was excellent with his hands. The printing paper for *MysIndia* came in wooden crates. Spratt would dismantle the empty crates, bring the pieces of wood back home on his bicycle, and then convert them into bookshelves. One son said his father's room resembled a modern supermarket, rows upon rows of open shelves running through it (stocking titles in English and French on philosophy, politics, and religion, rather than tins of tuna or packets of cereal). His favourite place in the city was Select Bookshop, which sold second-hand titles that he could afford. He spent long hours chatting with its owner, K. B. K. Rao.[21]

To make additional money to support a growing family, Spratt gave talks on All India Radio on books and literature, and even one on the joys and pains of fatherhood. He also began preparing guides for college students of English literature, one called *Selected Poems for University Students*, with excerpts from the works of Milton, Goldsmith, Shelley, Keats, another an introduction to a famous novel by Thomas Hardy. Both pamphlets had 'by P. Spratt, B. A. (Cantab.)' printed on the cover. His degree was actually in natural science; but his physics and maths having rusted beyond repair, it was far easier for him to offer instruction in literary subjects instead.[22]

Most of Spratt's articles in *MysIndia* were unsigned. Occasionally he published something in his own name, as in an essay on parenting, based on a talk he delivered at the Rotary Club of Bangalore in August 1945. This began by saying that, unlike most Europeans in India, he had spent most of his time with Indians, and with lower-middle-class non-Brahmins to boot. Based on what was now close to two decades of experience with one particular family (the Singaravelu Chettiars), and as a father of Indian children himself, he outlined the differences between, as the title of his essay had it, 'The Child in the East and the West'. He identified five fundamental differences: that weaning took place much later in an Indian home; that the baby was brought up not just by the mother but also by the several other women present in an Indian joint family household; that in contrast to 'the severe clocklike regularity of the small English home' the Indian household was more disorganized, even chaotic; that Indian parents (and especially mothers) were 'markedly more indulgent' of little children; and that there was far less privacy and hence far less segregation between the generations in Indian homes.[23]

V

Recall that Philip Spratt was released from prison after the colonial authorities had satisfied themselves that his 'political views have really changed and that he would be *most* unwilling to be drawn into politics again'. On his release, while Spratt had refused on principle to give an undertaking that he would eschew politics altogether, he did say, in writing, that he would not 'take part in any political activity or propaganda; except by means of writing for the press or publication, which may have some political reference, and for which I realise that I should be liable under the ordinary law'.[24]

In his first few years as a free man Spratt kept out of politics altogether. He published his book on Gandhi, got married, found a job, and began to raise a family. He wrote about current affairs in the press, but had no formal political affiliation. However, in 1940 or 1941 he met another lapsed Communist, albeit a far more celebrated one than himself. This meeting, and the friendship that developed, drew Spratt back into the orbit of politics.

The famous former Communist whom Spratt befriended was Manabendra Nath Roy. Born in Bengal in 1887, as a young man Roy joined a group of nationalists who believed in armed struggle. When the First World War broke out he went abroad seeking German help for his fellow freedom fighters. He landed in California via Japan, married an American woman, and embraced Marxism. In 1919 he helped found the Mexican Communist Party, before spending several years in Soviet Russia, where he had a famous debate with Lenin on the colonial question.

Spratt had first heard of M. N. Roy from Clemens and Rajani Palme Dutt, the half-Bengali brothers who recruited him into the Communist Party of Great Britain. They admired Roy for, among other things, being a truly international revolutionary, who had worked in several countries other than his own. However, while the Palme Dutts stayed loyal to Stalin, M. N. Roy was less impressed by Lenin's successor.[25] In 1930, he returned to India, and was almost immediately arrested because of his revolutionary past. He spent five years in jail, in prisons in Uttar Pradesh different from those in which Spratt was

Anne Besant sitting in the gardens of the Theosophical Society
with her newspaper, *New India*, *c.* 1917.

Annie Besant lecturing to a crowd after her release
from internment, Bombay, October 1917.

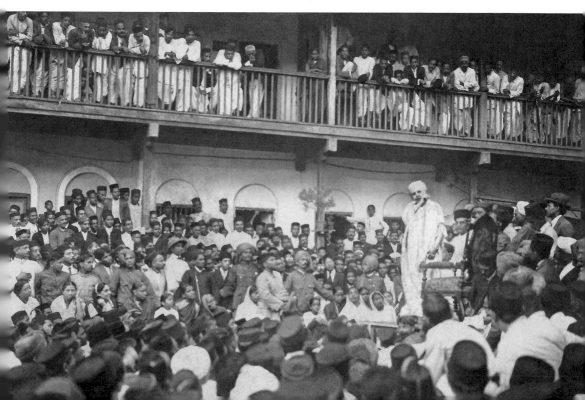

Studio portrait of Annie Besant, Madras, *c.* 1921.

Studio portrait of
B. G. Horniman,
c. 1918.

Madeleine Slade as a young woman
in London, early 1920s.

Samuel Stokes in his
Gandhian phase, *c.* 1921.

Satyanand Stokes with wife Agnes
and daughter Satya, *c.* 1940s.

Mira Behn being visited at her Himalayan ashram by the President of India, Rajendra Prasad, March 1950.

Mira Behn feeding a calf in her Pashulok Ashram, Rishikesh, c. 1947.

Mira Behn helping Gandhi repair his spinning wheel, Wardha, 1936.

Philip Spratt and his wife Seetha,
early 1940s.

Philip Spratt at work, Bangalore,
late 1940s.

R. R. (Dick) Keithahn and his wife Mildred,
Bangalore, early 1940s.

Peace Award conferred on **Dr. Rev. R. R. Keithahn,** by the peace-loving Citizens of Madurai District in the Public Function held on 30-1-1984, the SARVODAYA DAY, the 36th Death Anniversary of Mahatma Gandhi, at Gandhi Museum, Madurai, Tamil Nadu, India, under the Chairmanship of Dr. M. Aram, Vice-Chancellor, Gandhigram Rural University, Gandhigram, conferring the Title "அமைதிக் காவலர்"

"THE DEFENDER OF PEACE"

Born in a farm family in the year 1898 on January 26th in the United States of America, Dr. Rev. R. R. Keithahn was educated in the Carlton College. Then he came as a young missonary to India where he would not be confined to the Mission Compound. He went out to mingle with the people and identify himself with their aspirations. He sympathised with the Indian freedom struggle and soon become a close associate of Mahatma Gandhi.

Reverend Keithahn was expelled from the country by the alien Government, early to get back later with added glory when India won its freedom. After 1947, he joined the Sarvodaya Movement and actively participated in the Bhoodan–Gramdan Movement initiated by Acharya Vinoba Bhave.

Reverend Keithahn has always been on the frontiers, pioneering to build Gram Swaraj at the grassroots. He took creative initiatives in pre-school education and citizenship training. Of late he has been concentrating on the Gandhi District Movement which aims at transforming Madurai District into an Area of Peace.

Shanti Sena is a cause to which he has dedicated himself and he feels proud to be called a Peace Soldier. He has been a source of strength and inspiration in the building of peace in India and the world at large.

Having completed 86 years, Rev. Keithahn is still on the move pressing forward towards the ideal of a war-free world which he hopes to achieve by the turn of the century. Innumerable persons who came in touch with him have derived spiritual strength and solace from him.

In gratetul appreciation of all that Rev. R. R. Keithahn is and all that he has done, this gathering of peace loving public of Madurai District felicitate him on this sacred Sarvodaya Day, being death anniversary of Mahatma Gandhi, and declare and confer on Rev. Keithahn the title

"அமைதிக் காவலர்"

''DEFENDER OF PEACE''

(Read and Presented by Dr. M. Aram)

Citation of award presented to Dick Keithahn, Madurai, 1984.

Sarala Behn,
late 1940s.

Sarala Behn with
her students and
disciples, Lakshmi
Ashram, early 1960s.
Her successor Radha
Bhatt is second
from the right. The
solitary male in the
photograph is a
Gandhian visiting
from Gujarat.

housed, with each surely knowing about the other. On his release from prison, Roy joined the Congress but didn't last long, finding the wearing of khaddar (homespun cloth), and particularly Gandhi's censorious attitude to alcohol, problematic. The Mahatma's public displays of religiosity also disturbed him. So Roy left the Congress, preferring to start his own party, which, even if small to start with, would be run according to his principles and preferences.[26]

In the late 1930s, now married to another American, named Ellen Gottschalk, M. N. Roy relocated to Dehra Dun (coincidentally the town where the writer of this book was born and raised). With this town as his base, he made trips around the country, canvassing support (and supporters). He called his party the Radical Democratic Party, the name suggesting a halfway house between the extremist, anti-democratic Communists he had left behind, and the timid, conservative Congress he had tried but rejected. Roy's new political position appealed to Spratt, and so did his personality. Impressive to behold – he was more than six feet tall – and with his colourful past in three continents, and not least his connection to Lenin himself, he attracted many young intellectuals to work with him. When they first met is not clear, but by the early 1940s Spratt was seeing Roy as a political mentor, and Roy viewing him in turn as a favourite disciple.

Spratt joined M. N. Roy's Radical Democratic Party quite soon after it was formed, and began to contribute to its newspaper. In 1944, Roy started a new quarterly called the *Marxian Way*, which he said would 'subordinate ideological preoccupations to intellectual detachment'. As the journal's founding statement put it:

> In such conceptual fields as history and philosophy, sociology and economics, science and aesthetics, a responsible iconoclasm is the supreme need of the moment. For if this unhappy country is ever to occupy her rightful place in the cultural commonwealth of nations, she must be taken out of our abiding deference to authority, her past must be reinterpreted, her present reorganised, her future reoriented.[27]

In planning the journal, M. N. Roy reached out for advice to the celebrated Calcutta poet and critic, Sudhindranath Datta, and to Philip Spratt in Bangalore. Roy had enormous regard for Spratt's literary abilities, writing to a friend that the Englishman-turned-Indian was 'an extraordinarily talented person'.[28]

In January 1945 Roy wrote to Spratt asking whether he would move to Calcutta to edit *Marxian Way*, and help with launching a daily newspaper to be called 'People's Voice'.[29] Spratt was attracted by the idea of working with Roy, and the possibility of having a real impact on politics and intellectual life in postwar India. *MysIndia* was an obscure journal in what was then a provincial town; whereas Calcutta was one of the great cities of India. Seetha was less enthusiastic. They had two little children, with a third on the way, and Roy's letter to Spratt had not specified what he would be paid. 'In these troublous days', wrote Seetha to Roy's wife Ellen, 'surely it would be very disconcerting to find ourselves in a new place with no money.' She continued: 'Getting nearly Rs 400 a month we are just able to manage with not even adequate comforts of life in a comparatively cheap place like Bangalore. And what would it be in a place like Delhi or Calcutta? Our children would have to be in great discomfort – after all we have to see to their comfort and education first.'

Seetha outlined some other difficulties. If Spratt joined the staff of the party newspaper in Calcutta, she would be able to join him only after several months, once the third baby was born and had been weaned. She would have to give up her job in Bangalore as a wireless operator at WAC (from which she was currently on maternity leave). She asked Ellen Roy to 'kindly explain all these to Mr Roy and tell him that my husband's going north would mean great unhappiness to me and also financial difficulty'. She added: 'It is rather disturbing to write to someone about your difficulties about money but I had to explain all these points for the sake of our little ones.'[30]

Ellen Roy had little sympathy with Seetha's feelings. It was in Spratt's own interest, she said, to move north and work full-time for the party. He could thereby move from a 'quiet and retired life' and participate in 'history in the making'. The Roys thought 'Bangalore was not the fit place for him [Spratt] to work, and that he ought to be at the centre, either in Delhi or Calcutta'.

The break with Communism, wrote Ellen Roy to Seetha, had

made Spratt inbred and lonely. Perhaps he had no other friend but you. That is not good for any man. I believe he is no longer inbred, or tries not to be. I also believe that he thinks he might find friends – in fact, he has already found them, in our party. They will be also your friends, very much so!

To induce Spratt to come and work for them, the Roys were willing to pay him Rs 300 a month, a full 50 per cent more than other full-timers of the Radical Democratic Party were offered.[31]

Ellen Roy's letter to Seetha Spratt was well intentioned, but its tone was extremely patronizing, suggesting that all the Roys wanted to do was rescue Spratt from undeserved obscurity and give him a chance to make history afresh. This correspondence led to some long, and certainly intense and possibly heated, conversations in the Spratt household. In late February, a month after the proposal was first broached, Spratt wrote to Roy saying:

> I am afraid I have got myself into a mess about leaving Bangalore. I practically promised you to do so in April, but now it looks as if I shall have to back out, or at least postpone it. I thought my wife had agreed, but afterwards her opposition was as strong as ever. Women are difficult to deal with when pregnant. Perhaps I can smooth it out after the delivery (April). I shall try, of course, but for the present am making no promises![32]

Two months later, Spratt wrote to Roy as follows: 'My wife produced a daughter three weeks ago. As we had two sons this is what was wanted. In not having children you have missed one of the most impressive experiences in life. But it can have its drawbacks too.'

In reply, Roy congratulated Seetha and Spratt on the birth of a daughter, while adding: 'The experience of fatherhood may be most impressive, as you put it, but I would like to impress the world in other ways!'[33]

VI

The Roys were unsuccessful in persuading the Spratts to move up north to impress the world in ways other than bringing up children. However, Spratt remained a member of the Radical Democratic Party, contributing to its journals and attending its meetings. In September 1945 Spratt travelled to Bombay for the party's annual conference, where he was a featured speaker. While in Bombay, he also gave a public talk at the Sunderbai Hall on the 'British Labour Government and India's Freedom'.[34]

In May 1946, Spratt travelled to Dehra Dun to attend the annual summer camp of party workers held in the Roys' bungalow in the leafy locality of Dalanwala. Roy gave long talks every evening; when these were collected in book form, he asked Spratt to write a foreword. Spratt did so, in a long, twenty-five-page essay which began: 'No public man I know of, whether practical politician or mere observer, has been a more consistently correct prophet than M. N. Roy.' Roy, said his disciple, had been right about how events turned out in Europe, China, and India. It was, he continued, 'strange' that 'in a country so given to hero-worship' as India, Roy has not become a 'popular idol'. This, thought Spratt, was because Roy did not write like a journalist seeking a wide audience; rather, 'he writes for a limited circle who understand his style of thought and his background of ideas, and seems unconcerned whether he is intelligible outside it'.

Spratt also blamed Roy's lack of fame and honour in his own country on the insularity of the Indian mind. There was, he said, a revolution going on in the world, and

> India is part of the world and is involved in the revolution. Few looking at Indian conditions would care to deny this, yet that Roy always has this fact in mind is one of his graver crimes. He thinks in terms which apply first to the world as a whole, and then applies them to India with the necessary modifications. . . . Now this deeply annoys many nationalists, who at bottom do not think of India as part of the world; they think India is unique, that foreign or 'western'

ideas do not apply to her, and presumably therefore that she happens to be having a private revolution of her own.[35]

This interpretation was not wholly convincing. For there was Jawaharlal Nehru, likewise a modern-minded man, likewise a thinker who saw India as part of the world revolution, but who was nonetheless adored by his countrymen. Why did Nehru succeed where Roy failed? Spratt should have asked the question – since he didn't, I should briefly do so myself. Roy was away from India during the great countrywide protest movements led by Gandhi – the Rowlatt Satyagraha of 1919, the Non-Cooperation movement of 1920–2 and the Salt March of 1930. During these upheavals Nehru was at Gandhi's side, as his favourite disciple and anointed successor. The many years he spent in jail, and his fluency in Hindi, were further advantages Nehru had when compared to Roy.

With Nehru around, Roy simply had no chance to make a major impact on Indian politics after he returned to his homeland. He had been away too long. Spratt does not seem to have recognized this. In another essay of 1946, he praised Roy as the thinker most relevant to Indian conditions. The essay (published as a pamphlet) began by referring to a recent article by the lawyer K. M. Munshi, which had argued 'that the British concept of democracy is incompatible with the Russian'. Munshi claimed that the first model guaranteed individual liberty and 'the free interplay' of political parties, while the latter crushed liberties and freedoms through the will of an all-powerful state.

Spratt's pamphlet was written to combat this view; it suggested that a free India could combine the best of both models, taking liberty and freedom from Britain and economic and social justice from the Soviet Union. Spratt often referred approvingly to Roy; he saw himself as advancing and defending the viewpoint of his leader. While advocating political freedom and universal adult suffrage, Spratt claimed this had long been Roy's own view, 'that the "achievements" of bourgeois democracy are extremely valuable and must if possible be preserved'. While 'most Marxists in the twenties and thirties' thought otherwise, Roy's perspective, argued Spratt, was consistent with Marx's own thinking. For 'revolution by force and dictatorship are not essential parts of the Marxian scheme. Marx personally believed that they could be avoided in some circumstances and named America, Britain and Holland as countries where this might be possible.'

At the same time, said Spratt, Roy went beyond bourgeois thought in arguing 'that political democracy is not incompatible with economic planning and economic equalisation'. For Roy, and for Spratt, the constitution of a free India should guarantee 'limited hours of work, security for those unable to work, free education [and] free health services'. Spratt further thought that economic policy in India must lay down as 'fundamental principles' that 'ownership of natural wealth vests in the people; increase in productivity through technological improvements is a State responsibility; the credit system and basic industries are state-controlled, and other large industries and large-scale agricultural enterprises shall be undertaken by the State'.[36]

Spratt greatly admired M. N. Roy, and was extremely attached to his wife Ellen, writing to her often as well. In June 1946 he wrote to her of his failed attempt to meet the chief ideologue of the Communist Party of Great Britain, Rajani Palme Dutt, who was then on a visit to India. Spratt had hoped to travel to Bombay to see Dutt, but in the event could not get away from Bangalore. 'Anyway he would probably have refused to see me', he wrote to Ellen, 'knowing I am an R[adical] D[emocratic] P[arty] man. I did not want to discuss politics with him, but only to see him. I have never set eyes on him – and [wanted to] ask about old friends and so forth.'[37]

For her part, Ellen Roy continued to try to persuade Spratt to move to Delhi or Calcutta to work full-time with the party and its journals. In the last week of June 1947, the disciple wrote to his mentor's wife: 'There is so much resistance now [from his wife Seetha] that I cannot hope to get away. I feel very guilty about it, because I had promised to go, and you seem to be anxious that I should. I really don't want to let you down like this, but I really cannot manage it.'[38]

In August 1947 India finally became independent. The following January, Mahatma Gandhi was murdered by a Hindu fanatic. Spratt felt the loss very keenly, for reading Gandhi and meeting Gandhi had played a critical role in moving him away from the path of bloody revolution, and towards a more democratic and accommodative style of politics. From Bangalore, he wrote to Ellen Roy in Dehra Dun that the assassination of Gandhi was 'certainly a blow to me. I felt the sense of loss people speak of, and gloomy apprehensions for the future.' Then he added:

I read his stuff quite a lot at one time, and went to Wardha and had long interviews with him. My feelings were distinctly of the filial order. One likes to criticize a person of that type, just as one likes to criticize any firmly established institution – always subject to the proviso that one's critical suggestions are not carried out. That is the unspoken proviso attached to the fulminations of any British revolutionary.[39]

CHAPTER 12

From Samuel to Satyanand

I

We left the American renegade Samuel Stokes in 1924, spending Christmas with his family, having withdrawn from his involvement in the Indian National Congress. After his retreat from politics, Stokes concentrated on apple cultivation. Apples were first planted in the Simla Hills in the 1870s by an Englishman named R. C. Lee. However, these early experiments in apple cultivation were not successful; the fruit tasted sour. It was only after Stokes brought American varieties to the region that the industry took off. In December 1921, Stokes's mother Florence sent him a Christmas gift of Stark's Golden Delicious saplings. In a few years the trees were bearing fruit. In August 1926, reporting that the yield of the orchard filled twenty boxes, Stokes wrote to his mother: 'Next year, if I live, I am going to see that all boxes containing it go out marked with "Kotgarh apples", so that this place may come to be associated with good apples in the Indian fruit market.'[1]

By 1928 there were almost a thousand apple trees in Stokes's orchard in Kotgarh. He gave saplings to farmers in the neighbourhood, laying the basis of a prosperous and still flourishing industry. The fruit was transported to the market in Simla on the backs of mules. For years, Stokes lobbied hard for the building of a road with the authorities.[2]

Stokes had also started a school, originally for his own children, but soon embracing the children of the surrounding villages as well. In May 1925, by which time the school had sixty students, Stokes wrote to his mother in America:

By means of this little school which is drawing into touch with healthy and elevating ideals those who will constitute our children's social environment in the years to come, we are accomplishing that which is the most vital necessity for them – the building up of a group of neighbours and friends whose influence will tend to help their lives . . . This seems to be an inheritance more valuable than anything else I can leave them.[3]

In the spring of 1926, an American named Richard Gregg came to live with the Stokeses in Kotgarh. Born in Colorado in 1885, the son of a Congregational Minister, Gregg had taken a law degree from Harvard. He worked in a legal firm but, dissatisfied with commercial practice, chose to do trade union work instead. This too he found boring; so he went off to work on a farm in Wisconsin. After discovering Gandhi's writings in a Chicago bookstore, Gregg wrote to him. The Mahatma was in jail, but the letter was seen by C. F. Andrews, who on his friend's behalf invited the American to come to India.[4]

Gregg arrived in India in 1925, spent several months in the Sabarmati Ashram (where Gandhi gave him the Hindu name 'Govind'), and travelled around the country before reaching Kotgarh and Stokes, who he had heard about from both Andrews and Gandhi. He began teaching in the school that Stokes had started, while preparing instructional materials. In September 1926 Gregg wrote to Gandhi about his work in Stokes's school:

My time has been much occupied in preparing a re-arrangement of the text-books in both mathematics and physics for my pupils, such as will conform to their experience. All English text-books, and even the Indian ones, are apparently written for city-bred children and presuppose familiarity with machinery and manufactured apparatus of all kinds. These children here have never seen automobiles, steam engines, electric lights, pumps, water-pipes, or even bullock-carts. So the assumptions, pictures, technical terms and arrangement of the text-books of physics, and even of much of mathematics can have no reality and therefore no interest or educational value for them. Gradually, therefore, I am putting together what will be in effect a text-book on science and mathematics for Indian village children. Since most of the children of India are in the villages, I hope it will be useful.[5]

Gandhi replied that having good teachers was as important as having suitable textbooks. He asked Gregg to tell Stokes not to worry unduly about Government recognition for his school; it was how the institution was run that mattered, not by which official agency it was certified. In another letter to Gregg, Gandhi remarked: 'Please thank Stokes for the parcel of apples. They were certainly delicious to eat. They were not golden to look at. My teeth couldn't work through the apples without stewing them. I ate two. The rest were distributed among patients and persons whom you and Stokes would consider deserving.'[6]

II

In 1927, Stokes's mother Florence decided to come out to India. She was almost eighty, but determined to make the arduous journey, telling her son: 'I do feel as if I must see you all – the dear boys and girls and Agnes before I go to my long home.' She spent a month in Kotgarh, seeing her grandchildren for the first time. It was the month of April, so the weather was mild, the views fine, and the apple trees in blossom. On her return she wrote to Stokes:

How pleased your father would have been if he could have known what you have accomplished in your Indian life – in every direction. Agnes would have won his heart and his confidence and your wonderful house and marvellous outlook – the school, everything connected with it and your dear boys and girls, above all your ideals and the way in which you are carrying them out, would have so commanded his interest and his respect. Above all, he would delight over your apples – it is already proving such a success.[7]

In September 1928, Richard Gregg left Kotgarh after two and a half years with Samuel Stokes and his family. He took with him a copy of the manuscript of a book that Stokes was working on, a study in comparative theology that drew upon the writer's practice of Christianity and his readings of classical Hindu texts. Stokes was keen to find a Western publisher, and Gregg had promised to help in this regard.

The departure of his American friend sparked a long meditation on what of his original homeland still remained in Samuel Stokes's heart, mind and character. 'I love America', wrote Stokes to his mother,

> and feel she has wonderful gifts to give the world. I am inspired by much that I see of the way she is developing. At the same time I am fearful lest she become bewildered and let her peculiar genius for organising the good but fleeting things of the world blind her to that in which lies our hidden oneness and to those things that fade not away.

Stokes continued:

> For me, at least – an American born – the East has had a deep and soul-stirring message. My whole outlook has been transformed and life has assumed a meaningfulness that it did not before. As a conse-quence I walk fearless through the welter of flux and change, seeing Time and all that from the standpoint of Eternity.
>
> The result of my twenty four years in contact with the deeper life of India has not been to make me see all things from an Indian standpoint. That has profoundly influenced me, but my viewpoint as it has emerged at the end is neither completely Eastern nor completely Western, nor a 'mixture' of the two. Rather it is the result of the impact of the two . . . [I]t is a <u>new</u> philosophy of life though it has roots deep in the past of human experience and human thought. For me it is <u>the Truth</u> in so far as my spirit through years of deep expe-rience and earnest thought . . . has been able to approach it. It is this vision of what life has come to mean to me that I have tried to give in my book. It is true to <u>me</u>; what it will be to others remains to be seen.[8]

In 1929, Stokes briefly re-engaged with the world of national politics, writing to Jawaharlal Nehru that Congress should participate in the forthcoming Round Table Conference in London. He thought that the Viceroy, Lord Irwin, and the Labour Government then in power in Great Britain, were more sympathetic to Indian aspirations than their predecessors. Nehru, however, was unenthusiastic about the idea, and instead of going to London for the conference the Congress organized a fresh round of civil disobedience.[9]

III

As Chapter 4 documents, Stokes had become disenchanted with how Christian missionaries functioned in India. He found them arrogant, insular, and with absolutely no interest in Indian cultural and spiritual traditions. Over time, Stokes withdrew from mission life, and engaged less and less with the Church. He began closely reading classical Hindu texts, and interacting with Hindu thinkers – pre-eminently Gandhi, of course, but also representatives of that reformist sect, the Arya Samaj. He visited their schools and colleges, and had long discussions with their leaders.

His readings and conversations, as well as his own personal experiences, all fed into the manuscript in comparative theology that he had shared with Richard Gregg. He had given the book the title *Satyakama*, or '*True Desires*'. Gregg was unable to find an American publisher; meanwhile, C. F. Andrews was unable to find a British publisher either. Reading the work now, one can well understand why. As one modern scholar of religion comments: '*Satyakama* is a difficult book, clumsy in form, repetitious and non-systematic. The general reader might be antagonised by the welter of strange abstractions and Sanskrit terms.'[10] In so far as the book has a thesis or argument, it is that every seeker must find his or her personal path to self-realization, rather than have this dictated by scripture or priestly authority.[11]

Bearing the subtitle 'being thoughts on the meaning of life', *Satyakama* was published by a Madras firm in 1931. The next year, Stokes was approached by some leading Hindus of his area, who wondered if, having immersed himself so thoroughly in native life, he wished also to embrace their religion. Stokes pondered over the suggestion, and decided to accept it. His becoming a Hindu would be a natural culmination of the journey he had been making, a religious confirmation of becoming an Indian. His elder sons, now aged twenty and nineteen, were enthusiastic about the idea; although his wife Agnes initially was not, she later came round to the proposal.[12]

In July 1932, Stokes wrote to his mother alerting her of his decision to become a Hindu. He had, he said, been too long a 'benevolent outsider'; it was time to become part of the community itself. He told his mother (whose own Christian faith was deep and abiding) that 'no conscientious scruples would be involved for us, as they would be for you, in entering the Hindu community, and we feel that our family exists peculiarly for the service of these hills, which is almost exclusively Hindu'.[13]

Stokes and his family formally embraced the Hindu faith on 4 September 1932, through a small, simple ceremony conducted at his home by a Hindu priest from the Arya Samaj. Stokes was asked a series of questions to ascertain the depth of his commitment to his new religion; when he had answered them satisfactorily, he was asked to chant some Vedic mantras and the sacred syllable OM. The priest then sprinkled water over him, to cleanse him of his past as it were, before formally accepting him as a Hindu. While keeping his surname, Stokes exchanged 'Samuel' for 'Satyanand', meaning 'happiness in truth'.[14]

For some years past, the Arya Samaj had been vigorously seeking to bring back to the Hindu fold those Indians (often from lower castes) who had converted to the Christian faith. This programme was called 'shuddhi', or purification. Stokes's case was rather different; he had been born a Christian, in America. Having transgressed across the racial boundary, most emphatically by marrying an Indian, he now wanted to make his identification with his adopted homeland complete by adopting an Indic faith as well.

Shortly before the ceremony, Stokes wrote to an Indian Christian priest explaining his reasons. While acknowledging that 'my debt in spiritual experience to Christ is profound', he said that 'philosophically

I am far nearer to the general Hindu position than to the Christian'. His personal inclination apart, he saw the act 'as a social question'. He would be able to serve the people of the hills better if he adopted their faith too.[15]

After his conversion, Stokes issued a short public statement, where he likewise argued that the social service that was his calling 'could be best rendered from within the majority community'. His family's change of faith did not however imply that 'we consider Christianity a false religion and [the] Hindu religion a true one'. He himself believed that there was 'a deep underlying truth in all great religions' and that there was 'no single and exclusive path to deep spiritual experience'. Stokes continued: 'We know also the extent and depth of spiritual life that is to be found in the community we are leaving. Only in our own case the path has led differently and each of us must follow the light as it shines for him.'[16]

IV

Through the 1930s, Stokes scrupulously kept away from politics and public engagement. Towards the end of the decade, he wrote to a friend:

> There was a time when I too thought that I was worthy to be a teacher of others, but as I grow older and look at myself possibly with clearer eyes I lose all confidence in any fitness that I once thought I had to teach others, for I find in myself a thousand spiritual weaknesses and faults which show me that it is for me to learn not to teach – to humbly strive for even a little of the spiritual treasure of which I have been talking and writing most of my life. More and more I feel the urge to be silent and to learn in silence what I may, trying as best I can to win a communion in which there will be no place for littleness and unworthiness.[17]

This was written on 4 February 1939. Yet, a mere six weeks later, Stokes was compelled to seek to teach the three most influential nationalists in India – Gandhi, Nehru, and the person who was the current President of the Congress Party, Subhas Chandra Bose. His instruction took the form of letters on the current political situation in Europe and its implications for India and the world. Having left the Congress fifteen years previously, and retreated into family life, apple cultivation, and spiritual reflection, Stokes was now – by means of these letters – re-engaging with the political party he had been so devoted to in those five heady years, from 1919 to 1924.

The letters that Stokes wrote to these three leading Congressmen were phrased differently. However, all made the same argument: that sooner or later a war would break out in Europe between Britain and Germany, and that while both sides were committed to imperialism, Indians should not stay neutral in this conflict but should instead side with Britain. This choice was necessary, argued Stokes, because while Britain might, at the end of any such war, concede independence to subject peoples, the Germans – with their fanatical and absolute commitment to racial superiority – never would.

The letter to Bose was posted on 30 March 1939; the letter to Gandhi sent the next day; and the letter to Nehru dated 4 April. That Stokes wrote to them all is manifest of how urgent he considered the matter. All the letters are available in Stokes's collected writings; here, I am only reproducing chunks of the letter to Gandhi, because it was by far the longest, and because Gandhi meant much more to Stokes than either Nehru or Bose. The letter makes for remarkable reading, eighty and more years after it was written.[18]

Stokes began by apologizing for intruding into Gandhi's mailbox 'in the midst of all the stress and burden of your life at present'. But he had to, because of the 'sad state of things' in India and the world. For he saw a major global conflict emerging, between older imperial powers, such as Britain, and emerging imperial powers, such as Germany. As Stokes wrote to Gandhi,

> Germany, Italy and Japan simply cannot afford to accept the present basis of division of opportunity and privilege, with practically all the exploitable areas of the subordinated peoples reserved by Britain, France and two or three minor nations as preserves in which they are to enjoy preferential treatment for their trade and advantages

from which other outsiders are excluded. And the present holders of these areas cannot submit to a re-division of imperial spoils because it would almost certainly result in their own disruption as world powers and their economic and financial ruin.

With Britain and France determined to hold on to their colonial possessions, and Germany and Japan equally determined to wrest control of these territories from them, it seemed to Stokes that

the present holders cannot yield a share to others and yet survive, while the others cannot accept the present division and survive. The only way out – and I am convinced the only solution – lies in the termination of the entire imperial system and self-determination for all peoples large and small, weak or strong. This would doubtless involve very real hardship for the present enjoyers of empire and, at first, a much reduced standard of living until they had adapted their economy to the new conditions, but the world as a whole cannot afford [for] special nations the exclusive enjoyment of such privileges as the empire holders seek to retain, and in time they could so reconstruct their economy as to carry on without them.

While Indian patriots naturally wanted the whole system of imperialism to end, said Stokes to Gandhi, neither the British nor the German camp were

prepared for such a solution. They all want to enjoy empire and if there is a war it will be a war for empire – not for the ending of it. In such a war there would be no question of one side's fighting 'for the right' and the other for the wrong; both would be fighting, the one for the retention and the other for the acquisition, of what by right and justice neither should possess. It is this frame of mind that results in the impasse and makes war inevitable.

Stokes told Gandhi that his reason for writing this letter was 'to give you my views upon the question of what India's attitude and line of action should be in the event of war'. He added:

I know you will not mind my doing so; you were always so good about letting me express my views when I was with you in the days of the first non-cooperation [movement], and though I know you will reach your own conclusions in the end, if you have not already, still you will welcome an honest opinion which, whether right or mistaken, is the outcome of anxious study and prolonged consideration.

Preparatory to offering his suggestions on what India's attitude towards the coming war should be, Stokes suggested to Gandhi that a text they both knew and loved, the Bhagavad Gita, sanctioned the use of violence in certain circumstances. As he argued:

For all those who believe that 'ahimsa' implies of necessity complete physical non-violence upon all occasions and in every set of circumstances there can of course be no question of what their individual attitude must be. Like my own Quaker ancestors they will have no truck with war whatever, going to prison and to death rather than participate in it either directly or indirectly, though some might be ready, as the Quakers were in the last war, to work for the alleviation of suffering in the hospitals and in the ambulance corps.

On the other hand, continued Stokes,

there are others – possibly a greater number – for whom 'ahimsa' means a freeing of the spirit from hatred and anger and the desire for the harm of others, yet to whom Sri Krishna's exhortation to Arjuna includes, under certain circumstances, the duty of fighting in a literal sense. For them . . . it sometimes is a call literally to fight in a physical sense, but to do so not as the result of hot anger and resentment or hope of acquisition or in a spirit of egotism. In so far as such are true to their vision the considerations that would lead them to join in war would be what they felt it to be the good of all – 'Lokasamgraham' ['the greater good'] – and they would try to do so in a spirit from which hatred and selfishness had been cleansed away and their minds free from any taint of bitterness against those with whom the eternal law demanded that they should engage in battle. Before those who hold such a view of 'ahimsa' could enter a

war they would have to believe, rightly or wrongly, that . . . they would have exactly the same feeling of compassion and sympathy for those against whom they were fighting as for those on their own side. Such an attitude is of course terribly difficult to attain, but the spirit of 'ahimsa' in any form is as difficult to attain. By either path the ideal perfection is the goal we see far ahead and for which we haltingly strive.

Having outlined two forms of belief in *ahimsa* or non-violence, one absolute and rigid and the other more flexible and (as it were) pragmatic, Stokes continued:

I am not concerned here with which is the truer conception of 'ahimsa'; you would probably hold them both to be different aspects of the same thing, the one a higher aspect than the other. What I am anxious to bring out is that here in India, as everywhere else in the world, there are both classes of people to whom 'ahimsa' has a reality to which they seek, however imperfectly, to be true, and though in their attitude toward what the inner state of their soul should be they may be one, their dharma of <u>action</u> as it touches such a question as taking part in a war may really differ. In such a case – not of course in <u>every</u> war but in certain wars and under certain circumstances – the line of conduct that was the 'kartavya' [duty] for one class of 'ahimsak' [believer in non-violence] would be a failure in 'kartavya' for people of the other class.

While spiritually and philosophically minded people might debate between the merits of these two perspectives on non-violence, the relative versus the absolute, Stokes said that 'the rank and file of a nation' had 'not yet reached a stage in their spiritual experience where "ahimsa" has become a reality in either of these senses'. Their attitude towards war would not be dictated by deep philosophical belief but by mundane considerations.

Having outlined the ethical complexity of the matter, Stokes said that

in the event of war it will be for Congress to give the whole nation a lead as to the attitude and line this country should take. For I hold

that it would be calamitous for Congress to be unable to give the country a lead if war breaks out, and for India to be wallowing at such a crisis in confusion as to what attitude it should take. Whatever line is to be taken it should be a clear one and should be a means of teaching us to act and think as a united nation.

Stokes's heart-felt and necessarily expansive letter to Gandhi continued:

Even if the Congress should decide that it was in the interests of India to throw the whole weight of the country behind the British in the event of war that would not mean that individuals whose individual spiritual outlook called for absolute physical non-violence should be untrue to their 'svadharma' [individual conscience] and take up arms. Yet all might possibly be united in the conviction that it was not in the interests of the subordinated peoples of the earth that Germany, Italy and Japan should replace the present holders of empire. Those whose principles permitted them to fight might in that event do so and those who could not upon principle do so might work for 'Lokasamgraham' in accordance with their light, yet each with the same object in view.

I assume that whatever our individual dharmas may be regards war we are all convinced of the evils of imperialism by whatever names it may be called. So far as the subjugated races of Africa and Asia are concerned this empire is no less an empire because it calls itself a 'commonwealth of nations'. We would all agree that the goal of our aspirations is a world freed of imperialism, in which no nation rules another and the principle of self-determination governs the relations of all peoples. For the realization of that wider objective self-determination for India is what Indians have to strive for.

Stokes told Gandhi that 'my own conviction is that the terrible mess in which the peoples of the world find themselves has no solution but the ending of imperialism. We shall go on killing each other and sending out our young people to be killed until this thing is rooted out of the earth.' If that was the case, he continued, in the event of a world war what position should India take in the interest of bringing imperialism to an end as speedily as possible? I may be quite wrong but after long pondering and the most anxious consideration I believe she can do more toward forwarding that objective by throwing her whole weight without reservation or resort to bargaining behind the British and their allies.

Stokes then offered, to Gandhi, some weighty justifications for Indians to take the side of Britain against Germany in the war that he saw coming. As he wrote:

My reasons are these: – Britain and her allies represent the earlier wave of imperialism as opposed to the new one that threatens the world. The British Empire passed its zenith shortly after the last war when the colonies and India set out to industrialize themselves and become as far as possible economically self-sufficient. The great days of England, when the British Isles did all the manufacturing not only for the outlying parts of the world and other countries furnished her largely with the raw materials, are gone forever. She is no longer the leading manufacturing nation and with the loss of her position her merchant marine is dwindling as well as her urge to empire.

There was a time when the British really believed themselves God's appointed race to rule over non-European peoples and she was able to justify herself morally to herself with the thought that she was 'bearing the white man's burden', but that time is coming to a close. There is no longer the same conviction among her people of their right to rule others and as consequence her hand is slackening. She has relinquished control over the dominions and, even without war, her grip on India is slowly slipping from her grasp. Even now she does not find it easy to stand out against the demands of this country. If there should be a war with Germany I believe that Britain and her allies will be ultimately the victors, provided she can stand the first quick onslaught, for she and those who would be associated with her have resources that give them much greater staying power. But even if she comes out victor she will be so crippled and exhausted and war-weary that she will have neither the strength nor the heart to attempt to stand out against the demands of this country. India will then be able to insist upon complete self-determination and no one will be able to gainsay her.

As a Quaker and as an Indian, Stokes had been resolutely opposed to all forms of imperialism. Yet he clearly saw how much more awful the German variety was than the British. As he told Gandhi,

The new imperialism that threatens will be of quite another order. The Germans are a logical people, with a dangerous tendency to implement their philosophy in terms of life and carry it out to its logical implications. Their conception of themselves as the loftiest expression of the human race and of their right to dominate 'inferior peoples' is a religion with them. They need no salve to quiet their conscience in doing so. Under the influence of Hitler they have become a people 'with a mission' and that is to make the earth and its peoples subserve the needs and the glory of Germany. In the carrying out of that mission they have shown themselves capable of the utmost ruthlessness. They have not hesitated coldly and calculatingly to take measures that inevitably sentence the aged and women and little children to destitution and death and to carry them out in the most shockingly callous manner. . . .

This spirit of coldly calculating ruthlessness combined with the new race philosophy of the Germans makes me feel that they are now in a frame of mind that perfectly fits them to be perpetuators of the wrong of imperialistic domination. Should they win to such an empire I think they are fitted to hold it long and neither violence nor non-violence would avail us. We should become mere hewers of wood and drawers of water to a nation whose conscience would not be wounded by bending all our activities to subserve its ends. Our nascent attempts to supply our own needs by factory and village industry would be crushed, and along with other subordinated races we should be set to supply the Reich with raw materials in exchange for the manufactured products that they would force upon us. A new caste system, based on race and power, would become firmly established with the German 'Aryan' as Brahman and Kshatriya, the other European peoples as Vaishya, and the non-European peoples as the Shudras of the world. Surely we cannot contemplate such a prospect with equanimity.

Stokes continued:

All empires are Asuric [devilish] and we want to see the ending of them, but in this present movement of the Axis powers it seems to me we have a supreme up-boiling of the Asuric spirit which threatens to overwhelm the world. And I submit that in casting the whole weight of India into the scales against it we shall be working for the welfare not only of India but of all peoples, and opening the way to the speedy end of imperial domination by any race over any other.

There is no need to bargain with the British, selling her India's support in exchange for concessions no matter how great. The next war will either see the establishment of a new and ruthless imperialism by a people bringing fresh blood and a new enthusiasm to the task, or the end of imperialism. Britain will be in no condition to retain her hold over the peoples who do not want it and even her allies will refuse to let her do so. For even now all appreciate that it was the determination of a few powers to retain a large part of the earth for their own particular exploitation that has forced other great powers into a mood of desperation and led them to enter upon the path of empire themselves, thereby bringing out all the darkest qualities in their nature.

Stokes ended his letter by apologizing once more for trespassing on the time of the most important man in India, who perhaps got more unsolicited correspondence than any other person in the world. 'I do not know if you will have had the time and the strength or the patience to read so far', he wrote to Gandhi:

Forgive its length if you have. I do not write any more for the papers but I have felt I could not keep silent, for it seems to me that the fate of the world for quite a long time to come hangs in the balance today. God will, I know, give you wisdom as to the way by which you should lead the country when the time comes for it to make its decision.

He signed off by saying:

With love
Satyanand

It took two months for Gandhi to read this letter. This may have been because Stokes had posted it to his ashram in Sevagram, whereas Gandhi was travelling through much of April and May. In early June the Mahatma sent a short reply to Stokes, addressing him as 'My dear Satyanand'. The letter began: 'Pyarelal has preserved many letters for me to read when I can. I can just now find yours of 31 March in this bundle. I have devoured its contents with avidity simply because it is your letter.'

Gandhi then said:

As to the great question raised by you, my reading of the Gita and interpretation of *ahimsa* are different from yours. I do not believe that killing in war can ever be done without anger. As I believed in unadulterated ahimsa I am groping as to India's duty. I am shirking the national solution. . . . My own individual conduct is determined. But I quite agree with you that national can be the opposite. My present mood is to ask the [Congress] Working Committee to decide for itself.[19]

Gandhi did not respond to what was perhaps the *greater* question raised by Stokes – the fundamental difference between German imperialism and British imperialism. Jawaharlal Nehru, who recognized this difference more clearly than Gandhi (though not as clearly as Stokes), also replied, saying:

Generally speaking I am in agreement with your analysis of the situation. I feel, however, that we cannot, under present circumstances, go so far as you suggest, that is, agree to support any war against fascism. If we fight for democracy we must have democracy to fight for. Besides I distrust entirely [the British Prime Minister Neville] Chamberlain and I cannot conceive of a fight for democracy under Chamberlain's lead.[20]

There was no reply from Subhas Bose, possibly because he was busy, or because he knew Stokes far less well than did the other two, or perhaps because he would have been the least sympathetic to Stokes's line of argument. For Bose had come to view the British as the greater danger; he was soon to leave the Congress and go on to make common cause with the Nazis and the Japanese.

Satyanand Stokes's letter to Gandhi was both deeply insightful as well as extraordinarily prescient. While having no illusions about British imperialism, or about the British sense of superiority, Stokes understood that German imperialism was altogether more dangerous, based as it was on racial pride. He knew that the treatment by Germans of people they considered inferior partook of a savagery unprecedented in the history of the modern world. In the event, Stokes turned out to be exactly right – the British side won the war, but the victory left them too exhausted to cling on to their colonial possessions.

V

Five months after Stokes wrote to Gandhi, hostilities broke out in Europe. Stokes spent the war on his hilltop, with his family, watching his apples grow. Little of what he said or thought in these years is recorded. We do know, however, that in 1946 he bestirred himself to vote for a Congress candidate in the elections to the Punjab Assembly. Later that year he went to Simla to arrange for the sale of that season's apple crop; here, in what was still the summer capital of British India, he had an attack of diarrhoea, and was rushed to hospital. His family rushed down from Kotgarh, but the attack turned out to be fatal. He died on 14 May 1946, his wife and his children by his side.[21] Fifteen months later, the independence from colonial rule that Satyanand (formerly Samuel) Stokes had so nobly fought for finally came to India.

PART III
INDEPENDENT INDIANS

CHAPTER 13

The Elusive Search for 'Bapu Raj'

I

In February 1948 – shortly after Gandhi was murdered – his adopted daughter Mira Behn (formerly Madeleine Slade) sent a note to other close disciples of the Mahatma, outlining her own personal plans to honour his memory. She had identified a large area of land in the Himalayan foothills, between Dehra Dun and Rishikesh, which she wanted the State to acquire and run, under her supervision and direction, to promote Gandhi's economic ideas. The tract had forests, grasslands, rivers, fields and hamlets, and Mira's hope was that it would 'be developed beautifully as a model of Bapu's ideals through model villages, self-supporting agriculture, cottage industries, etc.' The project already had a name that Gandhi had approved of – *Pashulok*, the Abode of Animals. A prime focus would be on the animal most greatly beloved of master and disciple, the cow. Mira hoped that 'within a few years Pashulok should become a land of beautiful and happy cattle'.[1]

While Mira was seeking to create a rural utopia in Gandhi's name in India, some friends were urging her to return to the West, where the rivalry between the United States and the Soviet Union was now intensifying. Antoinette Boissevain, a Dutch artist based in London and a friend of Mira's from the 1920s, wrote to her saying:

I try to picture you in your Pashulok and I think that the idea of creating the 'good life' for man and animal such as Gandhi conceived it in that small area as a memorial for him a lovely and lofty one. But I do feel if you have the physical strength to do it, work in a far

greater area is to be done that only you can do; you seem to me too
young still, to go into semi-retirement and devote all your energies
and time and organising talent to Pashulok. You do not belong to
India alone. It is no coincidence that you were born in England. It is
much more a divine purpose to me, that you were born to both
continents. It may well be through you, that a great European peace
movement can be started which would interpret Gandhi's ideas to
the western world and Russia and America. You could do that better
than any other living soul. Now and in the next two years is the time.
Why don't you go to America? Come here, visit the Continent, get
in touch with the panicking politicians and speak to the people of
Europe who are in great despair. I believe in your unique power. You
are, as your mother once said, with a little sigh, an inspired soul.
Now more than ever. Since Gandhi's passing more than ever. Pashulok
could wait and be done as the final memorial at the end of your life
here, or perhaps be started during your absence.[2]

Mira was touched by her friend's letter. She got it typed and sent
it to Gandhi's close associate C. Rajagopalachari (Rajaji), Gandhi's
favourite son Devadas, and Gandhi's wealthy patron Ghanshyam Das
Birla. To each she sent the same covering letter, saying that Antoinette
Boissevain, in her affection for her, 'pictures far greater accomplish-
ments than would possibly result from a visit of mine to the West'.
The thought that she could lead a peace movement in Europe was
flattering, said Mira, but 'my heart and soul are in Pashulok, and it
is through the work that I can do here that I shall be able to speak
to the world best. The most I could contemplate in the West would
be some 4 or 5 months in the summer, when the rainy season here
brings development work here to a temporary stand-still.'[3]

So Mira would stay on in her adopted homeland, and work at
building the India of Gandhi's dreams.

II

Towards the end of 1948 Mira went to Delhi, where she stayed for
ten days with Devadas Gandhi and his family. One section of the

Mahatma's followers, led by Jawaharlal Nehru and Vallabhbhai Patel, were running the Government; another section were active in constructive work. Mira naturally saw herself as part of the second group; but worried that the activities of individual members were 'becoming as unconnected as ourselves'. In the columns of the Mahatma's own newspaper, *Harijan*, she issued this plaintive plea 'for unity':

> Bapu had been the central power round whose physical form we all foregathered in common devotion. Are we to lose that cohesion because the bodily presence has passed away? That would indeed be a tragedy of tragedies, for the first and the greatest memorial we can raise to Bapu is unity of purpose and action among ourselves.[4]

Mira was unhappy with the lack of cohesion of the Gandhian movement in civil society, and disenchanted with the priorities of the new Government. In January 1949, she wrote a short but pungent article with the telling title 'Development or Destruction'. The article began: 'Development schemes are going on apace in India today. But are they all wise and far-sighted? Are they all for the good of the people?' Mira thought they were not, adducing, among other things, the ploughing up of grasslands when fodder was so scarce, the water-logging and salinity caused by 'huge new irrigation schemes', and the preference for chemical fertilizers over compost manure, which increased dependence on foreign exchange while depleting the soil. She urged that technical experts collaborate closely with farmers, to ensure 'that development does not lead to destruction'.[5]

Some months later, in a letter to the Prime Minister, Jawaharlal Nehru, Mira unburdened herself of her reservations with the direction India was taking after Gandhi. She said the system of rationing and controls introduced by the State had increased corruption, adding that the Government's policies were 'very dangerous for the permanent well-being of agriculture and animal husbandry'. Her letter continued:

> Now that I have opened my heart to you about the food crisis and controls, I had better say the rest. As I feel it, India is being taken down the common road along which all countries are running to perdition; big industries, huge armies, centralization, mechanization

and the rest; and along with this the old Imperial Grandeur has never been thrown off. Every time I come to New Delhi it cuts me to the heart. What connection is there between New Delhi and the Mother – Rural India? None! We won our Freedom by means of Bapu's weapons. Why then have we so completely cast away Bapu's ideals in the consolidation of that Freedom? Perhaps the answer is that those who have capacity to rule have not that faith, and those who have that faith have not capacity to rule. What a strange thing it is! And for one like me, who came from the other end of the earth to serve Bapu's cause, it is a heart-rending tragedy.

'I have written all this', said Mira in conclusion, 'simply because I do not want to think these things, or say them to others, without saying them to you.'

Nehru took the criticisms of his fellow freedom fighter in good spirit. He replied that they were 'making some progress on the food front', though it was not as much as he would have liked. However, he thought controls were necessary, for otherwise opportunistic merchants would engineer artificial shortages and profit from them. As for Mira's broader disenchantment with the direction the nation was taking, the Prime Minister somewhat disarmingly remarked: 'I can understand your distress at the way things are working out. To some extent, I share it myself.'[6]

On 26 January 1950, India became a republic, shedding all ties with the British Crown. Mira's old friend and comrade, Rajendra Prasad, became the Republic's first President. In March 1950 he came to visit her, spending the night at her ashram.[7] For all the support she got from the formal Head of the Indian State, Mira found the politicians and administrators she had to deal with obstructive in the extreme. 'I must confess', she wrote in *Harijan*, 'that I am worn out by my long struggles with the machinery of Government.'[8]

Adding to Mira's troubles with the bureaucrats of the UP Government was a return of the malaria that had previously plagued her. She lay in bed for weeks with the illness; after she had recovered, Mira decided to move out of Pashulok into the inner hills, where the air was more healthy. In the valley of the Bhilangna river, she found a plot to build a new ashram, with a magnificent view of the snows. In the middle of a pine forest she laid out a vegetable garden; which prospered, until it was discovered by porcupines.

A young Garhwali who joined Mira as her secretary has left a vivid portrait of her at work in her new 'Gopal Ashram' in the Bhilangna valley. She lived in a small room, ten feet by twelve feet, with a string cot in the middle, where she slept during the night and on which she sometimes sat during the day. The room had 'two or three wooden cupboards containing books and odds and ends, and a couple of bamboo mats spread on the floor for visitors'.

In the mornings, Mira dictated letters to her secretary, after which she went to attend to the animals. The secretary recalled:

> First there were the cows – two or three of them. She spoke to each tenderly, stroked them, picked ticks off their backs and underbellies and let them out to graze. She then groomed the horse, petted the dogs and gave suitable instructions to the stable hands. The animals done with, she made for the compost pit. She spent quite a while mixing dung with other refuse to get the compost just right. Then it was time for the vegetable garden where she spent an hour and more, digging out stones, weeding, watering and caressing the plants.

After lunch – which consisted of two *chapattis*, and some *dal* and vegetables – Mira would take a short rest. A short tour of the premises followed, whereupon she would dictate more letters before dinner. After the meal – as simple as the first – she would read aloud from some of her favourite books, which included (as per the secretary's recollection) '*The Little Flowers of St. Francis*, Nehru's *The Discovery of India*, William Vogt's *Road to Survival*, Weston Price's *Nutrition and Physical Degeneration*, and a variety of tracts on organic farming'.[9]

III

Ever since she moved up north, Mira had sent a steady stream of articles to the *Hindustan Times*, the newspaper edited by Devadas Gandhi. The articles often dealt with environmental themes. An essay of October 1949 deplored the devastation of zamindari forests by large landlords whose properties were being taken over by the state. 'Lakhs upon lakhs of trees', she wrote in anguish, 'have fallen in this shameless scramble throughout India. Trees are the precious wealth of land, giving shelter, drawing rain, and protecting the soil. It takes no time to cut them down, but it takes years and years for trees to grow.'[10]

Another essay, published a few months later, dealt with the degradation of the forests of the Himalaya. This was, as she pointed out, 'not just a matter of deforestation as some people think, but largely a matter of change of species'. In the years that she had been living in the mountains, Mira had observed how, especially on the southern slopes, pine was replacing oak as the dominant species. Oak was immensely valuable to the rural economy – as a source of fuel and fodder – whereas pine was far more profitable for the Forest Department, since it yielded both timber and resin. So the Forest Department was quite happy to encourage and promote this change of species, to augment the state's revenue.

The promotion of pine over oak discriminated against the interests of the hill peasantry. It was socially unjust, but also, as Mira noted, environmentally disastrous. For oak forests had a dense undergrowth of bushes and creepers which effectively absorbed the monsoon rain, whereas the bare ground underneath pine trees led to rainwater crashing down the slopes, taking stones and mud with it, and leading to floods in the plains down below.

Mira urged that the Forest Department and the villagers cooperate to bring back oak at the expense of pine. For, as she remarked, 'the Banj [oak] forests are the very centre of nature's economic cycle on the southern slopes of the Himalaya. To destroy them is to cut out the heart and thus bring death to the whole structure.' Her article ended with this heartfelt plea: 'The forests of the Himalaya are the Guardians of the Northern Plains, which, in their turn, are the Granary of India. Surely such guardians deserve the utmost care and attention that the Government can give them.'[11]

Apart from articles in the press, Mira also wrote directly to the Prime Minister, urging him to take account of nature's laws in his plans for economic development. These letters are not available; but we do have his replies. Thus we find Nehru responding defensively to Mira's criticisms of artificial fertilizers, by saying: 'Reliance on them alone is, I think, dangerous, but there is no harm in some fertilizer being used in addition to organic materials. There is no doubt that they have produced good results in various parts of the country. What the long term result is likely to be on the soil remains to be seen.' Another letter acknowledges the receipt of a book sent by Mira, *Farming and Gardening* by the great prophet of organic agriculture Sir Albert Howard, adding that while he was 'terribly busy' he 'shall certainly look through this book, more especially the pages you have suggested'.[12]

IV

Jawaharlal Nehru was Gandhi's anointed political successor, chosen as Prime Minister of independent India because the Mahatma felt that, among the leaders of the Congress Party, he alone had the ability to appeal across religious, linguistic and regional lines, and to connect India with the world.[13] However, while Nehru followed Gandhi in his remarkable absence of parochialism and chauvinism, in one crucial respect he departed from his mentor – his approach to economic development. Gandhi wanted a free India to be built around self-sufficient villages; Nehru felt that mass poverty could only be tackled effectively by rapid industrialization and mechanization.

Mira had great personal affection for Nehru – which was reciprocated – while retaining grave doubts about some of the policies his Government was promoting. These reservations were shared by the economist J. C. Kumarappa, who had likewise been part of Gandhi's inner circle in the 1930s and 1940s. Kumarappa believed that what he termed an 'economy of permanence' had to be based on local use of local resources. As he once put it: 'If we produce everything we want from within a limited area, we are in a position to supervise the methods of production; while if we draw our requirements from the ends of the earth it becomes impossible for us to guarantee the conditions of production in such places.'[14]

Mira and Kumarappa had known each other well from their days together in Sevagram and Wardha. Their views on rural development were entirely congruent, and, crucially, opposed to Nehru's. There were other followers of Gandhi who thought likewise. In the winter of 1950–1, Mira wrote to Kumarappa that these Gandhians should adopt villages in a contiguous area, and here promote the best practices of rural renewal. She wrote:

> If only we could produce something approaching a Model State it would be a tangible thing for people to catch hold of, and it would be [a] glorious service to Bapu. But unless we are sufficient in number, and sufficiently experienced, we shall only make a mess of it, and that would be worse than anything for Bapu's cause, which is already suffering badly.[15]

Mira suggested that this microcosm of a Gandhian utopia could be nurtured in the area where she was then residing, Tehri Garhwal. After discussing her proposal with colleagues, Kumarappa reported back that one colleague thought that the Government might not agree as such a scheme would violate the Constitution, a second worried that funds might not be forthcoming, a third said that 'the present situation makes this region [Tehri] almost a frontier [with China] and with the conditions prevailing in the world today, it may even become a strategic frontier and therefore, he has his doubts about the feasibility of the scheme at the present time'.[16]

Mira, in reply, suggested that they shift the scheme away from the Himalayan borderland to a tribal district in central India. The 'scheme does not depend on Tehri Garhwal', she wrote to Kumarappa:

> It is the independent area amongst simple and responsive people that we require, and it may be from all points of view better that we seek out an area in a climate in which we can all thrive . . . This would mean, let us say, the Santhal country or somewhere in the Bhil region or if there is any better area which your people can think of. The Aborigines would probably be even better than the Himalayan population, and to create a Gandhian Ram Raj in their midst would perhaps appeal to everybody more.

Mira sent Kumarappa a sketch map of an area in central India that might be suitable for their Gandhian experiment. She wrote:

As you will see it is about as big as Ceylon and the beauty of it is that it has only one branch Railway entering it up to the depth of about 50 miles, and motor roads are very few . . . At the same time this area must be full of Aborigines. Don't you think it looks rather tempting.[17]

In pursuit of this scheme, Mira went to the Chotanagpur plateau in March 1952 to study the situation there at first-hand. She was deeply distressed by what she saw, by the poverty and ill health of the tribal communities in the Ranchi region. 'The whole thing makes one feel very ashamed', she wrote to Kumarappa:

Do you not think we should make a thoroughgoing survey of their economic conditions and the root causes thereof? Do we not owe it to Bapu to try and get to the bottom of these poor innocent and dumb people's suffering? A really strong statement backed by an economic report after direct investigations would be bound to have some effect on the Government . . .

While the conditions of tribals in Chotanagpur depressed her, by now Mira had reluctantly come round to the conclusion that, at her age and prone as she was to malaria, she could not really do intensive work anywhere in central India. 'My health became so bad in the Ranchi area', she wrote to Kumarappa, 'that I had to come back here quickly and even so, I had a high temperature all the way in the plains.' Now back in the mountains, she told her old Gandhian comrade that 'they alone will give me a resting place!'.[18]

V

In the first months of 1952, the Congress Party won a sweeping victory in India's first General Elections. The Congress campaign had been led by Jawaharlal Nehru, and the victory emphatically consolidated his position as Prime Minister. Also in the first months of 1952, Nehru's partially estranged comrade Mira Behn issued a series of short, numbered pamphlets bearing the title 'Bapu Raj Patrika'. Gandhi had often spoken of his dream of an ideal state which would deliver peace and justice to its people. He called this state 'Ram Raj' (after the mythical Hindu God-King); his disciple, however, chose to name her rural utopia after Gandhi himself. The first *patrika* (newsletter) Mira produced said that this Bapu Raj would have 'self-sufficient healthy villages in which man's primary needs of life are produced', where the peasantry would take their own decisions as regards their future, where there would be no exploiting lawyers, landlords, businessmen, contractors, or Government officials. Later newsletters spoke of the importance of village sanitation, cattle breeding, etc.[19]

In April 1952, Mira was visited by the Hungarian writer Géza Herczeg. She had come as an emissary of her compatriot, the Hungarian-born British film-maker, Gabriel Pascal. Pascal had made several films based on the plays of George Bernard Shaw, and now wanted to make a feature film on the life of Gandhi, for which he naturally wanted to consult (and in time feature) Gandhi's foremost Western disciple. Mira took the visitor around the villages of the Himalayan foothills, telling Herczeg about her vision for 'Bapu Raj'.[20] In the event, probably for lack of funds, Pascal's film on Gandhi was never made.

In August of the same year, Mira wrote 'An Open Letter to Congress Leaders', which charged her erstwhile colleagues with being indifferent to the plight of the peasantry.[21] However, even while scolding those in power, she continued to hope they would reverse their policies and priorities. Shortly after her 'Open Letter', she opened discussions with the Government on a 'Himalayan Project', a scheme for rural uplift in the hills focusing on land, pasture and forest. In November 1952 she wrote to J. C. Kumarappa that she would shortly go to Lucknow to finalize details with the UP Government. The Centre (probably at the prodding of both President Prasad and Prime Minister Nehru) had said it would finance 75 per cent of the estimated cost of the project, which was Rs 1.1 million. Mira was quite hopeful of the scheme coming through, telling Kumarappa:

My stipulation of no American money and no American experts has been willingly accepted, and I have had a free hand to draw up the details according to my own ideas. If this Project, by God's grace, leads to satisfaction of the peasantry, it will undoubtedly have considerable influence on the [Government-administered] Community Project people, and it will be a clear demonstration for the villagers. I shall, of course, be looking to Maganwadi [Maganwadi was the headquarters of the All India Village Industries Association, of which Kumarappa was the moving spirit] for help in various technical matters, and I know I can count on your affectionate assistance.[22]

These hopes slowly began to dissipate. The bureaucrats of the Uttar Pradesh Government sat on her file, and then put all sorts of questions and queries. Mira made several trips to Lucknow, but failed to get past these hoops and hurdles. In April 1954, a full eighteen months after the project had first been proposed, she wrote to J. C. Kumarappa in exasperation from her Gopal Ashram in Tehri Garhwal:

Can you believe it, but the Project for this area is still under discussion with the U. P. Government. It is an amazing demonstration of how our democratic Government functions through its bureaucratic officials. Three times I have sent in my resignation but the Government has not accepted it, nor has it begun work, though 13½ lakhs are sanctioned ready since last July. All that is happening is that a useless staff of officials is being paid. You can imagine how this has increased the mistrust of Government in the minds of the villagers. . . . It is now one and a half years since the discussions began! I am just about worn out, and finances are also nil.[23]

In the summer of 1954, Mira visited the Valley of Kashmir for the first time. She was enchanted by its beauty, like thousands of visitors before her. A spirited American woman who had once spent time in Gandhi's ashram, Nilla Cook, was working with Kashmiri craftsmen, and she showed Mira around.[24]

Mira was now in her early sixties. And yet, after two failed experiments in Uttar Pradesh, she now embarked upon a third one in Kashmir. She approached the state's Chief Minister, who – prompted perhaps by a word from Rajendra Prasad, or Jawaharlal Nehru, or both – allotted her a plot of land in a place called Kangan, in the Sindh Valley. She saw the plot, liked it, and began an experiment with cattle breeding. Mira ordered some Dexter cows from Europe, and went herself to Bombay to receive them, supervising their unloading from the ship and then putting the cattle on a train to Pathankot and taking them from there by road to Srinagar and on to Kangan.

In November 1954, Mira wrote to the Prime Minister inviting him to visit her 'in your own glorious country Kashmir', and take the break from his official duties she thought he so desperately needed. She described the landscape and the views, and assured him:

> You could be just as quiet and alone as you liked – and with good riding horses available from a neighbour. The Gangabal water is the best I have ever drunk, and the climate at this time of the year is grand – bright sun by day and white frost at night. Would it not be good for body and soul? Only give the word, and everything will be ready waiting for you.

Nehru wrote back saying he knew the area she was working in 'very well. I have stopped at Kangan more than once on my way up and down, so I can well understand how attractive your place of residence must be. But I fear I cannot go there for a variety of reasons.'[25]

Mira's first winter in Kashmir was fortunately very mild, with only seven inches of snow rather than the usual three feet. In the last week of January 1955 she wrote to an old friend in Delhi:

> We should be in the high grazing lands of Sonemarg from the end of May to the beginning of September. The altitude there is 9000 ft, just under the glaciers. Here we are at 6000 ft.
> The little Dexters are enjoying the cold and we are planning to carry the cross-breeding experiment up into Ladakh next summer.[26]

Later in the year, Mira was visited in Kashmir by the American pacifist Homer Jack. She was busy establishing her new ashram, whose name (Gaobal) demonstrated its main aim, the protection and strengthening of the cow. Jack was impressed by her deep engagement with her favourite animal, speaking of how 'this lady of the cattle' attended to a sick cow and lovingly took a group of women teachers around her terrain.[27]

In Kashmir, as in Uttar Pradesh, Mira found the state's politicians and bureaucrats difficult to deal with. And inter-departmental rivalries and turf wars disgusted her. She wrote in the *Hindustan Times*:

One of the tragedies in our development work is that most of the Ministers and officials know little or nothing about the real needs and proper handling of cattle. Another and fundamental difficulty is that forests, agriculture and animal husbandry are dealt with as separate activities, resulting in continual friction between these departments, which should, in fact, be all working for the benefit of the country as a whole through the full development of these three fundamental sources of a nation's wealth.[28]

Mira's Kashmir experiment was probably doomed anyway. It finally ran aground when the State Government called in an agricultural expert from Delhi, who told them that free-range cattle such as Mira's little Dexters were not the solution. Stall-fed cows of sturdier build should be promoted instead. Mira had a furious argument with the expert, but he was unyielding, and the administration took his side. What happened next is movingly described by one of her associates:

Mirabehn threw up her hands. If the Government were bent on the disastrous course of bringing in large-limbed cattle into Kashmir, she at least was not going to be party to it or be a witness to it. She must remove herself from the scene, the sooner the better. But first the herd of Dexters had to be disposed of.

This did not prove difficult. Under Mirabehn's urging the Government of Himachal Pradesh readily agreed to take the stocks off her hands. Lovingly she bade the animals adieu and stood watching till the trucks carrying them away disappeared around the bend.[29]

VI

In the summer of 1957, Mira left Kashmir and returned to Tehri Garhwal. She found herself a plot of land near the village of Chamma. This had, she told Devadas Gandhi, 'magnificent views of the Great

Himalayan Range, and with good grazing for cows'. She hired local artisans to build her a cottage, a cowshed, and prepare a vegetable garden. She told her adopted brother that 'I feel tremendously cheered up to think that I am going to get my roots into the soil again at last and have a cow or two.'[30] She had chosen to call her new ashram 'Pakshi Kunj', the Abode of Birds.

Sadly, if not unexpectedly, the enthusiasm soon dissipated. Mira was now in her mid-sixties, and found physical labour harder than ever before. Six months after moving back to Garhwal, she wrote to Devadas's father-in-law, C. Rajagopalachari, who lived in Madras. 'Though I am so much younger than you', she said, 'yet I am nearly 65, and I can no longer manage much physical work. As a matter of fact there is deep desire to go inwards, and contemplate and understand. I feel I am only now beginning just to sense the meaning of it all.'

Mira's letter to Rajaji continued: 'I have commenced to write a small book of Recollections, starting from earliest remembrances, and this has opened up a new vision which I have got to dwell on and try to reduce to words.'[31]

Mira was now old and weary, and disenchanted with how independent India was turning out. In February 1958 she wrote to Rajaji that 'the situation goes on deteriorating faster and faster. Every day when I open the newspaper, I brace myself for receiving any shock.' Their old comrade Maulana Azad had just died. He was the serving Minister of Education, and his death, observed Mira, 'must be a heavy blow to Jawaharlal'. She ended her letter with these despairing lines: 'We seem to be working up for an inevitable crisis. May God help us, for we are so little able to help ourselves under the present dispensation!'[32]

Two months later, Mira wrote to her devoted follower Krishna Murti Gupta – who had worked with her in several of her previous ashrams – that Pakshi Kunj, 'though quite the most beautiful spot in the Himalaya I have yet found, is going to be beyond me'. She added: 'Since a restless urge has been with me for some time that sooner or later I shall have to go West, I take it that I must accept the call now and do my best. In some ways I believe there is more response to Bapu's thought over there than in present-day India.' When Gupta wrote back expressing sadness and disappointment at her abandoning a country she had for so long thought of as her own, Mira replied:

> You don't seem to approve of my leaving India, but whether you
> agree or not with the spiritual reasons, there is no getting round the
> physical ones, for if one cannot keep one's health either in the heat
> or at high altitude, there is no other go but to seek a country where
> the lowlands have a temperate climate. I have come to the conclusion
> that it would be better to go to England at least in the beginning . . .
> In England also after all I have friends and relatives, and know the
> countryside quite well.[33]

To console herself and keep going, Mira had begun to write her own memoirs. In May 1958 she wrote to Rajaji that

> much has been evolving in my inner being. The writing of the book,
> which I have now termed 'The Spirit's Pilgrimage' – for that is what
> is has turned out to be – has brought me realization of fundamentals
> that had remained buried deep down in the depths of my heart. I am
> finding myself at last. And along with this has come an urge to go
> West, at least for a time. It is no good my trying to say *why* – I have
> never known exactly 'why' in my life beforehand. I have simply
> followed the inner instinct, and that I have to do now. God will show
> the way as the days go by.

Mira told Rajaji that she planned to stay in Garhwal till the autumn, by which time she would have finished her book. She would then go down to the plains for a few months, say goodbye to old friends, and set off for Europe. Of her last ashram in India, she wrote: 'This little place will be taken over by others. It is beautiful and peaceful, but when I think of remaining the Himalayas say "No, now that you have found yourself you have got to go forth and not fossilize here."'[34]

Mira was deep into writing her memoirs when, one day in 1958, the postman brought a book sent from France by the widow of Romain Rolland. This sparked many thoughts. She still had with her a copy of one of Rolland's several books on Beethoven, which the writer had presented to her when she went to Villeneuve with Gandhi in 1931. She took out the book, and began to read it. At first her French was rusty, but the more she read the more the language returned to her. And with it the spirit of Beethoven, 'the spirit of him from whom I had been separated for over thirty years that I heard and felt, but now with new vision and inspiration'.[35]

In October Mira sent Rajaji the manuscript of 'The Spirit's Pilgrimage', saying: 'In writing the book I have kept in mind the Western public, and have therefore addressed it more to the world than to India.'[36] Three weeks later Rajaji wrote back. He told Mira that her memoir was 'a most interesting human story, most readable and sure to be seized by readers with eagerness so soon as published – this apart from its value to those who hope to make this world better than it is today.'

Rajaji told Mira that he was 'glad you are going to Europe and England. You will of course be a welcome guest everywhere. God bless you – angel pure – I bless you on behalf of Bapu as well as of myself.'[37]

Mira received Rajaji's letter in Delhi, where she was staying in the Presidential Palace as a guest of Rajendra Prasad. She thanked him for his comments on her manuscript, saying: 'God willing it may open the way for me to help bring Bapu's spoken and written word nearer to the Western world.' The rights to the book had been sold by Mira's literary agent, Curtis Brown, to Longmans Green in England and India, and to Coward MacCann in America. She was now 'planning to prepare one or two small books of Bapu's thought for publication in America as a follow on, and have discussed the matter with the Navajivan people. Their publications do not get anywhere! Not even round India properly.'[38]

In January 1959, shortly before leaving India for good, Mira heard of a proposed memorial for Gandhi, to be erected on the spot he was cremated, on the banks of the Jamuna in Delhi. This was to take the form of an artificial hillock through which four tunnels were to be cut. In the cavernous insides of this structure were to be fresco representations of Gandhi's life story. Mira was appalled by the project, by its extravagance and its crudeness. In a letter addressed to her fellow Gandhians, she urged them to have the scheme scrapped, and replaced by something simple and understated. 'Let it be flowers and flowers, and trees and trees', she wrote: 'Above all let there be a sapling or cutting from the peepul tree at Sevagram by which Bapu always sat for his morning and evening prayers.' She added: 'We cannot add one iota to Bapu's greatness by elaborate memorials. Let his greatness be felt by the very simplicity of the sacred spot.'[39]

VII

Mira sailed from Bombay for England on 28 January 1959. The wheel had turned full circle. It was Beethoven who had brought her to India via Romain Rolland and Gandhi, and now – with Gandhi gone for ten years and more, and his influence steadily ebbing in his homeland – it was a letter from Rolland's widow which was bringing her back to Beethoven. She knew anyway that she was not needed in India any more.

In moving back West in 1959, did Mira recall her friend Antoinette Boissevain's letter to her of a decade earlier? That had urged her to present 'Gandhi's ideas to the western world and Russia and America', which she could do 'better than any other living soul'. At that time she was in her fifties; now, however, she was close to seventy. She no longer had the energy, nor possibly the desire, to travel from place to place, proselytizing on behalf of her dead mentor. What she wanted now was a quiet place to read, think, and write.

Mira had thought she would find such a place in her original homeland. However, she found England uncongenial, socially as well as spiritually. So she chose to move to Austria, to be where her original hero Beethoven had found so much inspiration. In September 1959 she wrote to Krishna Murti Gupta from a village near Vienna:

> This place is excellent. The climate is very good, the country is gently mountainous, with lovely forests and open green fields. The people are charming. . . . As for the interest in Bapu here, it is remarkable. . . The call that has brought me here is no false one, and I feel that this must be headquarters and later I can perhaps visit India. I feel too that Bapu would say that my place is in Europe today. Why have I been given this double knowledge of West and East if not to put it to use? I shall be more useful to the cause here than hidden away in

some remote Himalayan village, where all my strength (and there is not very much now-a-days) would go in trying to keep an establishment together under most difficult conditions.[40]

Mira had brought with her to England, and now to Austria, a Garhwali servant named Rameshwar Datt, since, as she told a friend, 'the last days of my life I want to devote to writing and contemplation, not to wearing myself out cooking, cleaning, sweeping and clothes washing'.[41] She rented a cottage in a hamlet near Vienna, from where she wrote to Rajaji in October 1960: 'I have settled down in this little village. Every day I walk in the glorious forests, and every evening I listen to Beethoven's music. Of all this I shall have to write more in the days to come.'[42]

Some months later, Mira wrote to her other great friend in Indian public life, the President of the Republic, Rajendra Prasad. What she 'was unconsciously seeking in the Himalayas', she said, 'I have found here in these forests, where Beethoven wandered with his note-book, in communion with God, and received the inspiration for his immortal music. As you know, it was he who first set me on the road to Bapu.'

The letter continued:

> Though I am outside India, I do not feel far away – really distance makes little difference now-a-days – and I watch with deep interest all that is going on. I read the *Hindustan Times Overseas Weekly*, and Rajaji's writings in *Swarajya*, so I get a general idea. The political temperature is evidently going to rise high during the preparations for the coming elections! No doubt that is a good thing in as far as it prevents stagnation, but politics are becoming a bit of a curse all the world over, and result in everything being looked at from the point of view of votes.

The letter ended: 'At present I am busy with a book about Christianity and Bapu, which I hope to make suitable for Western readers, and enable them to understand better a little more of his Hindu background.'[43]

However, the book on Gandhi and Christianity was abandoned, and Mira began working instead on an anthology of Gandhi's epigrams and short statements. This was published by Navajivan in

India, with Mira trying, unsuccessfully, to have editions brought out in European languages as well. Meanwhile, she was also trying to write a book on Beethoven and his music.[44]

In her years in the Himalaya, Mira moved around from place to place, establishing five different ashrams in the course of a decade and a half. In her years in Austria, Mira could not stay still either. She lived in five different villages in her time in the country, always however within reach of a good natural forest to walk in (and think of Beethoven). Each time, she was helped to settle in by two Viennese ladies who had adopted her as an aunt; Leo Calice, who ran a furnishings store in Vienna called 'Haus and Garten', and a countess named Rosetta Spalt.

In Austria, Mira was living on an allowance of Rs 300 per month given her by the Gandhi Smarak Nidhi, a public trust established by the Government of India in Gandhi's name. This was supplemented by an annuity bequeathed her by her grandfather which was approximately Rs 140 a month. Apart from meeting his living expenses, she also paid her servant Rameshwar Datt a salary from which he could send some money to his family back home. She found it hard to make ends meet, and in March 1962 wrote to the Trustees of the Gandhi Smarak Nidhi to increase her allowance to Rs 500 a month. That would, she said, 'relieve me of much physical and mental strain, and will enable me to handle the work here which is adding to my expenses day by day'.

In appealing for material help to the Gandhians in India, Mira told them that

> my coming to Austria is not a passing fancy which may change at any time. It is the natural fulfilment of my life's journey. It was Beethoven, through his music, who inspired me to fight for India's freedom and I have been drawn now to end my days in the forested countryside where he spent so much of his time. If I was restless during the later years in India, it was because there was a fundamental part of me unfulfilled. Bapu realized that for me there was something lacking, and I know no one would be gladder than Bapu that I have now reached my true self.[45]

The plea was heeded, and the Gandhi Smarak Nidhi increased Mira's allowance to Rs 500 a month.

VIII

In October 1962 war broke out between India and China. Reading the reports in the press, Mira was horrified by the jingoism of the Indian political class. 'I am utterly disgusted with what is going on in India', she wrote to her old associate Krishna Murti Gupta: 'Leaders talked so glibly about the duty of all nations to turn to world judgment to settle their quarrels, but the moment India's own toe is slightly trodden on, they flare up onto a mad war-fever.' Mira had written to Prime Minister Nehru asking him to appeal for international arbitration, and now she did likewise to her Gandhian comrades. So she told Gupta: 'I do not suggest that there should be a non-violent army of Satyagrahis to face the Chinese soldiers, no one has the power today, but I do suggest that cold-war language and attitude should be avoided, and that every effort should be made to bring about a settlement by international negotiation.'[46]

The India–China dispute led to a quarrel between Mira and her old friend C. Rajagopalachari. This long-time associate of Gandhi had now left the Congress and started his own party, named Swatantra. The new party fiercely opposed Prime Minister Nehru's foreign policy, for being excessively hostile to America, and his economic policy, for being excessively hostile to the free market. Rajaji, and Swatantra, wanted India to abandon its traditional non-alignment and place itself squarely in the Western camp during the Cold War.

Mira had a deep affection for Rajaji. In her years in the Himalaya, she had regularly corresponded with him, writing that 'it is such a consolation to have you there, though far away in the South, while I am perched on the northernmost mountains'.[47] Rajaji had been almost the first person she had shown the manuscript of her memoir to, and she was greatly cheered by his endorsement.

Now in Austria, Mira followed Rajaji's activities with an increasing dismay. He wrote a weekly column in the magazine *Swarajya*, where he excoriated Nehru and his Government in the harshest terms. While Mira herself had reservations about Nehru's policies, out of affection and loyalty she did not criticize him in public. Reading the nasty things said about Nehru and his Government in a magazine of which Rajaji was the moving spirit upset her. So she wrote an angry letter to the publisher of *Swarajya*, T. Sadasivam, cancelling her subscription.

Mira's action prompted this short and tender letter from Rajaji:

My dear Mirabehn,
   Your letter to Sri Sadasivam was read by me. I note you are disgusted with what appears in Swarajya and do not any longer wish to read it. Very probably I have disappointed you deeply. But I hope you will not be irreconcilably angry. God bless you.
   Yours affectionately
          C. Rajagopalachari.[48]

Mira wrote a long letter in reply, saying:

Angry with you I am not – how could I be?! Our ties are too deep and too true for that! But I am sad. Sad than one whose wisdom I so much cherished should have become shackled by the orthodoxies of a political party. Yours was the one, clear, balanced voice on international problems, unfettered by any isms or party slogans, Eastern or Western, and I always keenly watched for anything you might have to say. But this politics-business has blurred the clearness. With apologies to Shelley we might say of politics that 'They, like a dose of dingy-coloured glass, stain the white radiance of untrammelled thought'.

   It is true that I do not see eye to eye with you in the present situation, but that is a matter of opinion. No, what has induced me to stop subscribing to Swarajya is a matter of principle. I cannot any longer endure the paper's general tone, and particularly its cartoons (cartoons should always be humorous and good-natured). I feel I cannot – I must not – subscribe to such narrow-minded, third-class, degrading cold-war propaganda. There are many things in Communism which I do not like, and I also have never felt particularly drawn towards China. But my whole being rises against distorted, bitter and vulgar anti-propaganda! China is a great and ancient country, also Communism is a mighty force, and India, today, has made herself look petty and contemptible with her hate-campaign and second-hand cold-war mimicry (not only in Swarajya of course). All the more after the soaring heights of the Gandhian Period. To have you smeared round with this kind of stuff makes one sad indeed!

So that is how it is. What more can I say?! I thank God you are well, and pray that He may yet give back to India your true self.[49]

To this Rajaji responded with warmth and understanding:

My dear Mira,

So I have your reassuring and characteristically affectionate letter. I am relieved to see that you can still write to me in the old way. Be assured that I am just the same man as ever. I feel unhappy over what has come over India even as you do and no more. I have not fallen into any trap of politics. I don't like this huge machine of permits and licences and terrorism that is now ruling India. But let me not trouble you with these things. God bless you, dear Mira,

Yours affectionately
C. Rajagopalachari[50]

This is a moving as well as instructive exchange. Mira, based in Europe and now retired from social work, believed that a true disciple of Gandhi must promote international cooperation and global peace; Rajaji, based in India and still active in politics (despite being in his eighties), believed that a true disciple of Gandhi must hold his own Government to account for its betrayal of the ideals of the freedom movement. Both thought that, in acting as they did, they were best upholding the legacy of their common mentor. That they so profoundly disagreed perhaps only shows us how complex and complicated that legacy was.

CHAPTER 14

Reading from Left to Right

I

When Independence arrived, Philip Spratt was based in Bangalore with his wife Seetha and their three small children, with a fourth on the way. Through the 1940s and 1950s the family lived in rented houses in and around Fraser Town, a cosmopolitan locality of Muslims, Tamils, Mangalore Catholics, and others. All their homes were close to the Bangalore East railway station, so the hooting and shunting of trains was always in the background.

Every morning, Spratt cycled to the office of *MysIndia*, the English-language weekly for which he worked. This was in Brunton Road, two miles south of Fraser Town (as it happens, the premises of *MysIndia* adjoined the house this writer presently lives in). Spratt took his lunch with him, in a tiffin-carrier packed either by Seetha or her mother Sivakami who spoke only Tamil and referred to her British son-in-law as 'Durai' (Sir). The children remember the father as taciturn, absorbed in his world of reading books and writing articles. He told the boys to spend a little less time on athletics, and read the odd book instead.[1]

Spratt's life revolved around editing *MysIndia*, frequenting Select Bookshop and the local libraries, and giving talks at such places as the Institute of World Culture and the Mythic Society. Seetha also worked full-time, as a teacher and later principal in a city school. Even so, the family were never more than modestly off. Spratt always travelled by bicycle, and never owned a motor-scooter, still less a car. He still took on the odd freelance assignment to make a little extra money; as in agreeing to translate from a book by the great Indologist Louis Renou, although in this case the chance to practise his French may also have played a part.[2] As a young journalist who lived in the city in the 1950s recalled, this renegade Englishman in postcolonial India 'lived on a meagre salary, moved about on a rickety bicycle, and could be seen eating a vadai and imbibing a cup of coffee in dingy cafes while reading a book'.[3]

In a remembrance written many years later, Seetha spoke of how, given Spratt's revolutionary past, activists would come to their Bangalore home hoping he could advise them on their own political paths. 'They didn't know', wrote Seetha, 'that Spratt the man was a theoretician who loved his armchair to do his reading & writing on subjects that interested him – he was always a student – never fitted for a practical way – either as a politician or as a man of the world.' Seetha was his anchor; while she took care of the house and the children, he also depended, in matters of his own life and career, on what he termed her 'robust common sense'.[4]

Remarkably, despite his break with Communism, Spratt retained warm personal relations with those he had been in jail with, meeting them whenever they passed through town. Once, when a Bangalore writer asked the Communist Party leader S. V. Ghate, then visiting from Bombay, why he sought out Spratt, now a rabid anti-Communist, Ghate replied: 'Yes, officially he is anti-communist. But we are human beings. Our friendship and our joint struggles, his contribution to the cause – how can I forget him?'[5]

II

From Bangalore, Spratt carried on a sporadic correspondence with M. N. Roy, the far more famous lapsed Communist who lived in the sub-Himalayan town of Dehra Dun. In December 1947 Spratt told Roy he had been reading an article on Soviet biology by the British geneticist C. D. Darlington. This spoke of how scientists were killed in the Soviet Union for being on the losing side of an intellectual contro- versy. 'If true it is worse than Nazism', wrote Spratt to Roy, adding:

I must say I have read much elsewhere by apparently reputable people which confirms it. Is this the pass to which your (our) first love has come? If it is true, communism is a world menace more dangerous than fascism; and I think you – we – ought to speak out about it. We cannot be silent or ambiguous on such a fundamental matter.[6]

At this stage, Spratt still saw himself as a man of the Left, albeit of the democratic rather than revolutionary Left. When, in 1948, some radical Congressmen broke away from the party of the freedom struggle to start a socialist party, Spratt was hopeful that 'one contested general election, mainly between the Congress and the SP, in which there is general adherence to electoral propriety, etc, will be a very valuable lesson. It will create conditions in which other parties can hope for toleration.' Shortly afterwards, the Socialist leader Ram Manohar Lohia came to Bangalore. He met Spratt, who reported that he was 'very friendly' and had asked him to attend the forthcoming party conference in Rajasthan. Spratt had to decline, because of family commitments, but promised to write from time to time for the Socialist mouthpiece *Janata*.[7]

In distant Delhi, the Constituent Assembly was busy drafting a new constitution for the now independent nation. A draft was circulated in the summer of 1948; it left Spratt deeply disappointed. He wrote a short book expressing his concerns that the proposed constitution did not do enough to remove social and economic inequalities. He wished it had modelled itself on a document prepared by his own Radical Democratic Party, which asked for – among other things – state control of key industries and mineral resources, the provision by the state of education and health care for all citizens, social security for the old and the disabled, and the right for voters to recall legislators they believed had betrayed them.

Spratt thought that those in charge of drafting India's constitution were not radical enough. He saw them as liberals narrowly and even exclusively concerned with protecting individual rights. He wished they had instead focused their attention more on reducing the gap, within India, between an educated and propertied minority and the majority who had neither property nor education.[8]

At this stage, Spratt had not entirely abandoned the socialist ideal. His book on constitution-making had some nice things to say about the origins of the Soviet experiment, even if he acknowledged it had later gone very sour. In 1948 he was not a Leninist and not a classical liberal either. Rather, he was now what is conventionally known as a 'social democrat'; though he himself, following M. N. Roy, preferred to call himself a 'radical democrat'.

In 1949, as the Cold War intensified, Spratt began to lean towards the side of the United States. The proprietor of *MysIndia* visited America, and, as Spratt reported to Roy, was 'very enthusiastic; he ticked them off about their attitude to Negroes, but liked everything else'. Spratt then added this comment of his own: 'Neutrality is possible if the combatants will leave you alone. Personally I have no hesitation in choosing. There are promising signs in America. Truman's election for one. What I have read about their education impresses me.'[9]

Spratt's preference for one superpower over another led to a disenchantment with the Socialist Party, on whom he had once placed his hopes. He deplored both their opposition to the Western alliance and their protectionist economic policies. In an essay for a Madras weekly, he wrote:

An opposition party which hopes to replace the Congress on the strength of a rational platform must take up these two policies, of inviting American economic aid on the largest scale, and entering the American defence system. They fit together: they promise the best chance we can now see of escaping Russian imperialism, and at the same time offer us the only possibility in sight of overcoming our economic difficulties. Unfortunately the Socialist Party is strongly opposed to both of them.[10]

It appears that his mentor M. N. Roy scolded Spratt for this tilt towards America. His letter of chastisement is not available, but we do have Spratt's reply, where he said:

Don't think I have made up my mind on anything. I vacillate. I often have Gandhian moods, as you appear to (interesting!). I think I can say that my masochistic heart is in Gandhism, but I cannot persuade myself that it is a practical policy. Just as my nineteenth-century heart is with materialism-humanism, but I cannot move away the rational objections to it as a system or ignore its lack of appeal as an ideology.

I am also attracted by the policy of realistic non-Gandhian neutrality. Try to save something from the wreck. The difficulty is that (in most moods) I am not neutral. The communists won't leave anyone alone: they force one to choose. It ceases to be a private quarrel between them and America. If they win, neutrality won't save anything from the wreck, so unless one is willing to acquiesce in communism one must at least hope for their defeat. Then neutrality becomes rather like Orwell's 'making mock of uniforms that guard you while you sleep' – a common British failing. In fact, I think the line is Kipling. . . .

Thinking of these things, I sometimes get into a C[ommunist] P[arty] Mood. You do, too, I think. At least one would be spared the incompetence of the American leadership. What a mess they have got themselves into in Korea! I suppose it was a trap deliberately set for them. . . .[11]

This letter, written in July 1950, ends the extant correspondence between M. N. Roy and Philip Spratt. It ran through the 1940s, a formative decade for India, and the world. This last letter lays bare some of Spratt's own confusions as regards the Cold War. But while he could see some merit in America, Roy never would, because of his old loyalties to the ideals of the Russian Revolution and his personal memories of American financial and military assistance to the opponents of the Bolshevik regime. Mentor and protégé were already drifting apart. By the time of Roy's death in January 1954, Spratt had chosen to side decisively with the Americans.

III

After 1950, there are no letters between Philip Spratt and M. N. Roy. Nor, more importantly, are there any letters between Spratt and his wife Seetha, since they were now living under the same roof. Nor do we have the unpublished intelligence reports available for the 1920s and 1930s, since Spratt wasn't active in revolutionary politics any more.

What we do have for this period of Spratt's life are his own writings, which are rich and various. His oeuvre ranged widely across politics, economics, international relations, literature, culture, and psychoanalysis. While much of what he wrote for *MysIndia* was unsigned, he occasionally appended his name. He was also a prolific contributor to journals published in other cities in India.

A major focus of Spratt's work was to warn Indians against being seduced by the lure of Communism, which promised equality in theory, but delivered tyranny in practice. In 1951, Spratt was elected one of the Secretaries of the newly formed Indian Committee for Cultural Freedom. The ICCF was affiliated to the Congress for Cultural Freedom, founded the previous year as a platform for intellectuals, writers and artists opposed to Communism in general and to Soviet expansionism in particular.[12] (In 1966, it was revealed that the US Government's Central Intelligence Agency had funded this group, although the fact was unknown to almost all of its members at the time, and for many years thereafter.) There was among left-wing intellectuals in Europe and America a genuine disenchantment with Communism, which – especially in Russia – had revealed itself to be brutally intolerant of dissent and free thought. This disenchantment was most eloquently expressed in the volume *The God that Failed*, in which six celebrated writers – Ignazio Silone, Arthur Koestler and Richard Wright among them – explained why they had joined the Communist Party and why they had left it. The book was published in the United States in 1949 and in the United Kingdom in 1950. Spratt could (and perhaps should) have been one of the contributors to *The God that Failed*. Living in obscurity in Bangalore, he was not asked. In any case, by 1949 Spratt had – on the basis of his own personal experiences – already come around to the view expressed by its contributors.

That Spratt would join the Indian Committee for Cultural Freedom was not surprising. That a shy, reticent man like him would take on organizational responsibility perhaps was. It showed the depth of his commitment to his new cause, that of anti-Communism. As Secretary, he had to frequently correspond with the office of the parent Congress for Cultural Freedom, headquartered in Paris, as well as coordinate the activities of the different branches of the Indian unit.[13]

In the last week of March 1951, a meeting of the Indian Committee for Cultural Freedom was held in Bombay, at which some international delegates were also present. Afterwards, Spratt wrote an article in an anti-Communist weekly edited by a bitter critic of Nehru, the journalist D. F. Karaka. Spratt said here that 'illiberal tendencies' in Indian society, such as caste discrimination and communal conflict, 'become an immediate threat to freedom because of the opportunity which they present to communism'. He warned India against taking a neutralist position in the Cold War, arguing that 'in comparison with the threat of communism, the dangers from the expanding economic power, and cultural vulgarism of America, and from a survival of colonialism from the lesser capitalist powers are a lesser threat to cultural freedom'. If America could treat African Americans more fairly, if Britain ceased to support racial discrimination in Africa, and if France could grant self-government in places like Morocco and Pondicherry, then, said Spratt, 'India would cease to look with suspicion on invitations to support Western democracy against communist totalitarianism.'[14]

In the summer of 1952, Spratt was one of the five delegates from India to attend a conference of the Congress for Cultural Freedom, held in Paris. He took the opportunity to visit his family as well. He had been away from England for more than twenty-five years. He relished the opportunity to visit art galleries, and to attend music concerts. Writing about his trip for an Indian audience, he remarked that, compared to the Britain he had left, the Britain he now saw was infinitely superior –

> the standard of life of the ordinary people is higher, health seems to be better, towns and roads are better kept and cleaner; I fancied the social atmosphere was less snobbish; there is a good deal of evidence in architecture of a break with stuffy old ideas. The state of Britain is certainly testimony to the advantages of change by agreement.

The last sentence showed how far he had moved from his Communist credo, from his old commitment to change by violent revolution. However, even while appreciating the progress made, he found the British, and the French, insensitive to the plight of people in the less developed parts of the world. In his talks, he warned his audiences 'that their new colonial policies are still far from adequate to the situation of the 1950s, and that they will have to make further serious sacrifices if they are to win the friendship of the Asian and African peoples'.[15]

Three years later, Spratt travelled overseas again under the auspices of the Congress for Cultural Freedom. This time it was to a neighbouring country, Burma, the venue of a conference of writers and intellectuals from across Asia opposed to Communism and its works. Participants had come from India, Pakistan, Indonesia, Thailand and the Philippines, but not, notably, from China or Vietnam, already lost to the other side.

The conference carried the title 'Cultural Freedom in Asia'. Spratt was one of thirty speakers, his topic being 'totalitarian threats to cultural freedom'. He spoke of the dangers posed to freedom by statism, puritanism, religious fundamentalism and nationalist hysteria respectively, ending with the greatest danger of all, Communism, which he characterized as 'psychologically akin to a militant religion; it mobilizes class envy and ambitions as well as nationalistic fanaticism, and it is highly destructive of civil and cultural freedom'.

These were the words with which Spratt's talk in Rangoon ended. Earlier in his narrative he had remarked:

> The more clearly it is resolved to keep the process of change within civilized bounds – to adhere to constitutional methods, to respect defeated opponents, to compensate expropriated interests – the less will adherents of the old order fear change, the less bitterness will be provoked, and the less will those on either side be tempted to lessen freedom of expression or to abuse it.[16]

The Communist of 1935 who had become a social democrat by 1945 had since travelled further along the road from left to right. In 1955 he qualified in all senses as a 'liberal'.

IV

Philip Spratt may not have had the privilege of being a contributor to *The God that Failed*, and thus alerting its Western audience to the lessons of his own experience. But he was determined nonetheless to alert Indian audiences to the dangers of Soviet expansionism. In 1951 he published a thirty-five-page pamphlet warning gullible intellectuals not to be taken in by Russia's professions of peace and international cooperation. The Soviet Union, he said, was committed to the export of violence and terror; 'she presents the world with the alternatives of submission or war'. 'Far from desiring peace', he continued, 'Russia has directed her policy since 1945 at expansion and at preventing the return of peaceful conditions in the rest of the world.'[17]

The next year, Spratt wrote an even longer pamphlet on Communist designs in India. This carried an introduction by the liberal journalist E. P. W. de Costa, which, recalling how and why the author came to India, said that 'readers will more greatly appreciate the anti-Communist fervour of this pamphlet because it is written by one who knew Communism from the inside and once pledged his life for its success'.

De Costa continued:

> Philip Spratt continues to be one of us. India is his home. His wife is Indian and so are all his children. He has an equal stake with us in the danger that he apprehends. Only he apprehends it more clearly than we do because he has been through that process of disillusionment which is described in 'The God that Failed'. This is a record written by a man who might have joined the authors of that notable book.

Running to fifty pages in print, Spratt's pamphlet was at once a primer of Marxist theory, a brief history of the Communist Party of India, and a call to educated Indians not to succumb to this sweet-sounding but ultimately pernicious ideology. Having been stopped by the Americans from taking over the whole of Europe, the Soviets had cast their eye on the vast and populous countries of Asia. China had already fallen, and India might be next. The pamphlet pointed out that the economic achievements of the Russian Revolution were greatly exaggerated, and, such as they were, had been achieved at an enormous human cost. The system depended on forced labour, and 'the restriction of freedom has extended from politics to all aspects of intellectual life'. If India ever came under Communist rule, warned Spratt, she 'would have to submit to a terror of more than mediaeval intensity', and 'would undergo total subversion of her culture'. She 'would undergo the most profound demoralization under a system which has no regard for truth or personal integrity, is basically hostile to religion and to individuality, and extracts rigid conformity as the price of survival'.[18]

Spratt also wrote often about Communism in the press. In 1958 he appreciatively reviewed Milovan Djilas's book *The New Class*, where the formerly high-ranking Yugoslav Communist had argued that the party elite had become a new ruling class.[19] The next year he visited the southern state of Kerala, where a Communist Government had come to power through the ballot box. In power, wrote Spratt, the Indian Communists ruled through deceit, subterfuge and terror. When the Congress and the Church launched a movement against the Kerala Government, and it was dismissed by the Centre invoking a then rarely used constitutional provision, Spratt shed no tears, believing that his erstwhile comrades had met their just deserts.[20]

In the autumn of 1963 – a year after India's war with China – the Indian Committee for Cultural Freedom organized a conference in Bombay offering 'A New Look at Communism'. Spratt presented a paper, where he allowed that 'Marxism is not intellectually negligible', and 'has a contribution to make to most departments of the study of man'. However, for an intellectual to become a party member was to mortgage one's conscience and self-respect. For, as the experience of the Soviet Union showed, 'communism imposes restraints of varying degrees of severity on almost all kinds of intellectual activity'. The fiasco of Lysenkoism was but 'a small illustration of the lack of respect for truth which distinguishes communist intellectual life. Political propaganda always has first place.'[21]

V

Debunking Communism in theory and practice was one of Philip Spratt's obsessions in the 1950s. Debunking the Prime Minister of India, Jawaharlal Nehru, was a second. In unsigned editorials in *MysIndia*, and in signed pieces elsewhere, he savaged Nehru's policies at home and abroad. Thus, when the Prime Minister visited the People's Republic of China in 1954, Spratt charged him with betraying 'an old friend, Chiang [Kai-shek], who stood by us in the war', while 'turning a blind eye to Mao's policy of debauching neighbouring countries with drugs, and using crores of dollars thus earned to finance his fifth-columns within them; blindness to Mao's slaughter, in the best Stalin manner, of millions of his subjects for ideological deviations; and blindness even to military aggression which could have no other aim than to threaten India'. Spratt attacked both Nehru and his close aide V. K. Krishna Menon. He wrote sarcastically that Menon should be awarded 'the Stalin Prize for the Most Ingenious Invention in Linguistics', while Nehru should be given the 'Mao Tse-tung Medal for Dupes (first class)'.[22]

In 1955, Prime Minister Nehru committed his Congress Party, and by extension the Government of India, to a 'socialistic pattern of society'. Spratt argued in the columns of *MysIndia* that the embrace of socialism was a betrayal by Nehru of his mentor, the Father of the Nation, Mahatma Gandhi. 'That government is best, which governs least', Gandhi had proclaimed. How did his disciple's commitment to nationalization, to the public sector occupying what Nehru called the 'commanding heights of the economy', square with this? Gandhi, wrote Spratt, had a 'deep suspicion of governments – all governments, foreign and indigenous. He was the prince of individualists. That government is best which governs least.' By now Spratt had come round to the view that socialism made for bad economics. This was because 'it has no solution of the problem of incentives. A man will work for fear of starvation, or to gain wealth. But socialism rules out both starvation and wealth. Why then should a man work? The socialist's only possible answer is that the government must compel him to work by fear of punishment.' In its coercive and elusive pursuit of equality, wrote Spratt, 'socialism sets up a society of slaves and slave-drivers'.[23]

In his writings, Spratt represented Nehru as, in effect, a crypto-Communist. In an essay of 1963, he went so far as to claim: 'Nehru is a Communist in this broader sense. He accepts increasing governmental power, socialisation and mechanisation, as both inevitable and desirable. He is strongly attached to the existing Communist governments, and when they clash with other governments he almost invariably supports them.'

These sentiments were expressed in a foreword to a book by Sita

Ram Goel, a right-wing thinker whose animosity towards Nehru exceeded even Spratt's. The foreword continued: 'His [Nehru's] Communism has been clearly revealed in his foreign policy. He cannot go wholly over to the Communist bloc, but he will not take the protection of the free countries, so India remains defenceless. China's big attack came a year after Goel's articles, and fully bore out his warning.'

And further: 'His [Nehru's] Communism is also shown in his economic policy. Its deficiencies in Russia and China have become generally known in recent years, but he still persists with it. He is not even disabused of collective farming, despite its spectacular failure everywhere.'[24]

Notably, the owner of the paper that Spratt worked for was himself an admirer of the Indian Prime Minister. When Jawaharlal Nehru died, in May 1964, *MysIndia* ran an unsigned editorial titled 'A Great Star Eclipsed', saying that the nation had 'suffered the greatest tragedy since the assassination of Mahatma Gandhi'. Nehru, said the weekly, 'came to be identified so closely with everything in the country that he became synonymous with the nation itself'. The obituary spoke of Nehru's role in laying 'the foundations of a modern democratic state', in promoting economic development, and in mediating between the two superpowers during the Cold War. It then euphemistically commented that 'whether his policy in relation to China was right or wrong, there can be no doubt that in whatever he did his purpose was always to live up to the high ideal he had placed before himself, of peace and friendship'. This was the only ambivalent note in a tribute which hailed Nehru as 'the greatest Indian of our time', and which hoped that 'in the critical time ahead those who had the privilege of working with him [Nehru] will practise his ideals and carry forward the good work that he initiated but left incomplete'.[25]

This encomium was most likely written by the paper's proprietor, D. N. Hosali. Immediately following it was a signed article by Philip Spratt on Nehru and his legacy. Spratt began, as he had to, by seeking to understand the enormous popular appeal of a man whose policies he had himself so vehemently criticized. Here he took recourse to Max Weber's famous concept of 'charismatic authority'.

While the twentieth century had 'produced many and various leaders of this charismatic type' each of whom gained his position 'by his direct appeal to the feelings of the people', Spratt wrote that the politician 'whose quality most literally accords with the meaning of Weber's term is Jawaharlal Nehru'. Leaders like Churchill and de Gaulle had appealed to national greatness, and Gandhi to 'the supernatural power of holiness'. However, Nehru's appeal had overtones neither of national nor spiritual greatness; rather, 'he triumphed by sheer charm, grace, loveliness, charisma'. Spratt acknowledged that 'underlying the charm was a genuine care for the people', that Nehru was 'the kind of man whom ordinary people like and trust, and he owed his almost uniquely long period of power to the fact that the people had not misjudged him'.

The article then examined Nehru's domestic and foreign policies, and their often contradictory character. Spratt wrote that 'with typical Hindu eclecticism', Nehru 'espoused Communist economics and at the same time democratic politics, and strange though it will seem, he will be remembered as one of the chief architects of Indian parliamentarianism, constitutional liberties, and freedom of thought and expression'.

In this article, Spratt tried throughout to adhere to the dictum of *De mortuis nil nisi bonum* (speak no evil of the dead), or rather, as in this case, to give the most generous interpretation to Nehru's acts. Of their practical consequences of course he had been much more critical when Nehru was alive, both in unsigned editorials for *MysIndia* and in signed articles elsewhere. Now that the man was dead, Spratt heroically suppressed his personal animus and his polemical instincts, by writing of Nehru as a, or indeed *the*, representative Indian of his time, uniquely connecting the country's past with the country's present. His article concluded with this paragraph:

Nehru's ambition was to transform his ancient country into a part of the modern world without losing the idealism which distinguished the old culture. He was himself almost purely modern in education, and he obtained a somewhat detailed acquaintance with Indian history, literature and philosophy when he was in his fifties. It is interesting then to observe that despite this, his basic patterns of response to political situations ran true to the old cultural traditions. He may almost be described as an Indian inspite of himself, an Indian without knowing it. But though he may not have known it, the public recognised it, and having made him Prime Minister kept him in that position for seventeen years.[26]

VI

As the de facto editor of a weekly magazine, Spratt spent more time rewriting other people's prose than composing his own. His duties at *MysIndia* were wide-ranging – going through a large number of unsolicited submissions, writing polite notes of regret, reshaping articles deemed worthy of publication, composing editorials that went unsigned, having manuscripts typed, galleys proofed, et al.

Much of this work was tedious. Occasionally, however, an article came his way that it was a pleasure to publish. In August 1963, a week before the sixteenth anniversary of India's independence, *MysIndia* was sent an essay by a retired colonel of the Indian Army, recalling those 'British friends who, in the distant past, when freedom was a far cry, not only joined hands with us in our struggle but also taught us the very idea of independence and, indeed, acted as our torch-bearers'. The essay mentioned some names; such as John Bright, who spoke out in the House of Commons for equality between Indians and Englishmen; A. O. Hume and William Wedderburn, who helped found and nurture the Indian National Congress; C. F. Andrews, 'who became a "brother" to both Gandhi and Tagore'; Annie Besant, 'who adopted India as her motherland and organised a countrywide campaign for Home Rule in which the present writer proudly recalls taking part during his student days'; B. G. Horniman, 'brilliant editor of the *Bombay Chronicle*, who was deported in 1919'; and George Lansbury, 'the untiring exponent of our cause from the Labour benches of Parliament'.

The article continued:

The list given above is by no means exhaustive. There have been

many Britishers who quietly, unassumingly and yet effectively
assisted us in aspiring for Independence and attaining it. This article
is merely to draw attention to the galaxy of well-known Britishers
who were either with us or fought alongside us to obtain Freedom,
the attaining of which we celebrate annually and to remember
whom on this day is but natural for us, with our great philosophy
of love and gratitude.[27]

I quote here from the article as it appeared in print. One does not
know whether the draft as submitted to *MysIndia* included Philip
Spratt's name as among those Britishers who had 'quietly, unassumingly and yet effectively assisted' the Indian search for freedom. If
it did, then Spratt would have – quietly, unassumingly – removed
the reference, though at the time he was surely pleased to see an
article of this kind published in the columns of his weekly.

VII

In February 1964, India's elder statesman, C. Rajagopalachari, 'Rajaji',
praised Philip Spratt in the pages of his weekly *Swarajya*. He reproduced extracts from an article in *MysIndia*, saying that 'Mr. Spratt's
analysis and exposition given below are better than anything I can
write on behalf of the [Swatantra] Party's programme and its opposition to what the Congress is doing'. While singling out Swatantra's
critique of nationalization and its call for transparency in electoral
funding, Spratt had remarked of the programme of Rajaji's party that
'on those subjects, principally economic, which fall within its statement
of principles, it is bold, clear and convincing'.[28]

A few months later, Rajaji once more praised an article of Spratt's,
this one dealing with the Nehru Government's foreign policy, and
its sanctimonious and impractical nature. Rajaji characterized
Spratt as 'an experienced old hand not deceived by the pious voice
or a balance of phrases. He sees total contradiction between word
and action and writes somewhat bitterly in *MysIndia* . . .'[29] A few
months later still, it was Spratt's turn to praise Rajaji, as one who
had the courage and clarity to differ with the most charismatic

and powerful leader of the day, whether this be Gandhi before
Independence or Nehru after Independence. In praising Rajaji as
a dissenter, Spratt was reminded of his old mentor, M. N. Roy,
whom he called 'one of India's neglected great men'. To be sure,
'Roy thought in abstract, theoretical terms, and wrote a harsh
style', whereas 'Rajaji thinks in traditional Indian terms and writes
simply and charmingly'. Nonetheless, there were some striking
similarities between the two thinkers, 'because they both take long
views, they refuse to be overawed by power, and they do not let
words take the place of facts'.[30]

It is not clear when Rajaji and Spratt first met. What we do know
is that in 1965, after more than two decades with *MysIndia* in
Bangalore, Spratt moved to Madras to work with *Swarajya*. The
Spratts lived at first in an apartment in a complex owned by
Swarajya's proprietor, T. Sadasivam, and called Kalki Gardens after
a celebrated Tamil writer of that name. The other families living in
the complex were all Brahmins who could not abide the cooking or
eating of meat. One or other protested about the smells wafting in
from the Spratts' kitchen, so the family moved out and rented a
place in the locality of Kilpauk instead.[31] Spratt's own favourite spot
in the city was Moore Market, a building close to the Madras Central
Railway Station that contained a number of second-hand book-
shops.[32]

A younger writer who worked with Spratt in the *Swarajya* office
in the late 1960s remembers him as 'a man of gentle strength [and]
unlimited integrity', who would come to work every day by public
transport. Spratt introduced the apprentice to the works of, among
others, George Orwell.[33] In the paper itself, he was at first regarded
as an expert on international relations, though he soon came to
write on Indian affairs as well.

Spratt wrote a couple of articles a month for *Swarajya*, apart from
contributing book reviews. He also helped with the commissioning
and editing of articles by others. An early essay under his own name
expressed some sympathy with Gandhians and non-Marxian socialists
who advocated a society based on cooperation and not competition.
Thus he wrote: 'The competitive, atomized society is certainly unsat-
isfactory, and on the other hand, the solutions provided by State-run

socialism are equally bad. Is it not possible that Sarvodaya or Boimondeau or some other is on the right track?'[34]

Spratt argued that, unlike the Utopians, 'most Swatantra Party people' were not thinking of constructing a perfect society in the future, but 'are thinking about the next ten years – and it is arguable that there is good sense in such ideological modesty'. He believed that Gandhians and non-Marxist socialists should consider that they might share a 'community of interest with a party which has a practical economic policy, and whose basic principle is freedom'.[35]

In 1967 India held its fourth General Election. The Congress found its overall majority in Parliament significantly reduced (by almost eighty seats), while losing power in several major states, including West Bengal, Kerala, and Tamil Nadu. Spratt wrote that the vote against the Congress was partly a 'protest against economic hardship', and partly 'an assertion of local, especially linguistic, identities which the Congress has over-ridden'. Spratt hoped the election result would lead to a deepening of federalism, perhaps by amending the Indian Constitution to provide more powers to the states. He remarked that the Constitution had been framed when 'the wave of nationalism, and therefore of centralism, was at its height', whereas the 'States are now foci of potent linguistic loyalties'.

What Spratt hoped for most of all was the decentralization of economic decision-making, not merely from the Centre to the states, but from the State to the individual. 'There is no point', he said,

> in freeing oneself from the bureaucracy of Delhi, only to be enmeshed in the toils of the bureaucracies of Calcutta, Trivandrum or Madras. There are socialist federations, but their socialism negates their federalism, just as it negates their democracy. The aim of federalism is freedom, and the new turn in national affairs will come to nothing unless it promotes freedom.[36]

Spratt was often perceptive on domestic politics, but less so on international affairs, especially when commenting on the foreign policy of the United States. In May 1966, he wrote urging India to reconsider her opposition to America's war in Vietnam. In his own version of the domino theory, he remarked:

The facts are that North Vietnam is working together with China to extend communist power. North Vietnam has armies in Cambodia, Laos and Thailand. If America withdrew, these three countries would at once collapse and be taken over, principally by China. Moreover, Malaysia, Singapore and Burma would soon follow. The new regime in Indonesia would be weakened and might adapt itself to the changed situation. . . . Pakistan would cease to bother with America and would strengthen her ties with China.

In sum, claimed Spratt, 'America's withdrawal from Vietnam would be a major disaster for India. Why then does the Government demand it?' Spratt thought the Indian opposition to America's involvement in Vietnam was 'probably put on to please Russia, though Russia's attitude is itself in part a pose, put on to please Afro-Asia. It is doubtful if Russia really wants America to withdraw, for the result would be a big increase in the power of China . . .'[37]

This essay showed the blind spots of Spratt's Cold War partisanship, as well as his lack of understanding of nationalist sentiments within Vietnam itself. He thought that the Vietnamese Communists would always be loyal to their Chinese counterparts. They weren't, then, nor for ever thereafter.

In 1967, to mark the fiftieth anniversary of the Bolshevik Revolution, the *New York Times* ran a series of reports on Russia, and these were reproduced in Madras's leading newspaper, *The Hindu*. On reading them Spratt was puzzled by both the way they showed a strong revulsion against Stalin but somehow exonerated Lenin. By now, Spratt had come to the conclusion that 'though Lenin was a less unattractive personality, he did nearly all the terrible things that Stalin did, and made it possible to do worse'. In an essay in *Swarajya*, he explained how Lenin aborted the Constituent Assembly in which his own party had a minority, used terror to seize power and to silence critics, and persecuted the Church. Spratt outlined Lenin's essential culpability for the crimes of Stalin in this concluding paragraph:

Though Lenin was a disaster for mankind, one has a certain respect for him. He felt he had dirty work to do and did it, without hesitating but without exulting in it. There was no blood-lust or vindictiveness;

he was like a general ordering troops into battle. That cannot be said of Stalin, whom it is impossible to respect. But it is not easy to say more for Lenin. Indeed as the better educated and more sensitive man he is in a way more culpable. True, Lenin merely slaughtered millions, whereas Stalin slaughtered crores. But is there much moral difference. Moreover, it was Lenin who started the game of political slaughter. The Russian public are still being misled if they denounce Stalin while glorifying Lenin, the real author of their miseries.[38]

Spratt's assessment recalls this verse of Robert Conquest:

> There was once a great Marxist called Lenin
> Who did two or three million men in
> That's a lot to do in
> But where he did one in
> That grand Marxist Stalin did ten in

I don't know whether Spratt knew of this limerick (unlikely), but he did know of Conquest's definitive work on Soviet authoritarianism, *The Great Terror*, which he termed, in *Swarajya*, 'the most complete account hitherto, and probably for a long time to come, of the criminal side of Stalin's rule'.[39]

Another piece by Spratt, likewise sparked by the fiftieth anniversary of the Russian Revolution, allowed that socialism as originally conceived by Marx was 'in many ways admirable'. Yet in practice in the Soviet Union it produced 'such monstrous results'. Non-Leninist Marxists claimed that this was because Marx himself had argued that the establishment of socialism must follow rather than precede the development of an advanced industrial economy under capitalist auspices. Thus, had England or Germany become socialist, they might have been spared the horrible fate that had befallen Soviet Russia.

Spratt advised Marxists in India to 'forget Lenin and Mao, and read Marx and Engels' instead. Then he mischievously added: 'The clear implication for such a country as India of everything that Marx wrote is that before thinking of socialism, it must undergo a thorough development through capitalism. If Marx lived in India now, he would support the Swatantra Party.'[40]

In 1968, a British publisher brought out four volumes of the essays and letters of George Orwell. Spratt wrote a long and most interesting review essay in *Swarajya*, where he let on that he had borrowed the set from the British Library in Madras, this suggesting perhaps that he was hard pressed for cash, or had no space at home, or recognized that at this stage in life he had no need to acquire new possessions.

In his assessment of Orwell's oeuvre, Spratt wrote of his distinctly unsocialist interest in English cooking and in flowers (for which he was berated by his left-wing readers), and his plain, unadorned, style. He then considered Orwell's self-description of himself as a socialist. He observed that 'in fact his socialism is exceedingly vague, no more than an aspiration for something better'. And of course Orwell was a bitter opponent of Stalinism.

Spratt titled his essay 'Orwell's Retreat to Common Sense'. The last paragraph turned from a dead British writer to the live and contentious world of Indian politics. In September 1969, when the essay was published, Prime Minister Indira Gandhi was moving rapidly leftwards in her politics, cheered on by a large section of the Indian intelligentsia. 'Our enthusiasts claim that youth is on their side and that their leader is riding the wave of the future', remarked Spratt. He himself thought that the Prime Minister was

> riding a wave, but it is just one more of many waves which for fifty years past have been surging up the beach and then washing back again disillusioned. The attempt to realize socialism can have one of three results: chaos, Stalinism, or a retreat to common sense. Let us hope the current attempt will result in this last and least harmful outcome.[41]

Because of Rajaji's stature, and the Swatantra Party's growing challenge to the Congress, *Swarajya* had a national presence. It was an altogether more serious and substantial magazine than *MysIndia* had ever been, a far more worthy outlet for a writer of Spratt's calibre and experience. Considering the range and quality of his own work, one wishes he had had access to such a pulpit much earlier.

VIII

From the 1940s, Spratt had begun reading widely about psycho-analysis, the works of Sigmund Freud in particular. He had also begun immersing himself in the scriptural and mythological traditions of India. These studies persuaded him that in understanding the long sweep of Indian history, 'the unilinear Marxist doctrine is unsound', whereas 'a psychological approach is more promising'.

In the 1960s, Spratt published a series of essays exploring the 'Hindu personality' from a psychoanalytic point of view. There was, he argued, an absence of the Oedipus complex in India, 'little trace of the infantile fantasy of attacking, castrating and killing the father'. Rather, there were 'strong traces of the passive homo-sexual attitude to the father, and of propitiating him, submitting to him and castrating oneself in order to ward off his anger and gain his love'.

This submission of the child to the authority of the father, Spratt argued, explained the relative lack of rebelliousness in Hindu society. From the time they were born, boys were taught to revere the father and the ideas and institutions associated with him. Because tradition and custom had a hallowed, sanctified status, 'the eternal rebellious-ness of the West is conspicuously absent'.

This submission to older male authority, claimed Spratt, was also manifest in the devotion of the *shishya* (disciple) to the *guru* (teacher), and in the admiration for ascetics and holy men. 'Thus a society in which the yogi is honoured above everybody else will deprecate youth and honour age, and will eliminate at the source the self-assertion of the young against the old.'[42]

In 1968 Spratt reworked these essays into a full-length book, which he titled *Hindu Culture and Personality: A Psycho-Analytic Study*. This was based on wide and somewhat indiscriminate reading in Indian mythology, Indian philosophy, Indian history, and Indian sociology. The book's main thesis was that the Hindu personality was inward-looking and 'narcissistic', whereas the Western (or Christian) personality was outward-looking and 'punitive'. Spratt attributed this largely to differences in child rearing; unlike in the

West, children in India were indulged and spoiled excessively by the mother, and sons did not enter into a rivalrous relationship with the father.

Unlike Spratt's political and literary writings, his ventures into psychoanalysis were replete with technical jargon. His book is meandering and very long, yet it contains flashes of genuine insight. He argued that, because of their narcissism and self-absorption, and their veneration of male authority, social reform and political radicalism did not come easily to Hindus. Thus he wrote:

> Hindus are abnormally tolerant of their rulers, whether hereditary monarchs, indigenous upstarts, foreign conquerors, or the popular leaders of the present day. A leader once established seems sure of continued favour for their lifetime. Occidentals and Muslims are more changeable in their attitude to leaders: the latent hostility to the father is always apt to come to the surface.[43]

Spratt argued that, apart from practices of child-bearing, the institution of caste also explained why Hindus tended to favour the status quo, politically as well as socially. He observed:

> The general tendency of the narcissistic psyche towards conservatism is shown with special clarity in relation to caste because of its strong inclination towards attitudes of superiority. . . . The inward-looking libido inflates the ego and all with whom the ego identifies itself, in the first place the family and the sub-caste. No caste admits that it is without an inferior. The caste system is the narcissistic consciousness of superiority institutionalised.[44]

Not all of Spratt's comparisons favoured the West over the East. In a discussion of race relations, he pointed out that while Hindus were extremely colour-conscious, their prejudice against dark skins was less intense than that shown by white Americans against black Americans. The Hindu colour prejudice was 'completely satisfied by aloofness or withdrawal', whereas white supremacism in the United States was overtly aggressive in a physical and social sense.[45]

It is said that these Freudian explorations of the Hindu personality offended C. Rajagopalachari, who was a devout Hindu, and a somewhat puritanical one to boot. One hopes Rajaji did not read the book, with its references to such concepts as 'anal eroticism' and 'semen augmentation'. It is not known whether mentor and protégé had any arguments about its contents. In any event, it did not affect Spratt's position in *Swarajya*.

IX

Back in 1939, Philip Spratt had published a substantial and in parts most interesting book on Mahatma Gandhi. This fell stillborn from the press, because it was published just before the Second World War broke out. In later years Spratt continued to read and think about Gandhi, and references to his life and legacy pepper his articles in *MysIndia*, *Swarajya*, and elsewhere.

In 1969, the world, and India, observed the centenary of Gandhi's birth. To mark the occasion, an academic journal published in Cambridge brought out a special issue, and asked Spratt, himself an old graduate of the university, to write an essay. He provided an overview of Gandhi's successes – the achievement of Independence, the undermining of Untouchability, and the bringing of women into public life – and of his failures – notably, the partition of India on communal grounds. The assessment was fair-minded and judicious, except towards the end, when Spratt launched into a tirade against the Mahatma's chosen successor Jawaharlal Nehru, claiming that, as Prime Minister, he 'set about, in part deliberately, in part unwittingly, to erase almost all the effects of Gandhi's work'.[46]

Spratt also wrote on Gandhi in *Swarajya*, in the form of a review essay in an edited volume on his philosophy. The review began with these arresting sentences: 'Mahatma Gandhi was not so much a philosopher as a practical leader and inspirer, who mainly addressed his thoughts to ordinary people. Thus it is doubtful if any philosophical system can be put together out of his thoughts. But that does not mean that his thoughts were not important or instructive.'

Spratt argued that while there was no coherent Gandhian *philosophy*, there might yet be Gandhian postulates or prescriptions for an ethical life. Spratt looked at the question of means and ends, which Gandhi spoke of so often and which philosophers were now writing about. He thought the Gandhian dogma that the means adopted should be free from all evil was 'not a universally valid rule'. Rather, it was 'a common sense warning against superficial theorising and hasty action in social affairs, about which we have very imperfect knowledge and with the best of intentions can do enormous harm'. Gandhi, remarked Spratt, warned against being 'carried away by enthusiasm for apparently glorious aims which may prove to be far more expensive than we thought, or even altogether unattainable, while we overlook the ramifying evils caused by the means we adopt'.

According to Spratt, Gandhi's transformation from obscurity to greatness was enabled by his years outside the home and outside India. 'Being uprooted from family and community so early in life', Gandhi 'was deprived of the psychological support that others enjoy, and he had to supply them himself'. Through his faith in himself, and in God, Gandhi became 'a self-reliant individual, freed from dependence on society or tradition, accustomed to judge all things for himself'.[47]

The year of the Gandhi Centenary was 1969. The next year, India, and the world, observed the centenary of the birth of Spratt's youthful hero, V. I. Lenin. To mark the occasion, he wrote a short but deeply insightful essay, a model of its kind. Here is Spratt on Lenin the man:

> He had qualities which could have made him a moral leader of world stature. He had great force of personality and self-confidence, and an appealing freedom from self-seeking and vanity. But these advantages were outweighed by his narrowness of sympathy and his dogmatic, aggressive temper. His talent lay in the direction of division and conquest, not reconciliation and unity.

And here is Spratt on Lenin the politician:

> His ideas on the government of a socialist state, as they gradually revealed themselves, were not such as the progressive world found easy to stomach. Given that he could not or would not work with

other parties, he had to suppress them all. But from this he passed to suppression of dissidents in his own party, a strict control of the press, and a more and more rigid control by his ever more disciplined party over the popular bodies, the soviets and trade unions, through which the people might have expressed their desires.

And, here, finally, is Spratt on Lenin's legacy: 'Lenin's most original contribution was his technique of seizing and maintaining power. It has been widely imitated, by communists and anti-communists, and has imparted a distinctive character, totalitarianism, to a historical epoch. There can be no doubt about the sinister, indeed catastrophic, nature of his invention.'[48]

In his writings of the 1940s and 1950s, Spratt had sought sometimes to distance Lenin from Stalin. He would do that no longer. Though he does not reference her work, one presumes he had read Hannah Arendt, who had authoritatively drawn parallels between Leninism and Fascism, between the totalitarianism of the left and of the right. Spratt's analysis of how even right-wing parties are Leninists in inspiration speaks directly to how the Bharatiya Janata Party has exercised power in India today.

X

A year after Spratt moved to Madras, the once hegemonic Congress Party lost power in the state. It was defeated by a regional party, the Dravida Munnetra Kazhagam (DMK), that affirmed Tamil pride and Tamil identity. The DMK opposed Brahmin domination of Tamil politics and public life, and had till recently stood for self-determination via the creation of a separate nation called Dravida Nadu. In 1970 Spratt published a book called *The D. M. K. in Power*, which presented a history of the Dravidian movement and of its ascent to political power. The book was commissioned by a Bombay publisher. Spratt perhaps wrote it in part as a sort of homage to his wife's people, who were Tamils, and whose patriarch (the late Singaravelu Chettiar) was a political radical who had been opposed to the Congress. The book was studiedly non-polemical in tone, presenting a detached, factual account of the first major regional party to make a mark in Indian politics.[49]

The founder-editor of *Swarajya* was a man called Khasa Subba Rao. After he died in 1961, the paper was edited by Pothan Joseph, an experienced and much travelled hand who had once worked with B. G. Horniman before editing the Congress mouthpiece *Hindustan Times* as well as the Muslim League mouthpiece *Dawn*. Through the 1950s Joseph had edited the *Deccan Herald* of Bangalore, in the course of which he had published (and got to know) Philip Spratt.

In January 1970, Pothan Joseph told *Swarajya*'s patron saint, Rajaji, that he wished to step down. In his 'Dear Reader' column of 17 January 1970, Rajaji announced that Philip Spratt, then working as associate editor, would succeed Joseph. He did, though strangely the masthead of the paper never carried his name, although it had once carried the names of Subba Rao and Joseph. This may have been because Spratt was originally British, and a paper opposing the Government had to be careful not to overtly offend thin-skinned nationalists. The arrangement suited Spratt, a reticent man who never liked to thrust himself forward anyway.

The first signed piece by Spratt after he took over as editor rehearsed some favourite themes, albeit with new examples and new phrases. This explained how Marx's predictions about the growing impoverishment of the working class 'notoriously proved to be mistaken', as had Lenin's predictions about capitalist rivalries causing wars (which, Spratt argued, were caused by ambitious or adventurist politicians and businessmen, for 'real disputes between capitalists are settled by a deal').

For all its faults and failures, socialism still had enormous appeal across the world, not least in the India in which Spratt lived and worked. The last paragraph of his first essay as editor of *Swarajya* ran:

The remnants of the free economy of India are fighting for survival. 1970 is likely to bring serious defeats. This ought not to be the case, for the free economy is superior in every way to its rival, the Statist economy. But the free economy has never seriously and effectively tried to persuade the public of its merits. It is high time to begin.[50]

After he became editor, Spratt wrote much less often in *Swarajya*, one piece every two or three months instead of two or three pieces every month. The longest of these articles was published in May 1970, to mark the centenary of Lenin's birth. It covered three full pages of the magazine. Early on, the writer offered this dry epigram: 'Centenaries are not obituaries; after all this time sentiment can give way to truth.' His article took apart myths propagated in other centennial assessments: that Lenin was 'a man of peace' when in fact 'he burned with hatred and aggressiveness'; that he was a great Russian patriot when in fact 'he would gladly sacrifice Russia for international socialism'; that he was a great anti-colonialist when in fact he suppressed Ukrainian nationalism while re-colonizing Georgia, Armenia and Azerbaijan, as well as bringing Muslim Central Asia under the Soviet yoke.

Spratt argued that the 'moral debasement of politics is Lenin's worst gift to mankind'. In the nineteenth century, 'politics was becoming to some extent moralized'; but then, after Lenin came to power in Russia, 'over a large part of the world, domestic politics was pursued by means of wholesale slaughter, torture, deceit and indoctrination'. Spratt claimed that 'if there had been no Lenin there would have been no Stalin, Mussolini, Hitler, Franco, Mao or Ho. It was he who opened the way to that totalitarian tyranny which has devastated the world in the past half-century.'[51]

In another essay, Spratt perceptively pointed to the moral arrogance and vanity of the socialist intellectual and politician. Thus he wrote: 'One who desires the State to reduce inequality is apt to think of the State as a person, usually himself, placed in personal relations with all the poor of the country and dispensing charity to them. This fantasy of exercising power and distributing bounty attracts many.'

Spratt accepted that poverty is indeed, as the socialists argued, 'a great problem'. But the socialist remedy, of State-directed or State-enforced attempts at redistribution, was worse than the disease, for, as demonstrated in country after country in the socialist bloc, 'it destroys the most precious values of liberty, culture, personality and variety, and fails even to achieve the equality in the name of which it is undertaken'.[52]

In India itself, Prime Minister Indira Gandhi was steadily consolidating her power and pre-eminence. The nationalization of banks and the abolition of princely purses had created an aura around her, as a sort of messiah for the poor. 'It looks as if', wrote Spratt in *Swarajya*, 'the Prime Minister's audacity and freedom from scruple will succeed in wrecking all the other parties and restoring the Congress Party to a convincing appearance of its former glory.' He added: 'The Prime Minister is creating a stream flowing in her direction; her opponents, who know they are in the right, must emulate her will to win and stand firm against it.'

Spratt provided a penetrating, and in the event prescient, analysis of Indira Gandhi's personality and leadership style. 'In the situation of India at present', he said, 'the truly democratic leader reconciles himself to cooperation with parties of considerably different opinions; the attempt to destroy and dominate lowers the tone of public life and suggests the would-be-dictator.'[53]

In January 1971, Indira Gandhi announced the holding of General Elections, a year ahead of schedule. Spratt argued that 'the Prime Minister has designed it [the polls] as a referendum on her own merits as the national leader, and inevitably it has become a two-sided dispute between her admirers and her critics'. He offered four major criticisms of Indira Gandhi's record as Prime Minister since 1966. First, 'her premature espousal of the demand for equality at the expense of development'. Second, 'her failure to maintain order', as manifested in the rising incidence of violence. Third, 'her undemocratic ways', as manifest in 'her indifference to constitutional forms, culminating recently in threats to amend the Constitution and discipline the Supreme Court'. Fourth, 'her dangerous collaboration with the Communists and Russia'.

Spratt warned that if Mrs Gandhi prevailed, 'a political future like that of Egypt under Nasser or Indonesia under Soekarno' awaited India. But he was hopeful that she wouldn't prevail for, as he believed, 'the case against her continued leadership is strong, so strong indeed that even against all the obstacles – her control of the administration, and of far bigger resources – her heterogeneous and disputatious opponents ought to win'.[54]

This article, published on 16 January 1971, was the last piece Spratt wrote for *Swarajya*. Shortly afterwards he fell ill, and in early

March passed away. Days after his death the results of the 1971 election were announced. Contrary to Spratt's hopes, the Congress won a massive majority. Four years later, via the Emergency imposed by Indira Gandhi, the would-be-dictator became a real one.

XI

Philip Spratt passed away at his Madras home on 3 March 1971. His wife Seetha resolved that, since he was born a Christian, her husband would die a Christian. He was buried in the Kilpauk Cemetery.

Spratt's life in India had seen him live in Bombay and Madras, give speeches in Calcutta and Kanpur, and be incarcerated in jails in Meerut and Belgaum. However, it was in the city of Bangalore that he lived longest, and where Seetha and he had raised their children. The *Deccan Herald* of Bangalore did not forget this connection, carrying a lovely tribute by the writer P. K. Srinivasan, whom the Englishman had befriended and encouraged when he came to the city as a young man. Now, after Spratt had gone, Srinivasan remembered him as 'a fine example of the British non-conformist conscience', who 'in his own way, and without letting others know about it, helped many a lame dog over the stile'.[55] The journal *Freedom First*, an organ of the Indian Committee for Cultural Freedom in which Spratt had published some of his best essays, also carried a moving obituary, written by the scholar A. B. Shah, who had played a key role in persuading a Bombay firm to publish *Hindu Culture and Personality*. 'Though Spratt was never rich like the latter-day Marxists or Malcha Marg socialists', wrote Shah, 'his simplicity was the outer expression not of poverty but of the Rishi's unconcern with the trappings of worldly goods. One felt humbled in his presence.'[56]

In December 1972, a year and a half after her husband died, Seetha Spratt wrote to someone he had been in jail with in Meerut many decades previously. This was P. C. Joshi, who – unlike Philip Spratt – had stayed loyal to the Communist Party of India all his life, even after it had removed him from the prestigious post of

General Secretary in 1948 because he had nice things to say about the Congress Party and its fight for India's freedom. Seetha had heard that the Government of India was giving pensions to those who had been political prisoners during the British Raj, or – if they were no longer alive – to their widows. When she applied for one of these pensions, she was told that she would have to show a certificate that her husband had been jailed for political reasons, and that he had spent more than six months in prison. She had no such certificate; so she wrote to P. C. Joshi for help. In her letter she discreetly hinted at her own financial situation, writing: 'You must know Phil very well – his attitude to money & worldly and practical matters.'[57]

Joshi wrote back at once. 'You have not to introduce yourself to me', he told Seetha:

> I have heard of you from the time you were a young kid as the daughter [sic] of one of our best comrade[s] among the founders of the Party. Later I heard about you from Spratt in Meerut Jail when we used to walk round and round the jail walls, he was my best friend in jail and we continued our friendly relations even after he left the Party.

He therefore asked Seetha to 'treat me as your own brother or brother-in-law and whatever suits you for taking all the liberties with me. It will be a pleasure to help you in any way I can.'

Joshi appended to his letter a certificate signed by him, saying that as an accused in the Meerut Conspiracy Case himself, he was testifying that Philip Spratt had been one of his fellow prisoners. He had in his possession copies of all the documents of the case, with Spratt's name prominently mentioned, and therefore spoke with both 'personal and documentary authority'. His testament ended by saying: 'His wife deserves the Nation's sympathy and support.'

Joshi asked Seetha to submit this certificate to the Madras Government while he, for his part, would speak to a Cabinet Minister at the Centre, K. C. Pant, who happened to be related to him. If Seetha sent him copies of her application, he 'might be able to wangle it, cutting across all the other bureaucratic formalities'.[58]

P. C. Joshi was as good as his word. While Seetha submitted an application to Madras – to be forwarded to Delhi – Joshi wrote to Pant asking for help. He provided the Minister with this charming capsule account of Spratt's political career:

> Philip Spratt, a British Comrade, was my colleague in the Meerut Conspiracy case and sentenced to twelve years R[igorous] I[mprisonment] by the Sessions [Court]. He was really the main accused. He was not only a typical brilliant British intellectual but very human who went totally Indian. . . . Essentially a British pragmatist intellectual that Spratt was, . . . he began developing doubts with repeated 'Trials of Traitors' [in the Soviet Union] during the mid 30s. He struggled very hard to remain loyal to the Party but intellectual and moral integrity, as he understood it, came in the way. He became a free lancer and ended up as the de-facto editor of Rajaji's weekly Swaraj[ya] on a paltry salary.

Joshi told the Minister that Spratt had left his wife 'no savings and no property'. He hoped Pant and his ministry would 'consider hers a deserving case', and 'lend a helping hand in the good cause'. The Minister wrote back saying that Seetha's case was 'an interesting one and I shall have it looked into quickly'.[59] A few months later – a mere blink of an eye by the standards of the Indian bureaucracy – Seetha wrote to Joshi that she had been asked by the Madras Accountant General's office to come and collect the first instalment of her monthly pension. 'I must thank you also for your effort to give me hope', wrote Philip Spratt's wife to Philip Spratt's former cellmate, 'and thanks to whoever it was that acknowledged that Spratt did fight for India's freedom.'[60] And so he had, and for more than forty years; fighting for political freedom to begin with, and for social, intellectual, and economic freedoms thereafter.

CHAPTER 15

A Himalayan Heroine

I

On New Year's Day, 1946, Sarala Devi – formerly Catherine Mary Heilemann – wrote a letter to Mahatma Gandhi from her base in the Himalayan hamlet of Kausani. She was, she told him, now back in the hills after almost two years 'wander[ing] a lot in the plains, haunting the jails – six in all . . .' Sarala's letter continued:

> I am now busy with my plans for my work. I am hoping to be able to start the Vikas Grah [Development Centre] in a few months – & my own school when our men are released. I believe they will send their girls to me. For the time being, I am planning a summer rural contact camp for girl students if Sucheta [Kripalani] approves & can help me with a little equipment.[1]

Her travels in the hills before and after the Quit India movement had convinced Sarala of the importance of the education of girls. On 5 December 1946, she inaugurated the Kasturba Mahila Utthan Mandal (Kasturba Society for the Uplift of Women). Though named after Gandhi's wife, the organization was commonly known as Lakshmi Ashram (after the wife of the person who had donated the property). The ashram would educate and train girls in social service. After graduating they would work for three years in the villages, following which they were free to get married. The hope was that even while raising a family, these social workers would nonetheless find time to promote education, handicrafts, and economic self-reliance in their locality.

That Sarala chose the Uttarakhand Himalaya as the site of her experiment showed courage. For even by the standards of Hindu society, these hills were extremely conservative when it came to the rights of women. Most girls did not go to school; the few who did were withdrawn before they reached puberty. Within the family, women took on all the housework, all the child rearing, and – with so many men away working in the plains – often all of the agricultural labour too. As one of the village girls who joined the Lakshmi Ashram recalled, when she was growing up she was taught to believe that

> Woman is a slave. So she makes roti [bread] and she just works in the fields. That is why my elder sisters did not study and my brothers studied. They had a good education because our country is a *purush pradhan* country [a country run by and for men], and here in Uttarakhand this custom is even stronger. He's a boy, so he alone must study, he alone must have good food.[2]

Once she had established her society named after Kasturba Gandhi, Sarala was able to lease, from the Forest Department, a large tract which had oak trees as well as a patch of open ground on which some buildings could be constructed. But for this she needed money; so she asked her mentor Acharya Kripalani for advice. Kripalani wrote to his old freedom-fighting comrade Rafi Ahmad Kidwai, now a Minister in the Government of Uttar Pradesh in free India. Kidwai sanctioned a sum of Rs 10,000, and with this a hostel for girls was built. Some classrooms and a small office building were added on later.[3]

The first students to be enrolled at the Lakshmi Ashram were children of Congressmen who had been active during the Quit India movement. They respected and even admired Sarala, and were willing to entrust their daughters to her care. The daily routine was modelled in part on Gandhi's ashram in Sevagram. After waking up, girls and teachers swept and cleaned the premises. A prayer meeting followed by breakfast was next, and then, until lunch, the girls and teachers performed what Gandhi termed 'bread labour'. This took various forms; working in the farm and dairy, or spinning, or collecting fodder and fuel from the forest. Formal classes began only after lunch, extending until tea, after which the girls had an hour of games and physical exercises before evening prayers and dinner.[4]

The syllabus of the school was designed by Sarala, who also – at least to begin with – did most of the teaching. The subjects included science, mathematics, history and geography. The language of instruction was Hindi, and books and other educational materials were also in that language. When conditions permitted – which was much of the year – classes were held outdoors, in the warm glow of the Himalayan sun. The students did not appear for Government Board examinations, which Sarala regarded with the same distaste as Gandhi had. Rather, when they had reached the age they would normally matriculate (say fifteen or sixteen), they were sent for a year to Sevagram, where Sarala's old friends the Aryanayakams schooled them further in the Gandhian ethos.[5]

On 15 August 1947, Independence came to India. Five and a half months later Gandhi was murdered. As Sarala recalled, 'the children [of the Ashram] burst into tears upon hearing the news. In such a short time Bapu had found a home in their little hearts, and perhaps their minds were fixed on the hope of one day seeing him.'[6]

Shortly after Gandhi's death, Sarala got the girls to start a magazine in Hindi called *Suryoday* (Sunrise). For the first issue she wrote an editorial herself, where she said:

> Darkness was driven away, a new day came. A new age has been born in our country. Independence has arrived. Right now, all our hands are immersed in the sunrise of this new age. What shall we make of this sunrise? A shining sun or shadows of clouds?
>
> Particularly in our mountains, our village women and children are entrapped in the night of ignorance's gloom. Our Kasturba Mahila Utthan Mandal has been founded in Kumaon with this hope: that through our girls, rays of knowledge shall spread among the women of the hills. Seeing their hard work, labour, play, and happiness, the hope is born that when these girls grow up they shall spread this light throughout our hill villages. We shall found a new age.[7]

The girls who came to the Lakshmi Ashram were often no more than seven or eight years old when they first arrived. By peeling an apple for a child, or reading a book to her, or showing her a picture, Sarala gradually overcame the loneliness of her wards and made them feel at home.[8] One of her early students, Vimala Nautiyal, has written feelingly of Sarala's commitment to her cause. She would be up an hour before the girls, making herself ready for the day with a cold-water bath, even in the depths of winter. After working with her girls in field and forest, supervising classes, etc., she would stay up late at night doing the ashram's accounts. Vimala writes that on 15 August, celebrated annually as India's Independence Day, Sarala would urge the students to think of the tasks that lay ahead of them and their country. Freedom from British colonial rule, said Sarala, had been relatively easy to accomplish; India's emancipation from economic poverty, social prejudice and intellectual slavery would be far more arduous.[9]

Another ward recalled Sarala's love of manual labour. A group of girls had gone, early in the morning, to collect firewood from the oak forest. When they returned they saw Sarala digging up a patch of ground in preparation for cultivation. Embarrassed and shamed, they put down their (relatively) light bundles and sought to relieve the matriarch of the heavy iron fork (made locally) that she was using. Sarala shooed them away, saying that they must not think of her as a 'budiya' (old hag). She was then in her early sixties, but the zest for hard work was entirely intact.[10]

Like Gandhi, Sarala liked walking, long distances for choice. Rather than hire a male porter, she chose to carry her own rucksack, containing a change of clothes, writing paper, some food items, a sleeping bag, torches and other items she deemed essential. She began taking older girls for treks through the hills, where they spoke to the villagers and sought to understand their problems. On these tours Sarala also inspired young men to take up social work in the Gandhian mould. Several did; they usually ended up marrying a graduate from the Lakshmi Ashram, these couples then setting up bases in their own valleys, counting on Sarala for instruction and inspiration.

These treks served another purpose; they helped bring to the ashram girl students from all parts of Uttarakhand. By the early 1950s there were as many as eighty girls being trained on the hilltop

on the outskirts of Kausani. Girls from Brahmin and Dalit backgrounds lived and studied together, defying both social prejudice
and scriptural sanctions.

Meanwhile, the Bhoodan (Land Donation) movement of Vinoba
Bhave had reached the hills. Bhave was a close associate of Gandhi;
he had joined him as early as 1916, shortly after the Mahatma
returned from South Africa. After Independence, when a Communist
insurrection broke out in eastern India in 1948, Bhave had promoted
Bhoodan as a non-violent alternative.

Bhave was a considerable scholar, and a thoroughgoing ascetic.
His discipline and his learning impressed many people, Gandhi
among them. Sarala also fell under his sway. Although Bhoodan did
not have much traction in Uttarakhand (where land holdings were
small), like other social workers at the time she came to accept
Bhave as Gandhi's spiritual successor, who would be to Indian civil
society what Gandhi's acknowledged political successor, Jawaharlal
Nehru, already was to the sphere of Indian statecraft and administration.

Vinoba Bhave had coined the phrase 'jai jagat'; glory to the entire
world. This was a twentieth-century adaptation of the Sanskrit phrase
'Vasudhaiva Kutumbakam', the 'World is One Single Family'. Bhave
did not believe in nation-states, and had even travelled to East
Pakistan with his message of Bhoodan. As an Englishwoman of
German descent who had made her life and home in India, Sarala
was attracted by the idea of global citizenship, and soon began
starting her letters with the salutation 'jai jagat'. From time to time
she would take a break from Lakshmi Ashram and join Bhave on
his walking tours through the plains of India, seeking to persuade
landlords to part with a portion of their holdings for peasants to
own and cultivate.

II

Sarala's approach to community work was very different from large
organizations such as the British charity Oxfam, or the Government
of India's own Khadi and Village Industries Commission. Devendra

Kumar, a pioneering Gandhian technologist who knew her well, has nicely captured Sarala's distinctive philosophy of social work. As Kumar remarked:

> Sarala Behn believed in constructive workers living with the masses and becoming part of them, not as superior beings with special privileges. . . . Outward dynamic activity along with inner spiritual simplicity, were reflected in all that she did. . . . She did not care for large institutions. It was as a result of her 'tapasya' [selfless service] that young people, women and even men came up in Kumaon and Garhwal areas of Uttarakhand, for serving the poor and the needy. She believed that it was not so much the centrally-managed, well-financed and efficiently-run, large voluntary agencies, having mostly experts and employees carrying out given programmes, but self-evolved small bands of dedicated groups of individuals living among the common people, who jointly work in small areas, that would deliver the goods. If there were to be big agencies, their role in her opinion, should be secondary and tertiary, small active groups being the primary units of societal change. She was not happy, when in assessing achievements, planning strategies, executing programmes, the bigwigs acted as the prime movers. In all her life, therefore, she kept her distance from seats of power, even in the social work institutions.[11]

By the late 1950s, the graduates of Lakshmi Ashram had begun to start small ashrams of their own in different parts of Uttarakhand. Some stayed single; others married fellow Gandhians. They immersed themselves in the lives of the peasantry, running schools and clinics for them, and urging them to overcome religious and caste prejudice. From wherever they were, they kept in touch with the ashram in Kausani and its matriarch, seeking her counsel and advice as they went about their own work in the community.[12]

One student who chose to stay unmarried was Radha Bhatt. She joined Sarala and the Lakshmi Ashram at the relatively advanced age of eighteen, after refusing several marriage proposals that came her way. Her father, unusually for a hillman, encouraged his daughter in her independence. Radha had a sparkling intelligence and an almost inexhaustible energy, and Sarala soon identified her as the person she would eventually hand over the Ashram to.

This English disciple of Gandhi had inaugurated a quiet social revolution in Uttarakhand, a region that had not previously acknowledged women from peasant households to be independent beings, capable of thinking and acting on their own. Now, under Sarala's guidance and inspiration, these women of the Himalaya had become agents of change and transformation. One scholar sums up Sarala's achievement as follows:

> In the historical moment just prior to Indian independence in 1947, she offered rural girls from a marginal region a sense of inclusion, urgency, purpose, and importance. She told them that they would found a new age. She encouraged them to think in new ways about themselves and their position in wider hill society and the nation . . . The experience changed their lives.[13]

And the lives of others, too. The graduates of the ashram went on to make education and health care accessible to villagers. Sarala's protégées also became active in social movements, which promoted forest conservation and temperance, for example. Alcoholism was rampant in these hills, particularly among ex-soldiers, who after fifteen years of service retired to their villages with a pension and time on their hands. They drank, and drank even more, provoking fights within the family and outside it. It was Sarala's protégée Vimala Nautiyal, and her husband Sunderlal Bahuguna, who began what became a widespread campaign against the sale and consumption of liquor in Uttarakhand.

As one student of her work has written, Sarala Behn

> constructed a creative political style of women's empowerment that not only challenged patriarchy but also took Gandhian ideas to radical directions. She combined the Gandhian notion of Indian womanhood, which extols motherly virtues of self-sacrifice and traditional traits as nurturers or caregivers with the progressive values and social ideals of equality, freedom, and strong sense of independence that characterizes western social activist women.[14]

In her approach to community activism Sarala was very different from Mira, the other Englishwoman who lived in Uttarakhand in the 1950s. Mira was a loner, a restless spirit, moving from ashram to ashram and from cause to cause. Sarala, on the other hand, was an institution-builder, whose Lakshmi Ashram nurtured a cadre of social workers who, upon graduating, went out and lived among the villagers, seeking to reshape society.

When Mira first arrived in India, back in 1925, Gandhi assigned his secretary Mahadev Desai to teach her Hindi. But, despite three decades of trying, her command of the language remained imperfect. Sarala, however, spoke and wrote Hindi like a native. She also picked up the local dialect, Kumaoni. Unlike Mira, Sarala was very comfortable in Indian dress, salwar kameez for choice (which is far easier to walk in than a sari). As a marker of how thoroughly Indian she had become, one associate recalls that once, when she abruptly slipped and fell, Sarala uttered the Hindi exclamation 'Bap re Bap' rather than 'Oh My God' as one might have expected her to.[15]

In 1960, a Danish social worker named Marie Thoger, interested in studying the living legacy of Gandhi, was directed to the Lakshmi Ashram. Many years later, she penned this vivid portrait of her time with the ashram's founder:

Sarala was very inspired. I recall one morning when she and I went out from the Ashram at sunrise. Sarala wanted to go to a faraway hillside where some of the Ashram girls were cutting grass. The slope in this place was so steep and dangerous that the owner gave up the idea of doing the work himself. However the cows in the ashram needed the fodder and Sarala's girls did not mind going and getting it. They had stayed in this place for about a week, and now Sarala liked to see what was going on.

This was a morning I shall never forget. May be there had been a snow-storm that same night on Trisul– at least the peak was covered with fresh snow and its summit was painted beautiful shades of pink by the sun. The pine forest below was dark and the Garur valley was green. They were wonderful moments. Sarala was running like a hill woman along the paths, speaking about her fighting old customs, expressing her strong wish to keep this ashram free from western influence.

When the visitor expressed her appreciation both of the landscape and of the work being done there Sarala told her: 'Why do you want to go back? Stay on here, and we shall set these hills on fire, these beautiful hills.' Alas, Marie Thoger had to return to her homeland, but, as she recalled, 'ever since, these words have been a stirring reminder for me to fight – a peaceful fight against all injustice done to defenceless people – like Sarala fought for her hill women'.[16]

Shortly after Marie Thoger left, a Scotsman named Bill Aitken, who had done an MA thesis on Gandhi, arrived at Lakshmi Ashram. Aitken lived in the ashram for several years, teaching the children and labouring with them in field and kitchen. Many years later, he wrote of the ashram's matriarch, Sarala Behn, that 'she was not lovely to look at but God had given her the much greater gift of absolute integrity. I have never met another human being who was so totally honest to her ideals; who practiced exactly what she preached.'[17]

Aitken observed that 'the one thing that was like a red rag to the bull in Sarala was the occasional visitor who disturbed her labours with the phrase "Behenji, Ham Delhi se aiye hain" [Sister, we have come from Delhi] as though she ought to be impressed.'[18] While sometimes finding Sarala – as the children in the ashram did too – inflexible and unbending, Aitken wrote that 'her greatest achievement was to be that most elusive category: an honest citizen who thought of nothing but her adopted nation's moral advancement'.[19]

III

In 1962 a border war broke out between China and India, in which the Indian Army was comprehensively routed. In a belated bid to bolster defence preparedness, three new districts were created in Uttarakhand. Uttarkashi, Chamoli and Pithoragarh were thus carved out of the districts of Tehri Garhwal, Pauri Garhwal and Almora respectively. These new districts bordered Tibet – which had been colonized by China – and were categorized as Inner Line Areas, where those who were not Indian citizens were barred from entering.

Of the seven renegades featured in this book, Sarala was the only one who never visited her original homeland after coming to

India. Her commitment to her adopted country was absolute. Nonetheless, Sarala had not sought to obtain an Indian passport, looking upon herself as a citizen of the world. Technically, therefore, she was a 'foreigner'; who could not now so easily do what she had previously done – roam freely all over the hills. After 1962, to enter one of these three new districts she needed a permit – which she was disinclined to apply for.

In one of her last conversations with Gandhi, Sarala had promised him that she would give twenty years of her life to social work in the Himalaya. She resolved to honour the promise; confident that the ashram would be in the safe hands of her chosen successor, Radha Bhatt. In 1965 Radha went to Denmark on a study tour of progressive schools. The next year, Sarala handed over the ashram to her.

Not long after Radha took over the running of the Lakshmi Ashram, there was a meeting of Sarvodaya (Gandhian) workers in Joshimath. The town, which lay just short of the temple of Badrinath, was beyond the Inner Line, but the Sarvodaya stalwart Sunderlal Bahuguna had promised to get Sarala a permit. Sarala was then in Delhi, and drove up to attend the meeting with Devendra Kumar. They halted for the night at the ancient capital of the kingdom of Garhwal, Srinagar, sited on the banks of the Alakananda river. Here she learned that the Inner Line permit had not been granted. Radha had also arrived at Srinagar that night from Kausani, bound for the same meeting in Joshimath. She found her mentor in tears, weeping uncontrollably. Sarala was devastated at being considered a foreigner in a country to which she had given all. She told Radha that she would visit the Silyara Ashram of her pupil Vimala Bahaguna and then leave the hills for ever, so angry was she. Radha persuaded her to come to Kausani as well, to say a proper goodbye to the ashram she had built and tell the girls why she had to depart.[20]

After leaving Uttarakhand, Sarala travelled to Bihar, where she joined a group of Gandhians working on land redistribution and village renewal. There was a famine in Bihar in 1967, and she came face to face with the sort of destitution that for all the harshness of life there, the hill people of the Himalaya had never confronted. In Bihar, Sarala got to know Jayaprakash Narayan (always known as JP), a hero of the freedom struggle and formerly a firebrand socialist who had left party politics to join the Bhoodan movement. Sarala also travelled with Vinoba Bhave and his team in Madhya Pradesh, and on her own in Karnataka, getting to know South India for the first time.[21]

While journeying through the Indian heartland Sarala regularly wrote letters in Hindi to the girls at Lakshmi Ashram. Addressed to 'Priya Bacchon' (Dear Children) these chatty, conversational letters described the landscape, cropping patterns, and social customs of the districts she passed through. Ever the teacher, she sought to educate her wards about the history, geography and culture of parts of India so very different from their native Uttarakhand. And sometimes to stoke their social consciousness too, as in a letter from Mandla in Madhya Pradesh, which marvelled at the independence of spirit of tribal women, which was in such striking contrast to the submissiveness of their sisters in Hindu caste society. Another letter, written after a communal riot in Nagpur had made national headlines, told the girls to always disregard religious and caste identities in everyday life and in their dealings with one another.

These letters reveal, among other things, Sarala's deepening ecological consciousness. Thus she wrote feelingly about how dams built on the Kosi river in Bihar had interfered with natural drainage patterns, leading to waterlogging and floods, that devastated both crops and trees. She kept an eye out for flowering plants and shrubs, sometimes sending pressed flowers by post back to Kausani, saying that even if the flowers had lost their smell by the time they reached, the girls would nonetheless get some idea of their beauty.[22]

From these letters, and perhaps even more so from her autobiography, it is clear that Sarala revered Vinoba Bhave. She admired his powers of endurance, and his learning – he knew as many as twenty-two languages, for example. She thought that he was a second Gandhi, who would transform independent India through his message of love, sacrifice and renunciation. 'Vinoba was continually having new insights', she wrote admiringly. Of a Bhoodan camp in Bihar, she remarked: 'The atmosphere of the place where Vinoba was living was a source of great inspiration. It was as if it was a laboratory, seeking to create an explosion of a spiritual Love Bomb!' She even went so far as to claim that 'this experiment [of Bhoodan] was as important for the future of the world as was Gandhi's Satyagraha. Indeed, in the context of independence, this was a logical extension and expansion of Satyagraha.'[23]

Notably, Sarala's older contemporary Mira had a more sceptical, and arguably more realistic, view of Vinoba and Bhoodan. Characteristically, she expressed her reservations in public, in a long article in the *Hindustan Times*. Here Mira recalled that Gandhi, her mentor and Bhave's, had given his own pet project, the promotion of khadi, an organizational form through the establishment of an All India Spinners Association, which had active branches in districts across the country. By the same token, she suggested that those promoting Bhoodan should start an All-India Ploughmen's Association, to ensure that the land donated to them was properly cultivated. Mira was writing in 1955; by which time Bhoodan had been in existence for several years. That Bhave and his followers still had no organization to take their work forward showed to her that they were 'merely moralists and propagandists', not 'realists like Bapu'.

Mira wrote that 'it is good to recall how Bapu handled his constructive work, as it may help to show more clearly what is lacking in bhoodan'. She pointed out that before starting his khadi programme, Gandhi had made a deep study of spinning and weaving. On the other hand, Bhave and his followers had waded into the domain of land distribution without a prior analysis of the agrarian situation. Why, asked Mira, had they begun their campaign without 'a correct overall picture of the land tenure with a careful analysis of the different types of landlords and tenants, along with an equally careful analysis of the different types of land'? For, as she rather bluntly put it, 'one really has not the moral right to beg land from cultivators and redistribute them among landless peasants unless one is conversant with land and its intricate problems'.[24]

Unlike Sarala, Mira saw clearly that Vinoba was not a second Gandhi. This understanding came from having known Gandhi far better than Sarala did. The latter had just a few fleeting meetings with the Mahatma; whereas Mira was part of his inner circle, and had seen him closely at work over a period of twenty years. In this time, she had come to know Vinoba Bhave rather well too. Talking with him in Sevagram she had perhaps sensed what Bhoodan was to make clear; that while Gandhi was both a moralist and a realist, Bhave was merely the former.

Vinoba Bhave was, in generational and political terms, a colleague and contemporary of Mira's. They had grown up together in the freedom movement, under Gandhi. On the other hand, Vinoba was several years older than Sarala; and, within the Sarvodaya movement, unquestionably her superior and even mentor. All this – and the man's own learning and asceticism – perhaps blinded her to his limitations.

IV

In 1967 and 1968, as Sarala travelled through the Indian heartland, she missed the hills, but wasn't sure that she wanted to return. There was a shortage of Gandhian workers in central India, and there was pressure on her to stay on and train some. Also, the hurt at not being allowed to roam freely in Uttarakhand remained. A letter to Radha Bhatt, written from Indore in April 1967, has her saying: '*Philhal mera dil pahad ki aur jane ko bilkul nahin kahta. Main kahin seema ke nikat jana hi nahin chahti hoon.*' (At the moment I am in absolutely no mood to return to the mountains. I do not want to go anywhere near the border with China at all.) Radha wrote urging her to let bygones be bygones, but Sarala would not relent. Until the ban on her visiting the three border districts was lifted, she said, she would not return to Uttarakhand. She reminded Radha of how she had refused to ask for a pardon at the time of the 1942 movement, choosing to spend a year in the heat of Lucknow Jail instead. Her self-respect would not allow any compromise now either.[25]

While Sarala was away in the plains, the graduates and teachers of Lakshmi Ashram were in the forefront of the anti-alcohol movement in the hills. She followed their activities from afar, with pride and admiration. She wrote to Radha Bhatt that closing liquor shops was merely the first step; the transformation of social attitudes was what was really required. She also urged a renewed focus on the promotion of cottage industries, so that income and employment could be locally generated, within the hills.[26]

Sarala kept roaming across India, from Bihar to Madhya Pradesh to Karnataka and back again. In June 1968, after eighteen months on the road, she arrived at Vinoba Bhave's home ashram, in Paunar in Wardha district. From here she wrote to Radha Bhatt saying this ceaseless travel was taking its toll. Meeting new people every day was not the sort of thing she was accustomed to. Her body was tired; her mind was weary too. She was not sure what lay ahead of her.[27]

Three months later, now in Bangalore, Sarala wrote to Radha that she now had had enough of being a football, ferried from place to place by the Indian Railways. She wanted to stay in one place, in one environment, and seek the spiritual peace that these frenetic travels had denied her.[28]

Sensing her mentor's sadness, Radha Bhatt thought that she must get Sarala back to the hills she had made her own. But Sarala had insisted that she wouldn't return until she could travel freely within Uttarakhand once more. Radha knew that the surest way to make that happen was to get Sarala an Indian passport. She consulted Devendra Kumar, who suggested that she meet Morarji Desai, who was then Deputy Prime Minister of India. Morarji was known to be a fervent advocate of prohibition; so Devendra suggested that Radha should seek a meeting saying they were representatives of the anti-alcohol movement in Uttarakhand. She did, and the group led by her met Morarji and told him about their prohibition work. He was impressed, and asked if he could help them in any way. At this stage Radha brought up the question of Sarala not being allowed to travel freely in the hills. She showed Morarji her mentor's sorrowful letters, which so moved him that he immediately called the Home Minister, Y. B. Chavan, and urged him to get Sarala's passport sanctioned immediately.

Becoming an Indian citizen normally took years, but Radha Bhatt's enterprise and Morarji Desai's assistance got Sarala her papers within a month. However, there was another niggle. After the Home Ministry had conveyed their approval, Sarala set off for a meeting in Pithoragarh. She was stopped at the Inner Line checkpoint, where an official told her he had no information of her change of citizenship. She returned to Kausani very angry and feeling betrayed again.

Fortunately a phone call to Delhi and from there to the District Magistrate of Pithoragarh sorted matters out, and thereafter there were no restrictions on her movement.[29]

Back in Uttarakhand, Sarala became active in the prohibition and forest movements. In June 1969 she led a delegation to meet the state's Chief Conservator of Forests, conveying the popular disaffection with the state's forest policy. They asked that the system of awarding logging contracts to rich merchants be abolished, and local cooperatives be given preference in the allocation of forest raw material. Shortly afterwards, Sarala took a group of women to meet the first female Chief Minister of Uttar Pradesh, who was her old friend, Sucheta Kripalani. Kripalani was not unmoved by the arguments put forth by the delegation, and liquor shops were shut down in several places.[30]

Sarala chose to spend 2 October 1969, the hundredth anniversary of Gandhi's birth, in the small hill town of Berinag, where her protégées had helped establish a Gram Swarajya Seva Sangh (Society for Village Self-Reliance). She spent much of the winter season touring Kumaon, speaking every evening at a different village, on rural uplift and the relevance of Gandhi. She was in her late sixties, but still up to walking ten or twelve kilometres a day, from hamlet to hamlet, accepting whatever food was given her and spending the night in a peasant's hut or under the open sky. One day her slippers split wide open; she carried them in her hands, walking with bare feet till the next village where she could find a cobbler to repair them. One of the companions on this trip wrote of how her courage and commitment provoked wonder and admiration among the village audiences, for this white woman who, under Gandhi's inspiration, had come to serve and guide them.[31]

In 1970 there was a massive flood on the Alakananda river in Garhwal. The devastation of crops, cattle, houses and human lives was immense. The Sarvodaya activist Chandi Prasad Bhatt, whose Dashauli Gram Swarajya Mandal (DGSM) worked in the upper Alakananda valley, immediately connected the flood to the decimation of forests. So did Sarala. Speaking in a meeting of Sarvodaya workers in July 1971, she spoke of how the survival of humanity depended on a healthy forest cover. The next month she travelled

to Gopeshwar, where Bhatt and the DGSM were based. Here she
took part in, and addressed, a large demonstration of men, women
and children, asking for a ban on liquor, the eradication of
Untouchability, and an end to the industrial and commercial biases
of forest policy.[32]

Down in the plains, Jayaprakash Narayan had embarked on a
mission to get the dreaded dacoits of the Chambal valley in Madhya
Pradesh to surrender. He was remarkably successful, getting several
hundred bandits to give up their arms and accept a term in jail
before being reintegrated into society. Sarala was impressed by what
JP had done, and went to help with the rehabilitation. Some four
hundred dacoits who had given themselves up were now housed in
prison, where Sarala visited them daily, speaking about how they
could ease themselves back into society. Her brisk walk and sheer
energy belied her age; just as her Indian dress and flawless Hindi
ran counter to the colour of her skin. The erstwhile dacoits took to
Sarala immediately. She arranged for the food of their choice, and
for clothes and medicines too. When a colleague asked why she
showed such concern for these bandits, she sharply rebuked him,
saying that they were human beings just like him and her, who had
been tragically forced into criminality through lack of economic
opportunity.[33]

In the early seventies, Sarala contemplated settling down in
Belgaum, a town in the Deccan with a mild climate and a Gandhian
connection, for it was here that the Mahatma had been elected
Congress President for the first (and as it turned out last) time in
1924. While finalizing her plans, she spent some time in Tamil Nadu
with her fellow Sarvodaya workers. On a visit to the home of the
Gandhian activist Krishnammal Jagannathan she came down with
severe heatstroke. Dick Keithahn – Krishnammal's friend and hers
– now took Sarala off to Kodaikanal to recuperate. A spell in the
cool of the Anaimalai hills restored her to health, and it stoked a
yearning for her beloved Kumaon.[34] She now abandoned the idea
of living in Belgaum and decided to return to where she was always
most at home.

On her return to the Himalaya, Sarala followed, with keen interest,
the developing popular movement to protect the forests. It was being

led by Chandi Prasad Bhatt, in whom Sarala saw echoes of Jayaprakash Narayan, partaking of JP's ability to inspire the young and nurture a team of co-workers.[35] In 1973, under Bhatt's leadership, the now celebrated Chipko Andolan took birth. In villages across the Alakananda valley, peasants stopped forest felling by threatening to hug the trees. News of these protests quickly reached Sarala in Kumaon.

Sarala was now in her seventies. Her body was sending signals she could no longer ignore. She knew that the sort of travel that was once second nature to her lay in the past. She had henceforth to stay (mostly) in one place. This, however, could not be in or close to the Lakshmi Ashram, for she did not want to cast an overbearing shadow over Radha Bhatt. Her associate Sadan Mishra found her a suitable spot in the village of Dharamgarh, in Pithoragarh district, a full four hours away by road from Kausani. Here, in 1974, Sarala moved into a cottage which she named 'Him-Darshan', since it had a panoramic view of the snow peaks. It also had fine forests around. Sarala would live here, and read and write, while staying in touch with her wide network of protégées across Uttarakhand, her Gandhian colleagues across India, and her friends and admirers across the world.

CHAPTER 16

Keithahn Soldiers On

I

India became independent on 15 August 1947. Two months later, three individuals inspired by Mahatma Gandhi established a centre for rural education and research near Dindigul, a small town in South India, forty miles away from the city of Madurai. Two were a married couple, a medical doctor named T. S. Soundaram and her husband, the writer and activist G. Ramachandran. Dr Soundaram came from a family of wealthy industrialists, who donated some capital for this venture. The place was called 'Gandhigram', the village of Gandhi, and sought to promote village renewal through better education, better health care, and better agricultural practices.[1]

The third founder of Gandhigram was Dick Keithahn, who had lately returned from America with his family. Dr Soundaram was a native of Madurai, and had known the radical priest in his days there. Now, it was Keithahn who found the land and developed the blueprint for a university of rural education and innovation that would be worthy of Gandhi's name. He took to his new assignment energetically. The daughter of Gandhigram's agricultural superintendent has vivid memories of him carrying buckets from a well to water the saplings on campus. She remembers Keithahn leading interfaith prayers every Sunday, and running a crèche where she studied. She was particularly impressed by the American-turned-Indian's knowledge of, and interest in, agriculture.[2]

Unlike in China, peasants in India were unaccustomed to using night soil as manure. Caste taboos came in the way. In Gandhigram, however, Keithahn taught his colleagues how to reuse human waste to promote soil fertility. He dug a trench at a distance from their habitations, over which toilets with partitions were constructed, roofed by tin sheets and with wooden footrests placed several feet above the soil. Every morning, after using the toilets, the students of Gandhigram covered the excreta with mud and kitchen waste and allowed it to compost. The trench took a few months to fill up, whereupon the entire structure was moved to a new site, and the now well-composted mixture dispersed as manure for the fields. The results were deeply impressive – within a few years, paddy yields were far higher in Gandhigram than in neighbouring farms which used chemical fertilizers rather than organic manure.[3]

Keithahn worked in the fields, and he worked in the office, framing a vision and a curriculum for Gandhigram. A note in his papers outlines the scheme he designed for what would in time become a full-fledged university:

Founding of Gandhigram,
Training centre, priority for Girls, for Rural Development,
    another Shantiniketan . . .
A. Health & Medical: Village Health Centres . . .
B. Multipurpose Cooperative Societies
C. Children's Home
D. Seva-Ashram for Girls . . .
E. Agri – Dairy . . .[4]

II

A few months after Gandhigram was founded, Mahatma Gandhi was assassinated. How Dick Keithahn felt when he heard the news is not recorded. What we do have is an essay Keithahn wrote shortly afterwards, outlining the lessons of Gandhi's life for Christians in India who wished to take to the path of social service in their own 'Christian Ashrams'.

Keithahn began by saluting Gandhi as the 'most challenging saint [and] prophet' India had produced, before outlining 'six points at which I feel the passing of Bapuji does challenge the Christian Ashram'.

The first he termed 'stripped living'. Gandhi challenged the way of materialism, 'the way of dollar and pound power', with his own 'selfless living'. Christian ashramites had to follow this example and 'strip ourselves more fully'.

The second was that Gandhi showed that faith was relevant even in the atomic era, when 'the yeast of devotion must leaven the lump of society'. The passing of the Mahatma challenged Christian ashramites 'to make our devotional lives even more intensive, collective and individually'.

The third was Gandhi's 'respect for all religions'. In his prayer meetings, texts of all faiths were equally respected and read, while in his life 'a Charlie Andrews, Ghaffar Khan or any other devotee of another faith or culture was his brother-in-Truth'. Keithahn remarked that 'the evils of proselytism are not normally to be found in a Christian ashram. But I sometimes wonder whether the aggressiveness of a sectarian Paul is not more the example for Christians than the loving concerns of our Master for all who were in need.'

The fourth lesson was Gandhi's work and example as a 'bridge-builder', who fought for freedom and justice, but at the same time was 'a reconciler of caste and outcaste, of Hindu and Muslim, of colored and white, of all those divided by artificial differences'. This surely was an example for Christian ashramites to follow. Thus Keithahn pointedly asked: 'Cannot we make greater contribution to the solution of our caste, communal, sectarian and provincial conflicts as individual Ashrams or as an Ashram movement?'

The fifth was to be 'nation-builders'. Gandhi, wrote Keithahn, helped bring independence to India, but he knew that mere political freedom was not enough, that Indians had now to nurture and enable 'economic, social, religious and cultural freedom to all'. Here, the Christian ashramites could take forward Gandhi's Constructive Programme, through land redistribution, basic education, etc.

The sixth lesson was satyagraha, 'the chief contribution Gandhiji has made'. As Keithahn recalled a meeting with the Mahatma: 'Several years ago, I sat at his feet and humbly asked how we might help him most. "I have but started the technique of non-violence. I know little about it. Do help me carry on this work."' Gandhi had gone and India was now independent of colonial rule but, said Keithahn, 'perhaps the universal battle for freedom and justice has never been so tense as it is today. If the exploited tend to lag into complacency for a moment there are plenty to whip up new zeal and often for their own selfish ends with no profound sense of the true dignity of human life.'

Keithahn ended his essay by asking Christian ashramites to bestir themselves. As he wrote:

> I believe Christianity has still a chance to redeem itself in this gener-ation. But only if we, as true Satyagrahis, carry on a thorough revolution for Freedom for all men. This would draw unto ourselves the best of our youth. For who does not want to live a life of meaning and purpose! But I doubt, if I were a young man, the average Ashram or Church would give me the sufficient challenge. . . . Then some of us must leave our protected halls of comparative ease and vanguard the great movements of men for justice and freedom.[5]

In January 1949, as the first anniversary of Gandhi's martyrdom approached, Keithahn wrote an article in *Harijan* on what he and his colleagues were doing to honour the Mahatma's memory. After war broke out between India and Pakistan over Kashmir, some Union Ministers broached the idea of compulsory military training in schools and colleges. Keithahn urged that young Indians be trained instead in constructive work for the betterment of society. 'Here at Gandhi Gram', he said,

> we plan a Work Camp during the next long vacation. College students will be encouraged to come and help us build up our proposed Co-operative Agricultural Colony. They will work side by side with villagers who have come into the Colony. They will build dams, bunds for anti-soil erosion purposes. They will water the many fruit trees which have already been planted and thus engrain into their conscious-ness the importance of thinking and working for the future generation.[6]

In July 1951, an American doctor who wished to work in rural India came to visit Keithahn in Gandhigram. He was greatly impressed by what he saw, writing of how

Students and staff are taken in without regard to religion or caste; and while all religions are respected and there is daily worship in the Gandhian tradition, no caste distinctions or restrictions in type of work are tolerated. Every day they all gather together for eating in common, for worshipping together, for sharing the kitchen and sanitary chores, and for an hour of cotton spinning. Whenever any special job is necessary, such as harvesting a field or spreading fertilizer, they all drop their regular work to get the job done. Veterans of young people's work camps in the States will understand this sort of life, but here in India it is unprecedented.[7]

In Gandhigram, there were no distinctions of religion or caste. Outside the settlement Indians remained trapped in their sectarian identities. In the winter of 1951–2, campaigning began for India's first General Elections. Keithahn was dismayed to find that candidates were canvassing votes on the basis of sectional interests. In an article for *Harijan* entitled 'Whom to Elect?', he recalled Gandhi's own commitment to a classless and casteless society. He outlined a series of questions that 'all of us must ask when candidates seek our votes during the next two months'. These included: 'Does the candidate believe in economic equality? What will he do for it?'; 'Is he going to support every good social reform? For example, is he going to insist that women have equal rights with men?'; 'Does the candidate believe in a healthy and sanitary village? What has he done to promote such health and sanitation?'; 'Does the candidate believe in universal and life-centred education? Is he ready to promote whole-heartedly the accepted Basic Education programme in his State?'

Keithahn asked his fellow Gandhians to organize meetings where rival candidates would be asked such questions by voters. 'I take it', he said, 'that such an approach to the elections will be true to the spirit of Sarvodaya. Let us even from the beginning place our elections on a very high level.'[8]

III

Shortly after he joined Gandhigram, Dick Keithahn was brought back into the fold of the Church by the new Bishop of Madurai, a broad-minded theologian named Leslie Newbigin. Keithahn was, once again, a Presbyter in the Church of South India. However, in his own rural development work, he eschewed conversion completely; seeking to serve 'all needy people in a village'. At the same time, he sought comfort in the spirit of Christian fellowship. He attended services in church, while organizing interfaith prayers in the Gandhian manner as well.[9]

In 1955, Keithahn inspired the establishment of a 'Christian Fellowship Clinic' in a village called Oddanchatram, twenty miles from Dindigul. This was in a rain-shadow area, prone to drought and scarcity, which had no modern medical facilities at all. The clinic's prime mover was a doctor named A. K. Tharien, who had met Keithahn as a student in the 1940s, and come under his influence. Tharien gave up the opportunity to make money and win fame treating affluent patients, seeking to serve the rural poor instead. One room to treat sick villagers in time became a full-fledged hospital with up-to-date equipment and several hundred beds. Keithahn visited the place often, watching its growth, its services to labourers, artisans and peasants (of all faiths), and Dr Tharien's own commitment, with pride.[10]

While a practising Christian till the end (unlike Stokes), Keithahn was resolutely opposed to the practice, not uncommon during the period of British rule, of missionaries offering material incentives to low-caste or working-class Indians to convert. In an article of 1953 he pointed out that Hindus were 'more sensitive about these matters now that freedom has come and they are responsible for their own affairs. These activities will not be tolerated much longer.' Keithahn therefore urged his co-religionists to 'clean up their own act'. The Church in India, he wrote,

has a special responsibility to check on all their workers that there may be no material temptations offered for people to become

Christians. In fact, we ought to lean backwards in these matters. In other words, if there is any legitimate help to be given to others it should be on the basis of need and never on the basis of caste or creed.[11]

Within Gandhigram, Keithahn's closest associate was a remarkable social worker named Sankaralingam Jagannathan. A decade-and-a-half younger than Keithahn, Jagannathan had first met him in the 1930s, in an ashram in Tirupattur whose twin lodestars were Christ and Gandhi. Shortly afterwards Jagannathan moved to Bangalore, where he worked with Keithahn on the education of working-class children. Then the Quit India movement took place; whereupon Jagannathan was arrested and Keithahn deported. After the latter returned in 1947 from his forced exile in America, they met again, and became even closer. Jagannathan moved to Gandhigram, where, under Keithahn's direction, he established a Workers' Home to train constructive workers. The building was designed by Keithahn, and Jagannathan and he both helped in carrying stones and laying the foundations.[12] In July 1950, Jagannathan, who was from a family of landowners belonging to the powerful Thevar caste, married Krishnammal, a Dalit from a landless home, in an interfaith ceremony conducted under Keithahn's auspices. They exchanged garlands made of khadi, while vowing to be faithful to one another and to Truth and Non-Violence.[13]

In April 1953, C. Rajagopalachari, then Chief Minister of Madras State, wrote Dick Keithahn a letter of appreciation about the work he and his colleagues were doing in Gandhigram. Keithahn's reply showed how completely he saw himself as part of India's movement for national renewal. He told Rajaji that he regarded his letter as 'the blessing of the Annan [elder brother] to the Tambi [younger brother], the blessing of one of our revered leaders to a group who are deeply earnest about taking on at least a small bit of some of those tremendous burdens you have been carrying so gallantly these many years'.[14]

Even as Keithahn was acquiring a set of Indian co-workers, Christian as well as Hindu, he was becoming increasingly estranged from his American wife. Dick Keithahn had married Mildred McKie in the early 1930s, during his first banishment from India. She had come out with him when he was allowed to return; and in the two decades since they had raised a family together in Bangalore, Merom and Gandhigram, while he had trained students and social activists and she had cured patients.

After their return to India in 1947, Mildred moved with Keithahn to Gandhigram. Their children, no longer toddlers, were sent off as boarders to the American International School in Kodaikanal. While they were away Mildred researched and wrote a booklet called 'Natural Aids for Common Ills'. This invoked Gandhi's own interest in nature cure, and recommended yoga, mud baths, and a diet of whole grains, pulses and vegetables to keep healthy and fit, and thus reduce one's dependence on modern medicine.[15]

Within a few years, however, Mildred was weary of India, and longed to return to where she was, culturally and otherwise, more at home. One associate recalled that she found her husband's 'asceticism very difficult'.[16] Mildred would have liked the family to have some privacy; but Keithahn insisted that they live with everybody else in the Workers' Home in Gandhigram. Perhaps he was neglectful of her. Perhaps she thought that her children's future lay in America. We lack concrete details; we do know however that in the late 1950s they separated, and Mildred returned to America, where two of her children had gone to university, staying on thereafter. The eldest child, a doctor trained at the Christian Medical College, Vellore, worked in India for a while, but she eventually returned to America, too.

Keithahn himself had no desire to go back to the United States. He was devoted to India, and his work here. But his identification with his new homeland had come at an enormous cost; namely, physical and, in time, emotional separation from his family. A younger Gandhian who joined Keithahn after Mildred left told me that he missed his wife terribly. From time to time he would take out one of her saris and fold and re-fold it.[17] As A. K. Tharien recalled, 'their separation and subsequent divorce was the great pain of Keithahn's life'.[18]

IV

After his wife Mildred left India, Keithahn was adopted as an elder brother by Jagannathan and his wife, Krishnammal, whose commitment to Gandhi's ideals comfortably equalled her husband's. In 1956 the trio accompanied Vinoba Bhave on his treks through Tamil Nadu, acquiring donations of land (Bhoodan). Keithahn was impressed with Bhave, writing to a friend that he was now dropping all his other commitments to work full-time for the Bhoodan movement. He would focus first on 'softening up the sentiments' of the landlords, and, after some of them had gifted parts of their estate, on mobilizing poorer peasants to cultivate these lands cooperatively.[19]

In 1957, a violent clash between two religious communities broke out in the Ramnad District. The Jagannathans and Keithahn went there on a peacekeeping mission. Krishnammal later recalled:

We divided into groups of five women and one man – they were the padayatra, peace marches that we organized . . . [I]t took nearly three months to settle down all the people. Then Keithahnji told us, 'One-man padayatra – I will go round from village to village, talking to the people. We should not have a big gàthering, but I will go.' Nearly one month he went around and restored peace like this.[20]

To mark Keithahn's sixtieth birthday in 1958, his admirers, led by Jagannathan and Krishnammal, decided to establish an ashram near the village of Batlagundu. In this area, land had been collected in thirty-five villages under Bhoodan. Keithahn and Jagannathan settled artisans and labourers, and strove to improve their lives. They built homes, arranged for a water supply, found markets for the products of the artisans, and worked the land with intensive cultivation.[21]

Keithahn and the Jagannathans moved out of Gandhigram to work full-time in these new Bhoodan villages. They lived together in a modest home in a hamlet called Kannavaipatty. Now in his sixties, Keithahn retained his powers of endurance and his zest for physical labour. When, many years later, he was asked how this elderly man from the American Midwest had coped with the boiling heat of southern India, Jagannathan replied:

> Not only the heat, he used only village diet. That ragi, millet that the village people take. 'Why rice? No rice. I will only eat village food.' Then, he would go for only the cheapest vegetable, not the rich man's vegetable. Krishnammal would cook, and he would bring water and cut fuel. In the ashram, he did all the work. Carrying water, sweeping, gathering fuel for the kitchen. Very strong and hard-working man. A revolutionary.[22]

Within three years of the establishment of the ashram, it won a prize for agricultural work. Keithahn attributed the award to their farming methods. The land they had got under Bhoodan had a good well on it. They began immediately to compost all their wastes, including night soil, to use as natural fertilizer. Apart from using latrine pits, 'each morning and evening all of us try to go the fields and make our humble contribution'. They also planted green manure trees.[23]

Keithahn and the Jagannathans had a keen interest in adapting modern technology to the conditions of the Indian village. In the summer of 1962, two volunteers from Germany spent a few months with them in Batlagundu. They started a cooperative centre to service machines in the area and train mechanics. Of this experiment Keithahn appreciatively remarked:

> Here is where highly developed science and technology may come to the frontier of nakedness and hunger, producing the efficient little machine at the end of the electric line, in the mud hut, that will make poverty an unreality. Most of us sell ourselves to the production of big machines to exploit others. Cannot a few of us dedicate our lives to the discovery of the small machine that will serve the exploited?

The circular letter from which these lines are quoted went on to note that forty Harijan ('Untouchable') families had joined the Kannavaipatty Gramdan village. 'Now we must find land for them. Already integration of the castes is taking place.'

The letter then described their approach to living and working naturally:

> We insist on whole foods. We eat the rich millets of the area which our Indian friends tend to despise. We experiment with natural health aids. . . . We encourage life-centred rather than literary or academic education. We avoid septic tanks and compost all wastes. Thus we feed our fields with organic manure rather than with the unsatisfactory chemical 'pills'. We insist on working with all. God created all. All are potentially good. We refuse to recognise manmade boundaries and walls of separation.[24]

Keithahn did not – so far as I know – use the terms 'ecology' or 'environment', but he was an ecologist and an environmentalist before those categories came into common currency. In a fragment of memoir, he once wrote:

> We are robbing the next and future generations. Some warn us that we have only another generation of zinc or tin, etc. left if we continue to use our natural resources as we do today. A very small percentage of the population in the world in the USA use the major part of our natural resources. This is an impossible way of life for man in general. And yet most educated people, most leaders, seem to make this way of life their own – the assembly line way of life, shall we say!

Keithahn continued:

> Gandhi stood out against this way of life. He never started a movement against useful tools. But he did stress human values; he opposed all use of machines to exploit man. In that sense the old economic system must go; a new one must come. Kumarappa called the present economy a 'tiger economy'; he worked for the 'mother economy'. It is not important what terminology is used; it is important what are the values that guide our daily lives.[25]

V

In 1959, Keithahn travelled to the United States to see his children, and to raise money for his work. While he was away, Martin Luther King visited India, and even came to Gandhigram. Had Keithahn been in Batlagundu he would surely have gone there and tried to meet him.

Even though he could not meet Dr King, Keithahn had been following his struggle keenly. As someone who knew both countries well, he could see that racial discrimination in the United States was, in a structural sense, comparable to caste discrimination in India. His own impression was that the Indian political system had – at this stage – made more progress in affording dignity and self-respect to Dalits. In November 1960, after attending a meeting in Gandhigram, he sent a letter to friends overseas proclaiming:

> A small group sit about a dining table at the Gandhi Gram Anniversary. Among us, Jagjivan Ram, Minister of India's Railways, P. Kakkan, my old student and now a Minister of the Govt. of Madras, Sri Parameswaran, former Minister and now Member of Parliament – all Harijans! . . . And this within 15 years of freedom! In Andhra States the Chief Minister is a Harijan!
>
> What a judgment upon the U. S. A. which cannot match this even after 100 years of freedom for the Negro! Something is seriously wrong with American Christianity and Democracy![26]

This portrait was not inaccurate if confined to politics, where a constitutional quota of 15 per cent reserved for them had allowed Dalits to be represented in legislatures and ministries. No such quota existed for African Americans. However, in Indian society at large, caste discrimination was rampant, easily as rampant as racial discrimination in the United States. It may be that Keithahn's own self-identification as an Indian had compelled him to so emphatically elevate his adopted homeland over his original one.

In May 1961, the 'Freedom Rides' commenced in the American South, journeys of whites and blacks together in buses across state boundaries in defiance of the laws that then existed to enforce racial segregation. Reading about these rides in Batlagundu, Keithahn was deeply impressed. He wrote a letter to Martin Luther King, which began: 'For a long time we have been following your love and truth efforts with concern and with prayer. In my quiet time this morning it came to me that I must send a word of strength. We watch daily for reports of the "Freedom Riders". You have caught something of the real spirit of Gandhiji.'

The letter then informed Dr King of the ongoing Bhoodan campaign in India.

> We need a new wedding of 'Spirituality and Science': In other words every seeker of truth, in every realm, at every point of pioneering living, must join with his brother in this great modern search and adventure. Thus, while we in India, are building the new society on a sharing-of-land basis, so also must you formulate a great constructive program for both white and coloured.

The letter ended by saying: 'May God bless and strengthen you. You will also know that our prayers are with you.'

Dr King sent a brief reply, thanking Keithahn for his encouragement and support, saying it was 'of inestimable value' for the continuance of their struggle, as they 'gain new courage to carry on when we realize that persons of good will, such as you, are supporting us in the background'.[27]

Keithahn wrote a note for his Indian colleagues, explaining the meaning of the civil rights struggle in the United States. 'Throughout the world, nations and unprivileged groups are struggling for new freedoms', he said, adding: 'The Freedom Movement of which Dr. Martin Luther King is one of the leaders represents a new, creative expression of democracy and Christianity.'

Keithahn told Indians of other exemplary figures from within the African American fold. They included the labour leader Roger Baldwin, the singer Marian Anderson, and the statesman Ralph Bunche, apart from soldiers, aviators, and sailors. 'It is in such a day', he remarked, 'that Dr. King stands as a successful leader. He is the voice of a new Negro expression of and contribution to Democracy and Christianity. Historians in the future alone will be able to evaluate these significant contributions.'

Keithahn ended his note by linking King to Gandhi. Thus he wrote:

> It is good that you and I remember that all this is but a part of the great 'Children of God' [Harijan] movement of the world. Gandhiji enrolled each responsive person into this great 'Kingdom of God'. If we are truly appreciative of this great movement upward, we should identify ourselves with it and become true 'Harijans'. It is a noble name, it is a noble goal for each child of man. We must take this noble word out of the caste distinction level, to which it has been debased, and apply it to ourselves, thus including all of humanity. That will be our greatest recognition and expressed appreciation of this noble Negro leader, Dr. Martin Luther King.[28]

Gandhi had coined the term 'Harijan', 'Children of God', in the 1930s to replace terms such as 'Untouchables' and 'Pariah', which were felt to be degrading and demeaning. Yet by the 1960s, 'Harijan' was increasingly regarded as patronizing by those to whom it referred. Had Keithahn's suggestion been adopted, it may have rid the term of this pejorative and condescending connotation, by incorporating every human being on earth under its purview – regardless of race, caste, religion, and nation.

Notably, Dr King was not the only American radical of the day Dick Keithahn admired. There was also Cesar Chavez, whose work in organizing agricultural labour in California he had read about. Keithahn would often speak to his younger colleagues in Batlagundu about Chavez, urging them to non-violently mobilize landless labourers for better wages and working conditions.[29]

VI

In November 1964, writing to a Christian friend in Switzerland – who had apparently asked why he worked outside the Church rather than inside it – Keithahn remarked:

I always think of myself as a part of a great cultural group, in a great experiment for total freedom, carried on both in our Gramdan Sarvodaya [Village Service] Movement and at government levels. This all started when Gandhiji was our common leader. Therefore, I have assumed my duties as a citizen of the area in which I am a part. . . . In the same manner I have maintained my relationship with the Church of which I am a very real part. There is also an advantage of striving within a family for a larger ecumenical expression. Mankind in his struggle will always form new associations.[30]

Like his compatriot Samuel Stokes, Keithahn fell foul of the Church. Unlike Stokes, however, he did not change his religion and become a Hindu. He remained determinedly ecumenical, a position that confused (and sometimes angered) Hindu and Christian dogmatist alike.

In September 1965, Keithahn travelled to several parts of Tamil Nadu, speaking on the Gandhian concept of Sarvodaya (service for all) and on inter-religious dialogue. His talks went well, until he spoke to a group of earnest Christian seminarians at a town called Marthandam. What happened here is described in a circular letter he wrote shortly afterwards:

However, they [the Seminarians] found it very difficult to swallow my Sarvodaya approach. Yesterday noon, just before I left, I gave them a little time to ask me further questions about their doubts. After some discussion, one of them said, 'You are supporting Sarvodaya. Sarvodaya says all religions are equal. This is a great handicap in our evangelistic work. You are a great obstacle in our evangelistic work.' I rose up and said, 'If that is the blessing and gratitude that you give me, then let me go and work where my efforts are appreciated.' Then I went back, did my packing and got the next bus back here [to Batlagundu].

Writing of this unhappy experience to his Christian friends overseas, Keithahn remarked:

It is a tragedy if the young people who are being trained [to become] pastors still live in their textproof theology and compound. I tried to help them to see that every layman was out in the secular world daily and had to make some witness there – that I was in the same world, only I had the privilege of working on a spiritual basis and this could be more effective. That approach, they could not understand at all. One wonders what place such a Christianity can have in this world.

Keithahn's position on religion was impeccably and honourably Gandhian. Like the Mahatma, he stayed faithful to the religion in which he was raised, while seeking to interpret its tenets in (as it were) the interests of justice and non-violence. At the same time, there were many Hindus whom Keithahn befriended, and a few whom he greatly admired. They included three seers who lived in South India at the same time as he did. These were Sri Aurobindo of Pondicherry, Ramana Maharishi of Tiruvannamalai, and Swami Ramadas of Kanhangad.

In an essay published in the 1960s, Keithahn paid homage to this trio, with a particular focus on the last, who was then – and remains still – by far the least known. Unlike Aurobindo and Ramana, Ramadas was of working-class origin. He had been employed in a textile mill before starting an ashram in northern Kerala whose workings made a powerful impression on Keithahn. 'Ananda Ashram was always a place of great peace and joy', he wrote, adding: 'My wife said that very seldom did she find the family spirit more beautifully expressed than at this Ashram.' (The reference is deeply poignant, since Mildred had been back in the States for several years at this point in time, and was never to return.)

His experience of these Hindu saints and their ashrams had led Keithahn to conclude that

our whole Christian expression in India needs to be rethought in the light of the fact of these great Indian thinkers, leaders and saints. Again and again, at certain points, they are closer to the Eternal Christ than are most so-called Christians. Again and again, they take some expression of Jesus Christ, as Gandhiji took the expression of the power of love, they apply it to particular problems, they make us ashamed of our own Christian discipleship.[31]

VII

Through the 1960s, Keithahn and his comrades the Jagannathans worked tirelessly on rural renewal in southern Tamil Nadu. A letter of August 1964 to a Gandhian friend in Maharashtra has Keithahn writing:

Jagannathan and Krishnammal have been with us during this last week. Each night we go to one or two villages, hold Mahasaba [public] meetings and try to put the village into a more definite Gramdan Sarvodaya pattern. We have failed as yet to create a self-sufficient Khadi pattern in any village. That is partly the result of not having at least one good Khadi worker in this area. However, food is our first need and perhaps it is just as well that we concentrate at that point. It seems quite clear to me that Kottaipatti for example has increased its food production during the last five years by at least 300%.

The letter goes on to say:

My own health has been good. However, I have been trying to do too much. I must be stronger in saying 'no' to many requests. I must concentrate more on our own Ashram family and its positive expressions. I also want to do more writing. The younger generation and the villagers themselves must do more of the work at the village level.[32]

The following January, the Republic of India celebrated the fifteenth anniversary of its founding. On the morning of 26 January 1965, Keithahn raised the National Flag at the Government Free Hostel in Kannavaipatty. He then explained to the boys the symbolism of the colours of the flag. Thus

I reminded the young men that the saffron colour of the Indian flag symbolized the devotion that was necessary if we were to attain our goal. . . . Then I pointed to the white part of the flag and reminded the youth that white always symbolized purity. Finally, the green of our flag symbolizes courage. It takes great courage to hold to the ideals that the followers of Gandhi and Gramdan Sarvodaya workers hold today.[33]

Within a few days, however, Keithahn's mood had soured. From this day, 26 January 1965, English would no longer be used along with Hindi in the official business of the Government of India. The Tamils of South India feared the imposition of Hindi on them, and rose to resist it. All across the state of Madras there were massive and sometimes violent protests. Government offices were attacked, buses were burned, and railway stations were vandalized.

While acknowledging that the Government of India had erred in the unilateral imposition of Hindi, Keithahn was upset at the destruction of property by protesting students, egged on by political leaders. Thus he wrote:

> It should have been comparatively easy to discuss these matters quietly and constructively in our educational institutions. The students could have met with members of the Legislative Assemblies and Parliament, discussed these issues with them, sent their resolutions to the Assemblies and Parliament and made their contribution in a substantial and non-violent way. Surely we have not yet come to the point where we have to resort to demonstrations that might be exploited by irresponsible people.[34]

Fortunately, the Government backed off, and withdrew the order banishing English from official communications. The Tamils were mollified, since they had no objection to a language they regarded as neutral. English was acceptable to them, unlike Hindi, which they saw as the thin edge of the wedge of North Indian imperialism.

By the monsoon of 1965 the attention of Keithahn, and the Jagannathans, had focused back on the land question. They were particularly exercised by the allocation of 120 acres of land in a village named Vilampatti. Owned by the famous Meenakshi Temple of Madurai, this land had been handed over by the temple authorities to a single landlord. Jagannathan and Keithahn led a satyagraha to have these fields given instead to landless labourers of the locality. Every day, villagers and satyagraha workers organized prayer meetings. When the authorities did not yield, Jagannathan went on a ten-day fast. The authorities then said they would allocate the land to the villagers, and Jagannathan broke his fast.

The assurance was betrayed, and the land was allocated to cronies of the landlord. When these men came to prepare the fields, the Sarvodaya workers went along with local villagers and obstructed the interlopers, albeit non-violently. The state came down hard, arresting 350 protesters, including the Jagannathans and Keithahn, but also many women. This led to reports in the press, protest meetings in solidarity, and questions in the Assembly. Some district Congress leaders came out in support. After a week in prison, they were all released, and an assurance given that the 120 acres owned by the temple would be rented directly to landless agriculturists.

In the week they were in prison, Keithahn led interfaith prayers every evening. Here he would speak of Christ and Gandhi, and also of Ramana Maharishi, the great saint of the Tamil country whose *darshan* he had been privileged to have.[35]

Of their struggle in Vilampatti, Keithahn remarked: 'The significant aspect of this slight victory is that it indicates what must be done with the thousands of acres of Temples and Churches in the Tamilnad and India. They must go to the landless poor. They must be used with a high sense of responsibility. All exploitation must go.'[36] He urged that the struggle must not end with the donation or distribution of land. For once that was done, 'the land must be cultivated well. Organic material is most important. Good seeds are required.' He particularly emphasized the composting of wastes, chastising Sarvodaya workers 'who do not take such an approach seriously', who did not show 'a maximum concern for the fullest use of all waste materials that the soil might be fully enriched and the food products might be of the best quality'.[37]

VIII

The previous chapter has spoken of the somewhat different attitudes of Sarala and Mira towards Vinoba Bhave, the pre-eminent Gandhian after Gandhi. Keithahn also knew the man, and inclined more towards the Sarala point of view in this regard. He had marched with Vinoba through southern Tamil Nadu, and admired his commitment and powers of endurance. In camp-side conversations with Bhave he had marvelled at his knowledge of Hindu scriptures as well as of comparative religion.

Mira, who had lived with the Mahatma for twenty years, knew that Bhave was not cut from the same cloth as Gandhi. Keithahn, who like Sarala had met Gandhi several times, but had never been part of his inner circle, was more ready to accept that Vinoba was the Mahatma's 'spiritual successor'. The letters that Keithahn wrote to Bhave were redolent with adoration. One representative letter began:

I often think of you, enquire of you and always rejoice when there is word from you. You have made your own great pilgrimage and are still making it. We are most grateful for the new road of Gramdan Sarvodaya on which you have set us. This has taken our unique Movement several steps forward and closer to the people.

The letter continued with a report of their work:

As you know, Jagannathan has been giving us strong leadership as usual. For over two months he carried on a program of bhoodan distribution, etc in the Chingeput District. There is the need of a unique and strong effort to integrate the economy of Madras and the rural areas about. Today, perhaps one of the worst examples of the city exploiting the villager is to be found around Madras City. We might well lead India in solving this general and serious problem.

The letter ended with this deeply devotional paragraph:

I know you have in mind coming to us again. At the moment I feel we are not ready. Perhaps, in that sense we can never be ready. We have done so little since you have been with us. Most of us are so weak. Some of us waste our time and efforts by doing good things but not doing the important work you have set for us. Perhaps it is not easy to see your vision and task for us. And yet we hope you can come to us soon. Especially I look forward to this fellowship.

There are so many things to talk over; so many places where we need to make new steps forward. I am convinced when you come again we shall be more fully with you, shall have a program for ourselves that will challenge our very best.[38]

Jagannathan himself could see both sides of Vinoba – his learning and asceticism on the one side, and his lack of interest in organizational matters on the other. He appears to have communicated his ambivalence to Keithahn, since a few months after writing the paean above the latter became slightly less fulsome in his appreciation. When a Christian friend asked about the progress of Bhoodan and Gramdan, Keithahn replied that 'there has been some frustration among Sarvodaya workers in recent years'. He added:

I do not blame Vinobaji for the situation. He is not a leader in the Gandhian sense. He is primarily a man of the spirit. At that point he made an outstanding contribution to Gramdan Sarvodaya. Perhaps his weakness is that of all who sow good and strong seed and think that the manuring and nurturing and watering of the crop is not so essential. It is at the latter point that a person like myself feels he can make his best contribution.[39]

IX

In November 1965, Keithahn travelled to Sevagram, where he attended a meeting of Quakers, Gandhians and other peace-makers. He travelled to and fro by train, third-class sleeper. 'It was a thrill to be in Gandhiji's cottage', he wrote. At the meeting, his friend, the Quaker Marjorie Sykes, spoke of her work for peace and reconciliation in Nagaland. Keithahn hoped that 'the methods that are working in Nagaland can be used in the Kashmir Valley and later perhaps on the China frontiers. We must gain experience, gain strength and slowly formulate substantial programs.'[40]

Keithahn was well into his sixties, and decades of hard physical labour and arduous travel by bus and train were taking their toll.

Now, every summer he went off for a retreat to the hill station of Kodaikanal, a couple of hours' drive from Batlagundu. Here he would conduct training camps for younger social workers; these were a mixture of Christian prayer and Gandhian manual labour, with evening campfire chats on current events. Near the Kodai ashram was a massive rock called 'Suicide Point' until Keithahn renamed it 'Rock of Vision'. He liked climbing on top of the rock and holding court there, facing a wooded hill.[41]

In January 1968, Dick Keithahn turned seventy. The Jagannathans organized a celebration at the Sarvodaya Ashram in Kannavaipatty. The honorand was charmed and moved by the village drummers, the wind pipes, and the dancing of men and women. 'There is so much vim and speed in the music and dancing', he wrote, 'that one wonders how the people have the strength to do all of this.' Of these village musicians and dancers he remarked that 'if they keep on, if they have good training, they could go into this profession and make name and fame and earn a great deal of money. However, they will probably live their natural lives [in the village] as they should do.' He was himself 'tremendously interested in [these] local expressions of culture', which 'express themselves fairly well in the local natural atmosphere', but which 'never comes to fruition in the artificial city atmosphere'.[42]

Later in 1968 Keithahn formally took Indian citizenship, becoming in practice what he had long been in theory. He had first come to the country a full forty-three years previously. To mark the occasion, he wrote an autobiographical poem, where he spoke of his boyhood mentor Pastor Herreman, who 'set me on this pilgrimage when I was but 14', and of the 'vital vision', 'challenging training', and 'wider fellowship' that Carleton, Chicago, Yale and the Union Theological Seminary had provided him. The poem continued:

But it was India that brot *the greater blessings*:
blessings in Mission – the crossing of compound walls:
Tagore insisted, 'We are one humanity!'
Gandhiji took me out of the luxurious, imperialistic bungalow:
brot me into the non-violent and community building movement;
Vinoba led us on the pilgrimage of 'land to the landless';
'The earth is the Lord's and the fulness thereof' . . .[43]

The 2nd of October was the birth anniversary of Mahatma Gandhi. That day in 1968 was special, for it marked the beginning of the Gandhi Centenary year. Jagannathan and Keithahn decided that, on 2 October 1968, they would celebrate their hero's birthday by taking over vacant land owned by an absentee judge. The judge wanted to build a temple, but the Gandhians said they would build for him a *Mandapam*, 'a place of meditation and community living, that would be a place of simple beauty and great utility'. In relating their plan to friends, Keithahn remarked:

> I am becoming very strong that wherever people do not use their land or property in India, we have a right to take it over. We have started with the Government waste-land. We recovered 500 acres of waste-land in the Batlagundu Block. But I am saying frankly, wherever people have land fallow, we should simply water and get to work.[44]

One of the highlights of the Gandhi Centenary year, for India as a whole, was a visit by Khan Abdul Ghaffar Khan, the remarkable Pathan follower of the Mahatma. At Partition, Ghaffar Khan became a citizen of Pakistan, since the North West Frontier Province where he lived and worked was now part of that country. Having long fought for a united India he found himself adrift and bereft. He soon fell foul of Pakistan's rulers, and spent much of the 1950s in prison. In the 1960s he went into exile in Afghanistan. And it was from Kabul that he came to India in the winter of 1969–70.

Ghaffar Khan travelled across India, and among the places he visited was Batlagundu. Someone in Sarvodaya circles had told him about the work of the Jagannathans, and he went to see this in the first week of January 1970. This was, wrote Keithahn to a friend, 'an outstanding event naturally in the life of this area'. The next day, Ghaffar Khan spoke at the Madurai Gandhi Museum to a group of Sarvodaya workers. He minced no words, telling them (as Keithahn reported):

> that he sees the same poverty around us that he saw 22 years ago. He thinks we should have done much more in the removal of this poverty than we have done. I agree! However, unless we are stronger and more devoted; unless there is a more substantial leadership at

each point; these matters are not simple. Nevertheless, we constantly need the voice of the prophet to remind us of the world of poverty in which we live, to get rid of this complacency.[45]

X

Even as he continued his activist work with the Jagannathans, Keithahn was becoming increasingly attracted to the contemplative life. He had struck up a close friendship with Bede Griffith, a Benedictine monk of British origin who had come to South India in the 1950s, seeking to combine Hindu and Christian monastic traditions. Griffith based himself at an ashram in Tamil Nadu established by a French Benedictine monk who had taken the name Abhishiktananda.[46]

Inspired by his friend, Keithahn also took formal vows of monasticism. From the late 1960s, he began signing his letters 'Richard Benedictine', instead of 'R. R. Keithahn'. In the spring of 1970, his newly minted Indian passport in hand, Keithahn left for a long trip abroad. He spent time in a Trappist monastery in Rome and visited other parts of Europe before going on to the United States. He stayed with each of his children, the daughters, Mearl and Ruth, who were both doctors, and the son, Richard, who was a pastor. From the latter's home in Minnesota he wrote to a German friend: 'There have been happy summer days at my son's home; swimming – visiting many relatives and friends – speaking about India everywhere.' He was delighted that Richard and his wife Mary had, after having three children of their own, adopted an African American child.[47]

On his return to India after almost a year abroad, Keithahn moved out of the Batlagundu area for good. He now divided his time between his hill retreat in Kodaikanal and the Christian Fellowship Ashram in Oddanchatram. When in Kodai, he gave the occasional sermon on interfaith relations, sitting on his 'Rock of Vision'.[48] In Oddanchatram, the Thariens had arranged for him to have a small, independent house at the edge of the campus. Here he read, meditated and received visitors. He liked to wear khadi shorts and a khadi bush shirt, of the same colour; except while conducting

Communion, when he wore a khadi cassock. He was much loved by the hospital staff and gloried in their company.[49]

In his retirement Keithahn followed the activities of his friends the Jagannathans with interest and admiration. In June 1975, Indira Gandhi, the Prime Minister, imposed a State of Emergency, following which all those who opposed her rule, even if non-violently, were arrested. Among those sent to prison was Jagannathan. He was at first lodged in a prison in Bihar, but then moved to the Central Jail in Madras. Keithahn wrote to Jagannathan saying he wanted to come and see him. Only relatives were allowed to visit prisoners, so in his application the Tamil Gandhian listed his American-born mentor as his 'father'. When the prison guards saw a white man arriving to see an inmate, they at first refused to let him in, until Keithahn harangued them in his broken Tamil.[50]

The year 1975 gave way to 1976, and the Emergency was not lifted. Tens of thousands of political prisoners were still in detention. On New Year's Day 1977, Keithahn wrote a poem that exhorted the Sarvodaya workers still at large

> To return to the villages:
> To the hungry, the outcastes, exploited mothers, children;
> To be much more faithful to our accepted callings:
> The rule of the self-sufficient village;
> The pilgrimage on to 'One Humanity';
> With developing 'Mothers' Power'
> And universal 'soulforce'
> To be faithful Trustees of all God's Gifts.

Another verse spoke directly to the politics of the time. It went:

> We are striving together for the removal of Emergency:
> The Emergency of Hunger, Exploitation, Injustice:
> The declared 'Emergency' of the Government;
> The emergency of all Frontier living
> With faith, hope and love – these three![51]

CHAPTER 17

The Last Gandhians

I

In December 1964 – five years after she had moved to Austria – Mira got a letter from the Quaker Horace Alexander, an old India hand who had frequented Gandhi's ashrams and written books about him. Alexander was writing on behalf of a Gujarati friend in London, Motilal Kothari, who was keen that a film be made on the Mahatma's life. Kothari had persuaded the British director Richard Attenborough to take up the project. Now he asked Alexander to arrange a meeting with Mira, since her support and advice would be crucial to the venture. Of Gandhi's close associates, she was among the few who were still alive, and the only one based in the West.[1]

Mira agreed to meet Motilal Kothari, who went to see her in Austria in January 1965. He was nervous beforehand, since he had heard that Mira was 'very much opposed to the idea of making a film on Gandhiji'.[2] Fortunately, she was set at ease by Kothari's earnestness and sincerity. Her visitor was a Gujarati who knew Gandhi's cultural world intimately, and she thought he would give the director, Attenborough, the right sort of advice.

After Kothari's visit, Mira wrote to her friend Krishna Murti Gupta in Delhi:

My impression is they are going to do their best to make a really good job of it [the proposed film on Gandhi] . . . They are going to consult me further, and send me the text to look at and make any suggestions I like. The actress who will play my part will also come and see me here. I will do what I can to keep it on the right lines. . . . It is a huge undertaking, and now that it is actually under way, I think we should all try to help.[3]

Motilal Kothari had got Horace Alexander to smooth the path for him with Mira Behn, and now he wanted Mira to smooth his way with the Prime Minister of India, whose support would be absolutely crucial, especially if the film was to be shot in India. At the time of Kothari's visit to Mira in January 1965 the Prime Minister was Lal Bahadur Shastri, whom Mira knew only very slightly. It is not known whether she wrote to him. However, a year later Shastri suddenly died, and was replaced by Indira Gandhi. Mira had known her since she was a little girl.

Attenborough had commissioned Robert Bolt to write the script for the film. In 1966, when Kothari and Bolt planned a trip to India, Mira wrote to Indira Gandhi asking her to meet them. 'My dear Miraben', the Prime Minister wrote in reply, 'it was a pleasant surprise to hear from you. I have often wondered where you were and what you were doing.' She then added:

> I myself am greatly interested in the Gandhi film as I feel a good film on this subject would be of tremendous help to us, and it is probably easier for an outsider to make it. I shall certainly see Mr. Bolt and Mr. Kothari when they come to India if they are in Delhi at the same time as I am.[4]

In the event, Robert Bolt dropped out of the project. Then, in January 1970, Motilal Kothari died of a heart attack. Attenborough, however, was determined to make the film. In 1974 he wrote to Mira requesting a meeting. He flew to Vienna, and from the airport drove to her cottage at the edge of the woods. He later wrote:

> As the car drew up she came out of the door: amazingly tall, still very upright, with grey swept-back hair and a large pair of thick glasses. Well wrapped in heavy woollies, she strode down the path with her arms spread out in greeting, while standing discreetly in the background was Datt, her devoted Indian bearer.

Attenborough and Mira 'quickly developed a warm relationship, and she began to relate anecdote after anecdote'.[5] He returned to see Mira several times. He came, as Mira's Austrian friend Lea Calice recalled, 'to get the right angle and more details of the persons and indeed happenings concerned. She would carefully explain Gandhi's aims and attitudes and answer questions faithfully, often quoting his answers while describing an episode.'[6] Mira had thrown her weight behind the project; she wished, as she told her friend Nilla Cook, to show Attenborough 'the ways in which Gandhiji's larger mission was for the world'.[7]

Attenborough himself wrote that 'Mira's encouragement was unstinting, particularly during the period of Morarji Desai's Prime Ministership [1977–9] when Indira Gandhi was out of office, and she wrote to him urging Pandit Nehru's original approval of the film'. In January 1980, Indira Gandhi returned as Prime Minister, and sanctioned a large grant from the public exchequer for the project. In the winter of 1980–1, almost twenty years after the idea was first mooted, the film was shot on location in different parts of India. Attenborough sent Mira photographs from the shooting. After seeing them Mira wrote back, expressing 'her delight in their veracity, although she complained bitterly that Geraldine James, who portrayed her, was so much more beautiful than herself'.[8]

II

While Mira hoped, via Richard Attenborough's film, to bring Gandhi's vision to the world, she also sought to remind Indians themselves of the man and his legacy. In 1968, reading the news-papers from India, she was not impressed by the form that the preparations for the Gandhi Centenary were taking. She wrote to Krishna Murti Gupta:

> I don't feel particularly happy about the pamphlets, badges, and what not that are being prepared for 'carrying Gandhiji's message to the people'. Leaders have gone on talking about 'Gandhiji's Message' for the last 20 years, but with what result? What the people want is

tangible improvement in their economic and general condition. In their present plight, to carry to them paper messages is an insult both to Bapu and the masses!! Well – there it is, and what can one do about it?![9]

Mira made her disenchantment public, in the form of a long letter published in the *Hindustan Times*. She said that the best tribute to Gandhi in his Centenary year would be 'a combined effort by the [Gandhi Smarak] Nidhi and the Government [of India] for the removal of illiteracy down to the lowliest and poorest throughout India within a definite and short period, or with the help of modern scientific and technical knowledge, to turn every village or group of villages into a cloth producing centre'. She insisted that

> it is not seminars, lectures, photographs, pamphlets, badges and what not that will impress the Indian people, nor is it museums, libraries, and monuments in stone and brick which will carry Gandhiji's name down through the centuries to come, but it is the fulfilment of that 'revolution' which Gandhiji used to say had got to begin with after reaching independence, which is needed. Without that revolution his name will fade away into a sweet but sad remembrance of one who had divine ideals, but was, in fact, a failure.

In Mira's view, this revolution would consist of 'raising of the villages to their rightful place in the country's economy and culture', through the 'decentralization of industry, balanced distribution of both labour and transport . . . as well as an automatic check to the growth of cities'. Thus she argued:

> Unless the programme of carrying out this objective can be freed from the orthodox Gandhian cult of today, there is no hope of rousing enthusiasm. A new approach has to be made. Decentralization of industry must not have to mean hand-spinning and weaving of the old kind but spinning and weaving in the villages with the aid of modern, small-scale machinery capable of producing first-class cloth at economic rates. Cloth production has, of course, top priority because of India's cotton output, but there are also other industries which can be split

up and carried on in village homes. One of the essential things in this new approach is that scientific knowledge be brought to bear on all problems. Amateurishness and unscientific experimentation are all too common in Gandhian programmes. Finally it should not be thought necessary to associate rules for prayers, hymn-singing, diet, dress, etc., with this new approach. Honesty, courage and an enlightened love of Man and Nature (our Earth who gives us all) are what are needed.[10]

Mira was now too old and too frail to travel to India for the Gandhi Centenary celebrations. But a short flight to London was deemed feasible. In October 1969 she spoke about her own memories of Gandhi at a large meeting at the Royal Albert Hall, chaired by the last Viceroy of India, Lord Mountbatten. Afterwards Mountbatten wrote to her: 'You absolutely captivated and charmed the entire audience and stole the whole show: and deserved to do so too.'[11]

III

In Austria, Mira's modest living expenses were met through a pension from the Government of India, via the Gandhi Smarak Nidhi. Prime Minister Indira Gandhi came to Vienna on a state visit in October 1971 and met Mira, and asked for her to be invited to the official functions as well. The following January, when Mira fell sick, the Indian Government (as instructed by the Prime Minister) met her medical expenses. She was now in her eightieth year, and on the doctor's advice a pacemaker was inserted in her heart.[12]

Apart from sending her monthly cheques, the Gandhians in India also sent Mira news that might interest her, of activities, illnesses and deaths of constructive workers she had known, of water conservation and the planting of trees in her beloved Sevagram. She was also regularly visited by officials from the Indian Embassy, who remember her as retaining great fondness for India and Indians. She spoke a lot about her time in that country, as well as about her current passion, which was for the music of Beethoven.[13]

In January 1980 Indira Gandhi became Prime Minister once more, after three years out of office. Later that year Krishna Murti Gupta wrote to her suggesting the Government help Mira, who was in dire financial straits in Austria. She wrote back saying: 'I have known Mira all my life', adding: 'I shall . . . see what can be done.' Mrs Gandhi thereupon sanctioned an enhanced monthly allowance, and told the embassy in Vienna to take care of Mira's medical expenses.[14]

In the spring of 1981, Mira was visited in her Austrian home by two Englishmen she had known in India. These were Gilbert Laithwaite, the former Private Secretary to the Viceroy, and Wilfrid Russell, a former company executive in Bombay. They found Mira, aged eighty-eight, to be 'amazingly fit'. The visitors were impressed by 'her sense of humour as well as her vitality'. She was reading without glasses, and had a clear and sharp memory. Mira 'talked a lot about Richard Attenborough and the film of Gandhi he is making', and showed the visitors some pictures of the director and herself together. Then 'she described vividly how Gandhi had made her responsible for getting the new Ashram built at Wardha in the Central Provinces. . . . She only just got the hut ready for him to move into just before the monsoon broke. And it was she who got soaked!'[15]

In November 1981, Mira sent her old associate Krishna Murti Gupta a sheaf of her old articles, asking whether he could find for them a suitable publisher in India. In an introductory note to this selection, Mira remarked:

> Now, on entering my 90th year, I feel the urge to express once more my feelings about India. This has led me to read over articles which I wrote in the [19]40s and 50s, a selection of which I give below, because many of them are so relevant to present conditions in India and give one a sharp realization of the fact that 'Progress' has done little towards rectifying the three fundamental ills – damage to the precious soil, destruction of the precious trees and neglect of the rural masses (not the pampered rich farmers).
>
> India, like the rest of the world, is in the clutches of mechanized Big-Business seeking more and more Energy – energy of every imaginable kind *except* that ever present, ever renewable living Energy of humans and animals. The inevitable result is rapidly increasing unemployment and social unrest.

Progressively remove mechanization and chemical fertilizers from
agriculture! Resist Big-Business at every turn!

In Simplicity lies Salvation![16]

This was a succinct restatement of the environmental credo she had
so precociously outlined in her articles of the 1940s and 1950s.

In January 1982 Mira Behn was conferred with the Padma
Vibhushan, India's second highest civilian honour. This was on the
recommendation of Indira Gandhi. Mira was of course in no position to travel to New Delhi for the investiture, so the award was
conferred on her in her cottage by the Indian Ambassador.

Later that summer Mira fell seriously ill. Mira Behn of India,
formerly Madeleine Slade of England, died in Austria on 20 July
1982. She was cremated, not buried, and as per her wishes her ashes
were scattered in the Helenental, a section of the Vienna woods
where Beethoven had often walked. Her remaining assets went to
her devoted Garhwali servant Rameshwar Datt.[17]

When Mira left India, in 1959, she had hoped to proselytize about
Gandhi in the West by writing books and articles about him. The
one book she published (her memoir) did not attract a wide readership. She had little luck in placing articles about Gandhi in Western
newspapers either. Nonetheless, she met her aim, posthumously,
through the agency of Richard Attenborough. His film *Gandhi* was
released in November 1982, and was a spectacular success at the
box office, and won nine Oscars. For all its flaws, the film played
a major role in making Gandhi relevant and popular again. And
Mira's role in inspiring and encouraging its director was critical.

When Mira left India, in 1959, she also had a secondary ambition:
to write a major book on her first love, Beethoven. In the decades
that followed she read more about the man and listened afresh to
his music. At her death, in July 1982, a manuscript on Beethoven
was found in Mira's papers. Her aristocratic friends in Vienna were
able to obtain a foreword by the great violinist Yehudi Menuhin.
But even with this endorsement it was impossible to find a publisher
in the West; with reason, for the script lacked coherence or originality, being merely a long and rambling love letter to the composer
from a fan. Then Mira's friend Rosetta Spalt heard that an editor

in the Indian branch of Oxford University Press was obsessed with Beethoven. So she sent it to him, but he turned it down as well, for (as he was to later write) 'there was nothing in the script other than the passionate personal devotion that Beethoven's music – like Elvis Presley's – is known to excite in many listeners'.[18]

Mira's book on her favourite composer was, as it were, unpublishable, but it would not go unpublished. *Beethoven's Mystical Vision* by Mira Behn (with a foreword by Yehudi Menuhin) finally appeared in print in 1999, brought out by the Khadi Friends Forum, based in the southern city of Madurai. This was an act of grace, and of gratefulness; in honour of her decades of devotion to the Mahatma, the Gandhians in India would not let the world forget Mira's decades of devotion to Beethoven.

IV

After handing over the Lakshmi Ashram to Radha Bhatt in 1966, Sarala Behn spent several years working with Vinoba Bhave and Jayaprakash Narayan in the plains. In the early 1970s Sarala came back to the hills, and found herself a little cottage with a view of the snows, a fair distance away from the ashram that she had founded.

When Sarala returned to the Uttarakhand Himalaya, the Chipko movement was in full swing. She wrote to one Chipko worker that that 'I am a teacher by nature and by my habits, not a revolutionary or an activist.'[19] Even so, she enthusiastically supported the non-violent protests against forest felling. She was particularly pleased with the participation of women. Travelling the villages, she found that 'the sisters are firm . . . and will not let the contractors enter their local forests. Each sister is prepared to stick to each tree and is ready to suffer blows from an axe. But while alive they will not let a single tree be cut.'[20]

The Chipko movement had two major leaders: Chandi Prasad Bhatt, who was active in the Alakananda valley, and Sunderlal Bahuguna, who was active in the Bhageerathi valley. Both were Gandhians who belonged to the Sarvodaya family; both greatly admired Sarala, the acknowledged Mother of the Sarvodaya movement in Uttarakhand. Bahuguna and Bhatt had once worked closely together; however, as the Chipko movement grew and developed, and as it acquired national and even international recognition, they began to develop differences. These were partly on questions of tactics – Bahuguna believed more in propaganda, Bhatt more in grassroots work; and partly a question of personal rivalry: namely, who was to get greater credit for leading what was unquestionably the country's most celebrated 'environmental' movement. Bahuguna was several years older than Bhatt and – age being a determinant of hierarchy in most things Indian – resented the acclaim accruing to the younger man.

Sarala knew Sunderlal Bahuguna much longer. His wife Vimala had been one of her first students and protégées in Kausani. But over the years she had developed a healthy appreciation of Chandi Prasad Bhatt's abilities as well. In the autumn of 1977, as the rift between the two men became more visible, and began to affect the movement as a whole, she wrote to both urging them to mend fences. She told Bhatt that the future of Chipko depended on the 'unity visible among us'. She said that while she personally preferred his approach, 'of doing solid work among the people and developing the organization', Bahuguna's emphasis on 'extensive propaganda' was important as well. As she put it, 'each one has a particular nature and approach, and it is not necessary that they are in opposition. They could be supportive of each other.' It was thus that she was making this effort 'to repair the rupture between Sunderlal and yourself'.[21]

Sarala also wrote to Sunderlal Bahuguna. She told him that she was 'deeply impressed with Chandi Bhai's work, his character and truthfulness, his gravitas, power of organization, simplicity, affection and dedication and continuity of effort'. She was distressed by 'the distance that is growing' between the two, and urged Bahuguna to trust Bhatt's 'truthfulness and sincerity'. Sarala told Bahuguna that it was of vital importance, for the movement as a whole, 'that you and Chandi Bhai understand each other well, have goodwill and cooperate and support each other in work. That will give us a lot of power or else the feeling will grow that there is groupism brewing between us.'[22]

Sadly, Sarala's efforts to reconcile the two men failed. Chipko split into two wings, one led by Chandi Prasad Bhatt, the other led by Sunderlal Bahuguna. Within Uttarakhand and outside it, journalists, writers and activists took sides, dividing and weakening the movement further.[23]

V

Its divisions and schisms notwithstanding, Chipko inspired Sarala to devote her own attention to the protection of the Himalayan ecosystem and the hill forests especially. In October 1979 she sent a memorandum to the President of India on this question. The destruction of the Himalayan forests, she said, had led to floods and landslides and in turn to the devastation of farming in the plains. Apart from commercial tree felling, the building of roads, the laying of electricity cables and the construction of mega-dams had also led to a rapid thinning of forest cover. Sarala urged the Government of India to stop forest felling and promote mixed forests. There was a General Election imminent; Sarala hoped that candidates who favoured the conservation of the environment would get the votes of the people.

A few months later, Sarala established a 'Parvatiya Paryavaran Sanrakshan Samiti' (Society of Himalayan Ecological Conservation). She was its Convenor, and Vimala Bahuguna and Chandi Prasad Bhatt were among its members, with provision for members from Nepal and the eastern Himalaya too. The society defined its objects as:

The dissemination of educative and soundly based information regarding the danger at present arising to:

The natural environment due to the mass felling of the green cover of the hill areas, the construction of huge dams which interfere with the natural flow of the rivers, the use of heavy explosives used in the construction of these dams and of roads, the dangers to agricultural fertility arising from the degradation of the water supply due to the above activities and from the use of chemical fertilizers, pesticides and herbicides and the dangers from atmosphere and water pollution from the effluent of large-scale industry and the use of fossil fuel in all spheres;

The cultural environment arising due to a faulty system of education which estranges the students from the activities of daily life producing a white collar class;

The social environment from concentration in huge conurbations sapping man's faculties for spontaneous thought or recreation . . .

The society planned to publish books and pamphlets towards 'the establishment of an ecological library'; educate workers for spreading its message; and establish village institutions and promote cottage industries.[24]

Sarala was now writing a book herself on the ecological predicament facing humanity. She had been honoured with the prestigious Jamnalal Bajaj Award; she used the prize money to order books and pamphlets on environmental subjects from around the world. Based on these materials, and her own decades of field experience, she wrote a book in Hindi entitled *Sanrakshan ya Vinash* (Protection or Destruction), which was published early in 1981.

Even as she was writing a book with a global perspective, Sarala had important things to say about her own local environment. In 1980 she published a major essay on environmental renewal in the Himalaya. This asked for a complete overhaul of forest policy, away from the promotion of coniferous monocultures towards the nurturing of mixed forests with many different species. She urged that villagers, and women in particular, play a key role in forest management, to enable it to serve local needs rather than outside commercial interests. Sarala also wanted a moratorium on the building of large dams in the hills, with sun, wind and micro-hydro being used to fulfil energy demand instead.[25]

In the monsoon of 1981, Sarala had a most interesting exchange with Sri Madhav Ashish, a Hindu monk of British extraction who had lived in Kumaon as long as she had. Ashish was keenly interested in the revival of the hill forests, and in the role that village councils (panchayats) could play in this revival. He had worked out that 'if replanted and properly managed', panchayat-controlled forests could 'supply more than adequate fuelwood and fodder for the entire population and their animals in the whole U. P. hills'. Now he wrote to Sarala as follows:

> It is easy to plan for fuel & fodder forests. But how are they to be planted (a) when the Netas [political leaders] who control the panchayats want commercial forests, and (b) without full co-operation from the village women? The exceptional cases show us what can be done, but there are over 15,000 villages in the hills for which one cannot plan on the basis of exceptions. We have to have panchayats which represent the interests of the majority and, particularly, the interests of the women.
>
> As they stand, the panchayats appear as an institution for transferring development funds into the Netas' pockets.
>
> I am told that the students working for the Chipko movement are helping to build up village opposition to the Netas. This prepares the ground. At the top, people <u>seem</u> to be taking the hill problem seriously. What sort of institutional process is needed (Block, Panchayat etc) to link the top to the ground and cut out, as far as possible, the private short-term interests of the small politicians? Can you summon the energy to reply?[26]

The last query was because Sri Madhav Ashish knew that Sarala had recently been quite unwell. But, as it turned out, ill health would not deter her from engaging in a discussion on a matter close to her heart. While her eyes were giving trouble, she told Ashish, 'I am quite happy to have an opportunity of something to reply to!' Now, to his scheme for the renewal of the hill forests, she wrote these nine numbered paragraphs in response:

> 1) I should like to make it clear that I do not associate myself with any label, which one can stick on oneself & interpret at one's own sweet will. . . .
> 2) I think the ecological question is at root not a material but a spiritual, not a technical but an educational question, concerning man's adjustment with total nature, i.e. with God (if you choose to use the term).

3) In the name of a 'realistic' approach one may be either an optimist or a pessimist, depending mostly on the above alternative approaches.

4) I can quite believe that your calculations are correct, but how long even with an optimistic approach will it take you to achieve the required figure, & in the meantime, how do you slow down the rate of erosion & flooding. Therefore, I call for a moratorium on mass commercial fellings until the flow of silt, say at Hardwar in the rains, can be called 'normal' – i.e. a reasonable difference [from what it was at present].

5) The question of the conservation of forests calls for a change in the blind following of 'netas' & also in the approach of the average government servant of the Forest Dep[artmen]t. Both are difficult, but I am inclined to think that the 'uneducated' villager may change more quickly than 'educated' or semi-educated officials whose eyes have been blinkered by their so-called education.

6) I must admit that there is a considerable difference of approach between Garhwal & Kumaun, & the majority of constructive efforts in this connection have been in Garhwal. Here, owing to its traditional centres of pilgrimage, people are more easily moved to corporate action. . . . In Garhwal the approach has been a 3-day camp interpreting the Shrimad Bhagwat in terms of conservation & the garlanding with a 'rakhi' of the trees the women intend to protect and foster. The women respond far more readily than the men – they are more practical also.

7) The present organisation of the panchayats is a part of the vicious system of government by party politics. We envisage a different form – a part of complete reorganisation of life which the conservation movement calls for, ultimately placing the public good before personal profit. This would involve a delegation of the responsibility for planning, execution & utilisation to the villagers – guidance by specialists where necessary.

8) One must evolve new techniques of approach both to the public & to government servants. I believe on the whole public cooperation can be won through a cultural approach (as outlined above) but I am not clear as to how to awaken a new approach in the average government servant (at any level). I think that is a more difficult

& complicated matter. If effective, it could also help to solve the 'neta' problem.

9) At root, this is all part of the one problem of approach:

Politics + religion = Sarvanash

Science + religion = Sarvodaya[27]

The Hindi words *Sarvanash* (destruction of all) and *Sarvodaya* (welfare of all) were written in hand, in the Devanagari script.

This is a quite extraordinary letter, suffused with wisdom, understanding and (not least) hope, written by an ailing, elderly lady still seeking to leave a better world behind for those she had loved and lived with.

VI

The news of Sarala Behn's ill health in the monsoon of 1981 had reached other people, among them Indira Gandhi. Mrs Gandhi had offered to have her treated by Government doctors in a modern hospital in Almora or Nainital, and perhaps even in the plains. Sarala was touched by the concern, but said her co-workers were looking after her well, and that the clean air and fresh surroundings of the Himalaya were a great boon. She told the Prime Minister that she had belatedly learned a lesson, that social workers needed to take better care of their health in order that their work didn't suffer. In a mood of pensive reflection, she wrote:

When I came to India I resolved to live as simply and as austerely as possible. Although I never experienced real poverty, even so I made sure that I spent the absolute minimum on myself. But I could have done this while taking care of my health as well, so that I could have done the work I set out to do. Now that I am in this state, I realize my error, and have resolved that from now on I shall take better precautions [with regard to her health].[28]

In January 1982, a publisher in Nainital brought out the English edition of Sarala's book on the global ecological crisis. Entitled *Revive Our Dying Planet*, this appeared under the authorship of 'Sarala Devi (Catherine Mary Heilemann)', her original European name in brackets, perhaps as a reassertion of her world citizenship. It was 'dedicated to the coming generation in the hope that they may be inspired to play their part in the revival of the dying planet through a Constructive Ecological Revolution'.

The book drew on an eclectic range of reading: Western scientists and sociologists, Indian spiritualists and sacred texts. It covered a wide range of subjects, from the origins of life on earth to the ways in which humans had reshaped the planet down the centuries. Different forms of environmental abuse were discussed in detail, as well as methods of ecological restoration. However, the narrative was jerky and disconnected, abruptly jumping from one theme to another. Sarala strongly stated a preference for the countryside, against 'the concentration and centralisation involved in city life'. She thought India was still in a position to step back from wholesale industrialization, and focus on 'organic farming and ecological balance with a decentralised way of life'. While approving of an identification with the local community on the one hand and with humanity as a whole on the other, she was sceptical of nation-states and the divisive and violent feelings they engendered. She urged scientists to be more aware of the consequences of their research, and not to be secretive about their findings.[29]

In the second week of January 1982, the book was formally released in Delhi, in the presence of Sunderlal Bahuguna and the great ornithologist Salim Ali. A news report on the release said: 'Ms Sar[a]la who could not come for the function due to illness in a message from her hometown Pithoragarh stated that the origin of the book on ecological conservation was a childhood intuition confirmed later: the oneness of the whole of creation.'[30]

Sarala actually lived some distance away from Pithoragarh, near the hamlet of Dharamgarh. Nonetheless, the reference to that place as her 'hometown' would surely have delighted her, as acknowledging that it was in these hills of Kumaon that she had dug her deepest roots. In March, Vimala and Sunderlal Bahuguna went to spend a week with Sarala in Dharamgarh. After they left, Sarala wrote to Vimala asking her to return soon. In a month the flowers would be in bloom, and they could walk around the forest together, glorying in the beauties of nature.[31]

In early July, Sarala fell very ill and had to be shifted from Dharamgarh to a nursing home in Almora. It was clear her end was near. Her disciples and associates from across the hills came to see her for one last time. With her throughout was her devoted successor, Radha Bhatt. She drifted in and out of consciousness. One night, while at her bedside, Radha heard Sarala say, in English: 'Tell the Gandhians to be true.'[32] This was on 6 July 1982; she died two days later.

VII

While Mira was in Austria, and Sarala in the Himalaya, Dick Keithahn lived on in Tamil Nadu. Like them, as he grew older he became increasingly contemplative, watching his health decline and his contemporaries dying around him.

In 1978 Keithahn turned eighty. The next year the great hero of the struggle against Indira Gandhi's Emergency, Jayaprakash Narayan, died. This prompted Keithahn to put down on paper his impressions of three remarkable Indians he had known: Gandhi, Vinoba Bhave, and Jayaprakash. He wrote first of his visits to Sevagram when Gandhi was alive, and of the particular place that the Mahatma had in his own pantheon. Then he said:

> I will stand with the Carpenter of Nazareth whom we count as the Universal, Eternal, Christ. I am sure that Spirit was with the Buddha, etc. Therefore, I am reverent before them all. And I turn to the Mahatma, who emerged out of the Culture of India with all that means, to guide me as a Christian as I listen to Jesus, 'I was hungry and you fed me; I was naked and you clothed me; come into my Kingdom!' Does that not include the Gandhi, the Vinoba, the Jai Prakash, and many more?

It was in Sevagram that Keithahn had first met Vinoba Bhave. But he really got to know him only through his campaign for

Bhoodan, when 'it was impressive to see that tall, lean man walk through the nation, Development Block after Development Block, State after State!' In Vinoba's tours in Tamil Nadu in the 1950s, Keithahn and the Jagannathans had walked with him from district to district, getting donations from large landlords. Now, in this retrospective look-back from two decades later, a note of ambivalence crept into Keithahn's assessment. 'Vinoba was not a usual Sarvodaya man!' he remarked: 'He showed us what could be done; then went on his way to let his coworkers complete the task! Many of us never did! Vinoba strode on; it was not easy to keep up with him!'

Keithahn came, finally, to Jayaprakash Narayan, 'a real leader in his own right'. He remembered him as 'always a friend of the South and especially of the Tamil workers'. Keithahn's friend Jagannathan admired JP enormously, and went to Bihar to be with him. JP, in return, came several times to Tamil Nadu to support them in their work. 'He helped us in the urban areas', remembered Keithahn, 'in our conferences and seminars, in our rural areas: and always substantially. I always marvelled how he could talk to any of us, thoughtfully, almost in meditation, and hold our attention even for a couple of hours, although that generally included translation as well.'[33]

Keithahn was putting down a life's memories and a life's thoughts on paper, sometimes in prose, sometimes in verse. In February 1981 he sent Sarala in the Himalaya a long letter, which began with these lines:

> Spirituality is the acceptance of the Spirit of Truth;
> Spirituality is the doing of one's Duty – Dharma
> It is People's Power – Mother's Power;
> Such Power is invincible, that brings us to Peace:
> Such Power takes us to Abundant Living – Spirituality

and continued by giving his 'Dear Sister', his news and that of his colleagues. Thus

> Jagannathan is busy with Padayathras [walking tours], mostly in Naxalite-ridden areas in Dharmapuri and North Arcot Districts. Krishnammal has been busy similarly in Thanjavoor District. . . . In

the Batlagundu area we are starting a strong Adult Education programme . . . There are now 100 Balvadies [crèches] in the Tamilnad. Dr. Pankajam is guiding them well from Gandhigram.[34]

The next January, Keithahn wrote to Sarala again. His letter began: 'I regret you have not been well; I wish you might be here and receiving the healing ministrations of this devoted group of healers who do so much for so many of us.' He himself felt well enough, he told her, to make plans to go to Madras for a meeting, and travel to Vinoba's ashram in central India for a programme there. He was even planning

to go to USA in 1985 for a Grandson's graduation at Yale. Three of them are at important studies just now. My elder sister hopes also I may have some time with her. I have a good family and should give them a little time now and then altho I don't travel too well thru these long airports anymore.

Keithahn's letter continued: 'I am grateful for your book [Revive Our Dying Planet]. If I buy 10 could I get it [at] a cheaper price? How much? I am always giving such books out to important Gandhian institution libraries and groups of workers.'[35]

In the same week as she got this letter from Keithahn, Sarala heard from K. M. Natarajan, a respected Gandhian worker in Tamil Nadu. Natarajan had just recommended Keithahn for the Jamnalal Bajaj Award. Since Sarala had herself got the award recently, he asked her to write a letter of endorsement on Keithahn's behalf. Natarajan enclosed a copy of his own recommendation to the Bajaj Foundation, a five-page narrative account of all that Dick Keithahn had done for and in India. The account ended with his work in setting up crèches and a training centre for pre-school teachers, with 'a special emphasis on rural culture', promoting folk songs and stories linked to the agricultural cycle. It was, said Natarajan, Keithahn's 'firm belief that [a] new society can be built up only with new men; young children between 2 and 5 can be moulded in such a way that they become the new responsible citizens of the coming future'.[36]

Sarala was entirely willing to recommend her fellow seeker for an award she had herself got. 'I don't know whether this is a correct procedure', she wrote to the Secretary of the Jamnalal Bajaj Foundation, 'but I am giving my experience of two summers spent with him in Kodai, during which I had some opportunity to move about and see some of the work which is proceeding under his guidance.'

Sarala characterized Keithahn's approach to rural development as 'most pragmatic'. He had organized farmers' cooperatives, taking great care about 'the proper utilisation of funds'. She added: 'Inspired by his work the Tamil Nadu Gov[ernmen]t has taken up training for and the administration of Balwadis [crèches] on a large scale.'

Apart from his own work, said Sarala, Keithahn had inspired younger social workers to set up their own ashrams. 'Personally he lives a very frugal life spending the majority of his pension on scholarships for ten or twelve poor children', she said: 'He is a firm believer in self-supporting productive labour, and even at his age is active in forest and home.'[37]

Sadly, the recommendations were not heeded, and Dick Keithahn did not get the Jamnalal Bajaj Award.

VIII

Like Sarala, Keithahn saw himself as a citizen of the world. He worked in Tamil Nadu and carried an Indian passport, but his love and concern embraced all of humanity. In July 1982, he sent a letter to his friends overseas, offering 'suggestions for peace making throughout the world in the 80's and 90's'. He listed twelve goals, among them 'Uniting all peace work – workers – programs', 'Realising people's power – women's power – good citizenship', 'Community-Village centred planning – Development – self-sufficiency', and 'Form Academies of Peace at various Universities'. Keithahn wrote:

> Let each area and nation work out its own peace making steps laying stress on hill-tribes, out-castes, ordinary people, women and youth. . .
> They will have common goals such as village rule – 'Small is beautiful'

– 'soil is holy' – 'plant a tree' – 'terrace the hills' – the sun is our friend – 'solar energy' – water is precious – save it – a world without arms.[38]

Keithahn was now living in Oddanchatram, in the premises of the Christian Fellowship Hospital that his protégé A. K. Tharien had founded. In the summer of 1982, his son Dick, a pastor in the United States, came to India and tried to persuade his father to return with him. Keithahn, with dark visions of ending up in an old people's home, absolutely refused. 'Tharien has promised to look after me', he told his son. Dick then got him to draw up a will, which specified that all he had would be left to a Trust whose activities would be supervised by the Thariens.[39]

Keithahn not only refused to go back to the United States permanently but also he would not be able to go there to attend his grandson's Yale graduation. Towards the end of 1983 he fell ill and had to be hospitalized in Oddanchatram. He was in his eighties and clearly the end was near. His friends across Tamil Nadu decided to honour him and his work for his adopted country. So, on 30 January 1984, the thirty-sixth anniversary of Gandhi's martyrdom, they organized a public felicitation at the Gandhi Museum in Madurai, where Dr M. Aram, Vice Chancellor of Gandhigram Rural University, conferred the title 'THE DEFENDER OF PEACE' on Keithahn. A commemorative poster was also printed, which spoke of his having 'always been on the frontiers, pioneering to bring Gram Swaraj at the grassroots', his taking 'creative initiatives in pre-school education and citizenship training', and of his having inspired 'innumerable persons who came in touch with him [and] have derived spiritual strength and solace from him'.

Keithahn was fortunately able to attend this event in his honour. However, a few weeks later he had a fall in the bathroom in Oddanchatram. His old secretary from Batlagundu days, Sam Stawrence, came to be with him. Sam stayed on for the rest of the year, reading out to his sick mentor the letters that came for him. There was one from a Gandhian named K. Muniandi, an associate of J. C. Kumarappa's, which assured Keithahn that

your intimate connection with the Father of the Nation speaks volumes of your ability to identify yourself with noble causes and aspirations of the weaker sections of humanity. On your part you may justifiably feel that you have proved the secret of your birth on this ever-evolving planet. Your services to the most ignorant and diffident gentry of the Batlagundu area villages are worth inscribing on monumental pillars.

'God is great', continued Muniandi, 'in that He keeps us alive on this earth until His wishes are fulfilled through us. . . . I fully know that you, as a Gandhian Satyagrahi, will creditably pass the last minute tests with courage, conviction and equanimity.'[40]

Another letter came from his old friend from Gandhigram days, G. Ramachandran, now living in retirement in Kerala. This told his 'Fellow Spirit in the service of humanity' that

All your friends here remember you and revere you.
May the Grace of God lead you to eternal peace and joy in good
   time.
Your services to India will never be forgotten by any of us.
Please accept our love, reverence and prayers.[41]

In November, Dick Keithahn's companion and soulmate S. Jagannathan came to be with him. He fed and bathed him, attended to his bedsores, and slept at night on the floor in his room. Keithahn died on the evening of 7 December 1984, in his rooms in the Christian Fellowship Ashram at Oddanchatram, Jagannathan by his side. The next morning there was an interfaith prayer meeting in the open air, conducted according to the Sarvodaya practice. This was followed by a service in the hospital's little chapel, with Christians, Hindus and Muslims in attendance. Then the body, covered with a khadi cloth and decked with flowers, was taken for burial, in a procession led by a priest, with children following, and students, nurses and doctors bringing up the rear. A grave had been prepared amidst a copse of trees, on the edge of the campus, where Keithahn had liked to take his evening walk, contemplating the line of hills in the distance.[42]

Epilogue

In 1972, India celebrated the twenty-fifth anniversary of its independence from British colonial rule. To mark the occasion, a writer in Bangalore delivered a series of radio talks paying tribute to those 'who braved the wrath of their own countrymen and served, suffered and sacrificed for India's self-respect and Swaraj'. The talks were later published as a book, entitled *Foreign Friends of India's Freedom*, which profiled twenty-one individuals, beginning with the liberal Governor General William Bentinck (who oversaw the abolition of sati), and ending with the Labour Prime Minister Clement Attlee (who oversaw the transfer of power to Indian hands). The others included a founder of the Indian National Congress, A. O. Hume, the scholar Friedrich Max Mueller, and the theologian C. F. Andrews, as well as two individuals featured in the present book, B. G. Horniman and Annie Besant.[1]

The author of *Foreign Friends of India's Freedom* was named P. Kodanda Rao. He had, when young, been an associate of the prominent Moderate politician V. S. Srinivasa Sastri, a man who always saw the British connection with India as 'providential'.[2] So did Kodanda Rao, which led him to dwell on what some might consider the best, the most admirable, aspect of that connection. As he wrote in the book's preface:

> It was the bounden duty of Indian patriots to have striven and even suffered for India's Swaraj. They deserve the homage of all who have inherited the fruits of their efforts. . . . [But] the Americans and the

Britishers . . . had no obligation to work and suffer for India's freedom. And yet there were many of them who strove and sacrificed for India's freedom. They deserve Indians' gratitude even more.[3]

P. Kodanda Rao's book was little known in its day and is wholly forgotten in ours. It probably never circulated outside the town in which it was printed; and indeed it was in a second-hand bookstore in Bangalore that I stumbled across a copy in the early 1990s, some twenty years after it was published. The subject keenly interested me, for I was, at the time, working on a biography of Verrier Elwin, the son of a British Bishop of Sierra Leone who became the foremost authority on the tribes of central India.

The characters Kodanda Rao profiled included viceroys, civil servants, clergymen, social reformers, scholars and political activists. To invoke afresh the categories defined in the prologue to this book, they included *both* bridge-builders *and* rebels. However, Verrier Elwin was not one of them. That puzzled me, at the time, for Elwin was close to Mahatma Gandhi, and had written books and pamphlets supporting Indian independence. And no scholar, Indian or foreign, had written with greater authority or empathy about tribals, arguably the most disadvantaged section of Indian society. I later realized the omission was probably deliberate, when I discovered an old article by Kodanda Rao accusing the anthropologist of sowing seeds of division among the nationalist movement, by stressing the cultural distinctiveness of tribal people.[4]

Verrier Elwin does not figure in this book either. This is in part because I have previously published a four-hundred-page tome about his life and work, and in part because he was more a builder of bridges between Indians and Englishmen than a rebel against the Raj. That he never went to prison in the cause of India's freedom remained for Elwin a source of abiding regret. He knew Mira well, and fully intended to emulate her by following Gandhi into the jails of the British Raj. However, on a visit to England in 1932 to see his ailing mother, he was forced to sign an undertaking that permitted him to return to India only on condition that he eschew politics altogether. Since he already regarded India as his home, he decided, albeit very reluctantly, to pay the price.[5]

This book features seven rebels, whose lives I regard as being of unusual importance, and on whose work I was able to access original and (I hope) interesting material. But I must in this epilogue accord an honourable mention to four others. The first was Edith Ellen Gray, born in Cambridge in 1886. An Indian student at Downing College named J. M. Sengupta was a lodger at her parental home, and they fell in love, and got married. They decided to base themselves in Bengal, where Sengupta became a prominent nationalist. His wife, now known as Nellie Sengupta, was herself jailed for four months in 1931 for her part in the civil disobedience campaign. Two years later the annual session of the Indian National Congress was held in Calcutta. However, all the major leaders of the party, including the President-elect Madan Mohan Malaviya as well as J. M. Sengupta, were in jail, so Nellie was chosen to preside over the session in their absence. Her husband died shortly afterwards, but Nellie stayed on in the town of Chittagong in eastern Bengal, active in politics and social reform until her death in 1973. She served several terms as a member of the Calcutta Corporation, and was elected to the Bengal Legislative Assembly in 1946 from Chittagong, and to the East Pakistan Legislative Assembly eight years later, from the same constituency. Nellie Sengupta lived long enough to witness the birth of the independent nation of Bangladesh. A year before she died, she travelled to India, to receive a grateful nation's second highest civilian award, the Padma Vibhushan.[6]

Then there was Freda Marie Houlston, born in Derby in 1909, who went to Oxford to study, where she fell in love with an Indian student named Pyarelal Bedi, marrying him and returning with him to his native Punjab. In the early 1940s, Freda taught in a women's college in Lahore. After her husband was imprisoned for his left-wing views, she courted arrest herself, spending three months in jail. In 1947, following Independence and Partition, the Bedis moved to Kashmir, where they befriended the charismatic and controversial politician Sheikh Abdullah. Then, on a visit to Burma, Freda became interested in Buddhism, and this faith became the abiding passion of her life. She became close to the community of Tibetan exiles in India, working both with the Dalai Lama in Himachal Pradesh and with the Karmapa in Sikkim. Like Samuel/Satyanand Stokes, Freda

Bedi now chose to transgress in religious as well as racial terms. In 1972 she became a Buddhist nun, and acquired a new name. Thereafter she accompanied the Karmapa on his tours abroad, proselytizing in the West on behalf of her new faith. She died in 1977, in New Delhi.[7]

Finally, we have the radical couple, James H. Cousins and Margaret E. Cousins (née Gillespie), both born in Ireland in the 1870s, each growing up deeply inspired by the literary and political renaissance then underway in their country. They married in 1903, whereupon James came under the wing of the Theosophists, while Margaret joined the suffragette movement and became a leader of its militant faction, being arrested several times.

Among the remarkable Irish writers the Cousinses came to know were W. B. Yeats, George Bernard Shaw, James Joyce, and most significantly for their own lives, Annie Besant. In 1915, James Cousins wrote to Mrs Besant offering to work with her in India. By return of post came a letter inviting the couple warmly to Adyar, enclosing a cheque to cover the costs of their travel. They arrived in Madras in November of that year, with James being asked to work on Mrs Besant's newspaper, *New India*.

After a year in Madras, the Cousinses moved to the interior town of Madanapalle, where both of them taught at a Theosophical College established by Mrs Besant. In later years, James wrote prolifically on a variety of literary and spiritual subjects (like Stokes, he had a late life conversion to Hinduism), as well as on Indian art and architecture. Margaret was more active in social causes, in particular the emancipation of women. In 1927 she helped found the All India Women's Conference, which campaigned energetically for equality for women in all spheres, from family and community to education and politics.[8]

In December 1932, Margaret Cousins was arrested after she had criticized the Government in a public meeting held on Madras's Marina beach. Offered the choice between paying Rs 10,000 and executing a 'good behaviour' bond and going to jail, she chose the latter. Her months in Vellore Prison were mostly happy, as she made new friends and took civics classes, although, with no gramophone and records at hand, she confessed to missing her daily dose of 'high class western music'.[9]

Margaret Cousins died in 1954, her husband James two years later, in an India independent of British rule. Together and separately, they left a profound impress on the social and cultural life of the subcontinent. James was perhaps more of a 'bridge-builder' between the West and India, while Margaret was more decidedly a 'rebel against the Raj'.

These four lives were exemplary enough, but in one crucial respect their careers differ from those of the seven subjects of this book. Had Edith Gray and Freda Houlston not met and fallen in love with Indian students in England, they might never have left their homeland. It was the accident of romance that catalysed and encouraged the transfer of allegiance from one country to another. The Cousinses, for their part, came as a couple. On the other hand, the seven individuals featured in this book all chose to come out to India and become Indians unilaterally, on their own, *alone*.

In the prologue, I spoke of the International Brigade in the Spanish Civil War, and how these rebels against the Raj resembled that Brigade's members in fighting for the freedom of a country other than their homeland, and how they differed in making a *permanent* commitment to this country that was not originally their own. In the course of writing this book another comparison came to mind. This was with white South Africans who took a stand against apartheid and in favour of a multiracial democracy. These, as it were, renegades to their *race* (rather than nation) tended to be Jewish or Communist, often both. Their Jewishness made them marginal to the dominant Dutch and British ethos of white South Africa, while their Communism oriented them towards an identification with the poor and the oppressed.

The white renegades of twentieth-century South Africa include such well-known figures as Bram Fischer, Ruth First, Hilda Bernstein, Joe Slovo, and Albie Sachs. While all were broadly on the Left, and all risked their careers and often their lives in the battle against racism, their trajectories varied. Some died in jail in apartheid-era South Africa; others died in exile overseas without seeing the end of the regime they detested and had so bravely resisted; yet others returned from exile after apartheid fell, to contribute constructively to the building of a new South Africa.[10]

Unlike the subjects of this book, these South African men and women were born in the society they wished to change. Like them, they readily sacrificed the economic, social and political privileges that went with being members of the ruling race. Their idealism and commitment led them to identify with the *African* National Congress, in the same manner as the idealism and commitment of the Englishman Horniman or the Irishwoman Besant or the American Stokes oriented them towards the *Indian* National Congress.

One is tempted to extend the parallel further. There were white renegades in apartheid-era South Africa, and there were white bridge-builders too, men and women who, for reason of temperament or circumstance or belief, did not take to armed struggle or militant opposition to the ruling order, but instead worked quietly, patiently, but none the less heroically for a world in which there would be no oppression or discrimination on the basis of race. While the renegades tended to be members of the South African Communist Party, these bridge-builders were more often associated with the Liberal or Progressive parties. They include such figures as Alan Paton, Patrick Duncan, Clive van Ryneveld and Helen Suzman, whom we may plausibly see as the South African equivalents of the likes of Charlie Andrews, Sister Nivedita, Verrier Elwin and Marjorie Sykes in India.

India achieved its independence from British colonial rule in 1947. South Africa was liberated from white political domination in 1994. That the latter event is so much more recent may explain why the renegades of that country are still so actively remembered. How long will this last, one wonders? Will schoolchildren in South Africa fifty years hence have any knowledge at all of Joe Slovo and Ruth First, Albie Sachs, Bram Fischer and Hilda Bernstein? Still less of Helen Suzman or Patrick Duncan?

One hopes so. Perhaps South Africa will follow a different trajectory from India in this regard. Perhaps the capacious and cosmopolitan vision of its freedom struggle will not be as easily vanquished as the capacious and cosmopolitan vision of our freedom struggle.

In my country, the rise of nativism and xenophobia in recent decades has been both immense and intense. National and especially religious parochialism is rife. '*Garv se kaho Hindu ho*' – Proclaim with Pride that you are a Hindu – such is the leitmotif that has accompanied the rise to power of the political movement known as Hindutva. Hindus, it is now said, are destined to be the world's Vishwa Guru, teachers to the rest of humanity. They have apparently nothing to learn from or gain from the world in return.

Although this book has not been written for the nativists and xenophobes, I hope that some members of that tribe might read it too. For here are seven quite remarkable individuals, all foreign-born, all white-skinned, who identified so completely with Indian aspirations. In the course of fighting non-violently for India's liberation from colonial rule, all were interned or deported by the British. Yet it is not merely as 'freedom-fighters' that we should remember them. Quite apart from what they did in the sphere of politics, they each enriched and enhanced the life of the Indian nation in so many different ways.

Let us briefly rehearse their achievements. Annie Besant promoted the emancipation of women in a deeply patriarchal society. She cofounded one of the country's best-known universities, and helped focus scholarly attention on the culture and civilization of ancient India. B. G. Horniman ran one of the finest and bravest newspapers in India; promoted and encouraged young journalists; and campaigned tirelessly for the freedom of the press. Samuel, later Satyanand, Stokes helped abolish forced labour in the hills before laying the foundations of a horticultural industry that has sustained the economy of the state of Himachal Pradesh for many decades now. Madeline Slade, later Mira Behn, wrote pioneering environmental tracts and, by influencing the making of Richard Attenborough's film *Gandhi*, made the Mahatma's ideas of non-violence and interfaith harmony once more known around the world. Philip Spratt fought for the rights of workers before campaigning against the licence-permit-quota Raj that strangulated the Indian economy. Richard Ralph Keithahn helped found a rural university as well as a charitable hospital, and cultivated dignity and self-reliance among the oppressed. Catherine Mary Heilemann, later Sarala Behn, established a pioneering girls' school in one of the most backward regions of India, training and nurturing several generations of social workers, some of whom went on to lead that most celebrated of environmental movements, the Chipko Andolan.

Of my seven rebels, two, Besant and Stokes, died when the British still ruled India, while a third, Horniman, died shortly after the British left. The four who lived on continued to struggle nobly for the values and ideals they cherished. Under colonial rule they had fought for India's freedom; now that this had been achieved, they held the government of the day to account. Where lesser, or more insecure, people with white skins might seek to prove their 'Indian-ness' through fervent declarations of loyalty to the new nation, and sided with the State or the ruling Congress Party, these brave rene-gades stayed true to higher, universal ideals.

Till she left for Europe in 1959, Mira worked for rural renewal and environmental sustainability in India. Later, from her home in the Vienna Woods, she scolded her fellow Gandhians for jingoistically following the Government line in the country's dispute with China. Through the 1950s and 1960s, Spratt wrote and spoke against the creeping centralization of political power, against the Indian State's denial of freedom to entrepreneurs, its curbs on individual liberty, and its attacks on the federal structure of the Indian Union. Through the 1950s, 1960s, and 1970s, Sarala devoted her energies and her intellect to empowering village women, while warning against the environmental consequences of consumerism and industrialism. All through these decades, Keithahn, in deepest South India, was working as tirelessly as Sarala in the Himalaya. Some of their concerns over-lapped – village self-sufficiency and ecological renewal, for example – while others diverged, with Sarala focusing more on inequalities of gender and Keithahn more on inequalities of class.

Had Besant, Stokes and Horniman lived in independent India they would have surely followed the same sort of trajectory too. Besant might have campaigned to stop violence against women; Horniman against attacks on the press and sexual minorities; Stokes against aggressive and chauvinistic tendencies in his adopted Hindu faith. Like Mira, Sarala, Keithahn and Spratt, they would have been active conscience-keepers rather than unthinking nationalists in an India which had freed itself of British rule but whose people were still constrained by myriad forms of unfreedom.

These individuals came to India at different points of time, from widely varying backgrounds and with widely varying motivations. Once here, they lived in different parts of the country, and pursued different callings and obsessions. What unites them was, first, the courage and fearlessness they displayed in their personal lives; second, the depth and duration of their commitment to their new homeland; and third, the contemporaneity, indeed, timelessness, of what they lived and struggled for. So many years after the last of these rebels passed on, what they did and what they said still speaks to Indians today.

If only we could listen.

Acknowledgements

This book has its origins in some lectures delivered at the North-Eastern Hill University in Shillong more than twenty years ago. The lectures were named for the anthropologist Verrier Elwin, who had spent his last years in Shillong, and whose family still lived in the town. I had (I suppose) been invited to give these lectures because I had just recently published a book on Elwin himself.

My talks in Shillong travelled under the title 'The Other Side of the Raj'. The phrase had been coined by one of my early mentors, the sociologist Shiv Visvanathan, who had impressed upon me that while the patronizing, condescending attitude of British colonialists in India had been widely recognized (and justly criticized), now forgotten were the dissenting voices, of British scholars, scientists and administrators, who had studied and written about Indian culture and society in sympathetic (and empathetic) terms. And of course there were British political activists who had thrown in their lot with the Indian freedom struggle as well.

I had hoped soon to expand my Shillong lectures into a book. Indeed, in June 1998, even as my biography of Verrier Elwin was in press, I had written to a British publisher saying: 'I am now working on a sequel to the Elwin book. This would be a collective biography of about twelve to fourteen such characters from the "Other Side of the Raj". They include socialists, spiritualists, Gandhians, environmentalists, all of whom helped shape Indian politics and Indian culture.'

In the event, that sequel has been a long time coming. The reasons for this delay need not detain us here. But perhaps it was fortuitous, for, while working on other projects, I always had this one at the back of my mind, and thus filed away under 'Other Side of the Raj' nuggets I found in the archives while looking for something else altogether. As I did, I also narrowed down the list of potential subjects, from 'twelve to fourteen' to exactly seven, on whom I found enough material to tell what (I hoped) was a new (or new-ish) story.

As with my other books, the two *public* archives that have proved critical to my research are the Nehru Memorial Museum and Library in New Delhi and the British Library in London. I spent months in each, taking notes by hand or more lately on a laptop. At the NMML, apart from their holdings of private papers, I also took advantage of their unparalleled collection of Indian newspaper microfilms. Other institutional collections I worked in include those of the National Archives of India in New Delhi, the Theosophical Society in Chennai, the Uttar Pradesh State Archives in Lucknow, the Sabarmati Ashram Archives in Ahmedabad, the Library of Congress in Washington, the Martin Luther King Collection at Boston University, and the Swarthmore College Peace Archive. I am deeply grateful to the archivists and librarians in all these places for their assistance and advice.

In the making of this book I have also depended very heavily on the generosity of individuals with private collections. I am especially indebted to Bob Spratt for granting me access to the papers of his father, Philip Spratt; to K. M. Natarajan, Vinoo Aram, and Bhoomi Jegannathan for showing me the way to the papers of R. R. Keithahn, kept partly with his secretary Sam Stawrence and partly in a fellowship hospital in Oddanchatram where he spent his last years; to Manoj Pande for giving me access to the papers of Mira Behn, tucked away in a cupboard in the office of the Himalaya Seva Sangh in New Delhi; and to David Hopkins and Radha Bhatt of the Lakshmi Ashram in Kausani for sharing with me the correspondence of Sarala Behn.

It is said that one makes fewer friends when one gets older. That may not be the case with historians. In the last decade, I have had the privilege of working with a wonderful cohort of younger scholars, several of whom provided crucial inputs for this book. Thanks in particular to Aditya Balasubramanian, Abhinav Chandrachud, Kaberi Chowdhury, Venu Madhav Govindu, Prashant Kidambi, Akshaya

Mukul, and Dinyar Patel. I'd also like to thank Vijay Jain of Prabhu Book Service, Gurgaon, and K. K. S. Murthy of Select Bookstore, Bangalore, for sending me rare books and pamphlets by or about the seven renegades I have written about here. Other friends and colleagues who provided vital assistance to this project are Deepa Bhatnagar, N. Balakrishnan, Gopalkrishna Gandhi, Shekhar Pathak, Naresh Fernandes, Tridip Suhrud, Sachin Arya, Kinnari Bhatt, Suman Dubey, Jaishree Kannan, Andrew Rigby, Jairam Ramesh, Ashutosh Bhardwaj, Professor Vijay Stokes, Ajai Singh Mehta, Bill Aitken, Archana Nathan, Kalpana Raja, L. Raja, Devika Sethi, Joyce Riggs-Perla, William Beinart, Anil Nauriya, Saul Dubow, and Uma Dhupelia-Mesthrie. Two scholars no longer alive provided crucial tips – the anthropologist Rebecca Klenk and the historian Dharampal. And I am particularly grateful to Professor Dennis Dalton for his comments on a draft manuscript of the book.

My agents Gill Coleridge and Cara Jones have been wonderfully supportive throughout, and so has Melanie Jackson at the American end of things. And I have been especially fortunate in my editors, Dan Frank of Knopf, Meru Gokhale and Tarini Uppal of Penguin India, and Arabella Pike of William Collins, who have shaped the book and sharpened its arguments in critical (and always constructive) ways. Sadly, however, the publisher who commissioned this book, Sonny Mehta of Knopf, is no longer around to read it. Sonny was both a generous friend and a wonderful publisher, and I hope the book is not unworthy of the trust he bestowed upon its author.

As this book was going to press, Sonny Mehta's esteemed colleague Dan Frank also passed away. This was one of the last books he edited, with the care, attention, wisdom and sensitivity he brought to every manuscript that came his way. To have known Sonny Mehta and Dan Frank, and to have worked with them, has been one of the great privileges of my life.

'Last but not least' is a locution much favoured by Indians who write or speak in English, and it may not be out of place here. So, last, but certainly not the least, my thanks to Professor Mrinal Miri, the compassionate philosopher who, as Vice Chancellor of the North-Eastern Hill University in Shillong, invited me to deliver the Verrier Elwin Lectures back in the distant year 2001.

Notes

ABBREVIATIONS USED IN THE NOTES

AB/NMML	Annie Besant Papers, Nehru Memorial Museum and Library, New Delhi
AB/TS	Annie Besant Papers, Theosophical Society, Chennai
APAC/BL	Asia, Pacific, and Africa Collections, British Library, London
BC	*Bombay Chronicle* (newspaper published from Bombay)
BL	British Library London
BS	*Bombay Sentinel* (newspaper published from Bombay)
CWMG	*Collected Works of Mahatma Gandhi* (New Delhi: Publications Division, 1958-1994)
FR	Fortnightly Report
HT	*Hindustan Times* (newspaper published from New Delhi)
NAI	National Archives of India, New Delhi
NMML	Nehru Memorial Museum and Library, New Delhi
SAAA	Sabarmati Ashram Archives, Ahmedabad
SFP	Spratt Family Papers
SN	Serial Number
ToI	*Times of India* (newspaper published from Bombay)
TT	The Tribune (newspaper published from Lahore)
YI	*Young India* (weekly published from Ahmedabad)

PROLOGUE

1. See Adam Hochschild, *Spain in Our Hearts: Americans in the Spanish Civil War, 1936–1939* (Boston: Mariner Books, 2017), pp.336–7.

2. On the tradition of anti-imperialist dissent within Great Britain, see, among other works, A. J. P. Taylor, *The Trouble Makers: Dissent over Foreign Policy, 1792–1939* (London: Faber and Faber, 1957), and Priyamvada Gopal, *Insurgent Empire: Anticolonial Resistance and British Dissent* (London: Verso, 2019).

3. See *Collected Works of Mahatma Gandhi* (hereafter CWMG), LXXXII, pp.154–5.

4. The relevant secondary literature on these bridge-builders includes Benarsidas Chaturvedi and Marjorie Sykes, *Charles Freer Andrews* (London: George Allen and Unwin, 1949); Hugh Tinker, *The Ordeal of Love: C. F. Andrews and India* (New Delhi: Oxford University Press, 1979): Daniel O'Connor, *Gospel, Raj and Swaraj: The Missionary Years of C. F. Andrews, 1904–14* (Frankfurt: Peter Lang, 1990); Uma Dasgupta, ed., *Friendships of 'Largeness and Freedom'. Andrews, Tagore, and Gandhi: An Epistolary Account, 1912–1940* (New Delhi: Oxford University Press, 2018); Reba Som, *Margot: Sister Nivedita of Swami Vivekananda* (New Delhi: Viking, 2017); Gautam Bhatia, *Laurie Baker: Life, Work, and Writings* (New Delhi: Penguin, 2003); Marta Dart, *Marjorie Sykes: Quaker-Gandhian* (Hyderabad: Academy of Gandhian Studies, 1993); Ramachandra Guha, *Saving the Civilized: Verrier Elwin, His Tribals, and India* (New Delhi: Oxford University Press, 1999).

5. William Dalrymple, 'One sure way for Britain to get ahead – stop airbrushing our colonial history', *Guardian*, 3 September 2015. See also Dalrymple, *White Mughals: Love and Betrayal in 18th Century India* (London: Bloomsbury, 2003).

CHAPTER I: MOTHERING INDIA

1. Her Indian admirers occasionally called her 'Dr Besant', in recognition of an honorary (not earned) doctorate.

2. Arthur H. Nethercot, *The First Five Lives of Annie Besant* (London: Rupert Hart-Davis, 1961), p.87.

3. Isaac Lubelsky, *Celestial India: Madam Blavatsky and the Birth of Indian Nationalism*, translated from the Hebrew by Yael Lotan (Sheffield: Equinox Publishing Ltd, 2012), p.122.

4. Annie Besant, *An Autobiography* (1893: reprint Chennai: Theosophical Publishing House, 2008), p.244.

5. See Norman and Jean MacKenzie, *The Fabians* (New York: Simon and Schuster, 1977), pp.53–4.

6. Besant, *An Autobiography*, pp.300–11, etc.

7. See Stephen Hay, 'The Making of a Late-Victorian Hindu: M. K. Gandhi in London, 1888–1891', *Victorian Studies*, Autumn 1989, pp.83–4.

8. Nethercot, *First Four Lives*, pp.375–6, and passim.

9. Ibid., p.390.

10. 'History Sheet' of Annie Besant, compiled by the Criminal Intelligence Department in November 1917 (hereafter 'History Sheet'), in IOR/R/2 Temp No. 34/338, Asia, Pacific and Africa Collections, British Library, London (hereafter APAC/BL).

11. Annie Besant, *The Means of India's Regeneration* (Banaras: Theosophical Publishing Society, 1895), pp.5–6, 15–21, 23.

12. Annie Besant, *Education as a National Duty: A Lecture Delivered in Bombay on Monday, March 9th, 1903* (Banaras: Theosophical Publishing Society, 1903), pp.22–4.

13. Annie Besant, *The Education of Indian Girls* (Banaras and London: Theosophical Publishing Society, 1904), pp.2–10, passim.
14. Annie Besant to Gokhale, 1 May 1907, File No. 41, Gokhale Papers, National Archives of India, New Delhi (hereafter NAI).
15. Cf. Sumit Sarkar, *The Swadeshi Movement in Bengal, 1903–1908* (New Delhi: People's Publishing House, 1973).
16. Arthur H. Nethercot, *The Last Four Lives of Annie Besant* (London: Rupert Hart-Davis, 1963), p.108.
17. See Verrier Elwin, *The Tribal World of Verrier Elwin: An Autobiography* (New York: Oxford University Press, 1964), p.27.
18. Although a side-show to her career as a renegade, the story of Mrs Besant's relationship with Krishnamurti is fascinating nonetheless. For more details, see Mary Lutyens, *The Life and Death of Krishnamurti* (first published by John Murray in 1990: reprint Chennai: Krishnamurti Foundation India, 2006).
19. Kanji Dwarkadas, *Political Memoirs* (Bombay: United Asia Publications, 1969), pp.51–2.
20. Sri Prakasa, *Annie Besant as Woman and as Leader* (first published 1940: third edition, Bombay: Bharatiya Vidya Bhavan, 1962), pp.79–80. Sri Prakasa became prominent in public life, serving as independent India's first High Commissioner to Pakistan and also as Governor of Madras.
21. Quoted in Nethercot, *First Four Lives*, p.226.
22. Annie Besant, *England and India* (Harrogate: Theosophical Publishing Company, 1903), esp pp.7–8.
23. Arthur Lawley (Governor of Madras) to Mrs Besant, 20 February 1910; Private Secretary to the Viceroy to Mrs Besant, 25 February 1910, Reel 1, Annie Besant Papers, Nehru Memorial Museum and Library, New Dehli (hereafter AB/NMML).
24. PS to Viceroy (Lord Minto), to Mrs Besant, 6 February 1910, Reel 1, AB/NMML.
25. Quoted in Lubelsky, *Celestial India*, p.262.
26. Gokhale to Annie Besant, 26 June 1914, Annie Besant Papers, Theosophical Society, Adyar, Chennai (hereafter AB/TS).
27. Annie Besant to P. Kesava Pillai, 17 July 1914, P. Kesava Pillai Papers, NMML.
28. Annie Besant to Esther Bright, 16 July 1914, quoted in B. K. R. Kabad, 'Annie Besant', in *Some Eminent Indian Editors* (New Delhi: Publications Division, 1981), p.29.
29. Annie Besant to Bhupendranath Basu, 28 September and 24 November 1914, Bhupendranath Basu Papers, NMML.
30. Besant to Gokhale, letters of 15 November and 2 December 1914, File No. 119, Gokhale Papers, NAI.
31. Gokhale to Besant, 9 January 1915, AB/TS.
32. Bal Gangadhar Tilak to Annie Besant, 21 January 1915, copy in File No. 119, Gokhale Papers, NAI.

33. Gokhale to Besant, 26 January 1915, AB/TS.
34. Annie Besant to Gokhale, 23 January 1915, copy in File No. 119, Gokhale Papers, NAI.
35. A copy of the speech is in Reel 3, AB/NMML.
36. Annie Besant to 'Mr Wadia' (prob D. E. of the ilk), 20 June 1915, H. P. Modi Papers, NMML.
37. 'Home Rule for India', *New India*, 14 September 1915.
38. These paragraphs are based on Proceedings Nos 166–168, November 1915, Home (Political), NAI.
39. Cf. Dinyar Patel, *Naoroji: Pioneer of Indian Nationalism* (Cambridge, Mass.: Harvard University Press, 2020).
40. Annie Besant, *How India Wrought for Freedom: The Story of the National Congress Told From Official Records* (Madras: Theosophical Publishing House, 1915), pp.ii–iii, xxiii–xxiv, xxxi, li–lii, lv–lix (emphasis in original).
41. Letter of 23 December 1915 in Reel 4, AB/NMML.
42. See correspondence in Reels 3 and 4, AB/ NMML.
43. 'Preface to Third Impression' (1908), Annie Besant, *An Autobiography* (1893: reprint Chennai: Theosophical Publishing House, 2008), pp.ix–x.
44. Copy in Reel 3, AB/NMML.

CHAPTER 2: HOME RULER, CONGRESS PRESIDENT

1. On Gandhi's early admiration for Mrs Besant, see Eleanor Morton, *Women Behind Mahatma Gandhi* (London: Max Reinhardt, 1954), pp.29–33.
2. Gandhi to Annie Besant, 13 May 1905, CWMG, IV, pp.433–4.
3. CWMG, VI, p.310.
4. CWMG, XIII, pp.69, 75.
5. See S. R. Mehrotra, 'Gandhi and the Servants of India Society', *Gandhi Marg*, vol 34, no 4, Jan–Mar 2013.
6. On the history of the BHU, see S. L. Dar and S. Somaskandan, *History of the Banaras Hindu University* (Banaras: BHU, 1966); Aparna Basu, *The Growth of Education and Political Development in India, 1898–1920* (Delhi: Oxford University Press), Chapter 7, 'Banaras Hindu University'; Tejakar Jha, ed., *The Inception of Banaras Hindu University: Who was the Founder in the Light of Historical Documents?* (New Delhi: Partridge India, 2015).
7. For a fuller account of this episode, see Ramachandra Guha, *Gandhi: The Years That Changed the World, 1914–1948* (New York: Knopf, 2018), Chapter 2.
8. See Anon., 'The Banaras-Gandhi Incident', sd/ 'An Observer', Simla, 25 February 1916, in File 221 of 1916, General Administration Department, Uttar Pradesh State Archives, Lucknow.
9. Statements by Annie Besant in *New India*, 10 and 16 February, 1916.
10. See Hugh Owen, 'Towards Nation-Wide Agitation and Organization: The Home Rule Leagues, 1915–18', in Owen, *The Indian Nationalist Movement,*

c. 1912–22: Leadership, Organisation and Philosophy (New Delhi: Sterling Publishers Private Limited, 1990).

11. Annie Besant to P. Kesava Pillai, 23 July 1916, Kesava Pillai Papers, NMML.

12. Report by the Metropolitan Police, dated 18 July 1916, in A Proceedings 36–53, October 1916, Home (Political), NAI.

13. See for example, James H. Cousins, 'The Irish Leaders', *New India*, 4 May 1916.

14. See for example, A Proceedings 36–53, October 1916, Home (Political), NAI.

15. Cf. 'The Case of Annie Besant' in K. L. Gauba, *Famous and Historic Trials* (Lahore: Lion Press, 1946), p.43f.

16. Annie Besant, 'Lighting a Candle', *New India*, 29 May 1916.

17. Annie Besant, 'A Great Opportunity', *New India*, 7 June 1916.

18. Annie Besant to P. Kesava Pillai, 4 October 1916, P. Kesava Pillai Papers, NMML.

19. These paragraphs are based on the 'Report on the Native Newspapers of the Madras Presidency for the first half of 1916', L/R/5/121, APAC/BL.

20. *Bharati*, 7 July 1916, in 'Report on the Native Newspapers of the Madras Presidency for the second half of 1916', L/R/5/122, APAC/BL.

21. See Proceeding No. 25, December 1916, Home (Political), NAI.

22. See Fortnightly Report (FR) on the Political Situation in the Madras Presidency for the first half of November 1916, Home (Political), NAI.

23. Mysore FR, for the first half of March 1917, Home (Political), NAI.

24. Annie Besant, 'Three Reasons for Home Rule', *New India*, 1 March 1917.

25. One of those to whom Mrs Besant reached out for support was Mohandas Gandhi. See Besant to Gandhi, 14 May 1917, S. N. 6354, Sabarmati Ashram Archives, Ahmedabad (hereafter SAAA).

26. News clipping dated 20 June 1917 (name of paper not known), Reel 11, AB/NMML.

27. Chief Secretary, Madras Government to Home Secretary, Government of India, 23 June 1917, in Proceedings Nos 86–106, Home (Political), NAI.

28. Cf. 'History Sheet'.

29. Surendranath Banerjea, *A Nation in Making: Being the Reminiscences of Fifty Years of Public Life* (Bombay: Oxford University Press, 1925), pp.238–9.

30. Governor to Viceroy, 23 July 1917; Viceroy to Governor, 1 August 1917, in Progs 6–9, November 1917, Home (Political), NAI.

31. Emily Lutyens to Edwin Montagu, 30 July 1917, copy in AB/TS.

32. Andhrapatrika, 22 September 1917, as quoted in L/R/5/124, APAC/BL.

33. Annie Besant, 'Interview with Mr. Montagu', undated typescript, in Reel 7, AB/NMML.

34. Hugh Owen, op. cit., p.86.

35. I have used the printed text of Annie Besant's Presidential Address as available in Home (Political), Proceeding No. 10, May 1918, NAI.

36. Quoted in V. Geetha and S. V. Rajadurai, *Towards a Non-Brahmin Millennium: From Iyothee Thass to Periyar* (Calcutta: Samya, 1998), pp.6–7.

37. Cf. V. Geetha and S. V. Rajadurai, 'One Hundred Years of Brahminitude: Arrival of Annie Besant', *Economic and Political Weekly*, 15 July 1995.

38. *Justice*, issues of 19 April and 4 July 1917; *Non-Brahman*, issues of 18 February and 11 March 1917, in L/R/5/123, APAC/BL.

39. Annie Besant to P. Kesava Pillai, letters of 27 January and 16 April 1917 and 2 and 25 June 1918, in Kesava Pillai Papers, NMML.

40. Nethercot, *Last Four Lives*, pp.272–3.

41. See correspondence in Reel 11, AB/NMML.

42. Mahadev H. Desai, *Day-to-Day with Gandhi* (Varanasi: Sarva Seva Sangh, 1968), edited by Narahari D. Parikh, translated from the Gujarati by Hemantkumar G. Nilkanth, Volume I, pp.63–4.

43. Quoted in Erik H. Erikson, *Gandhi's Truth: On the Origins of Militant Non-Violence* (London: Faber and Faber, 1970), p.361.

44. See Sumita Mukherjee, *Indian Suffragettes: Female Identities and Transnational Networks* (New Delhi: Oxford University Press, 2018), pp.50–3; Geraldine Forbes, *Women in Modern India* (Cambridge: Cambridge University Press, 1996), pp.95–7.

45. See John Scurr to Mrs Besant, dated London, 11 February 1918, in Reel 4, AB/NMML.

46. A. A. Warrington, General Secretary of the Theosophical Society, to Woodrow Wilson, 31 October 1918, Reel 6, AB/NMML.

47. Annie Besant, *The New Era: An Epoch-Making Congress, 1918* (Madras: The Commonweal Office, January 1919), pp.5–6.

48. Jamnadas Dwarkadas to Annie Besant, 27 February 1919, Reel 11, AB/NMML.

49. Gandhi to S. Subramania Iyer, 23 March 1919, CWMG, XV, p.147.

50. Besant to Gandhi, 10 May 1919, S. N. 6605, SAAA.

51. Gandhi to Besant, 10 May 1919, CWMG, XV, pp.300–1.

52. Besant to Gandhi, 11 May 1919, S. N. 6605B, SAAA.

CHAPTER 3: FREEDOM-LOVING ENGLISHMAN

1. *'A Friend of India'*: *Selections from the Speeches and Writings of B. G. Horniman* (published by Lakshmidas Rowjee Tairsee and R. Venkat Ram, Bombay, 1918).

2. 'Biographical Sketch', *Bombay Sentinel* (hereafter BS), 16 October 1948.

3. P. Kodanda Rao, *Foreign Friends of India's Freedom* (Bangalore: The P. T. I. Book Company, 1973), p.159.

4. Quoted in Dwarkadas, *Political Memoirs*, p.227.

5. See *'A Friend of India'*, Introduction.

6. See Sandip Hazareesingh, *The Colonial City and the Challenge of Modernity: Urban Hegemonies and Civic Contestations in Bombay (1900–1925)* (Hyderabad: Orient Longman, 2007), pp.83–9.

7. Dwarkadas, *Political Memoirs*, p.109.

8. See Chimanlal H. Setalvad, *Recollections and Reflections: An Autobiography* (Bombay: Padma Publications, Ltd), p.468f.

9. See Hazareesingh, *The Colonial City and the Challenge of Modernity*, pp.115–18.
10. 'To Young India!', in *'A Friend of India'*, pp.9–11.
11. Ibid., pp.37–41.
12. B. G. Horniman to Jawaharlal Nehru, 1 July 1917, in *A Bunch of Old Letters: Written Mostly to Jawaharlal Nehru, and Some Written by Him* (Bombay: Asia Publishing House, 1958), pp.1–2.
13. For more details, see B. G. Horniman correspondence, Syed Hossain Papers, NMML.
14. *Times of India* (hereafter ToI), 9 January 1915.
15. CWMG, XIII, p.280f.
16. *'A Friend of India'*, pp.18f.
17. Cf. Gandhi to Horniman, 23 June 1918, CWMG, XIV, p.445.
18. *'A Friend of India'*, pp.179–82, 51–3.
19. Ibid., pp.34–5.
20. See Guha, *Gandhi*, Chapter 4; Ravinder Kumar, ed., *Essays on Gandhian Politics: The Rowlatt Satyagraha of 1919* (Oxford: Clarendon Press, 1971).
21. CWMG, XV, p.183f. In his speech, Gandhi read out resolutions demanding that the Rowlatt Act be withdrawn, asking the crowd to endorse them, to be sent 'weighted with the . . . promise that we shall continue to suffer by civil disobedience till the hearts of the rulers are softened'.
22. *Bombay Chronicle*, 11 April 1919.
23. Viceroy to Governor of Bombay, telegram dated 23 April 1919; Governor of Bombay to Viceroy, telegram dated 24 April 1919 (reply to above), in File 619–640, Home (Political), A Branch, National Archives of India, New Delhi, NAI.
24. See L/PJ/12/14, IOR, APAC/BL.
25. 'Memorandum by B. G. Horniman of the events relating to his arrest and deportation from India, April 1919', in L/PJ/12/11, IOR, APAC/BL.
26. Horniman to Gandhi, 27 April 1919, S. N. 6545, SAAA.
27. CWMG, XV, p.252.
28. Reports in L/R/5/126, APAC/BL.
29. 'Bombay's Silent Protest', *Young India* (hereafter YI), 14 May 1919.
30. This discussion is based on news reports in L/R/5/175, APAC/BL.
31. File 2992, L/PJ/6/1590, APAC/BL.
32. Telegram of 23 October 1920, in L/PJ/12/11, APAC/BL.
33. CWMG, XV, pp.252–3, 255–8, 263–5, 273–5, etc.
34. CWMG, XV, pp.336, 344.
35. CWMG, XV, p.384.
36. Horniman to Gandhi, 30 July 1919, S. N. 6780, SAAA.
37. CWMG, XVII, pp.330, 344–5.
38. B. G. Horniman, *Amritsar and Our Duty to India* (London: T. Fischer Unwin, 1920), quotes from, pp.70–1, 97, 122, 167, 169, 181, 192, 195–6.
39. *Manchester Guardian*, 12 May 1921.
40. Horniman to Gandhi, 23 September 1920, S. N. 7270, SAAA.

41. See File 9 of 1922, AICC Papers, First Instalment, NMML.
42. Report in ToI, 27 April 1921.
43. Correspondence in File 9 of 1922, AICC Papers, First Instalment, NMML.
44. B. G. Horniman, 'Slave Labour in Assam', *Daily Herald*, 29 May 1922.
45. B. G. Horniman, 'Britain and India', *Labour Monthly*, March 1922.
46. Correspondence in L/PJ/12/13, APAC/BL.
47. Viceroy to Secretary of State, telegram, 2 February 1924, in L/PJ/12/14, APAC/BL.
48. B. G. Horniman to S. A. Brelvi, 6 February 1924, Brelvi Papers, NMML.
49. *The Times*, 7 March 1924.
50. Imperial Legislative Assembly proceedings, 19 and 20 February 1924, in File 2992, L/PJ/6/1590, APAC/BL.
51. Extract from Proceedings of Bombay Legislative Council, 19 and 20 March 1924, in File 236 of 1924, Home (Political), NAI.
52. 'The Victim's Reply', *Bombay Chronicle* (hereafter BC), 21 May 1924.
53. B. G. Horniman to Arthur Field, 17 February 1924, copy in L/PJ/12/14, APAC/BL.
54. Note by New Scotland Yard, 19 February 1926, in L/PJ/12/12, APAC/BL.
55. Viceroy to Secretary of State for India, telegrams of 7 and 10 January 1926, in ibid.
56. Sir Leslie Wilson, Governor of Bombay, to Lord Reading, Viceroy, 13 January 1926, in ibid.
57. CWMG, XXIX, p.386.
58. Notes by Denys Bray, 25 March 1926; by M. I. Huk, 31 March 1926, both in File 34/29/1927, Home (Political), NAI.

CHAPTER 4: ANTI-COLONIAL AMERICAN

1. 'Historical Note', in S. E. Stokes, ed., *Letters of Nancy Stokes of Harmony Hall* (Kotgarh, 1916), p.11.
2. See Kenton J. Clymer, 'Samuel Evans Stokes, Mahatma Gandhi, and Indian Nationalism', *Pacific Historical Review*, volume 59, number 1, February 1990, p.55.
3. Letter of 11 September 1905 and undated letter, c.late September 1905, in Stokes Papers, NMML.
4. Undated letter, c.1906, in Stokes Papers, NMML.
5. C. F. Andrews, quoted in Asha Sharma, *An American in Khadi: The Definitive Biography of Satyanand Stokes* (New Delhi: Penguin Books India, 1999), pp.47, 53.
6. S. E. Stokes to C. C. Bardsley, 28 August 1911, quoted in William W. Emilsen, *Violence and Atonement: The Missionary Experiences of Mohandas Gandhi, Samuel Stokes and Verrier Elwin in India before 1935* (Frankfurt: Peter Lang, 1994), p.105.
7. 'Kotgarh' (pseud.), 'The Problem of Christianity in India', *Indian Social Reformer*, 21 December 1919.

8. Letters of 5 June, 19 June, 17 July and 18 September 1912, in Stokes Papers, NMML.
9. Letter of 28 May 1913, in Stokes Papers, NMML.
10. See Sharma, *An American in Khadi*, pp.110–13.
11. See Satyanand Stokes, *National Self-Realisation and Other Essays* (first published 1943; reprint New Delhi: Rubicon Publishing House, 1977), p.6.
12. Letter of 18 January 1914, Stokes Papers, NMML.
13. Letters of 9 May and 1 June 1914, Stokes Papers, NMML.
14. Letter of 15 June 1916, Stokes Papers, NMML.
15. Letter of 10 April 1917, Stokes Papers, NMML.
16. Letter of 7 May 1917, Stokes Papers, NMML.
17. Letter to his mother, c.November 1918, Stokes Papers, NMML.
18. Letter of 21 February 1919, Stokes Papers, NMML.
19. Letter of 5 June 1919, Stokes Papers, NMML.
20. Quoted in Clymer, op. cit, pp.58–9.
21. Letter to the *Times of India*, 19 March 1919, in Stokes, *National Self-Realisation and Other Essays*, p.15.
22. Stokes to his mother, 7 August 1920, Stokes Papers, NMML.
23. Stokes to his mother, 21 August 1920, Stokes Papers, NMML.
24. On the history of this practice, see Shekhar Pathak, *Uttarakhand Mein Kuli Begar Pratha* (The System of Coolie Labour in Uttarakhand) (Delhi: Radhakrishna Prakashan, 1987).
25. These letters are quoted in Sharma, *An American in Khadi*, p.134.
26. Ibid., pp.136–7.
27. See Stokes, *National Self-Realisation and Other Essays*, pp.40–51.
28. As recalled in Stokes to Gandhi, 25 March 1924, S. N. 8651, SAAA.
29. Stokes to his mother, 13 December 1920, Stokes Papers, NMML.
30. C. F. Andrews, 'Introduction', in S. E. Stokes, *The Failure of European Civilization as a World Culture* (Madras: S. Ganesan and Co., 1921), pp.viii–ix.
31. Stokes, *The Failure of European Civilization as a World Culture*, pp.11, 17–18.
32. Ibid., pp.47–8.
33. Ibid., pp.53–4, 56.
34. Mahadev H. Desai, *Day to Day with Gandhi*, edited by Narahari D. Parikh, translated from the Gujarati by Hemantkumar G. Nilkanth (Varanasi: Sarva Seva Sangh Prakashan, 1968), Volume 3, p.282.
35. Krishnadas, *Seven Months with Mahatma Gandhi: Being an Inside View of the Non-Co-operation Movement (1921–22)*, Vol. 1 (Madras: S. Ganesan, 1928), p.27.
36. Stokes to his mother, 13 August 1921, Stokes Papers, NMML.
37. 'The Shadow of Simla', *Young India*, 21 July 1921, in CWMG, XX, pp.408–9. 'Kala pani' was a reference to the dreaded Cellular Jail in the Andamans.
38. CWMG, XX, p.511.

39. CWMG, XX, pp.515–16.
40. Samuel Stokes, 'Latest Outrage on the Hindustan–Tibet Road', *Tribune* (hereafter TT), 31 August 1921; 'Oppression in the Simla Hill States', TT, 24 and 25 November 1921.
41. Stokes, 'Our Duty', BC, 4 August 1921.
42. Stokes, 'Our Duty', BC, 4 August 1921, emphasis in original.
43. Stokes, 'Begar in Simla Hills', TT, 23 July 1921.
44. Stokes to his mother, 3 September 1921, in Stokes Papers, NMML.
45. See Shekhar Pathak, 'The begar abolition movements in British Kumaun', *The Indian Economic & Social History Review*, volume 28, number 3, 1991.
46. CWMG, XXI, pp.138, 235–6.
47. Stokes to his mother, 30 October 1921, Stokes Papers, NMML.
48. See Stokes, *National Self-Realisation and Other Essays*, pp.106–14 (quote on p.110).
49. S. E. Stokes, 'The Acid Test of Loyalty', in two parts, *Tribune*, 1, 2 and 4 December 1921.
50. Stokes to his mother, 2 December 1921, Stokes Papers, NMML.
51. Stokes to his mother, 5 December 1921, Stokes Papers, NMML.
52. Stokes's statement is printed in full as an appendix to Sharma, *An American in Khadi*, pp.373–80.
53. Letters of 3 and 24 January 1922 and 7 April 1922, Stokes Papers, NMML.
54. Stokes to his mother, 9 December 1921, Stokes Papers, NMML.
55. C. F. Andrews, 'A Message from America', YI, 20 April 1922.
56. Quoted in C. M. Kashyap and Edward Post, 'Yankee in Khadi: The Story of Samuel Evans Stokes', *Span*, January 1961.
57. *New York Times*, 23 March 1922.
58. Stokes to his mother, 29 May 1922, Stokes Papers, NMML.
59. Letters of 26 July and 18 October 1922, Stokes Papers, NMML.
60. Letters of 27 March and 13 November 1923, Stokes Papers, NMML.
61. Gandhi to Stokes, 15 March 1924, CWMG, XXIII, p.250.
62. Stokes to Gandhi, 7 March 1924, S. N. 8458, SAAA.
63. Stokes to Gandhi, 4 April 1924, S. N. 8650, SAAA.
64. Gandhi to Stokes, 19 March 1924, CWMG, XXIII, pp.276–8.
65. CWMG, XXV, p.391.
66. Stokes to Gandhi, 5 November 1924, S. N. 11738, SAAA.
67. See CWMG, XXV, pp.316–17.
68. Letters of 22 and 29 December 1924, Stokes Papers, NMML.

CHAPTER 5: DAUGHTERING GANDHI

1. Mira, 'Preface', in *Bapu's Letters to Mira* (1924–1948) (Ahmedabad: Navajivan Publishing House, 1949), p.3.
2. Madeleine Slade (Mira Behn), *The Spirit's Pilgrimage* (London: Longmans, 1960), p.58.

3. See Guha, *Gandhi*, Chapter X.
4. Mira, 'Preface', in *Bapu's Letters to Mira*, pp.3–4.
5. Letter of 31 December 1924, in ibid., p.9.
6. Letter of 29 May 1925, S. N. 10541, SAAA.
7. Letter of 24 July 1925, in *Bapu's Letters to Mira*, p.10.
8. Madeleine Slade to Gandhi, 26 August 1925, addressed to 'Most Dear Master', in Subject File No. 1, M. K. Gandhi Papers, 5th to 10th Instalments, NMML.
9. *The Spirit's Pilgrimage*, pp.64–5.
10. Mira, 'Preface', in *Bapu's Letters to Mira*, pp.6–7.
11. Rolland to Mira, 17 December 1925 (translated by the latter), copy, S. N. 12158, SAAA.
12. Mira to Devadas, 18 December 1925, Devadas Gandhi Papers, NMML.
13. *The Spirit's Pilgrimage*, pp.73–4.
14. Mira to Devadas, 27 December 1925, Devadas Gandhi Papers, NMML.
15. Mira to Devadas, 28 December 1925, Devadas Gandhi Papers, NMML.
16. Letter of 11 December 1926, *Bapu's Letters to Mira*, p.15.
17. Cf. letters of 31 January, 14 February and 7 March 1927, *Bapu's Letters to Mira*, pp.24–8.
18. *The Spirit's Pilgrimage*, pp.89–90.
19. Letter of 2 May 1927, in Tridip Suhrud and Thomas Weber, eds., *Beloved Bapu: The Gandhi–Mirabehn Correspondence* (Hyderabad: Orient Blackswan, 2014), p.51.
20. Mira to Jamnalal Bajaj, 18 January 1928, Jamnalal Bajaj Papers, NMML.
21. Mira to Devadas, letters of 15 and 18 March 1928, Devadas Gandhi Papers, NMML.
22. Mira to Devadas, 16 April 1928, Devadas Gandhi Papers, NMML.
23. Mira to Devadas, 25 June 1928, Devadas Gandhi Papers, NMML.
24. Mira Behn to Hari Bhau Upadhyaya, dated Almora, 8 October 1928, Hari Bhau Upadhyaya Papers, NMML.
25. Mira to Devadas, 5 November 1928, Devadas Gandhi Papers, NMML.
26. Mira to Devadas, 10 November 1928, Devadas Gandhi Papers, NMML.
27. Mira to Devadas, letters of 4 and 6 December 1928, Devadas Gandhi Papers, NMML.
28. Letter of 6 January 1929, in *Beloved Bapu*, p.164.
29. Mira to Devadas, 27 January 1929, Devadas Gandhi Papers, NMML.
30. Letter of 5 January 1929, in *Beloved Bapu*, p.162.
31. Quoted in Mirabehn, *New and Old Gleanings* (second edition: Ahmedabad: Navajivan Publishing House, 1964), p.23.
32. Mira to Devadas, 28 February 1929, Devadas Gandhi Papers, NMML. Cf. also Mira to Gandhi, 23 February 1929, S. N. 15810, SAAA.
33. Letter of 12 April 1929, *Bapu's Letters to Mira*, p.93.
34. Mira to Devadas, 28 April 1929, Devadas Gandhi Papers, NMML.
35. Mirabehn, 'Khadi and Swaraj', S. N. 15316, SAAA.

36. Mira to Devadas, 18 August 1929, Devadas Gandhi Papers, NMML.
37. Mira, 'Unforgettable', YI, 21 November 1929.
38. Editorial note by Mira, in *Bapu's Letters to Mira*, pp.101–2.
39. Editorial note by Mira, in *Bapu's Letters to Mira*, pp.164–5.
40. Margarita Barr, 'MIRABAI: GANDHI'S ENGLISH DISCIPLE', *New York Times*, 15 November 1931.
41. 'Criminal Treatment of Political Prisoners', three-page ts signed 'Mira', Bombay, 20 May 1932, in Subject File 107, Purushottamdas Thakurdas Papers, NMML.
42. Mira to Purushottamdas Thakurdas, 23 May 1932, in ibid.
43. Mira to Gandhi, 16 January 1933, S. N. 20048, SAAA.
44. Mira to Gandhi, 29 April 1933, S. N. 21086, SAAA.
45. See, for details, Guha, *Gandhi*, Chapters XX and XXI.
46. 'The Parting of the Ways', a two-page note by Mira [Behn], dated Parnakuti, Poona, 27 August 1933, in Subject File No. 1, M. K. Gandhi Papers, 5th to 10th Instalments, NMML.
47. Mira to Devadas, 2 November 1933, Devadas Gandhi Papers, NMML.
48. Mira to Devadas, 12 December 1933, Devadas Gandhi Papers, NMML.
49. Mira to Devadas, 19 March 1934, Devadas Gandhi Papers, NMML.
50. Mira to Devadas, 10 May 1934, Devadas Gandhi Papers, NMML.
51. See *Beloved Bapu*, pp.397, 399.
52. See *The Spirit's Pilgrimage*, p.183f.
53. Report in BC, 28 August 1934.
54. Mira to Devadas, 3 August 1934, Devadas Gandhi Papers, NMML.
55. Mira to Gandhi (copy), 9 August 1934, Devadas Gandhi Papers, NMML.
56. Mira to Horace Alexander, 18 August 1934, Horace Alexander Papers, Swarthmore College.
57. Unsigned letter (almost certainly by Mahadev Desai), 27 August 1934, in Devadas Gandhi Papers, NMML.
58. Report in the *Warwickshire Advertiser*, 29 September 1934, copy in Devadas Gandhi Papers, NMML.
59. See *The Spirit's Pilgrimage*, p.185.
60. Winston Churchill to Mira (addressed to 'Miss Slade'), 21 September 1934, S. N. 31039, SAAA.
61. See correspondence in Box 5, John Haynes Holmes Papers, Library of Congress, Washington, D.C.
62. Letter of 12 October 1934, in *Beloved Bapu*, p.405.
63. H. MacGregor, Information Officer, India Office, London, to Angus Fletcher, British Library of Information, New York, 2 October 1934, in IOR/L/I/1/1517, APAC/BL.
64. Cf. 'Ocean Travellers', *New York Times*, 10 October 1934.
65. Circular Letter dated New York, 13 October 1934, Alexander Papers.
66. *The Spirit's Pilgrimage*, pp.187–8.
67. See Marie Falconer, Port Washington, Long Island, to Mira Behn, 16

October 1934, Subject File No. 318, M. K. Gandhi Papers, 15th Instalment, NMML.

68. S. J. Woolf, 'MIRABAI TELLS HOW SHE FOUND PEACE: Gandhi's English Disciple Rejoices at her Escape From Her Old Life and Urges the West to Learn From the East', *New York Times*, 4 November 1934.

69. See *Washington Post*, 18 October 1934.

70. Reports in the *New York Times*, 19 and 25 October 1934.

71. Mira, 'Notes on Interview with Sir Samuel Hoare', dated 2 November 1934, copy in Mira Behn Collection, Himalaya Seva Sangh, New Delhi.

72. As recalled in Mirabehn, *New and Old Gleanings*, p.16f.

73. Report in *Hindustan Times* (HT), 22 November 1934.

CHAPTER 6: BLOWING UP INDIA

1. Viceroy to Secretary of State for India, 28 January 1927; report by Scotland Yard, 3 February 1927, both in L/P&J/12/307, APAC/BL.

2. Letter dated 24 February 1927, by A. C. Seward, Master, Downing College, in L/P&J/12/307, APAC/BL.

3. Philip Spratt, *Blowing Up India: Reminscences and Reflections of a Former Comintern Emissary* (Calcutta: Prachi Prakashan, 1955), pp.6, 8.

4. Ibid., pp.19, 21–2.

5. Ibid., pp.29–31.

6. Weekly Report of Intelligence Bureau (hereafter IB), Home Dept, Government of India (hereafter GOI), 17 February 1927, in L/P&J/12/307, APAC/BL.

7. Cf. report in ToI, 1 October 1927.

8. IB report, 3 May 1927, in ibid.

9. Report in BC, 2 May 1927.

10. Letter from CID Punjab, to Home Dept, GOI, 30 June 1927, in L/P&J/12/307, APAC/BL.

11. These paragraphs on the case against Spratt for his India/China pamphlet are based on letters and documents in L/P&J/12/310, APAC/BL, and in File No. 27–I of 1928, Home (Political), NAI.

    B. R. Ambedkar's involvement in the case is documented in Rohit De, 'Lawyering as Politics: The Legal Practice of Dr. Ambedkar, Bar-at-Law', in Suraj Yengde and Anand Teltumbde, eds., *The Radical in Ambedkar: Critical Reflections* (New Delhi: Penguin, 2019).

12. See report in ToI, 24 November 1927.

13. Document P. 526, in Meerut Conspiracy Case Papers (hereafter MCCP), NMML.

14. P. Spratt, 'Introduction', in Shaukat Usmani, *Peshawar to Moscow: Leaves from an Indian Mujahideen Diary* (Banaras: Swarajya Publishing House, 1927), p.v.

15. Years later, Spratt remembered the Congressman's gesture with affection.

See *Blowing Up India*, pp.39–40. Exemplary for his courage, his decency, and his absolute lack of sectarianism, Ganesh Shankar Vidyarthi was murdered in 1931 while trying to stop a Hindu–Muslim riot in Kanpur.

16. See K. Murugesan and C. S. Subramanyam, *Singaravelu: First Communist in South India* (first published in 1975: reprint Chennai: Indian Universities Press, 2017).

17. The 'Simon Commission', named after its chairman, Sir John Simon, had been sent to India by the Imperial Government to discuss political reforms. However, since all its members were white, and English, the commission was boycotted by the Congress and by left-wing groups in India.

18. Spratt to Seetha, c/o Workers and Peasants Party, Bombay-4, 12 January 1928, Spratt Family Papers, in the possession of Bob Spratt, Bangalore (hereafter SFP). 'Vande Mataram' was a famous nationalist hymn originally composed in Bengali by Bankim Chandra Chattopadhyay. Seetha would have known the Tamil translation, as rendered by the great poet Subramania Bharati.

19. Spratt to Seetha, Bombay, 7 February 1928, SFP.

20. Cf. Muzaffar Ahmad, *Myself and the Communist Party of India, 1920–29* (Calcutta: National Book Agency, 1970).

21. Spratt to K. N. Joglekar, 23 June 1928, Document P. 1678, in MCCP.

22. These paras are based on IB Weekly Reports, 5 and 19 April, 3 May, 2 August and 6 September 1928, in L/P&J/12/308, APAC/BL.

23. See volume entitled 'Bengal Speeches in Connections with Strikes & Other Subjects', in MCCP, NMML.

24. PS to Seetha, Calcutta, 12 October 1928, SFP.

25. Viceroy to Governor of Bombay, 2 and 18 January 1929, in Mss Eur F 150/1, Frederick Sykes Papers, APAC/BL.

26. See reports in ToI, 22 and 23 March 1929.

27. *Blowing Up India*, p.46ff.

28. See ToI, 9 December 1929.

29. See File 27, Motilal Nehru Papers, NMML.

30. As recalled in P. C. Joshi to K. C. Pant, 25 April 1973, in P. C. Joshi Papers, Centre for Historical Studies, Jawaharlal Nehru University, New Delhi.

31. A copy of the prosecutor's speech is in the Meerut Conspiracy Case File, Motilal Nehru Papers, NMML.

32. *Communist Challenge Imperialism from the Dock: Meerut Communist Conspiracy Case: The General Statement of the 18 Communist Accused* (Calcutta: National Book Agency, 1987), quote from p.281.

33. PS to Seetha, District Jail, Meerut, 7 January 1930.

34. CWMG, XLII, pp.57–8.

35. Spratt, *Blowing Up India*, p.56.

36. Spratt to Seetha, District Jail, Meerut, 16 April 1930, SFP.

37. Spratt to Seetha, 4 December 1931, SFP.

38. See Gene D. Overstreet and Marshall Windmiller, *Communism in India* (Berkeley: University of California Press, 1959), p.136.

39. *Judgement delivered by R. L. Yorke, Esqr. I. C. S. in the Meerut Conspiracy Case* (Simla: Government of India Press, 1933), Volume II, pp.326–7.

40. See Muzaffar Ahmad, 'Introduction', in *Communist Challenge Imperialism from the Dock*.

41. Spratt to Seetha, c/o Central Prison, Naini, Allahabad, 9 June 1934, SFP.

42. Spratt to Seetha, c/o R. S. Pandit, Bar-at-law, 6, Cawnpore Road, Allahabad, 12 September 1934.

43. Spratt to Seetha, Bombay, 11 October 1934, SFP.

44. See Home Department notes 1 and 8 December 1934, in L/P&J/12/308, APAC/BL.

45. Spratt to Seetha, Wardha, 16 November 1934, SFP.

46. Home Dept, GoI to Secretary of State for India, 3 February 1935, in L/P&J/12/308, APAC/BL.

47. Spratt to Seetha, c/o The Fort, Belgaum, 17 February 1935, SFP.

48. Spratt to Seetha, c/o The Fort, Belgaum, 28 February 1935, SFP.

49. Spratt to Seetha, c/o The Fort, Belgaum, 13 March 1935, SFP.

50. Spratt to Seetha, c/o The Fort, Belgaum, 12 April 1935, SFP.

51. Philip Spratt to Home Secretary, Bombay Govt, 2 May 1935, L/P&J/12/308, APAC/BL.

52. Home Secretary, Bombay, to Home Secretary, Government of India, 20 June 1935, in File No. 7/8/35, Home (Political), NAI.

53. Spratt to Seetha, c/o The Fort, Belgaum, 29 May 1935, SFP.

54. Spratt to Seetha, c/o The Fort, Belgaum, 26 June 1935, SFP.

55. Spratt, *Blowing Up India*, p.59.

56. Spratt to Seetha, c/o The Fort, Belgaum, 24 July, SFP.

57. Spratt to Seetha, c/o The Fort, Belgaum, 21 August 1935, SFP.

58. Spratt to Seetha, c/o The Fort, Belgaum, 25 September 1935, SFP.

59. Spratt to Seetha, c/o The Fort, Belgaum, 24 October 1935, SFP.

60. Spratt to Seetha, c/o The Fort, Belgaum, 4 December 1935, SFP.

61. PS to Seetha, c/o The Fort, Belgaum, 8 January 1936, SFP.

62. H. B. Clayton, Commissioner, Belgaum, to Home Secretary, Bombay, 2 May 1936, in L/P&J/12/308, APAC/BL.

63. Spratt to Seetha, c/o The Fort, Belgaum, 12 June 1936, SFP.

64. P. Spratt, 'Some Notes on Jail Psychology', published in three parts, *Modern Review*, June, July, and August 1937.

CHAPTER 7: RETREAT OF THE MATRIARCH

1. See letter from Annie Besant published in the *Times of India*, 18 April 1919, in V. N. Datta, ed., *New Light on the Punjab Disturbances in 1919* (Simla: Indian Institute of Advanced Studies, 1975), Volume One, pp.439–40.

2. *West Coast Spectator*, Calicut, 5 April 1919, in *Report on the Native Newspapers of the Madras Presidency for the first half of 1919*, L/R/5/126, APAC/BL.

3. See Reel 4, AB/NMML.

4. Printed appeal, 17 August 1919 in Reel 4, AB/NMML.

5. CWMG, XVI, pp.201–2.

6. 'A Reply to Mrs. Besant's Appeal to the All-India Congress Committee', a fifteen-page letter by B. G. Tilak, printed at the Kesari Press, Poona, 16 April 1920, addressed to 'The President, Secretaries and Members of the All-India Congress Committee', in Reel 2, AB/NMML.

7. See extract from *The Theosophist*, August 1920, in *Annie Besant: Builder of New India: Her Fundamental Principles of Nation Building* (Madras: Theosophical Publishing House, 1942), p.91.

8. Undated typed copy of Mrs Besant's speech opposing the Non-Cooperation resolution of the Congress, Reel 2, AB/NMML.

9. Report in *Amrita Bazar Patrika*, 4 September 1920, in CWMG, Volume XVIII, p.224.

10. See correspondence in Reel 12, AB/NMML.

11. Presidential address by Annie Besant at the first Reform Conference, 1921, Reel 5, AB/NMML.

12. 'Winning Home Rule', Presidential address of Annie Besant to the Second Reform Conference, Bombay, 29/30 August 1921, in Reel 5, AB/NMML.

13. Annie Besant, *The Future of Indian Politics* (London and Adyar: Theosophical Publishing House, 1922), p.255.

14. Annie Besant to David Graham Pole, letters of 9 February and 9 March 1922, Mss Eur264/7, APAC/BL.

15. See papers in Reel 8, AB/NMML.

16. Brian Ross, c/o Theosophical Society, Adyar, to Mrs Besant, 10 February 1923, in Reel 8, AB/NMML.

17. Notes of a meeting between a deputation led by Annie Besant and the Secretary of State for India (Lord Olivier), London, 17 June 1924, Reel 5, AB/NMML.

18. See Reel 9, AB/NMML.

19. Nethercot, *Last Four Lives*, pp.348–9.

20. CWMG, XXV, p.59.

21. Annie Besant to Gandhi, 17 September 1924; Gandhi to Besant, 18 September 1924, copies in AB/TS.

22. See Devadas Gandhi, 'Eleven Days in Madras', YI, 18 December 1924.

23. A typed, unsigned copy of a letter by Annie Besant marked 'PRIVATE AND CONFIDENTIAL', dated 29 December 1924, in Besant Papers, TS.

24. See correspondence in Reel 9, AB/NMML.

25. A copy of this memorandum is in Besant Papers, TS.

26. Nethercot, *Last Four Lives*, Chapter 7 and passim.

27. George Lansbury to Annie Besant, 15 July 1926, Mss Eur C 888, APAC/BL.

28. See Reel 12, AB/NMML.

29. Gandhi to Besant, 2 October 1928, CWMG, XXXVII, p.324.

30. 'Convocation Address delivered by Mrs. Annie Besant at the Banaras Hindu University on the 1st of December 1928', in AB/TS.
31. See Reel 12, AB/NMML.
32. Annie Besant to Jawaharlal Nehru, 29 November 1929, in Nehru, *A Bunch of Old Letters*, pp.78–9.
33. Excerpt from *New India*, 20 February 1930, in *Annie Besant: Builder of New India*, pp.124–5.
34. Excerpt from *New India*, 17 April 1930, in *Annie Besant: Builder of New India*, p.95.
35. See File No. 426, Home (Political), NAI.
36. Typescript of press statement by Annie Besant, Bombay, 18 October 1930, Mss Eur64/9, APAC/BL.
37. Nethercot, *Last Four Lives*, p.446.
38. N. Sri Ram to Har Bilas Sarda, 26 August 1933, Sarda Papers, NMML.
39. Nethercot, *Last Four Lives*, pp.450–6.
40. CWMG, Volume LVI, pp.11–12.

CHAPTER 8: SEEKERS NORTH AND SOUTH

1. Sarala Devi, 'The Spirit of Nurture', in K. Arunachalam and Chris Sadler, eds., *On the Frontiers: Strategy for a New Social Order* (Madurai: Koodal Publishers, 1977), p.23.
2. Ralph Richard Keithahn, *Pilgrimage in India: An Autobiographical Fragment* (Bangalore: The Christian Institute for the Study of Religion and Society, 1973), p.8.
3. Ibid., pp.14–15.
4. Ibid., p.16.
5. Ibid., pp.21ff.
6. 'Mr Keithan [sic] On Mission Work in India', *Indian Social Reformer*, 23 August 1930.
7. *Pilgrimage in India*, p.42.
8. *Chicago Daily Tribune*, 20 June 1930.
9. *Pilgrimage in India*, p.10.
10. See V. T. Chandapillai, 'Rev. Dr. Ralph Richard Keithahn: Life and Work', in Arunachalam and Sadler, eds., *On the Frontiers*, pp.5–6.
11. See CWMG, Volume LXIV, pp.419–20.
12. K. Swaminathan, 'In His Presence', *Mountain Path*, April 1988, pp.104–5.
13. M. M. Thomas, 'Foreword', in Keithahn, *Pilgrimage in India*, pp.vii–viii.
14. Keithahn to Gandhi, 26 August 1941; unsigned copy of reply, 3 September 1941, M, K. Gandhi Papers, 15th Instalment, NMML.
15. *Pilgrimage in India*, pp.54–5.
16. R. R. Keithahn, 'A Call to Students', in D. G. Tendulkar, M. Chalapathi Rau, Mridula Sarabhai and Vithalbhai K. Jhaveri, eds., *Gandhiji: His Life and Work* (Bombay: Keshav Bhikaji Dhawale, 1944), pp.178–9.

17. Ralph Richard Keithahn and Mildred McKie Keithahn, 'Our Village Health', *Indian Journal of Social Work*, 1944, pp.52ff https://archive.org/stream/in.ernet.dli.2015.92700/2015.92700.The-Indian-Journal-Of-Social-Workvol61944-45_djvu.txt

18. CWMG, LXXVII, p.357.

19. This account of how and why Keithahn was deported from India is based on the documents in Parthasarathi Gupta, ed., *Towards Freedom; Documents on the Movement for Independence in India 1943–4* (New Delhi: Indian Council of Historical Research, 2007), Part II, p.2850ff.

20. 'An American's Fate in India', editorial in the *Indian Express*, 30 August 1944, copy in Box 70, Martin Luther King Collection, Boston University Library.

21. *Pilgrimage in India*, p.55.

22. Pamphlet, 1 December 1945, in Box 70, Martin Luther King Collection, Boston University Library.

23. Keithahn to J. C. Kumarappa, 19 March 1947, Kumarappa Papers, NMML.

24. Keithahn to Kumarappa, Karachi, 13 June 1947, Kumarappa to Keithahn, 24 June 1947, J. C. Kumarappa Papers, NMML.

25. Notes on Sarala Behn's early life, collected by Elaine Morrison, courtesy David Hopkins, Lakshmi Ashram, Kausani.

26. See, for more details, Sarala Behn (Catherine Mary Heilemann), *A Life in Two Worlds* (autobiography of Mahatma Gandhi's English disciple, translated from the Hindi by David Hopkins) (Nainital: Pahar, 2010), Chapter 1.

27. See transcript of the Oral History Interview with Dr Mohan Singh Mehta, NMML, p.164f.

28. See Mohan Singh Mehta, *The Story of Vidya Bhavan* (undated, privately printed by Vidya Bhavan Society, Udaipur), passim.

29. *A Life in Two Worlds*, p.39.

30. Asha Devi to Sarala, letters of 30 January 1939 and 5 February 1940, copies in Lakshmi Ashram, Kausani.

31. Letter 28 October 1939, copy in Lakshmi Ashram, Kausani.

32. This account is based on *A Life in Two Worlds*, Chapters 8 and 9; interview with Radha Bhatt, Lakshmi Ashram, Kausani, 29 March 2019; Sarala's own statement in court on 7 February 1944, in Volume 4, Part 1, Series 5, M. K. Gandhi Papers, 12th/13th Instalments, NMML.

33. See Shekhar Pathak, 'Sarla Behn: Ek Achachrit Gandhi Pravah' (Sarla Behn: A Lesser Known Gandhian Stream), paper presented at the seminar on 'Interpretations of Gandhi', Indian Institute of Advanced Studies, Shimla, March 1996.

34. Sarala Devi to Poornanand Sanwal, 5 August 1942, copy in Lakshmi Ashram, Kausani.

35. See the report by Sarala Devi and Shantilal Trivedi on the Quit India movement in the Almora District, c.December 1943, in Volume 4, Part 2, Series 5, M. K. Gandhi Papers, 12th/13th Instalments, NMML.

36. Conversation with Radha Bhatt, Lakshmi Ashram, Kausani, 29 March 2019.

37. Notice by J. C. Donaldson, District Magistrate, Almora, 21 December 1943; Sarala to J. C. Donaldson, 25 December 1943, in Volume 4, Part 1, Series 5, M. K. Gandhi Papers, 12th/13th Instalments, NMML.

38. Sarala to J. C. Donaldson, 19 January 1944, in ibid.

39. Statement in court, 7 February 1944, in Volume 4, Part 1, Series 5, M. K. Gandhi Papers, 12th/13th Instalments, NMML.

40. Sarala to J. C. Donaldson, 22 July 1944, in Volume 4, Part I, Series 5, M. K. Gandhi Papers, 12th/13th Instalments, NMML.

41. Sarala to Gandhi, 10 August 1944, in Volume 4, Part I, Series 5, M. K. Gandhi Papers, 12th/13th Instalments, NMML.

42. Quoted in *A Life in Two Worlds*, p.135.

43. Ibid., p.147.

44. See Gandhi to Vichitra Narayan Sharma, 6 November 1945, CWMG, LXXXII, p.34.

45. *A Life in Two Worlds*, p.175.

46. Ibid., pp.176–7.

47. Letter from Acharya Kripalani, c.November 1945, copy in Lakshmi Ashram, Kausani.

48. Sarala Devi, 'The Spirit of Nurture', p.23.

CHAPTER 9: THE SECOND INNINGS OF B. G. HORNIMAN

1. 'Mr. Horniman's Return: Reception in Bombay', ToI, 12 January 1926.

2. See Milton Israel, *Communications and Power: Propaganda and the Press in the Indian Nationalist Struggle, 1920–1947* (Cambridge: Cambridge University Press, 1994), pp.236–7.

3. BC, 17 October 1948.

4. Reports in ToI, 3 and 5 March 1926.

5. This account of the meeting at the Gaiety Theatre is based on a thirty-five-page pamphlet, entitled 'Mr. B. G. Horniman', published in Bombay in 1926 (publisher not stated), shelfmark IOL.1947.a. 2354, APAC/BL.

6. Report in ToI, 17 April 1926.

7. CWMG, XXXI, p.490.

8. 'Mr Horniman's Lecture: A Brief for the Congress', ToI, 8 November 1926.

9. *Indian National Herald*, 21 December 1926.

10. See, in this connection, the character sketch of Horniman in Pothan Joseph, *Looking Back* (Bangalore: Deccan Publications, 1950), pp.141–51.

11. See R/1/1/2010, APAC/BL.

12. B. G. Horniman vs Unknown on 19 September 1932 (1932) 34 BOMLR 1666; ToI, 26 July 1931.

13. G. N. Acharya, 'Syed Abdullah Brelvi', in *Some Indian Editors* (New Delhi: Publications Division, 1981), p.50.

14. Notes by S. A. Brelvi, 8 August, 1932, S. N. 19603, SAAA.

15. B. G. Horniman, 'Hoare Cuts the Painter: All Indians Now Free to Unite for Country's Freedom', BC, 15 July 1932, clipping in S. N. 18520, SAAA.
16. Cf. Ramachandra Guha, 'Gandhi's Ambedkar', in *An Anthropologist Among the Marxists and Other Essays* (Delhi: Permanent Black, 2000): idem, *Gandhi*, especially Chapters 20 and 21.
17. Entry of 15 July 1932, in *The Diary of Mahadev Desai: Volume I: Yeravda-Pact Eve, 1932*, translated from the Gujarati and edited by Valji Govindji Desai (Ahmedabad: Navajivan Publishing House, 1953), p.229.
18. B. G. Horniman, 'Tragedy Must be Averted', BC, 13 September 1932.
19. B. G. Horniman, 'Enthusiasm for Temple-Entry Must Not be Allowed to Wane', BC, 24 September 1932.
20. ToI, 17 September 1932.
21. A tribute entitled 'Affectionate Editor', by 'A Member of the Staff', BS, 16 November 1948.
22. 'Horniman Remembered', ToI, 12 May 1986.
23. K. Rama Rao, quoted in Rangaswami Parthasarathy, *Journalism in India: From the Earliest Times to the Present Day* (New Delhi: Sterling Publishers Private Limited, 1989), p.247.
24. See reports in ToI, 30 April, 13 and 25 June, and 10, 20 and 23 July 1934.
25. Joachim Alva, *Men and Supermen of Hindustan* (Bombay: Thacker and Co., 1943), pp.182–3.
26. Report in ToI, 4 November 1935.
27. See BS, 25 May 1937.
28. BS, 4 September 1939.
29. BS, 28 and 30 October 1939.
30. B. G. Horniman, 'Britain Must Think Again: Lord Linlithgow's Statement an Insult', BS, 17 October 1939.
31. BS, 28 March 1942.
32. BS, 31 March 1942.
33. Unsigned editorial, BS, 13 April 1942.
34. BS, 4 August 1942.
35. 'WHAT OF THE AFTERMATH?', BS, 10 August 1942.
36. 'WAR ON THE PEOPLE', BS, 13 August 1942.
37. ToI, 20 October 1942.
38. See letter in ToI, 6 October 1963; https://indiankanoon.org/docfragment/ 678456/?formInput=Horniman; https://indiankanoon.org/docfrag ment/980672/?formInput=Horniman.
39. ToI, 15 July 1944 and 7 February 1945.
40. ToI, 7 July 1948.
41. BS, 16 October 1948.
42. As reported BC, 17 October 1948.
43. BC, 18 October 1948.
44. *The Hindu*, 17 October 1948; 'The Late Mr. Horniman', HT, 17 October 1948.

45. Annie Besant, 'The C. I. D. or the P. D. D.', *New India*, 11 May 1916.
46. 'Biographical Sketch', BS, 16 October 1948.
47. Anonymous, 'B. G. Horniman (1873–1948)', in R. Srinivasan, ed., *Crusaders of the Fourth Estate in India* (Bombay: Bharatiya Vidya Bhavan, 1989), pp.110–11.
48. See BS, 19 October 1948.

CHAPTER 10: GOING SOLO

1. *The Spirit's Pilgrimage*, p.191.
2. Mira to Devadas Gandhi, 13 February 1935, Devadas Gandhi Papers, NMML.
3. Mira to Gandhi, 13 February 1936, in Correspondence File No. 31, M. K. Gandhi Papers, Ist and 2nd Instalments, NMML (one of many such letters written in this vein in 1935–6). [2nd?]
4. This account based on *The Spirit's Pilgrimage*, Chapters 48 and 49.
5. Mira to Devadas Gandhi, 28 August 1937, Devadas Gandhi Papers, NMML.
6. Cf. Baba Prithvi Singh Azad, *The Legendary Crusader: An Autobiography* (Bombay: Bharatiya Vidya Bhavan, 1987).
7. M. K. Gandhi, 'A Fellow Pilgrim', *Harijan*, 28 May 1938.
8. Mira to Devadas Gandhi, letters of 26 February and 1 June 1939, Devadas Gandhi Papers, NMML.
9. M[ahadev] D[esai], 'A Prisoner and Prisoners', *Harijan*, 2 September 1939.
10. Mira Behn to Prithvi Singh Azad, 26 October 1939, Prithvi Singh Azad Papers, NMML.
11. Letters of 1 and 2 November 1939, Prithvi Singh Azad Papers, NMML.
12. *The Spirit's Pligrimage*, pp.216–17.
13. Some years later, Prithvi Singh Azad decided to marry an Indian girl who was much younger than himself. Cf. Azad, *The Legendary Crusader: An Autobiography*, pp.260–2, 266–7.
14. Letter, 11 November 1939, Prithvi Singh Azad Papers, NMML.
15. Letter, 18 November 1939, Prithvi Singh Azad Papers, NMML.
16. Letter, 25 December 1939, Prithvi Singh Azad Papers, NMML.
17. Prithvi Singh Azad, *The Legendary Crusader*, pp.230–1.
18. See *Bapu's Letters to Mira*, pp.328, 331, etc.
19. Ibid., p.352.
20. Mira to Prithvi, c. early January 1942, Prithvi Singh Azad Papers, NMML.
21. Mira to Prithvi, 23 March 1942, Prithvi Singh Azad Papers, NMML.
22. Excerpts from a letter written by Mira to Gandhi in May 1942, from Orissa (intercepted by the censor), in R/3/1/322, IOR, APAC/BL.
23. Mira to Gandhi, 11 May 1942, Subject File No. 173, M. K. Gandhi Papers, 15th Instalment, NMML.
24. Mira to Mr Wood, Chief Secretary of Orissa, 5 June 1942 (copy), in ibid.

25. R. M. Maxwell, Home Secretary, to Private Secretary to Viceroy, 17 June 1942, in R/3/1/318, IOR, APAC/BL.

26. 'Note of interview with Miss Slade (Mira Behn) on 17th July 1942', sd J. G. Laithwaite (Private Secretary to Viceroy), IOR, R/3/1/293, APAC/BL.

27. *The Spirit's Pilgrimage*, p.246.

28. Mira Behn to Pandit Jagat Ram, PO Hariana, Dist Hoshiarpur, Punjab, 21 September 1943, in IOR R/3/1/307, APAC, BL.

29. See File No. 59 of 1943–4, Home (Special), Maharashtra State Archives, Mumbai (hereafter MSA).

30. Gandhi to R. Tottenham, Additional Home Secretary, GoI, 22 December 1943, in R/3/1/316, IOR, APAC/BL.

31. Note by R. Tottenham, 3 March 1944, in ibid.

32. H. V. R. Iengar, Home Secretary, Bombay Government, to Additional Home Secretary, GoI, 18 January 1944, in ibid.

33. *The Spirit's Pilgrimage*, p.255.

34. Note by R. M. Maxwell (Home Member, GoI), 14 March 1944, in IOR, R/3/1/320, APAC/BL.

35. Krishna Murti Gupta, ed., *Mira Behn Birth Centenary Volume* (New Delhi: Himalaya Seva Sangh, 1992), p.19.

36. Letter, 3 December 1944, *Bapu's Letters to Mira*, p.363.

37. *The Spirit's Pilgrimage*, Chapters 60 to 62.

38. Mira Behn to Gandhi, Kisan Ashram, P. O. Bahadurabad, via Jwalapur, near Haridwar, 7 November 1946, in Volume 138, Series 4, M. K. Gandhi Papers, 12th/14th Instalments, NMML.

39. *The Spirit's Pilgrimage*, p.277.

40. 'A Visit to Mirabehn's Ashram', HT, 27 January 1946.

41. Mira Behn to Gandhi, Kisan Ashram, P. O. Bahadurabad, via Jwalapur, near Haridwar, 18 and 22 November 1946, in Volume 138, Series 4, M. K. Gandhi Papers, 12th/14th Instalments, NMML.

42. Gandhi to Mira, Srirampur, 4 December 1946 (copy, not in CWMG), in ibid.

43. Mira Behn to Gandhi, Kisan Ashram, P. O. Bahadurabad, via Jwalapur, near Haridwar, 16 December 1946, in ibid.

44. Mira Behn to Gandhi, 7 March 1947, in Volume 125, Series 4, M. K. Gandhi Papers, 12th/14th Instalments, NMML.

45. Gandhi to Mira, Patna, 16 May 1945 (copy, not in CWMG), in Volume 124, Series 4, M. K. Gandhi Papers, 12th/14th Instalments, NMML.

46. *Bapu's Letters to Mira*, pp.352, 355, 361, 385.

47. *The Spirit's Pilgrimage*, pp.292–3.

CHAPTER 11: RECOVERING REVOLUTIONARY

1. Interview with Bob Spratt, Bangalore, 27 October 2012.

2. Mrs Spratt (Phil's mother) to Seetha, 15 October 1938, SFP.

3. Same to same, 11 January 1937, SFP.

4. Interview with Bob Spratt, Bangalore, 27 October 2012.
5. Spratt to Seetha, 'Glenrock', Coonoor, Nilgiris, 2 January 1937, SFP.
6. PS to Seetha, c/o *MysIndia*, 18, St Mark's Road, Bangalore, letters 3 and 11 April 1939, SFP.
7. Philip Spratt, *Gandhism: An Analysis* (Madras: The Huxley Press, 1939), pp.61–2, 150, 129.
8. Ibid., pp.513–15.
9. Ibid., p.7.
10. Ibid., pp.89–90.
11. Ibid., p.23.
12. Philip Spratt, 'Introduction', in N. G. Ranga, ed., *A Guide to Village Economic Survey* (Madras: All India Kisan Publications, 1939), p.2.
13. Spratt to Seetha, 12 October 1939, SFP.
14. Spratt to Seetha, 12 November 1939, SFP.
15. Spratt to Seetha, 8 December 1939, SFP.
16. Spratt to Seetha, 19 October 1940, SFP.
17. Letter of 14 September 1940, SFP.
18. Spratt to Seetha, 18 December 1940, SFP.
19. PS to Bertie, 31 March 1942, SFP.
20. PS to Seetha, 10 January 1943, SFP.
21. Interview with all four of Spratt's and Seetha's children, Bangalore, 2 February 2013; Interview with Bob Spratt, Bangalore, 27 October 2012.
22. P. Spratt, ed., *Selected Poems for University Students*; P. Spratt, ed., *Guide to the Return of the Native* (Thomas Hardy), both published in the 1940s by the Madras firm of P. R. Rama Iyar, neither carrying year of publication.
23. 'The Child in the East and the West', *MysIndia*, 1 September 1945.
24. Cf. Chapter 6 above.
25. Cf. John Patrick Haithcox, *Communism and Nationalism in India: M. N. Roy and Comintern Policy, 1920–1939* (Princeton, N.J.: Princeton University Press, 1971).
26. The scholar Sibnarayan Ray was working on a multi-volume biography of M. N. Ray, which lay unfinished at the time of Ray's death. An accessible short study is Samaren Roy, *M. N. Roy: A Political Biography* (Hyderabad: Orient Longman, 1997). For a revealing personal sketch, see J. B. H. Wadia, *M. N. Roy, the Man: An Incomplete Royana* (Bombay: Popular Prakashan, 1983). Also useful is R. M. Pal, 'Life of Iconoclast', *Mainstream*, Annual Number 1999, pp.99–108.
27. See 'Introduction', in R. M. Pal, ed., *Selections from* The Marxian Way *and* The Humanist Way (Delhi: Ajanta Books International, 1999).
28. Quoted in Pal, 'Life of Iconoclast', p.102.
29. Spratt to M. N. Roy, 31 January 1945, M. N. Roy Papers, NMML.
30. Seetha Spratt to Ellen Roy, 5 February 1945, M. N. Roy Papers, NMML.
31. Ellen Roy to Seetha Spratt, 19 February 1945, M. N. Roy Papers, NMML.

32. Spratt to M. N. Roy, 24 February 1945, M. N. Roy Papers, NMML.
33. Spratt to Roy, 23 April 1945; Roy to Spratt, 28 April 1945, M. N. Roy Papers, NMML.
34. Reports in ToI, 27 September and 1 October 1945.
35. Philip Spratt, 'Foreword', in M. N. Roy, *New Orientation: Lectures Delivered at the Political Study Camp held at Dehra Dun from May 8th to 18th, 1946* (Calcutta: Renaissance Publishers, 1946), quoted passages on pp.viii, x–xi.
36. Philip Spratt, *An Approach to Indian Constitutional Problem* (Calcutta: Renaissance Publishers, 1946), esp pp.14–15, 17–18. Cf. also Philip Spratt, *India and Constitution Making* (Calcutta: Renaissance Publishers, 1948).
37. Spratt to Ellen Roy, 21 June 1946, M. N. Roy Papers, NMML.
38. Spratt to Ellen Roy, 28 June 1947, M. N. Roy Papers, NMML.
39. Spratt to Ellen Roy, 20 February 1948, M. N. Roy Papers, NMML.

CHAPTER 12: FROM SAMUEL TO SATYANAND

1. Letter, 31 August 1926, Stokes Papers, NMML.
2. Asha Sharma, *An American in Khadi*, Chapter 18; Vijay Kumar Stokes, 'Rejuvenation of Apple Orchards; Experiments in Harmony Hall Orchards' (unpublished manuscript).
3. Letter, 6 May 1925, Stokes Papers, NMML.
4. Joseph Kip Kosek, 'Richard Gregg, Mohandas Gandhi, and the Strategy of Nonviolence', *Journal of American History*, Volume 91, Number 4, 2005. Gregg went on to write a famous book on the theory and practice of non-violence, which was read by (among others) Martin Luther King. See Richard Bartlett Gregg, *The Power of Nonviolence*, edited and introduced by James Tully (Cambridge: Cambridge University Press, 2018). The book was first published in 1934; and in revised editions in 1944 and 1959, the latter with a foreword by King.
5. Letter written early September 1926; extracts published in *Young India*, issue of 16 September 1926.
6. Gandhi to Gregg, letters 23 May and 2 October 1926, CWMG, Volume XXX, pp.472–3; Volume XXXI, p.469.
7. Quoted in Sharma, *An American in Khadi*, p.253.
8. Letter, 19 September 1928, Stokes Papers, NMML.
9. See Stokes, *National Self-Realisation*, pp.222ff.
10. William W. Emilsen, *Violence and Atonement: The Missionary Experiences of Mohandas Gandhi, Samuel Stokes and Verrier Elwin in India before 1935* (Frankfurt am Main: Peter Lang, 1993), p.21.
11. S. E. Stokes, *Satyakama or 'True Desires' (being Thoughts on the Meaning of Life)* (Madras: S. Ganesan, 1931).
12. See Sharma, *An American in Khadi*, Chapter 21.
13. Letter of 17 July 1932, Stokes Papers, NMML.

14. See Emilsen, *Violence and Atonement*, pp.228–9.
15. 'Letter to Padri Sahib (17 July 1932)', in Willian W. Emilsen, ed., *The India of my Dreams: Samuel Stokes's Challlenge to Christian Mission* (Delhi: Indian Society for Promoting Christian Knowledge, 1995), pp.190–5.
16. 'Statement to the Press (17 September 1932)', in *The India of my Dreams*, pp.196–7. See also Satyanand Stokes, 'Why Change Religion' (1938), in *The India of my Dreams*, pp.203–8.
17. Quoted in Sharma, *An American in Khadi*, p.332.
18. See *National Self-Realisation*, pp.239–43 (to Bose), 250–8 (to Gandhi), 259–62 (to Nehru). A copy of the letter to Gandhi is also in the Gandhi Papers in the NMML.
19. Gandhi to Stokes, 8 June 1939, CWMG, LXIX, pp.331–2.
20. See *National Self-Realisation*, pp.262–3.
21. Sharma, *An American in Khadi*, pp.356–7.

CHAPTER 13: THE ELUSIVE SEARCH FOR 'BAPU RAJ'

1. 'Pashulok Memorial Scheme', three-page typescript, c.February 1948, in File Number 69, C. Rajagopalachari Papers, Fourth and Fifth Instalments, NMML.
2. Antoinette Boissevain to Mira Behn, 30 March 1948, copy in File 69, C. Rajagopalachari Papers, Fourth and Fifth Instalments, NMML.
3. Letter, 10 April 1948, in ibid.
4. Mirabehn, 'For Unity', *Harijan*, 19 December 1948.
5. Mirabehn, 'Development or Destruction?', *Harijan*, 23 January 1949.
6. Mira to Nehru, 30 August 1949; Nehru to Mira, 16 September 1949, in Krishna Murti Gupta, ed., *Mira Behn Birth Centenary Volume* (New Delhi: Himalaya Seva Sangh, 1992), pp.213–14.
7. Cf. 'The President in Pashulok', HT, 12 March 1950.
8. Mira, 'The Unsolved Wild Cattle Catching Problem', *Harijan*, 30 September 1950.
9. J. P. Uniyal, 'Memories of Mira Behn', in *Mira Behn Birth Centenary Volume*, pp.253–4.
10. Mira, 'The Haldu Tree is no More', typescript of an article apparently published in HT, 24 October 1949, in Mira Behn Collection, Himalaya Seva Sangh, New Delhi.
11. 'Something Wrong in the Himalayas', article June 1950, reprinted in *Mira Behn Birth Centenary Volume*, pp.145–7.
12. Nehru to Mira, letters, 31 March 1956 and 28 February 1957, in Mira Behn Collection, Himalaya Seva Sangh, New Delhi.
13. See the chapter 'Sons and Heirs' in Rajmohan Gandhi, *The Good Boatman: A Portrait of Gandhi* (New Delhi: Penguin India, 2000).
14. J. C. Kumarappa, *The Gandhian Economy and Other Essays* (Wardha: All India Village Industries Association, 1948), p.10.
15. Mira to Kumarappa, 15 January 1951, J. C. Kumarappa Papers, NMML.

16. Kumarappa to Mira, 28 January 1951, in ibid.
17. Mira to Kumarappa, letters, 1 and 10 February, in ibid.
18. Mira to Kumarappa, 4 April 1952, in ibid.
19. Copies of these pamphlets are in the Mira Behn Collection of the Himalaya Seva Sangh, Rajghat, New Delhi.
20. See 'The Gospel of "Bapu Raj"', HT, 20 April 1952.
21. Mira Behn, 'An Open Letter to Congress Leaders', HT, 9 July 1952.
22. Mira to J. C. Kumarappa, 24 November 1952, Kumarappa Papers, NMML.
23. Mira to J. C. Kumarappa, 19 April 1954, Kumarappa Papers, NMML.
24. *The Spirit's Pilgrimage*, Chapters 70 to 72.
25. Mira to Nehru, 20 November 1954; Nehru to Mira, 24 November 1954, in *Mira Behn Centenary Volume*, pp.214–15.
26. Mira to Brijkrishna Chandiwala, 24 January 1955, Brijkrishna Chandiwala Papers, NMML.
27. Homer A. Jack, 'A Visit to Mirabehn', HT, 8 January 1956.
28. Mirabehn, 'The Milk and Fodder Problem', HT, 20 March 1955.
29. Uniyal, 'Memories of Mira Behn', in *Mira Behn Birth Centenary Volume*, pp.255–6.
30. Mira to Devadas, 30 July 1957, Devadas Gandhi Papers, NMML.
31. Mira to Rajaji, 12 October 1957, C. Rajagopalachari Papers, Fourth and Fifth Instalments, NMML.
32. Mira to Rajaji, 27 February 1958, C. Rajagopalachari Papers, Fourth and Fifth Instalments, NMML.
33. Mira Behn to Krishna Murti Gupta, letters 4 and 11 April 1958, quoted in *Mira Behn Birth Centenary Volume*, p.22.
34. Mira to Rajaji, 6 May 1958, C. Rajagopalachari Papers, Fourth and Fifth Instalments, NMML.
35. *The Spirit's Pilgrimage*, pp.314–16.
36. Mira to Rajaji, 16 October 1958, C. Rajagopalachari Papers, Fourth and Fifth Instalments, NMML.
37. Rajaji to Mira, 18 November 1958, in ibid.
38. Mira to Rajaji, 11 December 1958, C. Rajagopalachari Papers, Fourth and Fifth Instalments, NMML. Navajivan was a publishing house founded by Gandhi in Ahmedabad, which after Gandhi's death had fallen on lean days.
39. Letter to the editor by Mira Behn, printed in *Gandhi Marg*, volume 3, number 4, 1959, pp.312–14.
40. Letter to Krishna Murti Gupta, 21 September 1959, quoted in *Mira Behn Birth Centenary Volume*, p.22.
41. Letter to Krishna Murti Gupta, 15 February 1961, quoted in *Mira Behn Birth Centenary Volume*, p.22.
42. Mira to Rajaji, 25 October 1960, C. Rajagopalachari Papers, Fourth and Fifth Instalments, NMML.
43. Mira Behn to Rajendra Prasad, 30 May 1961, Mira Behn Collection, Himalaya Seva Sangh, New Delhi.

44. See Mira Behn to Krishna Murti Gupta, 29 April 1962, Mira Behn Collection, Himalaya Seva Sangh, New Delhi.
45. Letter, 31 March 1962, in Mira Behn Collection, Himalaya Seva Sangh, New Delhi.
46. Mira Behn to Krishna Murti Gupta, 28 November 1962, Mira Behn Collection, Himalaya Seva Sangh, New Delhi.
47. Mira to Rajaji, 27 February 1958, C. Rajagopalachari Papers, Fourth and Fifth Instalments, NMML.
48. Rajaji to Mira, 22 February 1963, in ibid.
49. Mira to Rajaji, 3 March 1963, in ibid.
50. Rajaji to Mira, 8 March 1963, in ibid.

CHAPTER 14: READING FROM LEFT TO RIGHT

1. Interview with all four of Spratt's children, Bangalore, 2 February 2013.
2. Louis Renou, *The Civilization of Ancient India*, translated from the French by Philip Spratt (Calcutta: Susil Gupta (India) Private Ltd., 1954).
3. P. K. Srinivasan, 'Philip Spratt: "Crystal Spirit"', *Deccan Herald*, 1 January 1984.
4. Seetha Spratt to P. C. Joshi, 30 December 1972, in P. C. Joshi Papers, Centre for Historical Studies, Jawaharlal Nehru University, New Delhi.
5. Jamadagni, 'Philip Spratt: The Man Who Came to Blow up India', *Freedom First*, January 1987.
6. Spratt to Roy, 5 December 1947, M. N. Roy Papers, NMML.
7. Spratt to Roy, letters, 19 April and 27 July 1948, M. N. Roy Papers, NMML.
8. Philip Spratt, *India and Constitution Making* (Calcutta: Renaissance Publishers, 1948).
9. Spratt to Roy, 9 December 1949, MN Roy Papers, NMML.
10. Philip Spratt, 'The Prospects of the Socialist Party', *Swatantra*, 8 April 1950.
11. Spratt to Roy, 8 July 1950, MN Roy Papers, NMML.
12. See Frances Stonor Saunders, *Who Paid the Piper? The CIA and the Cultural Cold War* (London: Granta Books, 2000). Cf. also Giles Scott-Smith, 'The Congress for Cultural Freedom, the End of Ideology and the 1955 Milan Conference: "Defining the Parameters of Discourse"', *Journal of Contemporary History*, volume 37, number 3, 2002.
13. See Correspondence in Folder 8, Box 173, International Association for Cultural Freedom Papers, Special Collections Research Centre, University of Chicago Library, Chicago.
14. Philip Spratt, 'Threats to Cultural Freedom', *The Current*, 11 April 1951.
15. Philip Spratt, 'After Twentysix Years', *Freedom First*, August 1952.
16. Philip Spratt, 'Totalitarian Threats to Cultural Freedom in India: An Inventory', in *Cultural Freedom in Asia: The Proceedings of a Conference Held at Rangoon, Burma, on February 17, 18, 19 & 20, 1955 and Convened*

by the Congress for Cultural Freedom and the Society for the Extension of Democratic Ideals (Tokyo: Charles E. Tuttle Company, 1956), pp.243–52.

17. Philip Spratt, *The Communist 'Peace' Appeal: Its Real Character* (Bombay: Democratic Research Service, 1951), pp.17, 34–5, etc.

18. Philip Spratt, *Communism and India* (New Delhi: Eastern Economist, 1952), quotes from pp.i–ii, 1, 43, 51.

19. Philip Spratt, '"The New Class" (A Review)', *Triveni*, July 1958.

20. Philip Spratt, 'Communism without Dictatorship', *Freedom First*, April 1959; idem, 'Kerala and the Amritsar Line of the C. P. I.', *Thought*, 15 August 1959; idem, 'Democratic Victory in Kerala', *Freedom First*, March 1960.

21. Philip Spratt, 'The Appeal to Intellectuals', in A. B. Shah and Nissim Ezekiel, eds., *A New Look at Communism* (Bombay: Indian Committee for Cultural Freedom, 1963), pp.9–13.

22. Philip Spratt, 'Licking the Boot that Kicks You', *The Current*, 22 September 1954.

23. P. Spratt, 'What Would Gandhi Say', *MysIndia*, 3 June 1956.

24. Philip Spratt, 'Foreword', dated 25 October 1963, in Sita Ram Goel, *Genesis and Growth of Nehruism: Volume I: Commitment to Communism* (a collection of articles that first appeared in *Organiser*) (https://voibooks. bitbucket.io/gagon/for/).

25. *MysIndia*, 31 May 1964.

26. P. Spratt, 'The Leader's Quality', *MysIndia*, 31 May 1964.

27. Colonel A. N. S. Murthi (Retired), 'Our British Friends', *MysIndia*, 18 August 1963.

28. 'The Swatantra Programme: Mr. Spratt's View', *Swarajya*, 15 February 1964.

29. C. Rajagopalachari, 'Our Adventure with Independence', *Swarajya*, 2 May 1964.

30. Philip Spratt, 'Rajaji the Dissenter', *The Indian Review*, January 1965.

31. Interview with Bob Spratt.

32. This was told to me by the late Hari Dev Sharma, the longtime Deputy Director of the Nehru Memorial Museum and Library in New Delhi.

33. Letter from Gopalkrishna Gandhi to the author, 4 August 1996.

34. Boimondau was then a celebrated French watch-making company run as a workers' cooperative.

35. P. Spratt, 'Swatantra and Utopia', *Swarajya* (hereafter S), 23 April 1966.

36. P. Spratt, 'Federalism and Freedom', S, 8 April 1967.

37. P. Spratt, 'Content to be a Satellite?', S, 7 May 1966. Cf. also P. Spratt, 'Murder in Vietnam', S, 26 January 1967; idem, 'Democracy's Stake in Vietnam', S, 15 April 1967.

38. P. Spratt, 'Stalin or Lenin?', S, 14 November 1967.

39. P. S[pratt], 'A History of Stalin's Purge', S, 1 February 1969.

40. P. Spratt, 'Marxism and Swatantra', S, 11 November 1967.

41. P. Spratt, 'Orwell's Retreat to Common Sense', S, 27 September 1969.

42. Philip Spratt, 'The Hindu Personality', *Freedom First*, October 1964; idem,

'The Impact of the West on India', *The Journal of Karnatak University – Social Sciences 1965*; idem, 'The Uniqueness of India', essay published in *Quest*, sometime in the 1960s.

43. P. Spratt, *Hindu Culture and Personality: A Pyscho-Analytic Study* (Bombay: Maniktalas, 1968), p.73.

44. Ibid., p.144.

45. Ibid., pp.174–5.

46. P. Spratt, 'Gandhi in Retrospect', *Modern Asian Studies*, Volume 3, Number 4, 1969.

47. P. Spratt, 'Delhi University Seminar on Gandhian Philosophy', S, 25 October 1969.

48. P. Spratt, 'Lenin', a printed text of eight pages, probably published in a book, copy in SFP.

49. P. Spratt, *The D. M. K. in Power* (Bombay: Nachiketa Publications, 1970).

50. P. Spratt, 'Read History Right', S, 14 February 1970.

51. P. Spratt, 'The Lenin Centenary', S, 23 May 1970.

52. P. Spratt, 'The Ethics of Inequality', S, 17 January 1970.

53. P. Spratt, 'What We Must Do to Save Democracy', S, 10 October 1970.

54. P. Spratt, 'A Four-Point Indictment', S, 16 January 1971.

55. P. K. Srinivasan, 'Profile: Philip Spratt', *Deccan Herald*, 14 March 1984.

56. A. B. Shah, 'Philip Spratt – A Tribute', *Freedom First*, April 1971. Malcha Marg is a road in the upmarket New Delhi locality of Chanakyapuri, where – at the time – lived some upper-class 'socialist' advisers of Prime Minister Indira Gandhi.

57. Seetha Spratt to P. C. Joshi, 30 December 1972, in P. C. Joshi Papers, Centre for Historical Studies, Jawaharlal Nehru University, New Delhi.

58. P. C. Joshi to Seetha Spratt, 2 January 1973, in ibid.

59. P. C. Joshi to K. C. Pant, 25 April 1973; Pant to Joshi, 3 May 1973, in ibid.

60. Seetha Spratt to P. C. Joshi, 18 September 1973, in ibid.

CHAPTER 15: A HIMALAYAN HEROINE

1. Sarala Devi to Gandhi, 1 January 1946, in Volume 33, Series 5, M. K. Gandhi Papers, 12th and 14th Instalments, NMML.

2. Devi Behn, quoted in Rebecca M. Klenk, *Educating Activists: Development and Gender in the Making of Modern Gandhians* (Lanham, Maryland: Lexington Books, 2010), p.95.

3. Shanti Lal Trivedi, 'Kuch Madhur Yaaden' (Some Sweet Memories) in Shanti Lal Trivedi and Radha Behn, eds., *Sarala Behn: Smriti Granth* (Kausani: Lakshmi Ashram, 1984), pp.172–3.

4. On the inception and early years of Lakshmi Ashram, see Radha Behn, 'Lakshmi Ashram: Pravah evam Pravratriyon ki mool Prernayain' (Lakshmi

Ashram: The Inspiration for its Main Trends and Themes), in *Sarala Behn: Smriti Granth*, pp.59ff.

5. See Rebecca Klenk, 'Gandhi's Other Daughter', *Himalaya*, Volume 34, number 21.

6. Sarala Behn, *A Life in Two Worlds*, p.197.

7. Quoted in Klenk, *Educating Activists*, p.29. (I have slightly modified the translation.)

8. Shyama Pancholi, 'Smriti Shesh' (Abiding Memories), in *Sarala Behn: Smriti Granth*, p.112. This book, a posthumously published festschrift, contains a rich range of reflective essays on Sarala Behn in Hindi, written by her wards, students, and colleagues.

9. Vimala Bahuguna (née Nautiyal), 'Manav Shilpi Behenji' (Behenji, the Artist of Humanity), in *Sarala Behn: Smriti Granth*, pp.94–5.

10. Bhavani Kunjwal, 'Sanskar ki Pratikriya' (Responses to Tradition), in *Sarala Behn: Smriti Granth*, p.119.

11. Devendra Kumar, 'Sarala Behn: A Tribute', in *Sarala Behn: Smriti Granth*, p.197.

12. For more details, see Klenk, *Gandhian Activists*, Chapters Three to Five.

13. Klenk, *Gandhian Activists*, p.96.

14. Bidisha Mallik, 'Sarala Behn: The Silent Crusader', *Deportate, Esuli, Profughe*, number 37, 2018, p.109.

15. Shanti Lal Trivedi, 'Kuch Madhur Yaaden', in *Sarala Behn: Smriti Granth*, p.71.

16. Marie Thoger, 'Sarala', in *Sarala Behn: Smriti Granth*, p.200.

17. Bill Aitken, *Seven Sacred Rivers* (New Delhi: Penguin Books India, 1992), p.27.

18. W. M. Aitken, 'Sarala Behn: A Study in Self-Respect', in *Sarala Behn: Smriti Granth*, p.204.

19. Bill Aitken, 'Traveller to the East', unpublished memoir, Chapter XI.

20. Conversation with Radha Bhatt, Lakshmi Ashram, Kausani, 29 March 2019.

21. See *A Life in Two Worlds*, Chapters 26 to 29, etc.

22. Diva Bhatt, ed., *Tumhari hi Behenji (Sarala Behenji ke patr)* (Your Loving Sister: The Letters of Sarala Behn) (Almora: Katyuri Prakashan, 2001), pp.27, 29, 34, 39, 42, 61–2, 67–8, etc.

23. *A Life in Two Worlds*, pp.191, 268, etc.

24. Mirabehn, 'Some Reflections on the Bhoodan Movement', HT, 28 November 1955.

25. Sarala to Radha, letters 26 April and 3 June 1967, in *Tumhari hi Behenj*, pp.88–9, 93.

26. Radha Behn, op. cit., in *Sarala Behn: Smriti Granth*, pp.67–9.

27. Sarala to Radha, 17 June 1967, in ibid., p.101.

28. Sarala to Radha, 30 September 1967, in ibid., p.105.

29. Conversation with Radha Bhatt, Lakshmi Ashram, Kausani, 29 March 2019.

30. See Shekhar Pathak, *The Chipko Movement: A People's History*, translated from the Hindi by Manisha Chaudhry (Ranikhet: Permanent Black, 2021), pp.79, 85.

31. Sadan Prasad Mishra, 'Sarala Behnji: Jitna Mein Samjha' (My Understanding of Sarala Behn), in *Sarala Behn: Smriti Granth*, p.103; Hari Singh, 'Diary', in ibid., pp.192–3.

32. Pathak, *The Chipko Movement*, pp.93–4.

33. Ramchandra Mehrotra, 'Aastha Ka Nam: Sarala Behn' (A Testament to Faith: Sarala Behn) in *Sarala Behn: Smriti Granth*, pp.104–5.

34. Sarala Devi, 'The Spirit of Nurture', in Arunachalam and Chris Sadler, eds., *On the Frontiers: Strategy for a New Social Order* (Madurai: Koodal Publishers, 1977), pp.23–4.

35. Cf. letter by Sarala addressed to social workers, 'Priya Sathiyon', 12 May 1981, copy in the possession of Shekhar Pathak.

CHAPTER 16: KEITHAHN SOLDIERS ON

1. Cf. *Golden Jubilee of Gandhigram – 1947–1997* (Gandhigram: Gandhigram Press, 1997).

2. Conversation with Dr G. Pankajam, Gandhigram, 5 November 2018.

3. Personal communication from Bhoomikumar Jegannathan, 8 November 2020.

4. A seven-page handwritten note, undated, entitled 'High Points on the RRK Pilgrimage', Keithahn Papers, in the author's possession.

5. R. R. Keithahn, 'Gandhiji, and the Christian Ashram', *Ashram Review*, April 1948. Cf. also R. R. Keithahn, 'Nation-Building in a Free India: Rural Reconstruction and Rural Welfare', Sectional Chairman's Address to the Annual Indian Conference on Social Work, Jamshedpur, 23 December 1950, text in Keithahn Papers.

6. R. R. Keithahn, 'Superior to Military Training', *Harijan*, 2 January 1949.

7. Note by Ed Riggs, 23 July 1951, copy provided by Joyce Riggs-Perla.

8. R. R. Keithahn, 'Whom to Elect?', *Harijan*, 3 November 1951.

9. Cf. Circular Letter (hereafter CL) from R. R. Keithahn, 10 November 1953, in Shankarrao Deo Papers, NMML.

10. See Jesudas M. Athiyal, *An Adventure in Faith: The Story of Dr. A. K. Tharien* (Tiruvala: Christava Sahitya Samiti, 2010).

11. R. R. Keithahn, 'Shall We Continue to Proselytize?', *Harijan*, 5 December 1953.

12. On Jagannathan, see especially Andrew Rigby, 'The Nonviolent Activism of the Radical Gandhian Jagannathanji (1912–2013)', in David Hardiman, ed., *Nonviolence in Modern Indian History* (Hyderabad: Orient Blackswan, 2017).

13. R. R. Keithahn, 'A Brahmin (sic)-Harijan Marriage', *Harijan*, 5 August 1950.

14. Keithahn to Rajaji, 6 April 1953, in C. Rajagopalachari Papers, Fourth and Fifth Instalments, NMML.

15. Dr Mildred W. McKie, M.D., *Natural Aids for Common Ills* (Kodaikanal: 'Arogyalayam', c.1950–1).

16. Notes from an interview conducted by Andrew Rigby with Dr A. K. Tharien, 10 April 1997.

17. Conversation with K. M. Natarajan at the Tamilnadu Gandhi Smarak Nidhi Office, Madurai, 5 November 2018.

18. Notes from an interview conducted by Andrew Rigby with Dr A. K. Tharien, 10 April 1997.

19. Note by Ed Riggs, 29 October 1956, copy provided by Joyce Riggs-Perla.

20. See Rigby, 'The Nonviolent Activism of the Radical Gandhian Jagannathanji', pp.191–2.

21. R. R. Keithahn, 'Gramdan Sarvodaya at Batlagundu', note c.1965, in Keithahn Papers. For an account by an American visitor of the work of Keithahn and Jagannathan in the Batlagundu area, see Franklin Zahn, *Deserter from Violence: Experiments with Gandhi's Truth* (New York: Philosophical Library, 1984), Chapter 20.

22. Transcript of interview of S. Jagannathan by Andrew Rigby, 15 December 1995, Worker's Home, Gandhigram.

23. CL by Keithahn, 12 March 1962, addressed to 'Friends of the Sarvodaya Ashram', Keithahn Papers.

24. CL by Keithahn, 16 November 1962, addressed to 'Friends and Co-Workers', from Sarvodaya Ashram, Batlagundu, in Keithahn Papers.

25. See *A Pilgrimage to India*, pp.67–8.

26. CL, 1 November 1960, Keithahn Papers.

27. Keithahn to King, 7 June 1961; King to Keithahn, 15 June 1961, both in Box 70, Martin Luther King Papers, Boston University.

28. Note entitled 'Dr. Martin Luther King', c.March 1965, Keithahn Papers.

29. Conversation with K. M. Natarajan, Madurai, 5 November 2018.

30. R. R. Keithahn to Richard Fichter, 27 November 1964, Keithahn Papers.

31. R. R. Keithahn, 'Modern Temple Bells of South India', typescript in Keithahn Papers.

32. R. R. Keithahn to Shankarrao Deo, 3 August 1964, Shankarrao Deo Papers, NMML.

33. CL, Sarvodaya Ashram, Batlagundu, 26 January 1965, Keithahn Papers.

34. CL, 19 February 1965, Keithahn Papers.

35. Deborah Keithahn, 'Sr Ramana Maharishi's Influence on Keithahnji', *The Mountain Path*, June 1998.

36. Ralph Richard Keithahn, 'Vilampatty – Victory', note, 9 August 1965, Keithahn Papers.

37. 'Some Thoughts – Land and Food Problem – India and the World', c.1965, Keithahn Papers.

38. Keithahn to Vinoba Bhave, 10 May 1964, copy in Keithahn Papers.

39. Keithahn to Dom Bede Griffith, 17 October 1964, copy in Keithahn Papers.

For Jagannathan's considered views on Vinoba, see Rigby, 'The Nonviolent Activism of the Radical Gandhian Jagannathanji', pp.189–90.

40. CL, 5 November 1965, Keithahn Papers.

41. Conversation with Dr Kuruvilla Varkey and Dr Susan Varkey, Christian Fellowship Hospital, Oddanchatram, 6 November 2018.

42. CL, 30 January 1968, Keithahn Papers.

43. Letter addressed to 'Revered Coworkers', 1 October 1968, Keithahn Papers.

44. CL, 1 October 1968, Keithahn Papers.

45. Keithahn to Dr Odilla Konig, 5 January 1970, Keithahn Papers.

46. On Griffith and Abhishiktananda, see Susan Visvanathan, *Friendship, Interiority and Mysticism: Essays in Dialogue* (Hyderabad: Orient Longman, 2007).

47. R. R. Keithahn to Dr Odilla Konig, letters 1 October 1970 and 4 April 1971, Keithahn Papers.

48. Cf. Richard Benedict (Keithahn), *Out unto Christ-Centred Frontiers* (Madurai: Rock of Vision Publication, 1979).

49. Conversation with Dr Kuruvilla Varkey and Dr Mrs Susan Varkey, Christian Fellowship Hospital, Oddanchatram, 6 November 2018.

50. Personal communication from Bhoomikumar Jegannathan, 8 November 2020.

51. Untitled poem in Keithahn Papers.

CHAPTER 17: THE LAST GANDHIANS

1. Horace Alexander to Mira Behn, 13 December 1964, Horace Alexander Papers, Swarthmore College.

2. Motilal Kothari to Horace Alexander, 10 December 1964, Horace Alexander Papers, Swarthmore College.

3. Mira Behn to Krishna Murti Gupta, 10 January 1965, Mira Behn Collection, Himalaya Seva Sangh, New Delhi.

4. Indira Gandhi to Mira Behn, 24 November 1966, in Mira Behn Collection, Himalaya Seva Sangh, New Delhi.

5. Richard Attenborough, *In Search of Gandhi* (London: The Bodley Head), pp.152–3.

6. Undated, untitled note by Lea Calice, Mira Behn Collection, Himalaya Seva Sangh, New Delhi.

7. See Nilla Cram Cook to R. R. Diwakar, 14 February 1974, Mira Behn Collection, Himalaya Seva Sangh, New Delhi.

8. Attenborough, *In Search of Gandhi*, pp.153–4.

9. Mira to Krishna Murti Gupta, 14 February 1968, Mira Behn Collection, Himalaya Seva Sangh, New Delhi.

10. Letter in HT, 30 November 1968.

11. Quoted in *Mira Behn Birth Centenary Volume*, p. 43.

12. V. C. Trivedi (Indian Ambassador to Austria) to R. R. Diwakar, Chairman, Gandhi Smarak Nidhi, 4 January 1972, in Mira Behn Collection, Himalaya Seva Sangh, New Delhi.

13. Telephone interview with Ranjan Mathai, 2 June 2018.
14. See *Mira Behn Birth Centenary Volume*, pp.45–6.
15. Record by Wilfrid Russell of a meeting with Mira Behn, 7 April 1981, in Mss Eur C343, APAC/BL.
16. See *Mira Behn Birth Centenary Volume*, p.53.
17. See *Mira Behn Birth Centenary Volume*, p.299.
18. See Rukun Advani, 'Beethoven or the Mahatma', *The Telegraph*, 23 March 2002.
19. Sarala Behn to Dhoom Singh Negi, 5 February 1977, in the collection of Shekhar Pathak, Nainital. These and other letters cited from this collection were originally written in Hindi.
20. Sarala Behn to Rajiv Lochan Sah, 19 February 1978, in the collection of Shekhar Pathak.
21. Sarala Behn to Chandi Prasad Bhatt, 18 September 1977, in the collection of Shekhar Pathak, Nainital.
22. Sarala Behn to Sunderlal Bahuguna, 10 October 1977, in the collection of Shekhar Pathak, Nainital.
23. See, for more details, Pathak, *The Chipko Movement*.
24. See Subject File Number 1, Sarala Behn Papers, NMML.
25. Sarala Devi, 'A Blue-print for Survival of the Hills', supplement to *Himalaya: Man and Nature*, volume 4, number 6, November 1980.
26. Madhav Ashish to Sarala, 13 August 1981, in Subject File Number 1, Sarala Behn Papers, NMML.
27. Sarala to Madhav Ashish, 18 August 1981, in Subject File Number 1, Sarala Behn Papers, NMML.
28. Indira Gandhi to Sarala Behn, 30 July 1981; Sarala Behn to Indira Gandhi, letters of 18 July and 6 August 1981, Correspondence Files, Sarala Behn Papers, NMML.
29. Sarala Devi [Catherine Mary Heilemann], *Revive Our Dying Planet: An Ecological, Socio-Economical and Cultural Appeal* (Nainital: Gyanodaya Prakashan, 1982), pp.63, 119, 133, 251, 256.
30. Press clipping from *National Herald*, 13 January 1982, in Subject File 2, Sarala Behn Papers, NMML.
31. Vimala Bahuguna (née Nautiyal), 'Manav Shilpi Behenji', in *Sarala Behn: Smriti Granth*, p.76.
32. Radha Behn, 'Antim Chitra', in *Sarala Behn: Smriti Granth*, pp.145–6.
33. An untitled ts of 15 pages, c.1980, in Keithahn Papers.
34. Keithahn to Sarala Devi, 11 February 1981, Sarala Behn Papers, NMML.
35. Dick Keithahn to Sarala Devi, dated New Year 1982, Sarala Behn Papers, NMML.
36. K. M. Natarajan, Secretary, Tamilnad Sarvodaya Mandal, Madurai, to Sarala Devi, 29 December 1981, Subject File Number 3, Sarala Behn Papers, NMML.
37. Sarala Devi to V. S. Mohan Roy, Honorary Secretary, Jamnalal Bajaj

Foundation, 8 January 1982 (copy), in Subject File Number 3, Sarala Behn Papers, NMML.

38. Letter addressed to 'Friends of Peace', July 1982, Keithahn Papers.
39. Notes from an interview conducted by Andrew Rigby with Dr A. K. Tharien, 10 April 1997.
40. K. Muniandi, Secretary, Gandhi Niketan Ashram, T. Kallupatti, to Keithahn, 20 October 1984, Keithahn Papers.
41. G. Ramachandran to Keithahn, 20 October 1984, Keithahn Papers.
42. These last rites are movingly described in a little pamphlet, 'A Grain of Seed' (Oddanchatram: Christian Fellowship, n.d.)

EPILOGUE

1. P. Kodanda Rao, *Foreign Friends of India's Freedom* (Bangalore: The P. T. I. Book Company, 1973).
2. See https://www.thestatesman.com/opinion/a-questioning-mind-1502806 176.html
3. Kodanda Rao, *Foreign Friends of India's Freedom*, pp.v–vii.
4. P. Kodanda Rao, 'Aboriginalisthan: Anthropologist's Imperium', *Social Science Quarterly*, volume 30, number 2, October 1943.
5. See Guha, *Savaging the Civilized*, pp.72–7.
6. See Phulrenu Guha, 'Nellie Sengupta (1886–1973)', in Sushila Nayar and Kamla Mankekar, eds., *Women Pioneers in India's Renaissance* (New Delhi: National Book Trust, 2002); https://www.thebetterindia.com/162806/nellie-sengupta-freedom-struggle-history/
7. For more details, see Vicki MacKenzie, *The Revolutionary Life of Freda Bedi: British Feminist, Indian Nationalist, Buddhist Nun* (Boulder, Co.: Shambala, 1997); Andrew Whitehead, *The Lives of Freda: The Political, Spiritual and Personal Journeys of Freda Bedi* (New Delhi: Speaking Tiger, 2019). Pyarelal and Freda Bedi had three children, one of whom is the actor Kabir Bedi.
8. The couple wrote a compendious joint autobiography, running to almost eight hundred pages in print. See James H. Cousins and Margaret E. Cousins, *We Two Together* (Madras: Ganesh and Co., 1950). On Margaret's feminism, and her influence in both Ireland and India, see Catherine Candy, 'Relating feminisms, nationalisms and imperialisms: Ireland, India and Margaret Cousins's sexual politics', *Women's History Review*, Volume 3, number 4, 1994.
9. *We Two Together*, p.585.
10. See, among other works, Glenn Frankel, *Rivonia's Children: Three Families and the Cost of Conscience in White South Africa* (New York: Continuum, 1999); Stephen Clingman, *Bram Fischer: Afrikaner Revolutionary* (Auckland Park, S. A.: Jacana Media, 2013); Alan Wieder, *Ruth First and Joe Slovo in the War against Apartheid* (New York: Monthly Review Press, 2013).

Index